KABUL

KABUL

THE UNTOLD STORY OF BIDEN'S FIASCO
AND THE
AMERICAN WARRIORS WHO FOUGHT TO THE END

JAMES HASSON
FORMER CAPTAIN, U.S. ARMY

JERRY DUNLEAVY
REPORTER, *WASHINGTON EXAMINER*

CENTER
STREET®

NEW YORK   NASHVILLE

Center Street
Hachette Book Group
1290 Avenue of the Americas, New York, NY 10104
centerstreet.com
twitter.com/centerstreet

First Edition: August 2023

Center Street is a division of Hachette Book Group, Inc. The Center Street name and
logo are trademarks of Hachette Book Group, Inc.

The publisher is not responsible for websites (or their content) that are not
owned by the publisher.

The Hachette Speakers Bureau provides a wide range of authors for speaking
events. To find out more, go to hachettespeakersbureau.com or email
HachetteSpeakers@hbgusa.com.

Center Street books may be purchased in bulk for business, educational, or
promotional use. For information, please contact your local bookseller or the
Hachette Book Group Special Markets Department at special.markets@hbgusa.com.

Library of Congress Cataloging-in-Publication Data has been applied for.

Interior book design by Timothy Shaner, NightandDayDesign.biz

ISBNs: 9781546005308 (hardcover), 9781546005322 (ebook)

Printed in the United States of America

LSC-C

Printing 1, 2023

To the thirteen Americans who gave their lives in Kabul on August 26, 2021, so that others might live. To the 2,448 other Americans killed in action in Afghanistan before them. And to every American service member who served beside them.

CONTENTS

PROLOGUE

T he crowd was packed shoulder to shoulder. Every man, woman, and child shouted and waved pieces of paper—their contents indiscernible—in frantic attempts to gain the attention of the US Marines and Air Force special operators standing on the wall above them. The promise of a new life lay just beyond the Americans guarding the gates. Sunset was less than an hour away, but the temperature exceeded 90 degrees F, and the air was filled with the stench of sweat and human excrement from the desperate souls who had been waiting outside for days with nowhere else to relieve themselves. There was no respite other than a dry wind periodically blowing from east to west, away from the gate and down the canal full of civilians struggling to shove their way to the front.

Most of the crowd had no reason to be there. They had no connection to the US government and no legitimate claim to US protection. Many had remained on the sidelines during the decades-long fight against the Taliban. But most of them posed no active threat, either. They knew that Afghanistan's US-backed government was no more and that sharia law enforced by the Taliban was on the horizon, and they desperately wanted to find a way out. Some had showed up because they had sincerely believed social media posts saying that the Americans would take anyone who wanted to leave.

For men such as "Amir," the others' motives didn't matter. He had a right to be there, and he was trying to push through the throngs to take his wife and four children to safety. He had served as an interpreter for US special operations units and the Defense Intelligence Agency (DIA) for nearly a decade. As such, he had an advantage over the hordes holding up clearly forged "admission documents." US troops were looking for him and had given him a call sign to confirm his identity. The US veterans and intelligence operatives he'd served alongside, now back in the United States, had arranged it.

Amir could see Abbey Gate. He took a picture of the troops standing on the wall, so they'd know where to look, and another of the call sign he'd been told to paint on a placard: PALE RIDER. Then he took one more of his two sons and two daughters standing below him in the crowd. His younger son stood on the far left of the frame, and his two daughters stood on the right. His older daughter, six years old with soft brown eyes, gazed directly into the camera with an inquisitive smile. His younger daughter, the baby of the family, was distracted by the ongoing commotion and blissfully unaware of the moment. Between his younger son and daughters stood his oldest child, an eight-year-old boy with large eyes, tousled hair, and a troubled expression. He seemed to be the only one who realized that things weren't okay.

At 5:30 p.m., Amir sent the photos to his handlers in the United States, who in turn would relay them to the troops waiting for his family. His family was a hundred feet away from freedom. The US-based operatives acknowledged his message and replied with further instructions. But Amir's transmissions went silent.

A few minutes later, 3rd platoon of Echo Company, 2nd Battalion, 1st Marines (known as "2/1"), gathered 1,250 feet away for a group photo. In less than an hour, they'd begin their final shift at Abbey Gate. Their platoon sergeant tried his best to capture a moment to commemorate what they'd endured together. He took a few shots, then told the platoon to turn ninety degrees and face toward the gate, where the fading sunlight offered the best picture. The Marines first saw a flash of light, then felt the concussion of a blast in their chests. For a few seconds, everyone remained frozen in place while their brains attempted to process the sensory overload. Reality set in as body parts started raining down on the cement around them. The entire platoon sprinted toward the gate.

By nightfall, military officials announced that thirteen US service members had been killed in action in a suicide bombing at the entrance to the airfield: eleven Marines, a Navy corpsman, and an Army staff sergeant from a special operations unit. At least 170 civilians were killed in the blast as well. Amir's oldest son was among them.

The deaths of the thirteen American heroes of Abbey Gate—and those of the innocent civilians they were attempting to save—were neither inevitable nor the product of good-faith decisions poorly executed. The same goes for the thousands of Americans and tens of thousands of Afghan allies left behind in Afghanistan on August 30, 2021. Those outcomes were caused solely by the Biden administration's toxic combination of ignorance and self-assurance.

The wisdom of the overarching decision to withdraw US troops from Afghanistan is immaterial. Plenty of Americans—and plenty of Afghanistan veterans—hold differing views on that topic in good faith. No matter which side you choose in that debate, one thing is painfully clear: things didn't have to turn out the way they did.

And unlike the tens of thousands of Americans and Afghan allies abandoned in Afghanistan on August 31, 2021, the consequences of the administration's failures in Afghanistan have not remained in Kabul; they've unleashed a dangerous new global dynamic that will be felt for some time to come.

This book tells that story.

ONE

WRONG ABOUT EVERYTHING

J oseph R. Biden, Jr., was first elected to the US Senate in 1972, the year Richard Nixon won his second term as president. Over the subsequent half century, he adopted many public, and often paradoxical, personas, ranging from an apologist for Dixiecrat segregation to a purportedly lifelong civil rights crusader. But he has been remarkably consistent in one respect: he has been wrong on every major foreign policy issue he confronted, from Vietnam, Cambodia, and China to Afghanistan and Russia. And he has consistently changed his story, after the fact, to cover his failures.

"NO OBLIGATION"

Biden's initial foray into foreign policy as a thirty-year-old senator ominously foreshadowed the crisis that would unfold under his watch five decades later. In April 1975, the South Vietnamese government was collapsing under a sustained offensive by communist forces from the North. Only a few thousand US soldiers remained in the country, and President Gerald Ford ordered a massive rescue effort to save thousands of South Vietnamese who had helped the United States during the war. Ford believed that the United States had a moral obligation to honor its commitment to its South Vietnamese allies, who "had been very loyal to the United States" until the bitter end.[1] It was a foreign policy imperative as well: if the United States' allies were to trust US leadership in the future, our government needed to keep its word.

Biden, a foreign policy novice, disdained Ford's moral concerns and dismissed the potential damage to the United States' relationships with her allies. Too late to play a prominent role in the antiwar movement, he made his mark by becoming the Senate's most strident opponent of US assistance to South Vietnamese refugees. He strenuously opposed Ford's evacuation plan and request for refugee resettlement funds. During a Senate Foreign Relations Committee hearing on April 14, 1975, he declared, "I do not believe the United States has an obligation, moral or otherwise, to evacuate foreign nationals. . . . The United States has no obligation to evacuate one, or 100,001, South Vietnamese."[2] In a meeting in the White House later that afternoon, Secretary of State Henry Kissinger protested that Biden's posture meant abandoning the Vietnamese "to whom we are obligated." Biden conceded that the United States would be abandoning its allies, but he doubled down anyway: "I will vote for any amount for getting the Americans out. I don't want it mixed with getting the Vietnamese out."[3] Exactly forty-six years later, he would announce his Afghanistan withdrawal plan, which unfolded with similar, coldhearted indifference to our allies.

Rather than evacuating US allies, Biden sought "a negotiated settlement" with the North Vietnamese, naively trusting the North Vietnamese to guarantee that "endangered South Vietnamese" allies would be afforded "safety in place."[4] Wiser heads prevailed, and the Senate overwhelmingly approved Ford's request for evacuation funds over Biden's objections. Still, thousands of South Vietnamese allies were left behind when Saigon fell on April 30, 1975. Despite Biden's rosy assumptions, the North Vietnamese had no intention of providing "safety in place" to any South Vietnamese who had fought alongside the United States. Most ended up in reeducation camps, where they were abused, tortured, and/or killed.

Biden similarly downplayed the related, looming disaster in Cambodia. In early 1975, months before Pol Pot launched a genocidal campaign that murdered millions and killed or exiled 40 percent of his nation's population, Biden declared that there was no reason to think that Pol Pot would be any worse than any other Cambodian leader. He opposed aid to Cambodia, saying "I may be the most immoral son of a gun in this room," but "I'm getting sick and tired of hearing about morality, our moral obligation."[5]

During the forty-six years from the Vietnam pullout to the Afghanistan withdrawal, Biden apparently learned little. The parallels between his glib assertions that the Taliban could be trusted and his naive willingness, decades earlier, to trust the North Vietnamese are impossible to miss.

A BLIND APOLOGIST

Vietnam was Biden's first foreign policy failure, but it was hardly his last. In 1979, the future commander in chief visited China, beginning a decades-long campaign of arguing that the totalitarian nation's rise would be a plus for the United States.[6] Over the next forty years, the Chinese Communist Party (CCP) showed little interest in cooperation and outright hostility to any notions of freedom and self-governance. Ten years after Biden's visit to China, the CCP massacred thousands of pro-democracy protestors in Tiananmen Square. But his conviction was as unshakable as it was unfounded.

In a press conference with Chinese state media in Shanghai in 2000, Biden declared that "China is not our enemy" and there was "nothing inevitable about China and the United States not being as cooperative as other nations."[7] As vice president, he lavished praise on China during a state visit in August 2011: "Let me be clear: I believed in 1979 and said so then, and I believe now, that a rising China is a positive development not only for the people of China but for the United States and the world as a whole." During the same visit, he refused to condemn China's brutal "one-child" policy, telling an assembly of Chinese students, "I fully understand and I'm not second-guessing one child per family."[8] The communist government enforced the population control edict through mass surveillance, unwilling sterilizations, and coerced abortions, but Biden was either ignorant of or indifferent to those realities.

Biden played apologist for the Chinese government on other occasions as well. During a May 2019 speech to Iowa voters, he extolled the virtues of the Chinese government and concluded his lecture with the inexplicable claim that "they're not bad folks." And as late as January 2020, he guffawed, "We talk about China as our competitor? . . . Give me a break."[9]

BLUNDERING ALONG: "I'M GROPING HERE."

As chairman of the Senate Foreign Relations Committee, Biden's response to the 9/11 terror attacks presaged his reaction to the fiasco in Kabul twenty years later. In both instances, his first instinct was to lie about his own foresight and to project blame outwards. Hours after the World Trade Center collapsed, he falsely (and shamelessly) claimed to ABC News that he'd predicted the attacks the day before.[10] Less than a month later, the future president launched into a rambling "stream-of-consciousness monologue" in a meeting with Senate Foreign Relations Committee staffers before finally conceding, "I'm groping here . . . but it seems to me this would be a good time to send, no strings attached, a check for $200 million to Iran."[11] He apparently believed that the unsolicited payment to the Middle East's greatest state sponsor of terrorism would buy the United States some "goodwill" in the Muslim world.[12] The 9/11 Commission later concluded that the Iranian regime had facilitated the travel of several 9/11 hijackers and was protecting al-Qaeda leaders. Iran's alliance with the al-Qaeda leadership continues to this day.

"THE MILITARY DOESN'T FUCK AROUND WITH ME"

Biden's career in public office has spanned eight presidents, five popes, and pop artists from the Bee Gees to Beyoncé. Through it all, he has consistently voiced distrust of military leaders. Ahead of a key meeting with the Joint Chiefs of Staff early in Barack Obama's presidency, Biden warned the new commander in chief, "You've gotta stand up to these guys, because if you don't, they're going to treat you like you're their puppy for the next three years." Obama coolly replied, "You know, Joe, it'd be fun to let you be president for just five minutes to see how you'd handle it."[13] Biden told others in private in 2009 that "the military doesn't fuck around with me."[14]

Biden repeatedly urged Obama to reject the military's advice. He harbored deep-seated grudges against the generals who rejected his positions, telling Obama that the Pentagon was producing "bullshit" on the war in Afghanistan. In private conversations, he routinely expressed the belief that Obama had been overpowered by the military, describing the joint chiefs as "fucking outrageous." "They thought they were outsmarting everybody," he said of the Pentagon. But he saw himself as wielding greater influence over Obama: "They're all over there having war games, but I was having lunch games."[15]

Time and experience failed to improve Biden's foreign policy judgment. In 2009 he said, "We're assuming that if al-Qaeda comes back into Afghanistan, where it wasn't, it would be welcomed by the Taliban. Is that a correct assumption? We have no basis for concluding that." He insisted that "we have to differentiate" between various factions within the Taliban, arguing that the group was not a monolith and included only a small number of true believers.[16] He echoed that statement in 2015, when he claimed that "the Taliban per se is not our enemy"—seemingly ignoring the fact that the Taliban had happily provided al-Qaeda a safe haven in Afghanistan before 9/11, refused to hand over Osama bin Laden and other al-Qaeda leaders after the attacks, and killed thousands of American soldiers in the years that followed. Despite downplaying the threat the Taliban posed, he acknowledged that a Taliban takeover of Afghanistan would certainly create "a problem for us."[17]

Robert Gates, a highly respected secretary of defense who served under both President George W. Bush and President Obama, wrote at length in his autobiography *Duty: Memoirs of a Secretary at War* about Biden's involvement in the Obama administration's decision making on Afghanistan. "Not too many meetings had occurred in the Situation Room before the president started impatiently cutting Biden off," he wrote, adding "I think he has been wrong on nearly every major foreign policy and national security issue over the past four decades."[18]

Gates reported that Biden had seemed overly focused on the political fallout of the Afghanistan conflict. After one June 2009 meeting on Afghanistan, Gates said, he felt "discouraged less about the skepticism regarding more troops than about the total focus on the politics. Biden was especially emphatic about the reaction of the Democratic base." Biden remained hyperfocused on politics in the ensuing months, Gates intimated, as he reacted to planned troop increases by saying "The Democrats hate the idea, and the Republicans will just say you're on your own."[19] Biden's judgment on Afghanistan was affected not only by political myopia but also by ignorance of the realities on the ground. Gates highlighted Biden's inability to grasp the implications of the "fighting season" in Afghanistan—a blind spot that would come back to bite him as president when he ordered the military to reduce its defensive posture just as the Taliban ramped up its fighting season in spring 2021.

"FUCK THAT"

In hindsight, Biden's fateful decision to break faith with tens of thousands of Afghan interpreters who had slept, eaten, and fought alongside our troops (and at times saved their lives) was predictable. According to Richard Holbrooke, Obama's special representative for Afghanistan and Pakistan, Biden insisted, as far back as 2010, that the United States needed to leave Afghanistan the same way it did in Vietnam. When Holbrooke responded to Biden with concern for the plight of women under a Taliban regime, "Biden erupted," Holbrooke wrote. Visibly angry and almost rising up from his chair, Biden said, "I am not sending my boy back there to risk his life on behalf of women's rights. It just won't work. That's not what they're there for."[20] Beau Biden, who died of brain cancer in 2015, figured prominently in Biden's withdrawal decision as president. Biden's refusal to keep the United States' promises to foreign allies was deliberate—and emotion driven.

When Holbrooke raised the idea of leaving a residual force in Afghanistan to train the Afghan forces, Biden responded dismissively that Holbrooke didn't "understand politics." He ranted that the administration was already "facing a debacle politically" due to high unemployment and that the war in Afghanistan was just another "issue that could pull us down." He said the administration needed "to be on our way out" and "to do what we did in Vietnam." Holbrooke, taken aback, responded that he "thought we had a certain obligation to the people who had trusted us."[21] Biden mocked the notion: "F— that, we don't have to worry about that. We did it in Vietnam, Nixon and Kissinger got away with it."[22]

RUSSIA RESET

Biden's ineptitude in foreign matters was not restricted to the Middle East and Asia; it extended to Russia, too. In 2010, FBI director Robert Mueller informed the White House that the bureau had identified four Russian "spy couples" living in the United States and asked permission to arrest them. Vice President Biden forcefully opposed the idea, arguing that "our national security interest balance tips heavily to not creating a flap" with the Russians.[23] Biden was speedily overruled. The Russian sleeper agents were arrested and sent back to Russia in a prisoner exchange.

During the 2012 presidential election, Biden repeatedly mocked Republican candidate Mitt Romney's warnings that Russia and Russian president Vladimir Putin posed a threat to US interests. He was particularly scornful of Romney's claim that Russia was "our number-one geopolitical foe." He ridiculed Romney as a "Cold War holdover" with an "apparent determination to take US–Russian relations back to the 1950s."[24] Biden believed that Russia was a possible ally for the United States' efforts against Iran but that it certainly wasn't a threat anymore.

In February 2014, two years into Obama and Biden's second term, Russia annexed Ukraine's Crimean Peninsula and launched military incursions into eastern Ukraine. Eight years later, in February 2022, it launched a full-scale invasion of Ukraine under Biden's watch.

REWRITING HISTORY: FROM "DON'T GO" TO "GO"

"I said, among—with others, we'd follow Osama bin Laden to the gates of hell if need be," President Biden boasted in April 2021 as he announced his disastrous withdrawal. "That's exactly what we did, and we got him."[25] Except that was not what had happened, and Biden had admitted it nine years earlier.

At a House Democratic Party retreat in January 2012, Biden had said that when Obama had been making his decision about whether to authorize Operation Neptune Spear, he had told the assembled advisers, "We owe the man a direct answer. . . . Mr. President, my suggestion is: Don't go." By 2015, Biden had fully reconstructed his account of the events, changing his advice from "Don't go" to "Go." According to his new narrative, he had privately encouraged Obama to approve the operation. During the 2020 campaign, he offered a slightly different version, claiming he had quietly told Obama to go with his gut.[26] That revisionist history, however, is flatly contradicted by the public accounts of Hillary Clinton, Secretary Gates, former CIA director Leon Panetta, Obama administration staffers, and even Obama himself: "Joe also weighed in against the raid."[27] Gates wrote in his memoir: "Biden's primary concern was the political consequences of failure. . . . Biden was against the operation."[28] Optics, not tactics, guided Biden's decision making, and taking credit for other people's work was a habit he'd practiced since his first year in law school.

DEAD WRONG ON IRAQ

As vice president, Biden spearheaded the Obama administration's Iraq policy. He confidently predicted in 2010 not only that Iraqi prime minister Nouri al-Maliki, whose reelection he had supported, would extend the status of forces agreement but also that Iraq would be "one of the great achievements of this administration."[29] Both predictions were dead wrong. The agreement with Iraq didn't materialize, and Obama pulled all US troops out of the country the following year. ISIS swiftly capitalized on the power vacuum and seized control of large swaths of Iraq and Syria. During the self-described Islamic Caliphate's three-year reign of terror, ISIS fighters enslaved thousands of Yazidi women—many of whom were sold to the highest bidder in open-air markets—and executed captured adversaries by burning them alive, beheading them, or strapping them in chains and drowning them in oversized water tanks. Who can forget the image of the Christian martyrs in orange jumpsuits paraded onto the beach for their execution?

The general in charge of the US withdrawal from Iraq was Biden's future defense secretary, Lloyd J. Austin III. Incredibly, Biden pointed to Austin's track record in Iraq (and Austin's friendship with Beau Biden) as the key reason for selecting him in late 2020 to lead the Pentagon. "General Austin got the job done. He played a crucial role in bringing 150,000 American troops home from the theater of war," he wrote in December 2020, adding "Today, I ask Lloyd Austin to once more take on a mission for the United States of America."[30] Austin's next withdrawal operation—this time in Afghanistan—would result in another terrorist takeover.

In sum, nothing in Biden's forty-eight-year political career before his presidency provided any reassurance that he was capable of navigating a national security decision such as the withdrawal from Afghanistan. As his former boss President Obama bluntly cautioned, "Don't underestimate Joe's ability to fuck things up."[31]

TWO

DOHA

The Trump and Biden administrations' pursuit of a "peace deal" with Taliban representatives in Doha paved the way for the slow-moving train wreck that unfolded in August 2021. Time and again, US "negotiators" made substantial concessions in exchange for the Taliban's vague (and wholly unreliable) promises to "consider" a potential cease-fire and to ensure that al-Qaeda didn't pose a threat from Afghanistan—things the Talibs never intended to follow through on.

There's plenty of blame to go around for the Doha debacle, but a small group of individuals played outsized roles in the failure. Trump's secretary of state, Mike Pompeo, amplified politically palatable narratives about the discussions instead of providing clear-eyed assessments of the Taliban's true intentions. Biden's point men, National Security Advisor Jake Sullivan and Secretary of State Antony Blinken, provided case studies in naiveté and wishful thinking.

And the utter incompetence of the chairman of the Joint Chiefs of Staff, General Mark Milley, and the State Department's special representative for Afghanistan reconciliation, Zalmay Khalilzad, spanned both administrations. The US officials overseeing the Doha talks were a veritable who's who of foreign policy failures. However, nearly all the national security officials we spoke with who worked with Khalilzad (often called just "Zal") expressed the feeling that he distinguished himself through a unique combination of mendacity and ineptitude.

As a former high-level US intelligence official with years of experience in Afghanistan and direct knowledge of the Doha talks remarked to us, "The beginning of the end was when Zal Khalilzad got involved in the negotiations."

Biden officials repeatedly claimed that their administration's hasty withdrawal had been predetermined by a binding agreement negotiated by their predecessors, but that is simply not true. The Trump administration brokered a flawed yet conditional deal with the Taliban that would take effect only after the Talibs fulfilled several concrete obligations. The Biden team simply ignored those conditions altogether and chose to withdraw on its own accord—with predictably disastrous effects.

MOAB

When Donald Trump entered office in January 2017, the United States had roughly 11,000 troops in Afghanistan, down from more than 100,000 during Obama's surge. Trump promised to bring US troops home from Afghanistan, but, on the advice of Secretary of Defense James Mattis, he increased the number of US forces there starting in September 2017, with troop totals reaching 15,000 by the end of his first year in office.

Trump also drastically increased US air strikes against the Taliban and ISIS-K. The now-famous "Mother of All Bombs"—MOAB—was dropped on an ISIS-K stronghold in eastern Afghanistan in April 2017, killing about a hundred ISIS-K terrorists.

ZAL

In 2018, President Trump ordered the State Department to resume direct talks with the Taliban. He tapped Zal to lead the negotiations—a decision that proved to be a disaster. From the outset, the "special representative" appeared to be more concerned with the Taliban's and Pakistan's interests than with zealously advocating for the United States'. He began the process by asking Pakistan to release Abdul Ghani Baradar, the Taliban's cofounder and second in command, ostensibly as a sign of goodwill to jump-start the process.[1] Baradar had been in captivity since the CIA had captured him in Karachi in 2010.

In a lunch meeting at a luxury resort in Doha shortly afterward, Zal laughably told Baradar, "I've studied you. I know you're a man of peace." In fact, Baradar was anything but peaceful. He'd commanded all Taliban forces in northern Afghanistan after 9/11, led the fight against US forces and the Northern Alliance, and continued to direct attacks against US troops in the years after. The Taliban number two, however, was happy to let Zal's false characterization go uncorrected. He simply replied, "I realize that I would not be sitting at this table if it weren't for you."[2] Members of the "Taliban Five"—the military commanders held at Guantánamo Bay until they were swapped by Obama in exchange for the return of Army deserter Sergeant Bowe Bergdahl in 2014—joined Baradar across the negotiating table soon after his release. Within a few years, they would all be holding key posts in the new Taliban government.

By January 2019, Zal was already bragging to colleagues that he'd secured a peace deal. Without a shred of evidence, he claimed that "the Taliban have committed, to our satisfaction, to do what is necessary that would prevent Afghanistan from ever becoming a platform for international terrorist groups."[3] Afghan president Ashraf Ghani's chief of staff, Abdul Matin Bek, warned Zal that he was being played, but Zal dismissively replied, "I've cornered them. There will be a political settlement."[4] Yet it was the US military and the Afghan government that Zal had painted into a corner. Bek later told us, "I don't know if he was just naive or Taliban himself." Either way, he added, "this man is responsible. He is responsible for what is happening today in Afghanistan."

Biden would inexplicably keep Zal in charge, with Blinken calling his work "vital."[5]

"PEACE" AGREEMENT

Trump said in August 2019, "We're working on negotiating a deal right now, as you probably have heard, and you know, at some point, we want to get out as quickly as we can."[6] But negotiations were briefly paused after the Taliban killed a dozen people, including Sergeant First Class Elis Angel Barreto Ortiz, in a car bomb attack near the US Embassy in Kabul in September. Trump had planned to hold a meeting at Camp David with Taliban leaders around the eighteenth anniversary of 9/11, but that was scuttled because of the Taliban attack. By 2019, the number of US troops in Afghanistan had fallen to 15,000.

On February 29, 2020, the so-called Agreement for Bringing Peace to Afghanistan, or the Doha Agreement, was signed by the United States and "the Islamic Emirate of Afghanistan which is not recognized by the United States as a state and is known as the Taliban." The deal committed the United States "to withdraw from Afghanistan all military forces of the United States" by May 1, 2021, and included the release of up to five thousand Taliban prisoners. Most of those five thousand immediately returned to the battlefield.[7] In exchange, the Taliban would take "steps to prevent any group or individual, including al-Qa'ida, from using the soil of Afghanistan to threaten the security of the United States" and its allies. The Taliban had no intention of keeping those promises. Edmund Fitton-Brown, the coordinator of the United Nations' Analytical Support and Sanctions Monitoring Team for al-Qaeda activity in Afghanistan, told us that his group had observed frequent and high-level coordination between the Taliban and al-Qaeda throughout 2020 and 2021. Fitton-Brown's team was not alone in that analysis. When the special inspector general for Afghanistan interviewed Zal for a report about the Taliban's adherence to the peace deal conditions, Zal insisted that "we have succeeded in getting [the] Taliban" to break with al-Qaeda. The Pentagon, however, told the IG the exact opposite: that al-Qaeda "maintains close ties to the Taliban in Afghanistan."[8]

Misguided as they were, Zal's efforts drew vocal support from one senior member of the Trump administration: Mike Pompeo. The secretary of state was the Doha Agreement's biggest cheerleader within the Trump cabinet and repeatedly claimed that the Taliban was "prepared to break with their historic ally al-Qaeda." He even asserted that the Taliban would "work alongside us to destroy" al-Qaeda. A collection of intelligence reports nearly the size of a phone book reported that the fever dream of Taliban cooperation was simply false, but Pompeo continued to promote the false narrative. Pompeo also falsely claimed that the Taliban "recognized that military victory was impossible" even though the Taliban saw the battlefield as its surest way of taking over.[9]

The Trump administration's Doha deal was inadvisable at best, but it carried one silver lining: the agreement was conditional. The Pentagon and NATO were in full agreement: if the Taliban didn't fulfill their end of the bargain, the United States had no obligation to withdraw. Even Pompeo—who repeatedly cast the Taliban as good-faith negotiators—pointedly noted, "Our commitment to reduce our forces to zero is conditioned on them executing their obligations under the agreement."[10]

"VICTORY"

The Taliban, of course, had no intention of following through on anything discussed in Doha. Its supreme leader, Haibatullah Akhundzada, trumpeted the agreement as a "collective victory of the entire Muslim and Mujahid nation" and described the "complete withdrawal of all foreign forces" as "undoubtedly a great achievement."[11] As soon as the ink was dry, the Taliban published a fatwa, or religious decree, stating that "there cannot be another ruler of Afghanistan" besides Akhundzada.[12] Al-Qaeda likewise called the deal a "historic victory" and reaffirmed its allegiance to Akhundzada, telling its fighters to join the training camps in Afghanistan.[13]

The United States quickly collected convincing evidence that the Taliban did not intend to follow the terms of the deal.[14] In May 2020, a UN monitoring team concluded that al-Qaeda remained in Afghanistan, was still close to the Taliban, and was happy about the deal. The team warned, "The Taliban remain confident that they can take power by force."[15] The Pentagon's inspector general noted in March 2020 that the Taliban had "ramped up attacks" on the Afghan military "almost immediately after signing" the Doha Agreement. The watchdog concluded, "Taliban levels of violence escalated throughout Afghanistan, raising questions as to the future of the agreement."[16]

General Milley dutifully defended the Doha Agreement and repeatedly downplayed the significance of Taliban attacks against Afghan forces and US troops. He boasted, "This is a significant step forward, this agreement, and it's going to lead to intra-Afghan dialogue, and it ultimately leads to a peace agreement."[17]

A BAD IDEA ABANDONED

Toward the end of his term, President Trump strongly considered removing all US troops from Afghanistan. He even signed a (quickly withdrawn) order to that effect in late 2020. Still, he ultimately chose to keep a small contingent of 2,500 to 3,500 troops in the country, avoiding the mistake that Biden would soon make.

During a speech on October 8, 2020, National Security Advisor Robert O'Brien announced a reduction of US forces to 2,500 by early 2021. In early November 2020, Secretary of Defense Mark Esper sent Trump a classified memo saying that a precipitous withdrawal from Afghanistan was a bad idea.[18] Christopher Miller took over as secretary of defense when Trump fired Esper by tweet just after Election Day.

Trump apparently soon signed a directive calling for a full US troop withdrawal by early 2021—which he quickly reversed after pushback from his officials. The aborted withdrawal effort was spearheaded by John McEntee, the director of the White House Presidential Personnel Office, and retired Army colonel Douglas Macgregor, who had been interviewed by McEntee about becoming a senior adviser to Miller.[19] McEntee provided Macgregor with a note on November 9, 2020, that allegedly relayed Trump's wishes, including "1. Get us out of Afghanistan."[20] Macgregor helped McEntee with the language for an order from Trump, which stated, "I hereby direct you to withdraw all US forces . . . from the Islamic Republic of Afghanistan no later than 15 January 2021."[21]

In 2022, General Keith Kellogg, Vice President Mike Pence's national security advisor, testified to the January 6th Committee, "An immediate departure that that memo said would have been catastrophic. It's the same thing what President Biden went through. It would have been a debacle."[22]

Miller told the January 6 Committee that the order he had received from Trump on the evening of November 9, the day after he was made acting secretary of defense, "was to draw down to 2,500 in Afghanistan" and called that "completely achievable."[23] He had been blindsided by the full withdrawal memo. Milley and Miller quickly met with O'Brien at the White House. O'Brien and White House counsel Pat Cipollone talked with Trump about their concerns,[24] and Miller, Milley, and O'Brien opposed the plan during an Oval Office meeting, telling Trump that it would look terrible if one of the final images of his presidency was of the Taliban taking over Afghanistan—which ended up happening under Biden. Trump withdrew the full withdrawal order, avoiding the mistake that Biden would soon make.[25]

THREE

HOW QUICKLY CAN WE GET OUT?

Joe Biden promised during his run for the Democratic Party nomination in 2019 and then in his race against Donald Trump in 2020 that he would withdraw most US troops from Afghanistan—but he also repeatedly vowed that he would leave a residual US force behind in the country to help fight al-Qaeda and ISIS-K. During Democratic Party primary debates and in foreign policy speeches and articles, he promised to keep a small presence in Afghanistan to fight terrorism. This promise was not kept.

"We cannot allow the remnants of Al Qaeda in Afghanistan and Pakistan to reconstitute, and we must destroy the Islamic State presence," he said in July 2019.[1] During a December 2019 debate, he said that he would leave US special forces in Afghanistan.

In January 2020, Biden made a promise to bring only the "vast majority" of US troops home from Afghanistan, narrowing the mission to defeating al-Qaeda and ISIS-K. That same month, he argued for keeping a small US force in Afghanistan, saying that "smaller-scale missions are sustainable."[2]

In a February 2020 debate, he cautioned against pulling all US troops out of the Middle East and attacked Trump over Syria, warning of ISIS, "Close your eyes, everybody. Remember what you saw on television. You saw a woman standing up there holding up her baby, Kurds saying,

'Please don't leave us.' And our military women and men standing at, going out in their uparmored Humvees with their heads down ashamed of what they did."[3] The picture he painted sounded eerily like what would happen in Afghanistan under his watch.

Still, when he was asked on *Face the Nation* that month if he would bear any responsibility if the Taliban took control again and women lost their rights, he answered, "Do I bear responsibility? Zero responsibility."[4]

Biden's repeated vows to leave US troops behind to fight terrorism in Afghanistan ended up being false. During his first week in office, he asked his team, "How quickly can we get out of Afghanistan?" The meeting, recounted to us by a senior intelligence official, made clear that the commander in chief wanted to shape the realities of the battlefield around his decision instead of vice versa.

"WE WILL LEAVE"

The first weeks and months of the Biden administration in 2021 were dominated by the mantra "America is back." But the United States was in fact leaving Afghanistan to the Taliban. During his Senate confirmation the day before Biden's inauguration, Antony Blinken said that Biden wanted to bring troops home from Afghanistan—but indicated that some should stay to combat al-Qaeda.[5] That didn't happen. Blinken, Jake Sullivan, and other soon-to-be Biden officials had sent the president-elect a memo during the transition advising that the negotiations with the Taliban in Doha were unlikely to bear fruit.[6] Biden nevertheless hinged his strategy on a peace deal that would never materialize.

On January 23, Sullivan told Afghan president Ghani's national security advisor, Hamdullah Mohib, that the United States would "support the peace process" with the goal of "a durable and just political settlement and permanent ceasefire" and that the United States was reviewing whether the Taliban was fulfilling its Doha Agreement obligations.[7] Once again, the Biden administration had no intention of following through on its promises.

The book *Peril* by Bob Woodward and Robert Costa provided insight into Biden's deliberations. Biden brought his national security team together February 3 to set the stage for pulling all US forces out of Afghanistan. He made it clear that he had long wanted to leave Afghanistan but promised to listen to suggestions. He also made it clear that he was uninterested in delivering "a death blow to the Taliban."[8]

Biden tasked Sullivan to run a national security review of the Afghan campaign. Even then, he loaded the dice. "If the mission is to preserve the Ghani government, I would not send my own son," he said.[9] Despite his promising to keep an open mind, a national security official told us that Biden had been committed to leaving Afghanistan regardless.

Publicly, Biden acted as though he was still weighing the decision. He said on March 16 that he was still "in the process of making that decision now as to when they'll leave."[10] Just a week later, however, he let his hand slip. He botched Ghani's name in a White House press conference, referred to him as Afghanistan's leader in scare quotes, and told reporters, "We will leave. The question is when we leave."[11]

Even though the outcome was predetermined, Biden asked for both best- and worst-case scenarios. Sullivan and his NSC staff compiled two memos—one on what they claimed was the most powerful case for remaining in Afghanistan and the other on what they considered the strongest case for a total withdrawal. The president's directives and planning for the withdrawal were never put into a national security memorandum, despite that being the standard process for major national security decisions, especially one as significant as ending a two-decade-long war.

ZAL'S "VITAL WORK"

Biden's first move was to keep Zal Khalilzad in charge of the withdrawal negotiations. The decision would have been illogical if Biden's goal had been anything other than getting out of the country as quickly as possible, consequences be damned. (Still, his decision to retain the architect of the Doha Agreement is ironic, given his later attempts to blame the agreement for his own disastrous decisions.) Many individuals who worked with Zal described him to us as a pernicious figure who was either hoodwinked by the Taliban or actively working for its interests.

A former high-level US intelligence official with lots of experience in Afghanistan told us that the Taliban had "suckered Zal hook, line, and sinker." Suspicions about Zal's judgment and motivations even led to a heated debate within the CIA about whether to self-censor the intelligence it shared with him, because agency officials were concerned that he would pass it on to the Taliban. The agency ultimately decided against that course of action, but its fears were eminently reasonable. According to several officials with direct knowledge, Zal frequently relayed requests from the Taliban for advanced notice and operational details about planned US raids against al-Qaeda or ISIS. He urged the intelligence community to grant the requests, and on at least one occasion, he argued, according to the source referenced above, "How could it hurt? You're not attacking them [the Taliban]." Military and intelligence officials curtly explained how intelligence-sharing with the Taliban would "hurt": the same source said, "You're gonna get dead Americans."

One of Zal's first acts under Biden was to try to rally support to push Ghani out of office. The effort backfired and destroyed any remaining trust between the Afghan government and the United States. In early 2021, members of the Afghan negotiating team accused Zal of "taking the side of the Taliban" and said that it was "very clear" that Zal "wanted the Taliban to be the head of the government."[12] The most charitable interpretation of Zal's actions was that he foolishly believed that the Taliban wanted only a power-sharing agreement instead of total control and that Ghani was an impediment to that outcome.[13] Nevertheless, Blinken used his first press conference as secretary of state to praise Zal for "the vital work that he is performing."[14]

Zal told Congress that the Taliban was breaking with al-Qaeda and that a military takeover by the Taliban was out of the question.

"HE'S NOT LISTENING TO ANYBODY"

Biden's attempt to preabsolve himself of responsibility for the consequences of his decision would have been galling on its own, but it was even worse considering that military and intelligence leaders repeatedly warned him about what was to come. Indeed, Biden did not receive a single military recommendation or intelligence assessment telling him that a full US withdrawal would be anything but a disaster. He was warned from the start of his presidency that a precipitous US troop withdrawal from Afghanistan—combined with the pulling out of US air support, the drop in air strikes, and the retrograde of contractors necessary to keep the Afghan air force flying—would likely result in a swift Taliban advance and the disintegration of the Afghan military.

In late 2020, the Pentagon commissioned a report from current and former special operations leaders assessing whether the Afghan military could repress an anticipated Taliban offensive if US forces withdrew. The report, designated top secret but briefed to us, stated in no uncertain terms that Afghan security forces would rapidly collapse. Several other groups—from the congressionally mandated Afghanistan Study Group[15] to the Office of the Director of National Intelligence (ODNI)[16]—issued similar warnings around the same time. The study group insisted in February that the Taliban could be held at bay by a small US and NATO presence, while the ODNI warned in April, just before Biden's withdrawal announcement, that the Afghan government "will struggle to hold the Taliban at bay if the coalition withdraws support." An outside net assessment published by the Combating Terrorism Center at West Point concluded that the Taliban would have a "slight military advantage" over the Afghan military if the United States withdrew, with the advantage likely growing "in a compounding fashion."[17]

In March 2021, the special inspector general for Afghanistan, John Sopko, warned that the Afghan government was facing an existential threat from the Taliban, pointing to the key role that Pentagon contractors were playing in keeping the Afghan military on the battlefield and the Afghan air force flying, with the Afghan air force likely to crumble quickly without US support. Sopko told the House that Afghanistan "may be fighting for its very survival" and that "it is not an overstatement to fathom that if foreign assistance is withdrawn and peace negotiations fail, Taliban forces will be at the gates of Kabul in short order."[18] That was exactly what happened.

Military leaders also repeatedly warned Biden against a full withdrawal from Afghanistan. General Austin "Scott" Miller, the Resolute Support Mission commander of US forces in Afghanistan, spent several months before Biden's April withdrawal announcement warning the administration that a swift Taliban takeover would be the likeliest result of a rapid US pullout.[19] Miller "strongly argued" that a small number of US troops must be kept in Afghanistan to prevent a Taliban takeover,[20] and he told Secretary Austin, General Milley, and General Kenneth F. McKenzie, Jr., the CENTCOM commander, that he strenuously opposed Biden's total withdrawal proposal.[21] McKenzie, in turn, told Biden that a full withdrawal would lead to the collapse of the Afghan government and advised the commander in chief to keep 2,500 troops in the country to ensure stability. General Milley later told Congress, "My assessment was, back in the fall of 2020 and it remained consistent throughout, that we should keep a steady state of 2,500."[22]

Even Taliban deputy leader Sirajuddin Haqqani said in February that if support from foreign "invaders" was taken away from the Afghan government, its "dissolution" would be "imminent."[23]

Biden ignored all of those warnings. Colonel Seth Krummrich, a twenty-two-year Green Beret who served as the chief of staff for Special Operations Command Central (SOCCENT) during the withdrawal, told us that military officials had repeatedly warned Biden, "If you start to withdraw, the Taliban are going to come pouring in and there's nothing that's going to stop them." The president, who privately claimed for years that he knew better than the Joint Chiefs of Staff despite decades of evidence to the contrary, had other ideas. "The president decided, 'We're

going to leave,'" Krummrich said. "And he's not listening to anybody."
A Biden official later admitted that the decision "came down to where
the assessment they were receiving from the military in Afghanistan
did not support the preferred policy decision that the administration
and certainly the State Department wished to pursue."[24]

When push came to shove, however, most of those generals chose
to toe the party line even though they knew what it entailed. After
publicly addressing the House Foreign Affairs Committee on June
13, General McKenzie met the committee's ranking member, Michael
McCaul, in a congressional Sensitive Compartmented Information
Facility, or SCIF. The congressman told us that the general told him,
"This is going to be a big mistake." Still, he never resigned. Milley didn't,
either. Unsurprisingly, the leaders' silent acquiescence to a plan that put
US troops in harm's way didn't sit well with the officers and enlisted
troops under their command. Krummrich, for example, told us that
if the generals had truly believed it would be a disaster to go to zero,
they should have resigned or gone public with their concerns. "None of
those four stars fell on their sword," he said. "Hey, man, there's no fifth
star. So you don't have to keep butt-snorkeling these guys. Feel free to
really put your foot down and make a stand. You really will never get
another opportunity in your lifetime to be able to do this. If you truly
believe something, then you need to stand up and do it. Nobody did."
He added that at least one of the generals should have stood up to Biden
and told him that if the United States conducted a hasty withdrawal,
"we're going to leave Americans behind."

THE TERRORIST ALLIANCE ENDURES

The alliance between the Taliban and al-Qaeda remained as strong as
ever as Biden made his withdrawal decision—despite its violating the
Doha Agreement. The Treasury Department revealed in early January
2021 that al-Qaeda was "gaining strength in Afghanistan while continuing to operate with the Taliban under the Taliban's protection."

The assessment concluded that "Al-Qaeda maintains close contacts with the Taliban, providing advice, guidance, and financial support" and that "the Taliban and al-Qaeda maintained a strong relationship and continued to meet regularly." The report also said that "senior Haqqani Network figures have discussed forming a new joint unit of armed fighters in cooperation with and funded by al-Qaeda."[25] A Taliban spokesman released a statement rejecting the assessment as "warmongering" and "propaganda."[26]

Despite its vocal denials about their ongoing ties, the Taliban continued to praise al-Qaeda in early 2021,[27] and al-Qaeda was present in roughly two-thirds of Afghan provinces when Biden announced his withdrawal.[28] In fact, the US and Afghan militaries killed several key al-Qaeda leaders operating in Afghanistan in the months before and after Biden's announcement.[29] The United Nations found that "Al-Qaeda and like-minded militants continue to celebrate developments in Afghanistan as a victory for the Taliban's cause."[30]

THE TALIBAN'S ADVICE TO JOE BIDEN

The Taliban was intently focused on the new Biden administration and on attempting to convince Biden to leave Afghanistan.[31] After Biden beat Trump, they immediately warned him to withdraw US forces from Afghanistan—accompanied by a promise to conquer Kabul.[32] They supplemented those warnings with something of a charm offensive. One Taliban official went out of his way to note that "Biden was the first U.S. official to start negotiations with the Taliban when he was working in the Obama administration."[33]

In January 2021, after Biden's inauguration, the Taliban posted a video saying "Our advice to Joe Biden would be to own Trump's policies by withdrawing his forces. He shouldn't trouble himself, nor his country. He doesn't have another option, either." To avoid any misunderstanding, the message concluded, "This is both a message and a warning. . . . We'll enter Kabul in victory, God willing!"[34] When Biden publicly suggested in late March that he was still contemplating whether he would go through with the withdrawal, and as NATO countries made clear that they didn't want the pullout to happen, the Taliban lashed out, telling Biden not to listen to "flawed advice and incitement by warmongering circles."[35]

Biden soon did what the Taliban demanded.

THE TALIBAN "PEACE GOVERNMENT"

The Taliban always made it abundantly clear that it wasn't interested in power sharing with the Afghan government. The Taliban repeatedly demanded Ghani's removal for any supposed power-sharing agreement, but Ghani insisted that he would leave only after a democratic election.[36] Blinken and Zal appeared willing to accommodate the Taliban's request if that meant the United States could get out sooner.

In late February, the Biden administration engaged in a bizarre Hail Mary diplomatic effort, pushing for a power-sharing "peace government" between the Afghan government and the Taliban that was dead on arrival.[37]

Through a series of overtures in the weeks prior, Blinken and Zal had tried to prep Ghani for what was to come, telling him that he had a "historic opportunity for peace." The Taliban was never interested in peace—there was no such opportunity. Blinken reported that they had had a "great meeting" with Zal on February 4, saying that they had discussed the "way forward in Afghanistan: continuing to protect the United States against the threat of terrorism, achieving a just and durable political settlement there, and cementing a permanent and comprehensive ceasefire."[38] All those things were fantasies.

Blinken told Ghani that a key aspect of the plan was to bring together Russia, China, Pakistan, Iran, India, and the United States to oversee the formation of a new government, implausibly claiming that "these countries share an abiding common interest in a stable Afghanistan."[39] The secretary of state reiterated that Zal was performing "vital work" for Biden and shared a draft document from Foggy Bottom that he believed would "jumpstart Afghanistan Peace Negotiations."[40] Zal provided the proposals, signed by Blinken and dated February 28, to the two sides.[41]

The Biden administration's peace agreement included calling for "a new High Council for Islamic Jurisprudence"—seven members picked by the Afghan government, seven by the Taliban, and one by the president of the "peace government." The president of the peace government would be someone agreeable to both sides. How the Biden administration proposed to find a president mutually agreeable to two sides who had been killing each other for twenty years was left unexplained. The peace government's executive branch, parliament, and judiciary would be filled by both republic and Taliban officials. The Biden proposal also said that the "Afghanistan Independent Human Rights Commission" would include Taliban members. The farcical proposal was quickly rejected by both the Afghan government and the Taliban, and Biden announced the US withdrawal a month and a half later.

Austin flew to Afghanistan in late March and met with President Ghani, General Miller, and US chargé d'affaires Ross Wilson. Austin said that the United States was "mindful of the timelines and the requirements that the Taliban has kind of laid out." He refused to say whether he thought that the Taliban was in compliance with the Doha Agreement, even though it wasn't. He also touted his role leading the US military withdrawal from Iraq under Obama—despite the ISIS invasion that had soon occurred as a result. "There's probably nobody who understands the physics associated with moving troops and equipment out of a place better than me."[42]

Blinken directed Zal to ask the Taliban about delaying the US withdrawal beyond May 1, but the Taliban said no. The president claimed he had had a tough time coming to his ultimate conclusion to withdraw US forces, but Sullivan did not believe it had been a hard decision for him. Biden called Obama before he made the withdrawal decision, and the former president was supportive of the current one.

"QUADRAPHONIC SOUND"

The NATO allies, who had 10,000 troops from roughly three dozen nations stationed in Afghanistan, were pointedly less supportive. On January 27, 2021, UK General Sir Nick Carter warned NATO's defense chiefs that a full withdrawal would be seen as "a strategic victory for the Taliban."[43] On February 14, 2021, NATO secretary general Jens Stoltenberg stated that "our presence is conditions-based" and the Taliban "must reduce violence, negotiate in good faith and live up to their commitment to stop cooperating with international terrorist groups" before NATO could leave.[44] The Taliban never met any of these conditions.

Five days later, on February 19, 2021, Biden promised that his administration was "committed to consulting closely with our NATO Allies and partners on the way forward in Afghanistan,"[45] but that commitment—like so many of his other promises about Afghanistan—was empty.

During NATO's ministerial meeting in Brussels on March 23 and 24, Blinken was ambushed by NATO allies firmly opposed to a full withdrawal. The secretary of state took notes for three hours during the closed-door meeting and called Biden back in Washington when it ended.[46] He told Biden that he had heard pushback in "quadraphonic sound"—i.e., it had been blasting him from all four corners of the room.[47] NATO wanted the United States to use its troop presence as leverage with the Taliban, conditioning any withdrawal on the Taliban's taking good-faith steps toward a political settlement. After the NATO meeting, Blinken advised Biden to delay any US troop withdrawal announcement until after an upcoming summit with Taliban leaders in Turkey.[48] The Taliban never showed up, so Biden simply declared soon afterward that the United States was leaving.

In an April 14 statement, NATO reluctantly went along with Biden's decision to withdraw, noting that its troops had gone into Afghanistan to support the United States after the 9/11 attacks.[49] The NATO officials' meeting in April related to both the United States' Afghanistan withdrawal announcement and a Russian military buildup around Ukraine (a buildup Russia would repeat and follow through on with an invasion less than a year later).[50] Blinken and Austin traveled to Brussels and stood alongside Stoltenberg as they announced the US–NATO withdrawal from Afghanistan, which they said would be done in a few months.

Blinken declared, "Our plan was in together, adjust together, out together—and today, we began to hammer out what 'out together' looks like." Austin again said, "I know a thing or two about executing a drawdown, or what the military calls retrograde."[51] Thus did the US–NATO mission in Afghanistan begin its end—which would conclude with the Taliban in charge before the end of summer.

Two days after the fall of Kabul, Sullivan would tout the fact that NATO had ultimately signed on to Biden's decision to withdraw. Unmentioned was NATO's opposition to the withdrawal up until the moment Biden made his decision. UK general Nick Carter said that Biden's withdrawal announcement "is not a decision that we hoped for, but obviously we respect it."[52]

Andrew Hastie, the Australian shadow minister for defense and an Afghanistan war veteran, told us, "The response from NATO and Australia was simply to follow the US lead in Afghanistan. . . . The US was the one great power anchoring the security effort in Afghanistan. Once the US had decided to withdraw from Afghanistan, the strategic options for allied partners to remain were very limited. We followed suit and left Afghanistan as well."

On August 18, British prime minister Boris Johnson said, "The West could not continue this U.S.-led mission—a mission conceived and executed in support and defense of America—without American logistics, without U.S. air power, and without American might."[53]

"WE'RE COMING HOME"

On April 14, 2021, Biden formally announced the decision he had made months, if not years, earlier. "I'm now the fourth United States President to preside over American troop presence in Afghanistan: two Republicans, two Democrats. I will not pass this responsibility on to a fifth," he declared in a speech from the White House Treaty Room.[54] He noted that it was the same spot where Bush had announced US military operations in Afghanistan in October 2001. He flubbed the number of US service members who had been killed during the war and confused Iraq and Afghanistan several times.

His speech was premised on demonstrable falsehoods and bizarrely scheduled the withdrawal date to coincide with the 20th anniversary of 9/11. He later moved the withdrawal date up to the end of August, perhaps recognizing the poor optics of the decision.[55] But whether August 31 or September 11, the withdrawal date was bizarre for another reason: it was right in the middle of the Taliban fighting season. "They didn't plan very well and they did it during the middle of a fucking fighting season. Like, why are you doing this in the summer? Because you want to get out before 9/11. But that's not smart," a former senior station chief in South Asia told us. "They would have done better if they'd waited until November, December, January, February time period, when it's easier to get people in and out and you're not in the middle of the fighting season."

Biden promised that he would "not conduct a hasty rush to the exit." That was insincere. He also contended that he had "inherited a diplomatic agreement"—the Doha Agreement—that had forced him to make that decision.[56] That was false. But the Doha Agreement had been predicated on conditions that the Taliban had never met, including that it would stop al-Qaeda from using Afghanistan to threaten the United States. He even admitted on August 19, just days after Kabul fell, that even without the Doha Agreement, "I would've tried to figure out how to withdraw those troops," so the deal cannot be blamed.[57] He also claimed in his April speech that "we accomplished that objective" of ensuring that "Afghanistan would not be used as a base from which to attack our homeland again" and that "al Qaeda is degraded."[58] He went even farther, falsely claiming that al-Qaeda was "gone" from Afghanistan.[59]

He also insisted that the Afghan military was 300,000 soldiers strong, a claim he would continue to make in the months to come even though it was demonstrably false.[60] It was actually vastly smaller due to "ghost soldiers" (existing only on paper) as well as to deaths, attrition, and capitulation and surrenders to the Taliban during the fighting.

Biden clung to the fiction that the Taliban was interested in a peace deal, promising in his April 14 speech that the United States "will support peace talks." He also called on a number of foreign adversaries— namely Russia and China—"to do more to support Afghanistan." He also said that Pakistan—which had helped give the Taliban safe haven and supported the Taliban and Haqqani Network—should do more. He said that those countries "all have a significant stake in the stable future for Afghanistan."[61]

"Throughout this process, my North Star has been remembering what it was like when my late son, Beau, was deployed to Iraq," he declared.[62] Right after his speech, he traveled to Arlington National Cemetery's Section 60, where thousands of US service members who were killed during the wars in Iraq and Afghanistan had been laid to rest. When asked what the moment meant to him, Biden brought up Beau again: "I'm always amazed at generation after generation, the women and men who prepared to give their lives for their country. . . . It means that I have trouble these days ever showing up at a veterans cemetery and not thinking of my son Beau."[63] He insisted that the withdrawal had not been a hard decision to make.

Biden was surprised to see negative coverage about his withdrawal decision. Blinken and Sullivan met with Biden in the Oval Office a few days after he made the decision. "Mr. President, this was an incredibly hard decision," Blinken told the president. "I admire the fact that you made it." Biden tapped on the Resolute Desk and said, "Yeah, the buck really does stop here."[64] White House chief of staff Ron Klain told colleagues that when a book was written about the war in Afghanistan, it would start with the attacks of 9/11 and would end on the day that Biden had said, "We're coming home."[65] Klain was correct, but not for the reasons he believed.

On April 15, Blinken met in Kabul with Ghani and the chairman of the High Council for National Reconciliation, Abdullah Abdullah, to discuss Biden's decision. He told Ghani that the United States "remains committed to Afghanistan and its people" and that "a negotiated political settlement remains the only way forward." He also claimed that "we'll retain substantial assets in the region" and "we'll hold the Taliban accountable to its commitments."[66] None of it was true.

A TALIBAN VICTORY LAP

The Taliban was ecstatic when Biden announced the full US withdrawal, responding the next day with tacit praise—"the efforts of warmongering circles have failed"—as well as with a warning for the United States if it stayed beyond May 1.[67] In July, the special inspector general for Afghanistan reconstruction revealed that the Taliban's tone had been "resoundingly triumphant" following Biden's withdrawal speech, noting that "the Taliban focused on achieving a military victory."[68] Then, in May 2022, the inspector general concluded that "the single most important factor" in the collapse of the Afghan security forces in August 2021 had been Trump's signing of the Doha Agreement, followed by Biden's April announcement that the United States would be pulling the plug.[69]

Matin Bek, who would soon become Ghani's chief of staff, was part of the Afghan negotiating team in Doha when Biden gave his speech, and he told us that the Taliban had been thrilled with Biden's withdrawal announcement. "I remember how relieving it was for Taliban. When we saw them in the lobby of the hotel where we all stayed, they were smiling and happy. Biden's announcement killed the little available window for an imagined peace," he said. "Biden's announcement of a withdrawal date sent a wrong signal to Afghans. . . . Unfortunately, Taliban were able to use this effectively."

The greatest debacle of Biden's presidency was on the way.

FOUR

BAGRAM

O nce Biden announced the withdrawal, Generals Austin and Milley sought to conduct a lightning-fast retrograde, aiming to get essentially all US forces out of Afghanistan by mid-July, even though the deadline wasn't until September 11 (it was later moved up to August 31). They successfully got US troops out quickly—and helped speed the collapse of the Afghan military in the process. The "go-to-zero" order by Biden and this rapid withdrawal approach by the Pentagon brass meant that support for the Afghan military and air force simply wasn't a priority on the way out the door. The removal of US troops also meant pulling out thousands of US and international contractors upon whom the Afghans relied to fight the Taliban.

The retrograde also required the military to give up Bagram Air Base—the linchpin of US operations in Afghanistan and the region— which meant giving up US air capabilities to strike ISIS-K and al-Qaeda and to stop Taliban advances. It likewise left the prison inside the airfield, which was full of ISIS-K terrorists and thousands of Taliban fighters, under the sole protection of the shaky Afghan military. The Taliban freed all of those prisoners when they took the base, and one of them would later murder thirteen Americans at Hamid Karzai International Airport (HKIA), just outside Kabul. Biden's decision to abandon Bagram had several immediate repercussions: it not only drastically limited the ability to bomb Taliban units, it also nixed the capacity to effectively conduct a mass evacuation with proper protection. If a Noncombatant Evacuation Operation (NEO) became necessary, the military's only option would be to evacuate tens of thousands of civilians using the single runway twenty-five miles away at HKIA.

Bagram is a massive air base, with 10,000- and 12,000-foot-long runways, parking spots for more than a hundred fighter jets, huge hangars, a large hospital, bunkers, and barracks, all guarded by high walls and guard towers. The base had a twenty-year history as the nerve center of US and NATO military operations in Afghanistan and had also been the tragic site of deadly Taliban, ISIS-K, and "green-on-blue" (Afghan military on US military) insider attacks over the years. HKIA, by contrast, is located in Kabul. It has a single runway capable of accommodating military aircraft, and in the summer of 2021 it was protected only by barriers and perimeter fencing. HKIA, with its single runway, accommodated fewer aircraft and was more difficult to defend than Bagram. Additionally, it was right next to the home of 4.5 million civilians—and soon would be under Taliban rule and swarming with ISIS-K.

As chaos spread in late August, US intelligence officers and military veterans shared a darkly humorous meme attributing a fake, snarky quote to Sun Tzu's *The Art of War*: "Always abandon your most strategic air base right before an evacuation."[1] Abandoning Bagram was a big mistake—but it wasn't the only one. All the mistakes together accelerated the Taliban's advance toward Kabul—giving both Americans and Afghans even less time to leave the country.

"300,000 STRONG"

Biden and his top officials repeatedly lied about the size of the Afghan security forces, in 2021 claiming that they totaled 300,000, even though the real number was much smaller. The US strategy (including getting Americans and Afghan allies out) relied upon the Afghan military to continue fighting after US troops withdrew—but it was based on fake numbers.

In February, Afghan government sources acknowledged that there were large numbers of "ghost soldiers" in the Afghan military.[2] But Sullivan nevertheless declared on April 15, "We've trained and equipped 300,000."[3]

Biden and Milley also prevaricated about the size of the Afghan army in the months leading up to the fall of Kabul, citing numbers that did not take into account ghost soldiers, casualties, captures, and capitulations. In a July 8 speech, Biden claimed that the Afghans had "nearly 300,000 current serving members of the military."[4] On August 16, the day after the Taliban takeover, he said, "We trained and equipped an Afghan military force of some 300,000 strong—incredibly well equipped—a force larger in size than the militaries of many of our NATO allies."[5] He repeated the lie constantly. Milley got the size of the Afghan National Defense and Security Forces (ANDSF) wrong during Senate testimony on June 17, claiming that "the government of Afghanistan is holding and they have approximately about 325,000 to 350,000 person security force—Army and police force."[6] Those numbers were inflated, at minimum, by 25,000 to 50,000—although, as the special inspector general for Afghanistan Reconstruction (SIGAR) pointed out, the numbers were likely much farther off due to "ghost soldiers" and the collapse of the Afghan forces.

A report released in August 2021 by the Center for Strategic & International Studies said that "only a small fraction of the 182,071 personnel supposedly in the Army and Air Force could be used effectively."[7] NATO said in May 2022 that the ANDSF was "only able to provide evidence of 254,000 troops."[8] And a 2021 report by the International Institute of Strategic Studies concluded that Afghanistan had only 171,500 members in the army and 7,300 in the air force, and only 99,000 "paramilitary" forces—its national police (which are not typically included in the military figures of other nations).[9]

"SHITTING IN A TRENCH"

The withdrawal had an instant impact. When Biden pulled the plug, US special forces were still advising Afghan forces in Helmand, but Afghan lieutenant general Sami Sadat would soon be fighting without US support and with only a dysfunctional Afghan government backing him.[10] Lieutenant Colonel Matthew Chaney remarked that Sadat was a key Afghan leader: "We're in this together." But one US special operator soon thereafter said he had just been told that Austin had "made the decision to pull everybody out starting immediately."[11] It was a ten-day retrograde. Americans shook their heads in disbelief. "We had a huge setback today," Sadat remarked. "Morale has been crushed."

The US troops held a meeting with the Afghan forces they would soon be leaving, telling the Afghans that they, too, had been blindsided by the news. The Afghans looked despondent, with some saying that the Taliban would hunt them down. "I felt like it was like musical chairs," Krummrich told us. "Like at any point, that could have been any one of us Green Berets having to sit there and tell them, but the music stopped and that team was the one stuck without the chair."

The same scene repeated itself at bases across Afghanistan in 2021. The US soldiers destroyed computers, papers, and weapons, piling up rifle ammo, mortar rounds, and boxes of machine gun rounds, pouring gasoline on them, and blowing them up. "Retrograde means you're shitting in a trench," one US special operator said.[12] Sadat remarked, "I think the Taliban are waiting for the Americans to leave Helmand. And then they will attack." He was right.

"FOOT ON THE GAS"

The Pentagon was much more focused on ensuring that the Taliban didn't attack US forces on their way out of Afghanistan than it was on helping the Afghan military fight the Taliban—and it never came up with a workable plan to assist the Afghans from afar.

A former senior US intelligence official in Afghanistan remarked to us, "You're either retrograding or you're enabling—and enabling fell by the wayside." Congressman Mike Waltz, a former Army Green Beret who was part of a congressional delegation to Kabul prior to Biden's announcement, told us that McKenzie declared to him, "If we get the green light to withdraw, I'm going to do it as fast as possible because we will be vulnerable." Waltz replied that McKenzie's approach was like "looking at the issue with a soda straw on just the military operation" and that it had failed to take into account NATO partners, support for Afghan security forces, US contractors, the US Embassy, and the languishing Special Immigrant Visas (SIVs). McKenzie replied, "I'm putting my foot on the gas to get the heck out of there."

In the wake of Biden's decision, military and administration officials admitted that they didn't yet have a plan to execute it. Twelve days after the announcement, Pentagon press secretary John F. Kirby candidly admitted, "We don't have all the answers right now" on continuing to assist Afghan forces. On May 3, he again made it clear that "we're still working our way through the details" on supporting the Afghans.[13] In June, Austin was "still chewing over" how to support the Afghans from afar.[14] Austin falsely said the month after the Taliban took over that "we planned for just such a contingency."[15] That was untrue; the Biden administration had not planned for the fall of Kabul, and it showed.

On June 12, McKenzie wrongly claimed that "the fighting is see-saw right now." In fact, the Taliban had been making steady gains for months. He added, "We will still do everything we can to keep pressure on ISIS and al-Qaeda from our over-the-horizon locations. . . . That will be a very difficult thing to do."[16] In mid-June, Milley said that the collapse of the Afghan forces wasn't a foregone conclusion, although the Afghan military was reeling. He said that the United States did not plan on helping the Afghan military fight the Taliban and would be focused only on al-Qaeda and ISIS-K.[17] "There's a range of outcomes here," he told the Senate on June 17, adding "Will that military disintegrate, will the government collapse, will the Taliban come in?" But he said that it was Biden's intent to "keep that situation from devolving into the worst case."[18] The worst case happened—quickly.

Plan or no plan, the Pentagon would not be dissuaded from its swift retrograde even amid a Taliban takeover, saying it had to follow Biden's orders. On June 14, McKenzie said that "zero means zero."[19] He repeated that the United States would strike only al-Qaeda or ISIS, not the Taliban. On June 21, Kirby said that the US forces would be out by August 31 regardless of what happened on the ground. Kirby said that there was "still active discussion" on how to "actualize" over the horizon, and admitted that the Biden administration hadn't yet figured out how to help the Afghan air force keep fighting.[20] He also said that the United States' ability to assist the Afghan military directly in its fight against the Taliban was lessening and would soon disappear. Also in June, a Pentagon spokesperson said that jets from carrier strike groups in the region had gone after the Taliban but "targeting for these strikes has been—and will continue to be—limited."[21]

The Defense Department also announced that a new organizational structure in Afghanistan would be built around three key entities— tellingly, the Pentagon inspector general later wrote that the details still hadn't been worked out when Kabul fell.

On his way out the door in July, Miller issued his final warnings: "The Taliban are on the move. We're starting to create conditions here that won't look good for Afghanistan in the future if there is a push for a military takeover." When asked if the United States should leave a small force behind, he demurred, "The uh—Let me hold on that one." And when asked about leaving Afghan partners behind, he said, "I don't like leaving friends in need."[22] He also implied that the Taliban takeover of Kabul was a near certainty. He gave a lengthy interview later that month saying that the Afghan military was in serious jeopardy.[23]

Miller handed over command to McKenzie during a July 12 ceremony at Resolute Support Mission headquarters in Kabul. McKenzie said that his first goal was protecting the US diplomatic presence in Afghanistan (the US Embassy in Kabul was shut down a month later as the Taliban took Kabul). His second was enabling the safe operation of HKIA (the US military would briefly lose control of the airport when it was overrun by thousands of Afghans). The third was providing assistance to the Afghan military (it was disintegrating). And the final goal was supporting counterterrorism (al-Qaeda and ISIS were rejuvenated by the Taliban takeover). Kirby said that it was "clear" that the Taliban had "governance designs certainly of a national scale" and the Talibs "believe there is a military solution."[24]

Milley insisted on July 21 that a Taliban takeover was "not a forgone conclusion" but the "strategic momentum appears to be sort of with the Taliban."[25] It's fair to say that "sort of" wasn't a strong enough phrase.

THE HANDOVER

The US military's retrograde from Afghanistan was quick. US forces handed over Camp New Antonik in Helmand province to the Afghan military on May 2, German forces handed over Camp Mike Spann near Mazar-e-Sharif on May 5, and US forces handed over Camp Morehead on the outskirts of Kabul and New Camp Brown in Kandahar province on May 11. US forces left Kandahar Airfield on May 13. In a controversy that would be repeated when the United States left Bagram at the start of July, Afghan military officials said that the US departure from Kandahar had come as a surprise, although the US government insisted that it had been coordinated with the Afghan government.[26] The New Kabul Compound and the Blockhouse in Kabul were handed over on May 28.

The Pentagon's retrograde updates now suddenly began to include references to the deteriorating situation. Their spin was that the United States' departing the country and handing bases over to the Afghans would help them fight the Taliban. On June 1, Camp Stevenson in Mazar-e-Sharif was handed over, and on June 7, CENTCOM announced that more than half the retrograde was finished. Camp Dwyer in the Helmand River Valley was handed over on June 15, Camp Arena in Herat on June 28, and Camp Lincoln next to the main airport in Mazar-e-Sharif on June 29.

The vast majority of NATO and other allied troops—more than 4,800—departed by the end of June.[27]

"JENGA!"

US and foreign contractors were the lifeblood of the Afghan military—especially for the deeply flawed Afghan air force—and the troop withdrawal meant the departure of contractors, too. Retired lieutenant general David Barno told the Afghanistan IG that "it was like pulling everything out of a Jenga pile when you took the contractors out."[28] Miller later said, "The companies are not going to keep people there if they don't have blanket protection either from the U.S. or the NATO forces."[29]

In late July, the Afghanistan IG said that the withdrawal of contractors "could significantly impact ANDSF sustainability, in particular their ability to maintain aircraft and vehicles."[30] The Afghan air force was the key advantage over the Taliban—but pulling out US advisers and contractors would be the death knell for the flying force. An Afghan military officer in charge of UH-60 helicopter operations worried that when contractors left "it'll be very bad."[31] In January 2021, SIGAR sent the Pentagon a classified report warning that the Afghan air force would likely fall apart without US support and contractors.[32] In January 2022, Kirby insisted that the Afghan air force's looming catastrophe had been "well known to us" at the time.[33] But the United States had never taken the steps necessary to keep the Afghans flying and effective against the Taliban.

Afghan Army chief of staff and acting minister of defense general Mohammad Yasin Zia said he had learned in May that CENTCOM would be trying to use "aircraft 'tele-maintenance' by video, on iPads" to assist with maintaining Afghan aircraft.[34] That plan predictably failed horribly. In June, a senior State Department official said that "you could see there wasn't going to be anything there" to keep the Afghan air force functional.[35]

The Defense Intelligence Agency said in a report spanning April to June that the Afghan Army "likely lacks the capability to carry out its missions without coalition support" and relied heavily on the crumbling Afghan air force.[36] The watchdog warned in July that accidents, battle damage, and the withdrawal of US and contractor support was "damaging the health" of the helicopter fleet.[37] Nevertheless, the US military was providing only "limited" over-the-horizon support to the Afghans "since most of the command's activity was focused on the withdrawal."[38]

In July, the Afghan government sent a memo to the White House "urgently requesting additional aircraft and imploring that the U.S. continue to fund critical contractors."[39] The White House blew them off.

In January 2021, there were 18,214 contractors in Afghanistan, including 6,346 Americans. In April, CENTCOM was focused on "go-to-zero" planning. By July, the drop in contractors was dramatic—just 7,795 contractors left, among them 2,656 US citizens (a drop of nearly 3,500 Americans). CENTCOM said that contractor efforts were now "focused on Afghanistan contractor retrograde and mission transition" rather than enabling the Afghan military, calling the retrograde the "highest priority."[40]

Krummrich told us that pulling out US troops and contractors had had an "absolutely catastrophic impact—total destruction. They caved within weeks or months of us leaving." Kirby bizarrely insisted on August 16 (the day after the Taliban takeover) that up until the week prior, the United States was "still meeting our commitment to support their air force." A year after the fall of Kabul, McKenzie said that the US military had made "heroic" efforts to help the Afghan air force, but "none of those things work particularly well."[41]

"NOT OPTIMAL"

During the spring and summer, Miller handed over seven bases to the Afghan armed forces, ending with the closure of Bagram Airfield (BAF) on July 2. The Taliban's military advances spanned Afghanistan, including in Parwan province. The Pentagon briefly paused its plans to close Bagram in mid-June as the White House considered whether it was wise to give up such a strategic base. Biden quickly doubled down.

A senior officer tasked with executing the Bagram withdrawal said, "To call it haphazard would be generous. Our planning relied on the assumption that we weren't going to abandon our dominant tactical position. We didn't get a formal directive one way or the other for months. Once the order came down, we scrambled to pack up our most valuable equipment and destroy the sensitive items we couldn't take."

In September 2021, Milley testified that the military had created options for keeping Bagram open, but Biden had rejected them.[42]

Numerous US military members raised serious concerns about closing Bagram, and Bagram had been included in US military plans in 2021, but the base was abandoned in favor of running the NEO solely through HKIA. "I knew throughout the planning process that once Bagram went away the battlespace would be massive. HKIA security was not optimal," one high-ranking service member later told investigators. "Bagram was more defensible, so concerns about threat could not have driven that decision."[43] A US military medical professional later told investigators that he had conducted a predeployment site survey at Bagram in May to look into setting up a theater hospital, but when Bagram had closed, that had been moved to HKIA.[44]

Bagram was also widely seen as a strategic asset for the United States in Afghanistan, not just for combating the Taliban and conducting counterterrorism operations but also for keeping an eye on nearby China.

"THEY ARE FUCKED"

The Pentagon did not properly communicate what was happening at Bagram to US contractors in Afghanistan—or to US troops on the ground. One US contractor at Bagram said in May, "So far, nothing is changing." Another said, "No one has told us shit." "Good luck to the Afghan guys left here with the Talibs. To be honest, they deserve more, but all I can say is, they are fucked," a third said.[45] Without US contractors and without Bagram, they were.

An Army official involved in the Bagram retrograde told us he had been blindsided by the decision to shutter Bagram. He had been overseeing the construction of a new US forces–Afghanistan headquarters building at Bagram, only for the order to be reversed suddenly in June. He had installed sensitive equipment at Bagram in the summer only for it to be ripped out and sent back. "It was like, one day it was there, one day it wasn't," he said. "That's how fast it happened. Because at no point do I remember them ever mentioning BAF shutting down, at least not like that. . . . And then all of a sudden BAF is gone, which was our main support." He said that the base had been the key to stopping the Taliban from taking Kabul. "They wouldn't have done shit if we still had a presence there," he said. "Even if they were pissed off and they started attacking again, they still wouldn't have gotten all the way into Kabul."

"SHROUD OF SECRECY"

The US military left Bagram in the middle of the night. The United States had airlifted tens of thousands of pieces of equipment out of Bagram, while thousands more had been destroyed. Some military equipment was smashed by US soldiers in the final days before closing Bagram.

Afghan officials said that the US military had left without alert-
ing the incoming Afghan base commander, General Mir Asadullah
Kohistani. "We [heard] some rumour that the Americans had left Bagram . . . and finally by 7:00 a.m., we understood that it was confirmed,"
Kohistani said.[46] He said he had not found out that the US forces had
left until several hours after their 3:00 a.m. departure from the base.[47]
Darwaish Raufi, the Afghan district administrator for Bagram, claimed
that the US departure had occurred without being coordinated with
Afghan officials. US forces left behind hundreds of trucks and cars,
as well as dozens of armored military vehicles, small weapons, and
ammunition. The items left behind at Bagram were valued at more
than $565 million. The Afghan military said that 3,000 Afghan forces
stationed nearby would be taking the base over.

The Taliban celebrated. "We consider evacuation of all U.S. forces
from #Bagram a positive step & seek withdrawal of foreign forces
from all parts of the country," Taliban spokesman Zabihullah Mujahid
tweeted on July 2.[48] The Taliban insisted, "Right now it is not part of
our strategy to capture the military bases like Bagram as our plan is to
seize small compounds and installations outside the cities."[49] Bagram
was seized in just over a month and other Afghan bases much sooner.

Waltz tweeted of Bagram's closure, "It's by far the biggest symbol of
our 20 years of blood and treasure we have expended for all veterans that
have served there. As our only base sandwiched between China, Russia,
and Iran it's a huge strategic asset. Why are we just giving it away?"[50]

On July 6, when pressed, Kirby defended the way the US forces had
left Bagram, saying "I can't speak for how Afghan leadership briefed
their people" but "there was coordination with Afghan leaders both
in the government, as well as in the Afghan security forces about the
eventual turnover of Bagram Air Base." He denied that the handover
had been done in a "shroud of secrecy."[51]

He then, incredibly, claimed that it was not "helpful" to be "hy-
pothesizing" about a potential Taliban takeover—even though that was

on the verge of happening. He contended, "We still have the authority to assist the Afghans in the field if they need it—the way you've seen it being conducted in the past, through airstrikes." But US air strikes had been cut drastically in June and dropped even further in July. He also admitted that the Biden administration was "still working out" how to support the Afghans. He added that the small US military force remaining in Kabul would not be there to help the Afghans fight the Taliban.[52]

"HAPPY THINGS, MAN!"

On July 2, just after Bagram was shuttered, Biden gave a speech as part of the White House's attempted summer victory lap on jobs and covid-19. He repeatedly expressed frustration with reporters' questions about Afghanistan—he really didn't want to talk about it. He didn't mention the Taliban once, placing blame for the deteriorating situation on the Afghan government. "We're on track exactly as to where we expected to be," he said of the retrograde. He said he was concerned about the Afghan government's ability to maintain itself. A reporter attempted to follow up on Afghanistan, and Biden interjected, "I want to talk about happy things, man."

The president was asked if the United States was going to give the Afghans the air support and military support needed to stop Kabul from falling. He replied, "We have worked out an over-the-horizon capacity that we can be value added, but the Afghans are going to have to be able to do it themselves with the air force they have, which we're helping them maintain." The United States was pulling out the contractors the Afghan air force relied upon in droves.

When another reporter tried to bring up Afghanistan, Biden again displayed frustration, raising both his hands. "I'm not going to answer. Any more quick questions on Afghanistan. . . . Look. It's Fourth of July. . . . I'm concerned that you guys are asking me questions that I'll answer next week, but I'm—it's the holiday weekend. I'm going to celebrate it. There is great things happening." He added, "We're bringing out—bringing our troops home. We have—all across America, people are going to ballgames and doing good things. This is good. I'll be—I'll answer all your negative questions—not negative—your legitimate questions."[53] The president left to host the World Series champion Los Angeles Dodgers at the White House.

"COLLAPSE"

Days after the Taliban took Kabul in August, Milley defended the decision to abandon Bagram, saying that the military had had to "collapse" either Bagram or HKIA due to troop number constraints. He called HKIA the "better tactical solution," given the reduction of US forces to six or seven hundred.[54] The US military leadership testified that Biden's go-to-zero order had meant that keeping both Bagram and HKIA open had become an impossibility. Austin was the only Pentagon leader to insist that Bagram wouldn't have been helpful, bizarrely claiming that the base "would have contributed little to the mission that we had been assigned: to protect and defend our embassy."[55] In fact, the opposite is true: abandoning Bagram was what had put the US Embassy and all of Kabul at grave risk. Keeping US assets at Bagram would have helped the Afghan military continue to fight the Taliban, enabled the United States to pummel the Taliban with air strikes, and stopped the Talibs from seizing Kabul. Bagram was also obviously a better position to be in during a NEO than inside HKIA surrounded by the Taliban.

The US withdrawal from Bagram had crushed Afghan military morale further. "A lot of times the Afghans have told us, 'That really changed my calculus. Now I realized you probably are leaving.' And so it started modifying them into survival mode," said Afghanistan IG analyst in charge James Cunningham in September 2022.[56] Bagram's closure also made it vastly more difficult for the United States to support Afghan forces, to conduct effective air strikes in Afghanistan, and to keep other US government operations there working smoothly. It was the final nail in the coffin for the Afghan military's chances against the Taliban. Earlier in the summer, CENTCOM had been claiming that handing bases over would help the Afghan military fight the Taliban, but curiously, just days after Bagram was shuttered, the US military was no longer claiming that.

AIR STRIKE STRIKE-OUT

At the end of June, Miller told reporters that the US military still had the weapons and abilities to assist the Afghan military, but "what I don't want to do is speculate what that [support] looks like in the future."[57] During a July 25 visit to Kabul, McKenzie said, "The United States has increased airstrikes in the support of Afghan forces over the last several days, and we're prepared to continue this heightened level of support in the coming weeks if the Taliban continue their attacks."[58] Bagram was closed, so the Biden administration's resumption of manned air strikes required flying US aircraft from the sea and bases in the Gulf.[59]

Statistics from the US Air Force show that US air strikes in Afghanistan dropped dramatically in 2021—at the exact moment they were most needed to help the crumbling Afghan military push back on the Taliban.[60] The number of sorties in Afghanistan dropped to 5,533 in 2020, down more than 3,000 from their height during Trump's presidency. The number of sorties declined by more than half in 2021.

The decrease in air strikes was even more dramatic. There were only 801 total US air strikes in 2021, the fewest in more than a decade. The United States deployed 142 aerial weapons in January, 126 in February, 116 in March, and 119 in April, dropping to 72 in May, 55 in June, and a paltry 18 in July despite massive Taliban gains. The Biden administration increased the number to a woefully insufficient 153 strikes in August, but it was far too little, too late, and the Taliban took the country—and Kabul—halfway through the month.

INDIRECT FIRE

After the fall of Kabul, US military leaders, including Milley and Austin, testified to Congress that the Taliban had broken every term of the

Doha Agreement except one—its promise not to attack US and NATO forces. That testimony was false, because in fact the Taliban had attacked US and NATO bases in Afghanistan numerous times before and after Biden's withdrawal announcement, including at Bagram.

Milley told the Senate on September 28, "The one that was met was the most important one—which was do not attack us or the coalition forces. And they did not." He repeated this to the House. Austin falsely testified that "the only thing that they lived up to was that they did not attack us."[61]

Both Milley and Austin were lying. In fact, the Taliban violated each piece of the Doha Agreement—not only its promise to break with al-Qaeda but also its promise not to attack US facilities. In August, the Pentagon inspector general said that from April through June, the Taliban had "executed a few ineffective indirect fire attacks in the direction of U.S. or NATO bases." The Pentagon watchdog stated that the "Taliban conducted limited attacks on coalition bases" and that "The Taliban fired rockets toward a coalition military base in Khost province in the early morning of April 2. . . . The Taliban fired rockets at an airport in Khost where U.S. troops were based. U.S. forces responded by conducting clearing operations in the vicinity."[62] The Khost Protection Force said that the "Taliban fired indiscriminate rocket missiles on the military headquarters of coalition forces in Khost." Several Afghan news outlets said that the US and coalition base in Khost had been targeted by Taliban rockets. The Taliban claimed that the Doha Agreement had been broken and so "today these invaders were targeted" as it cheered the attack.[63] "A large number of rockets were launched in the vicinity of the center of Khost province on the old airfield of that province, which is the main center of the enemy's mercenary forces," Taliban spokesman Zabihullah Mujahid tweeted on March 30. "The missiles hit specific targets, and as a result, the enemy suffered heavy losses in life and property."[64]

The Pentagon inspector general also said, "On April 7, the Taliban launched another rocket attack, this time against Kandahar air base, where several hundred U.S. troops were still based."[65] The Taliban celebrated the attack: "Kandahar airbase, a key enemy military center, targeted with multiple missiles noon hours today. Missiles have hit targets, causing heavy human & material losses."[66]

That day, a reporter said that the Taliban had attacked Kandahar Airfield and Camp Chapman and asked Kirby what the US military was doing to stop attacks on US and NATO troops. "We condemn to-day's attack on Kandahar Airfield, home to several hundred U.S. and coalition personnel," Kirby said. "While the attack resulted in no casu-alties or damage, the Taliban's decision to provoke even more violence in Afghanistan remains disruptive to the opportunity for peace." The reporter noted that Kirby hadn't actually said what the US military was doing about the Taliban attacks. "We always have the right of self-defense for our troops, but our focus right now is on supporting a diplomatic process here to try to bring this war to a negotiated end," Kirby added. He was asked whether a Taliban attack on Kandahar Airfield and US forces there would be a violation of the Doha Agreement. "I'm not prepared today to give an assessment of this attack as balanced against the Doha Agreement, okay?"[67]

Biden's withdrawal announcement came a few days later, and the Taliban attacks continued.

The Pentagon watchdog said, "An explosion inside Bagram Airfield on May 1 killed one and wounded 24 Afghan personnel." A Defense Intelligence Agency (DIA) spokesperson said, "The Taliban launched two rocket attacks against coalition forces at Kandahar Airfield on May 2." US military spokesman Colonel Sonny Leggett said on May 1, "Kandahar Airfield received ineffective indirect fire this afternoon. . . . U.S. Forces conducted a precision strike this evening, destroying addi-tional rockets aimed at the airfield."[68] Taliban spokesman Zabihullah Mujahid tweeted that the Taliban would "take every counteraction it deems appropriate against the occupying forces."[69] An Afghan news outlet reported that security officials in Parwan had said that "one person was killed and 24 others were wounded in an explosion while security force members were offering prayers at a mosque inside Bagram base." The security chief for Parwan police said that the casualties had been Afghan forces.[70]

Kirby repeatedly downplayed the Taliban attacks—but acknowledged that there had been some. "What we've seen are some small, harassing attacks over the course of the weekend," he said on May 3, adding "We've seen nothing thus far that has affected the drawdown."[71] He repeated the statement on May 13. Miller then bafflingly claimed on June 7 that the Taliban hadn't attacked the United States during the retrograde: "To date—we have not seen that."[72]

The Pentagon's after-action Abbey Gate Report also revealed the Taliban had conducted an "IDF on BAF"—an indirect fire attack (most likely a rocket attack) on Bagram—on June 28, three days before the United States ended its presence at the base.[73] The report said that the same day, Mullah Mohammad Fazl, one of the "Taliban Five" and a Talib commander, had told the United States to stop conducting air strikes. The next day, the US military told the Taliban that it must stop its indirect fire against US bases.

Despite a documented history of Taliban attacks on US and NATO bases in 2021, the Pentagon first tried to downplay or ignore them as they were happening, then denied that they had ever happened at all after Kabul fell.

"HERE COMES THE RED BLOB"

All signs pointed to the impending fall of Kabul. The US military brass and the Biden administration's missing that during the retrograde was inexcusable.

Krummrich told us that he had been tracking Taliban advances from the SOCOM ops center all spring and summer. "As we're pulling back, you begin to see the blob moving towards Kandahar and moving towards Kabul. . . . Here comes the red blob. Every day I come and look at the ops center, and everyday the blob would grow bigger. Momentum really starts to shift. The Taliban take more ground, the Afghan forces start falling back and just disappearing, and the Taliban are moving at the speed of their logistics."

The Afghan Analysts Network said that when US troops had begun a full withdrawal on May 1, the Afghan government had controlled 210 of 241 district centers, although the reality on the ground had been worse because "it was not uncommon to find" Afghan forces isolated in a district center with the Taliban controlling the surrounding territory.[74]

Only four district centers fell to the Taliban in May, but 119 district centers fell in June. The calamity accelerated in July and into August, ending with the seizure of Kabul, and the Biden administration acted as though it had never seen it coming. The Taliban ramped up its violence in 2021, especially following Biden's withdrawal announcement in April.[75] A US government–funded assessment confirmed a stark rise in violence in Afghanistan in April and then as the Taliban went on the offensive.[76]

FDD's Long War Journal's real-time assessment of the Taliban takeover showed that as of May 1, the Taliban controlled 73 of Afghanistan's 407 districts.[77] The Taliban controlled 88 districts by May 25 and 106 by June 14. But on June 23, Milley told Congress that the Taliban controlled just 81 of the 419 districts—even though it actually controlled far more.[78] By June 29, the Taliban controlled 157 districts.[79] By July 15, it controlled 221, and it was assessed that Afghanistan "is at risk of complete collapse if the government and military do not get a handle on the security situation, and quickly."[80]

District centers fell to the Taliban in fairly rapid succession as US forces retrograded, and the Biden administration never properly responded. By July 4, the Taliban also seized more than a dozen districts in northern Afghanistan. The Afghanistan IG said that the Taliban military conquest had reached a key turning point on July 31, when the Taliban conducted significant attacks on major airports in Kandahar and

Herat provinces.[81] The Taliban captured seven provinces in northern Afghanistan over a five-day period in early August.

The IG said that "six of the seven Afghan military corps had either disintegrated or surrendered by the time the Taliban took Kabul, with only the 215th Corps in Helmand Province continuing to fight the Taliban for two more days, after which it was ordered to stop fighting too."[82] The Taliban captured Afghanistan's final provincial capital of Panjshir province on September 7 and declared its new "interim government" the following day.

"After Biden announced the withdrawal, however, there was no longer any brake on the Taliban; they had no incentive to hold back in the hope of gaining more concessions from Washington or out of fear of drawing the US military back into the war," the Afghan Analysts Network noted. ". . . Khalilzad had gambled it all on the Taliban genuinely wanting to negotiate. He never had a Plan B of what to do if the insurgents were playing for time and actually intent on military conquest."[83]

"MANIFEST VICTORY"

Afghan special forces and commandos were attempting to fill the void left by Afghan troops who had abandoned outposts across Afghanistan as the Taliban advanced. Lieutenant Colonel Ayatullah Parwani in Kandahar province said that he had previously coordinated the US and Afghan air support deployed against the Taliban there—but the US air presence had basically left. Captain Masoud Karimi of Afghanistan's Special Mission Wing said that his special forces teams were conducting double or triple the number of air missions they had in the past.

Thousands of Afghans in a host of provinces said in 2021 that they would be taking up arms against the Taliban. The Afghan government, desperate in its fight against the Taliban, claimed to support the nascent, ragtag resistance efforts.[84] It was a total failure. The Afghan Ministry of Defense contended, "Mobilization of the people in support of the security and defense forces has had a considerable role in retaking territories."[85]

In June, Ghani held a high-profile meeting at the presidential palace with a host of Afghan power brokers as part of his unsuccessful efforts to mobilize support against the Taliban.[86] The Afghan government never provided any real support to the militia efforts.

The attempted mobilization was led largely by former mujahideen commanders, as well as former Northern Alliance figures.[87] The Taliban condemned the militia movement, saying "the attitude of the Islamic Emirate towards them will be stern and they will be deprived of amnesty."[88]

Miller said in July, "Afghan government officials are not aligning themselves with militias because they fail to see the risks involved. They are doing it because they think such alliances are necessary for their survival."[89] Afghan minister of the interior General Abdul Satar Mirzakwal claimed, just days before the Taliban took Kabul, that the Afghan government was arming local militias.[90] None of it worked.

On June 16, Colonel Sohrab Azimi, a well-regarded, US-trained Afghan special forces field commander, was massacred along with twenty-two of his men by the Taliban.[91] As the Taliban made significant gains and Afghan forces folded, the Afghan military was increasingly relying on Afghan special forces leaders such as Azimi. The death of Azimi and his squad, executed in cold blood by the Taliban while defending a base as they awaited reinforcements, was a significant blow to Afghan military morale.

The Taliban celebrated its victories in late June, calling its "manifest victory and triumph" against the Afghan military "the victory of the entire Muslim and Mujahid Afghan nation." The group reiterated its "hope for the full realization of the goals of sacred Jihad."[92]

"DOWNHILL"

After US troops left, Afghan general Sadat tried to fend off the Taliban, largely without US support and with a dysfunctional Afghan government not doing what it needed to do. He remarked that the fighting was tiring "because our bases are surrounded by the Taliban, and we don't have strong air power."[93] Things got worse as the summer went on. The Afghan commander traveled to the capital of Helmand province, where Afghan efforts to fight the Taliban were being stymied by lack of US help and Afghan government incompetence.

On August 25, the *New York Times* published an opinion piece by Sadat blasting the Biden administration:

> For the past three and a half months, I fought day and night, nonstop, in southern Afghanistan's Helmand Province against an escalating and bloody Taliban offensive. Coming under frequent attack, we held the Taliban back and inflicted heavy casualties. Then I was called to Kabul to command Afghanistan's special forces. But the Taliban already were entering the city. It was too late.
>
> I am exhausted. I am frustrated. And I am angry. . . .
>
> It's true that the Afghan Army lost its will to fight. But that's because of the growing sense of abandonment by our American partners and the disrespect and disloyalty reflected in Mr. Biden's tone and words over the past few months.

He said that the withdrawal of US troops, the vast reduction in US air strikes, and the pulling out of US contractors had been the death knell for the Afghan forces in their fight against the Taliban, adding "Mr. Biden confirmed in April he would stick to Mr. Trump's plan and set the terms for the U.S. drawdown. That was when everything started to go downhill. . . . We lost our superiority to the Taliban when our air support dried up and our ammunition ran out."[94]

ZEROS AND THE BATTLE OF KANDAHAR

A senior Afghan official said that Ghani had been warned in early July that only two out of the seven Afghan army corps were still operative and Ghani had asked the CIA to use Zero Units to protect Kandahar city from being overrun.[95] The Zeros would soon be relied upon to help secure HKIA after the Taliban takeover, after they fell back to the capital of Kabul from Kandahar and elsewhere.

In early August, small groups of Afghan commandos were overwhelmed by massive Taliban forces at Kandahar.[96] The Taliban took the city quickly in a counteroffensive with the fighting finishing on August 13. Zero units surrounded the Kandahar airport and said they would fight to the death against the Taliban, with perhaps 1,000 Zeros arrayed against 2,000 or more Taliban. But then they announced a truce. The Afghan commandos surrendered millions of dollars of military equipment in exchange for safe passage on Afghan government flights out of the Kandahar airfield to Kabul.

A former senior US intelligence official in Afghanistan told us that the CIA had begun planning a year and a half before the fall of Kabul and planned to use Zeros to move rapidly to Kabul to defend the capital. At least six carrier planes pulled thousands of Afghan military units out of Kandahar into Kabul—which itself fell in less than forty-eight hours.

GROUNDED

During the summer fighting, Afghan pilots' ammunition began to run low. Mohib said that the Afghan air force had faced a significant shortage of laser-guided bombs in the waning weeks of the Afghan republic. The Pentagon had stopped a planned delivery of some laser-guided bombs ahead of the Taliban takeover.

Following a June meeting between Ghani and Biden, the Afghan government announced that the United States had promised to provide thirty-seven Black Hawk helicopters and two A-29 Super Tucano fixed-wing attack aircraft to Afghanistan, to add to the more than 160 helicopters and aircraft the Afghan air force already had.[97] The Afghan government also said it had been promised that roughly two hundred US and international contractors would stay in Afghanistan until September, mostly to assist the Afghan air force. "We have very limited air support, the helicopters have been busy with moving supplies and evacuating our dead and injured forces," Afghan interior minister Mirzakwal said on August 11.[98]

"LIKE A FLOOD"

Ghani's scrambling continued on August 2, when he presented the Afghan parliament with a new security plan. "The reason for our current situation is that the decision was taken abruptly," he said, blaming the Biden administration's withdrawal.[99] The Taliban called Ghani's plan "nonsense" as it threatened, "Declarations of war, making accusations and providing false information cannot prolong Ghani's life."[100]

The US military purposely chose not to work with the Afghan military on plans to secure HKIA ahead of a potential evacuation. "We didn't want to let the cat out of the bag and let them know we were planning for a NEO," Rear Admiral Peter Vasely, the commander of U.S. Forces Afghanistan–Forward later told investigators.[101] Roughly three dozen Afghan battalions had dissolved around the start of the month.

The weeks leading up to the Taliban takeover of Kabul may have been the deadliest time frames for Afghan forces since 2001.[102] The International Committee of the Red Cross said on August 10 that 4,042 patients wounded by weapons had been treated at fifteen Red Cross centers that month.[103] Afghan general Mohammad Yasin Zia said that data from July 1 through August 15 indicated that 4,000 Afghan forces had been killed and another 1,000 had gone missing. A military hospital doctor in Kabul described the arrival of wounded Afghan troops as "like a flood" during the final weeks of the war.[104]

"Contrary to popular perceptions, in many cases and places, the ANDSF fought valiantly to defend the country," an outside report published by West Point said in October 2021. "It is true that in the immediate aftermath of the United States beginning its withdrawal, some ANDSF units deserted or surrendered without a fight. But all across the country in the months that followed, ANDSF members fought and died in battles against the Taliban."[105]

The Afghan government never truly believed that the United States would fully withdraw. Mohib said in late 2021, after the fall of Kabul, "We didn't read the writing on the wall. The writing on the wall was that a withdrawal will take place no matter what."[106]

SECRET DEALS

Over a period of years, the Taliban laid the groundwork for its rapid takeover of Afghanistan by cutting deals with local Afghan leaders and negotiating potential surrender agreements. It ramped up that surreptitious activity in 2021, especially after Biden made his withdrawal announcement. Biden administration officials testified that they hadn't seen those negotiated surrenders coming.

US and Afghan officials said that the Taliban had purportedly tendered cease-fire offers to local Afghan officials, police, and military units in 2020 and increased their efforts in 2021, effectuating what were essentially negotiated surrenders, using a mixture of bribes and threats of violence to convince Afghan police and troops to lay down their weapons or abandon their posts when it advanced. In December 2021, the Afghan Analysts Network said that "negotiations and surrender played a major role in the Taliban victory."[107] Austin, incredibly, had already admitted in September 2021, "We did not anticipate the snowball effect caused by the deals that Taliban commanders struck with local leaders."[108]

"DID NOT COLLAPSE IN 11 DAYS"

McKenzie later said that the full US troop withdrawal—against the military's advice—had been the main reason the Afghan military and government had collapsed and the Taliban had taken over.[109]

In October 2021, an outside report published by West Point said that the Afghan military had lost its ability to sustain itself logistically because of Biden's withdrawal.[110] In August 2022, the Army War College said that the US withdrawal had undermined the Afghan government and military.[111] In October 2022, SIGAR said that "the single most important near-term factor" in the Afghan military collapse had been the US decision to withdraw the US military and contractors from Afghanistan through the Doha Agreement—signed by Trump but followed through on by Biden.[112]

Austin and Milley testified after the fall of Kabul that no one predicted the collapse of the Afghan government "in eleven days." The Afghan collapse had been happening for weeks and months, though. In October 2021, an outside report published by the Combating Terrorism Center at West Point bluntly concluded, "The ANDSF did not collapse in 11 days." The analysis concluded that at least fifteen of Afghanistan's thirty-four provincial capitals had been "effectively surrounded by Taliban-controlled areas" in early 2021. That meant that even prior to Biden's withdrawal announcement, the Taliban was well positioned around many of Afghanistan's major cities.[113]

The outside report stressed, "The ANDSF's collapse—while it occurred over the course of nearly four months and was surprising to serious observers even on that timeline—had been years in coming." The report added, "Contrary to General Milley's statement to this effect, the ANDSF did not wholly collapse in a matter of days. . . . some ANDSF units were overrun—while others began to withdraw or surrender their positions to the Taliban—immediately after the United States began its withdrawal and the Taliban launched their offensive. These scenes were repeated across the country in the months that followed. The result was a domino effect."[114]

FIVE

KABUL FALLING

T he Biden administration had known for months before Kabul fell that an evacuation would be necessary to save Americans and Afghan allies. US troops were swiftly retrograding. American contractors were being pulled out. The Afghan military was reeling. The Taliban was on the march. But the State Department and the White House never did the basic things to ensure that Americans and Afghan allies would get out.

During a tabletop exercise at the end of June, McKenzie stated that a Noncombatant Evacuation Operation (NEO) was "going to happen."[1] Nevertheless, the State Department locked down the embassy in May and June, citing the spread of covid-19. The embassy largely refused to process new SIV applicants until they felt the risk had subsided. The decision was yet another example of misplaced priorities when American and Afghan civilians were facing an increasingly dire situation.

As the Taliban advanced, the White House and the State Department not only refused to consider the possibility of a meltdown in Kabul but also actively suppressed attempts to warn about it. The Kabul embassy's regional security officer drafted a statement in early August warning US civilians that Kabul would likely fall to the Taliban within a few weeks. Embassy officials were livid. When the officer refused to change it, the statement was watered down and buried.[2]

To the White House, the closing of the embassy would be an unacceptable political failure. During a National Security Council tabletop exercise on August 6, the US Chargé d'Affaires, Ross Wilson, stated, "If we have to conduct a NEO, we have failed." According to a senior military official, "POTUS was publicly making it clear this was a priority. Ambassador Wilson began stating 'I am maniacal about the embassy remaining in Kabul' in direct support of Afghan government."[3] During planning meetings, State Department officials frequently corrected senior military officers: "Don't say NEO" and "We're not planning a NEO." The embassy then refused to fully participate in evacuation planning until a week prior to the fall of Kabul. That critically undermined any efforts to prevent the catastrophe barreling down the tracks.

The NSC and State Department still refused to plan for a NEO or even acknowledge the possible necessity of one. More than four thousand diplomats were then on the ground. In fact, in August 2021, the Kabul embassy was the United States' largest official diplomatic mission in the world. Despite that, Biden had assigned only 650 US troops to protect and facilitate a potential evacuation. According to Pentagon documents, military officials had recommended roughly five times as many personnel just to secure HKIA.

In the first week of August, after repeated requests from military officers watching the Afghan resistance to the Taliban rapidly disintegrate, State grudgingly agreed to reduce the number of personnel at the embassy to 2,500. Only a few days later, the embassy submitted a formal request for increased military assets to prepare for—lo and behold—a NEO. The request triggered the mobilization of units such as the 82nd Airborne Division and the 2nd Battalion, 1st Marines.

The failure to properly plan for a NEO would be a costly one— but the Biden administration had its eyes closed all summer. A State

Department official later admitted that "not once did we plan for Kabul to be overrun" as quickly as it had been.[4]

"A SUMMER OF FREEDOM. A SUMMER OF JOY."

Throughout the spring and summer of 2021, the Biden administration continued to cling to the useless Taliban peace talks. On May 14, Secretary of State Blinken spoke with President Ghani about "efforts to advance the peace process," claiming that "we support our partnership and Afghan security forces."[5] On June 2, the US Embassy in Kabul celebrated Pride Month by tweeting a picture of a rainbow flag flying. (Any freedoms gays might have had would be gone a month and a half later.) On June 4, Blinken announced $266 million in humanitarian assistance to Afghanistan, calling it "the latest concrete example of our deep commitment to a peaceful, stable future for Afghanistan."[6] But the Afghans needed military assistance far more.

On June 2, while Afghanistan crumbled—and the safety of the Americans living there became increasingly tenuous—Biden promised a fun-filled summer ahead for Americans: "Because of our vaccination program and our economic response . . . America is headed into the summer dramatically different from last year's summer: a summer of freedom, a summer of joy, a summer of get-togethers and celebrations."[7] The summer in Afghanistan was not so joyous.

Blinken was dismissive when pressed on June 7 about the failure to evacuate Afghan interpreters. "We are not withdrawing, we are staying, the embassy is staying," he wrongly claimed. "If there is a significant deterioration in security, that could well happen—we have discussed this before—I do not think it is going to be something that happens from a Friday to a Monday. So, I would not necessarily equate the departure of forces in July, August, or by early September with some kind of immediate deterioration in the situation."[8] But that was exactly what happened.

"1861 MOMENT"

A few days before Biden hosted Ghani at the White House on June 25, Taliban spokesman Suhail Shaheen touted a "victory" and falsely claimed that the Taliban wasn't pursuing a violent takeover. He contended, "We do not have any intention of running over those [provincial] capitals and taking them. A military takeover is not our policy."[9] That was an obvious lie.

Shaheen refused to promise that the Taliban wouldn't destroy religious artifacts and wouldn't execute religious minorities and women as it had in the 1990s. But he did lie when he said that schools would remain open to women and girls.

During their meeting, Biden "emphasized enduring United States support for the Afghan people." He also "expressed his concern about the recent increase in covid-19 cases in Afghanistan" and promised, "Our troops may be leaving, but support for Afghanistan is not ending." He added, "Afghans are going to have to decide their future of what they want. . . . But it won't be for lack of us being a help."[10]

For his part, Ghani honored the 2,448 Americans "who paid the ultimate sacrifice" and said that the United States "has not spared any effort in blood or treasure." He said, "The Afghan nation is in an 1861 moment, like President Lincoln, rallying to the defense of the republic." Ghani quipped, "I hope that nobody does the Bernard Shaw on us—exaggerating our death." Biden told Ghani, "We're not walking away." The Afghan president said, "The most important ask I have for Afghanistan is that we have a friend in the White House." The US president replied, "You have a friend."[11] Yet when Ghani asked Biden to provide more helicopters and to ensure that US contractors would continue to support the Afghan military, Biden was noncommittal.

Ghani also met with Austin. "We will make the transition to a new relationship with Afghanistan and the Afghan forces," Austin said. The Afghan president was also asked about intelligence reports that his government might not survive six months after the United States' departure. "There have been many such predictions, and they've all turned out false,"[12] Ghani said.

"NONE WHATSOEVER"

On July 8, Biden dismissed the chances of a Saigon-like situation: "None whatsoever. Zero. . . . The Taliban is not the South—the North Vietnamese Army. . . . There's going to be no circumstance where you see people being lifted off the roof of an embassy in the—of the United States from Afghanistan. It is not at all comparable." He added, "The likelihood there's going to be the Taliban overrunning everything and owning the whole country is highly unlikely."[13] The Taliban did just that a month later.

Blinken tweeted that the United States would be delivering 3.3 million doses of covid-19 vaccines to Afghanistan "to help lead the global fight against COVID-19. #EnduringPartnership."[14] But the Afghans needed contractors and air strikes more than jabs.

State Department officials pointed to the fruitless talks in Doha and argued that "only a negotiated settlement" could end the war.[15] The Taliban, however, believed that the conflict could be ended by force.

Blinken also repeatedly thanked Qatar (which had been double-dealing in Doha for years) and Pakistan (which more than any other country had been responsible for the Taliban takeover) for their roles in the "peace" process.

The Biden administration clearly had skewed priorities. On July 19, the State Department announced that it was releasing Guantánamo Bay detainee Abdul Latif Nasir, a key al-Qaeda leader and bin Laden associate who had spent years fighting alongside the Taliban in the 1990s and against the United States after the invasion of Afghanistan. State stated that the terrorist "is the first detainee to be repatriated to his country of origin during the Biden-Harris Administration" and reiterated Biden's promise to shut down Gitmo.[16] The White House press call made no mention of the Taliban, al-Qaeda, Afghanistan, or 9/11.

A "PERCEPTION" PROBLEM

Biden and Ghani held a call July 23—three weeks before Kabul fell—during which the Afghan president begged the US president for more US air strikes. "We are facing a full-scale invasion, composed of Taliban, full Pakistani planning and logistical support," he said. "What is crucial is close air support." The Afghan president said Abdullah Abdullah had gone to negotiate with the Taliban but the Talibs "showed no inclination" in real negotiations. Ghani said, "We can get to peace only if we rebalance the military situation."[17]

Biden replied, "Look, close air support works only if there is a military strategy on the ground to support. . . . We will continue to provide close air support, if we know what the plan is." US air strikes had plummeted to almost negligible numbers. He also said, "The perception around the world and in parts of Afghanistan, I believe, is that things aren't going well in terms of the fight against the Taliban. And there's a need, whether it is true or not, there is a need to project a different picture." He also falsely told Ghani, "You have 300,000 well-armed forces versus 70,000 to 80,000" Taliban.[18]

Milley, Sullivan, and McKenzie also spoke with Ghani, with Milley telling him, "The perception in the United States, in Europe, and the media sort of thing is a narrative of Taliban momentum, and a narrative of Taliban victory. And we need to collectively demonstrate and try to turn that perception, that narrative around."[19] There was the perception of a rapid Taliban takeover because that was the reality.

"WE GOT ALL KINDS OF CABLES"

The State Department inspector general found that in the period starting with Biden's April announcement of withdrawal to the suspension of the embassy's operations in August, State "approved and issued just 1,754 (eight percent) of the 22,085 SIVs issued since 2009."[20] The 8 percent figure for 2021 was just barely higher than one-thirteenth of the total over the thirteen years. The watchdog found that visa issuance had increased from just 45 in April to a peak of 685 in August—a fraction of what was needed.

State was asked in late July about estimates that there were up to 70,000 Afghan allies and their families who might need to leave Afghanistan, but a State official wrongly acted as though the number was much smaller—just 20,000—saying "I'm not sure where the 70,000 number comes from."[21]

An internal dissent cable was signed by two dozen US Embassy members in Kabul and sent to State on July 13, warning that Kabul could collapse soon after the US troop withdrawal. The dissent cable, sent to Blinken, warned about the collapse of the Afghan military and a potential near-term Taliban takeover, urging State to speed up evacuation planning, do more to deal with the SIV applications, develop systems for processing locally employed staff, help keep safe those who had assisted the United States, and provide stronger condemnations of Taliban violence.[22] The cable was authored by Elisabeth Zentos, a deputy political counselor who had previously been on the Obama NSC, and Anton Cooper, the political unit chief at the embassy.[23] The cable also warned that the embassy would likely be overrun if Kabul fell.

On July 30, Biden announced that the first group of SIV applicants brought out of Afghanistan as part of Operation Allies Refuge had arrived in the United States—just over two weeks before Kabul fell. On August 2, less than two weeks before Kabul was overrun, Blinken said that the second flight of Operation Allies Refuge evacuees had just arrived. Tens of thousands would be left behind.

On August 20, after Kabul fell, Biden dismissed the significance of the dissent cable: "We got all kinds of cables, all kinds of advice. If you notice, it ranged from this group saying—they didn't say it would fall when it would fall, when it did fall—but saying it would fall to others, saying it wouldn't happen for a long time, and they'd be able to sustain themselves through the end of the year. I made the decision. The buck stops with me. I took the consensus opinion. The consensus opinion was that, in fact, it would not occur, if it occurred, until later in the year."[24]

A US official familiar with the dissent cable said, "By then, everything was blinking red. It takes a lot for folks to go around leadership."[25] Blinken spoke about the dissent cable in September 2021 but said that making it public would have a "chilling effect": "This dissent channel is something that I place tremendous value and importance on. It is a way for people in the State Department to speak the truth, as they see it, to power." Blinken said that the cable had expressed "real concerns" about the durability of the Afghan government forces and called upon State to speed up the SIV-granting process.[26] The White House repeatedly refused to share the cable. McCaul, blasting Blinken's continued "bullshit" excuses for not handing the cable over, subpoenaed the State Department for it in March 2023.[27]

COMING FOR KABUL

The Taliban ramped up its attacks on Kabul in early August ahead of conquering the capital. Its "martyrdom battalion" conducted a deadly attack against the home of Afghan defense minister Bismillah Mohammadi in Kabul on August 4, although Mohammadi escaped assassination. Two days later, Taliban gunmen assassinated Dawa Khan Menapal, the director of the Afghan government's media and information center, killing him on a Kabul street.

On August 3, Blinken spoke with Ghani "to reiterate the strong and enduring U.S. commitment to Afghanistan" and spoke of the need "to accelerate peace negotiations toward an inclusive political settlement that respects the rights of all Afghans, including women and girls."[28] That was a fantasy. When announcing additional US air strikes that day as the Taliban continued its march, General Joseph Votel, the deputy commanding general (operations) of the 82nd Airborne Division, said, "This is about buying time. It's about blunting and slowing down the

Taliban and helping the Afghans to get a little more organized."[29] It was too late.

On August 5, Blinken spoke with Abdullah to repeat the "commitment to seek a just and durable political settlement" as Blinken "condemned continuing Taliban attacks."[30]

On August 9, the online comedian "Benny Drama" (real name Benito Skinner) posted a jokey viral video on TikTok that he had recently filmed with White House press secretary Jen Psaki and others about his day-in-the-life experience as an intern at the White House.[31] He had filmed it a few weeks prior. The unserious video, featuring him typing with acrylic nails and generally being obnoxious, was variously embraced and mocked, but to many it showed the misplaced priorities of the White House.

Kirby was asked that day if the Pentagon would allow US air strikes beyond August 31, and he demurred, saying "Where and when feasible, we'll continue to support them with airstrikes." He stressed that the United States was focused on withdrawing by the end of the month and added, "We have fewer capabilities now than we did before the drawdown, but as we have them, and I have them available, we'll use them where and when feasible." He repeated the favorite falsehood about there being 300,000 Afghan forces: "They have an Air Force, the Taliban doesn't. They have modern weaponry and organizational skills. The Taliban doesn't. They have superior numbers to the Taliban."[32] Most of those purported advantages had long since disappeared.

Psaki and Kirby continued to argue that a Taliban takeover wasn't inevitable, even as the Taliban rushed toward Kabul. "No particular outcome is inevitable," Kirby said on August 10. "We will continue to coordinate airstrikes with—and in support of—Afghan forces when and where feasible."[33]

State Department spokesman Ned Price spent a number of minutes that day repeatedly dodging questions about whether the Taliban had violated the Doha Agreement (it obviously had done so repeatedly). He stressed that Zal was working on a deal in Doha. He offered up something of a defense of the Taliban, pointing to "the proviso that they not target U.S. or coalition forces—the Taliban had not done so."[34] That wasn't true; the Taliban had attacked US and NATO bases.

The same day, Psaki said that Biden "continues to believe that it is not inevitable that the Taliban takes over Kabul." "We will continue to provide close air support, making sure the air force functions are operable," she said the next day. "We are closely watching the deteriorating security conditions in parts of the country, but no particular outcome, in our view, is inevitable."[35] The US air strikes—belatedly ramped up—were not nearly enough. Ned Price also continued the Biden administration's fixation on the fictional 300,000 figure.

The Biden administration remained in denial about what the Taliban actually wanted. On August 11, Psaki said, "The Taliban also has to make an assessment about what they want their role to be in the international community."[36] There was never any reason to think that the Taliban cared about those empty threats.

The Biden administration stubbornly clung to the fiction that the Taliban was interested in a political settlement rather than military conquest. On August 12, Blinken tweeted that he and Austin had spoken with Ghani, insisting that the United States was "committed to supporting a diplomatic solution."[37] Austin told Ghani that a "cohesive ANDSF is the linchpin of peace and security in the face of a heavy fighting season." By that time, the Afghan military had largely disintegrated. Both Austin and Blinken promised Ghani that the United States "remains committed to maintaining a strong diplomatic and security relationship" with the Afghan government (which ceased to exist three days later).[38]

During the second week of August 2021, Vice President Kamala Harris filmed a YouTube Originals space series with child actors flying in and filming at Harris's residence at the Naval Observatory that Wednesday through Friday—two days before the Taliban took Kabul.[39]

"RANGE OF POSSIBILITIES"

Austin later claimed that "we planned for a range of possibilities" but "we certainly did not plan against a collapse of the government in eleven days."[40] The collapse had been happening for months, though.

During congressional testimony, General Milley defended the US military's planning, pointing to "4 key synchronizing events"—an "Afghanistan Retrograde Rehearsal" on April 28, a "senior official rehearsal of concept" on May 8, a "working level interagency table top exercise" on conducting a NEO on June 11, and a "senior official interagency table top exercise on NEO" on August 6—just over a week before the Taliban took Kabul.[41]

Austin agreed with Senator Tom Cotton that the ROC drill was an important one.[42] He said that the Pentagon's leadership—himself and Milley included—had attended, as had Sullivan, CIA director William Burns, and others. But Cotton pointed out that Blinken had not attended, and neither had Deputy Secretary of State Wendy Sherman. Instead, the highest-ranking State Department official present was Blinken's number three deputy, Brian McKeon, who was overseeing the US Embassy in Kabul.

Just before Kabul fell, the Treasury Department froze an Afghanistan-bound plane on the tarmac thanks to warnings from a top Treasury Department official, Marshall Billingslea, who led the fight in combating terrorist financing and who told us, "Luckily, at the very last minute, the Federal Reserve actually stopped the cash flight so that they did not wind up replenishing the Central Bank of Afghanistan with hundreds of millions in banknotes that would then have fallen right into the Taliban's hands."

On August 13, Kirby was still saying "It still is a moment for Afghan National Security and Defense Forces" and "no outcome has to be inevitable." He implausibly claimed, "Kabul is not, right now, in an imminent-threat environment."[43] It fell two days later.

One intelligence community analyst who briefed the NSC on the deteriorating situation in Afghanistan in the summer of 2021 told us that some Biden national security officials hadn't seemed to understand how dire the situation was. The analyst said that Biden administration officials still hadn't seemed to grasp the possibility that Kabul might fall over the weekend when warned about it on Friday the thirteenth.

Leaked notes from an NSC meeting in the White House Situation Room on the afternoon of August 14 reveal that the Biden administration was still scrambling to come up with plans for the most basic things necessary for a functional NEO at HKIA, even as the Taliban was less than a day away from taking Kabul.[44] The meeting notes suggest that the Biden administration was still operating under the delusion that the Taliban wouldn't be taking Kabul in the extreme near term—let alone the next day. It was agreed that "the priority [be] given to U.S. Embassy personnel, U.S. citizens, and allied personnel with whom the U.S. Government has agreements for evacuation."[45] The meeting notes also discussed forming plans for the yet-languishing SIV applications. An NSC meeting to continue discussions was set for the next day, but Kabul fell. Kirby later said he wouldn't comment on the damning leaked NSC meeting documents.

Blinken continued to cling to the fictional idea of peace with the Taliban even on the eve of the fall of Kabul. He tweeted about a "productive call" with Abdullah and thanked him for the Afghan government's "every effort to reach a political settlement." He also spoke with Ghani about "our urgent diplomatic and political efforts to reduce violence."[46]

On August 14, Biden gave a speech in which he sought to defend his withdrawal while shifting the blame for the debacle to Trump, declaring "I have authorized the deployment of approximately 5,000 U.S. troops to make sure we can have an orderly and safe drawdown of U.S. personnel and other allied personnel, and an orderly and safe evacuation of Afghans who helped our troops." He also said he had told Blinken to support Ghani and other Afghan leaders "as they seek to prevent further bloodshed and pursue a political settlement."[47] The Taliban took Kabul the next day.

"By June, it was clear to me that this thing was done, that the stupid plan of 'We're going to keep this embassy in sort of this defended route to HKIA so we have a lifeline there,'" Krummrich told us. "'We're going to keep all that open. And we're going to keep advising these guys. Hey, maybe we can even, you know, keep a small special operations footprint.' It's just bullshit, right? It was the most wishful thinking you ever heard of."

SUMMER VACATION

Biden had planned a two-week vacation starting on August 9, although that was quickly ruined by the Taliban takeover. He began the week in Wilmington, Delaware, then was in the nation's capital from August 10 to 12, spending the morning of August 13 in Wilmington again before flying to Camp David in the afternoon. On August 9, a White House official said that Biden was expected to be in DC and Delaware the following couple weeks.[48]

The Biden team was heavily focused on pushing its $1.2 trillion infrastructure bill, and the Senate passed it on August 10. "After years and years of 'Infrastructure Week,' we're on the cusp of an infrastructure decade that I truly believe will transform America," Biden said during a White House speech that day.[49] The White House was ecstatic, but the victory lap was cut short by the Taliban rampage.

In his speech touting the passage of the bipartisan Infrastructure Investment and Jobs Act on August 10, Biden again brought up the fictional 300,000 number and said that "there's still a possibility" that Kabul would not fall. On August 11, Blinken and Sullivan joined to promote the Biden administration's upcoming Summit for Democracy in December. Afghanistan's democracy ended a few days later.

Before leaving for his planned vacation, Biden held a meeting in the White House Situation Room with Harris, Austin, Milley, Sullivan, Klain, Director of National Intelligence Avril Haines, and others. Austin, Blinken, and Sullivan led discussions on options for the security of

Americans in Afghanistan. Biden told Austin and Milley to ready a plan to send more troops to assist with the coming evacuation. The president also told Blinken to step up State's efforts to evacuate Afghan allies.

"Some of the outlying provincial capitals had begun to fall, and he was increasingly concerned about what might happen in Kabul," Sullivan later said. "The president posed a series of direct questions to his national security team about whether we had to activate the contingency planning that we had put in place over the course of several months. The Chairman of the Joint Chiefs of Staff and the secretary of defense recommended to him that we put the forces that we had already set in place, that we put them on what's called a prepare to deploy order."[50] The deployment order still hadn't been given.

Austin told Sullivan late on the eleventh or early on the twelfth, "It's now my judgment that it's gone past prepare to deploy. We need to deploy."[51] Sullivan helped lead the August 12 meeting as cabinet members joined by videoconference. Biden wasn't there. Intelligence officials were warned at the start of the meeting that the Taliban could take Kabul within weeks or even days. Sullivan went to the Oval Office after the meeting, and Biden called Austin and directed him to deploy US troops into HKIA and begin the NEO. Blinken also called the embassy in Kabul and said that many operations would need to move to HKIA. The orders were given just three days before Kabul fell.

The Friday before Kabul fell, many in the White House were starting their long-awaited summer vacations, with Blinken already in the Hamptons. Biden, along with his wife, Jill, and a small number of staffers, jumped onto Marine One on the thirteenth just after 1:30 p.m. By the time he returned, three days later, the Taliban were ruling Kabul.

The president spent the weekend at Camp David (Saturday, August 14, was the final full day of the Afghan republic, and Sunday, August 15, was when the Taliban seized Kabul) before returning to the White House on Monday, August 16, to deliver brief remarks, before immediately flying back to Camp David. The next morning, August 17, he woke up at Camp David but flew back to the White House, where he stayed for the rest of the week.

Psaki was on a previously planned family vacation, so she wasn't in the nation's capital when Kabul fell. An email query about Biden's plans to address the debacle that was sent to Psaki the evening of August 15 prompted an automatic reply that she "will be out of the office" through the next weekend.[52] However, she returned on Monday. Biden's absence prompted criticism among Republicans.

The White House tweeted a photo Saturday afternoon, August 14, of Biden sitting alone in an empty room at Camp David, with members of his national security team viewable on a TV display. On Sunday afternoon, the fifteenth, the White House tweeted out a similar photo: Biden, alone at a conference table, speaking to his distant team via videoconference as the Taliban was taking Kabul. Blinken hit the Sunday talk show circuit to discuss the administration's handling of Afghanistan, saying "This is not Saigon" and "This is manifestly not Saigon."

White House officials spent Sunday considering whether Biden should return to the nation's capital on Monday to deliver a speech about the Taliban's rapid advances. By the time Monday rolled around, the Afghan government was no more. The Biden administration treated the unmitigated disaster as a political and public relations problem, illustrated by Democratic House speaker Nancy Pelosi blasting out White House talking points on Monday.[53]

The mood inside the White House was dark. Biden returned briefly on Monday, finished his East Room speech that afternoon shortly after 4:00 p.m., and Marine One was wheels up for Camp David again before the clock struck five.

Military leaders at U.S. Central Command in Tampa were launching renewed air strikes against the Taliban forces sprinting toward Kabul, but to no avail. A US military officer said that there had been "51 kinetic strikes" against the Taliban between August 8 and August 15, killing an estimated 331 Taliban and destroying twenty vehicles that the

Taliban had stolen from Afghan forces. The commander of U.S. Forces
Afghanistan–Forward (USFOR-A), Navy Rear Admiral Peter Vasely,
said of the Taliban that by August 14, "We were killing them in bunches,
destroying tactical vehicles, and they kept coming."[54] Krummrich told
us that the Taliban knew they had won, characterizing their thoughts
as "Oh, fuck, this is great. Hey, let's just keep going. Yeah, they're gonna
keep drone striking us, those dicks, but we got patience and people, and
I got more gas, so let's keep going, and pretty soon, they're not gonna
have a place to drone strike us from."

BACK CHANNEL

On August 15, Ghani fled the capital by helicopter as the Taliban entered Kabul. It was the end of the Afghan republic and the start of the
Taliban's new reign. In the lead-up to that fateful decision, Ghani used
Abdul Salam Rahimi, an Afghan government envoy in Doha, to develop
a back channel to the Taliban's leaders, including not just Baradar but
also Haqqani Network leader Sirajuddin Haqqani and Mawlawi Yaqoob,
a son of the Taliban's deceased founder, Mullah Omar.[55]

Rahimi returned from Qatar and met with Ghani and Mohib on
August 12. He told them about the Taliban's offer, which was for all
intents and purposes a negotiated surrender ending with the Taliban
back in power: the Taliban would agree to a two-week cease-fire, and
the Afghan government would send representatives to Doha to work
out a transitional government led by the Taliban; then Ghani would
call for a traditional Afghan council—a *loya jirga*—that would ask
the Talibs to create a new government. The Taliban was supposed to
remain outside Kabul.

Zal's team in Doha knew of the back channel, and they received
calls from Rahimi and Mohib after the discussion with Ghani. Blinken
spoke with Ghani that night, and a US diplomat said that Blinken had
been relieved when Ghani had said he would agree to the deal. Blinken

and Austin spoke to Ghani on August 12, but there was no mention in the State and Pentagon readouts of any back-channel deal.

On August 14, Ghani called a meeting at the palace to meet with Afghanistan's top power brokers, including former president Hamid Karzai. Ghani told his underlings to head to Qatar. He spoke with Blinken again that night, and the surrender agreement was discussed yet again.

Zal asked Ghani to put together a group led by Abdullah and Karzai to work out a transition with Baradar and the Taliban. Blinken told Ghani to send the Afghan delegation to Doha ASAP. Ghani asked Blinken to tell the Taliban, "This is not a surrender" and asked the Biden administration to "lean as much as you can on a dignified process." Blinken insisted, "Dignified is exactly what we want as well."[56]

That evening, Ghani gave an address claiming that "the remobilization of our security and defense forces is our top priority."[57] He fled the country the next day.

GHANI'S FLIGHT FROM KABUL

Hamdullah Mohib said that Khalil Haqqani had called him on August 15 and asked him to surrender. "They were set on a military victory," he said. He called Zal's deputy, Special Representative for Afghanistan Tom West, who said not to take the meeting. In Doha, Abdul Ghani Baradar lied to Zal that the Taliban had "agreed that they will not enter Kabul" and would withdraw "hundreds" of Taliban infiltrating the city.[58] Zal relayed that to Rahimi, who in turn relayed it to Ghani. Interior Minister Mirzakwal put out a message saying that the Taliban takeover would be peaceful. Bek posted a Twitter message: "Don't panic! Kabul is safe!"[59] The Taliban bragged that "all parts of the country have come under the control of the Islamic Emirate" but claimed that they "do not intend to enter the city by force."[60] They were already inside the city gates. A Taliban spokesman said that they had been ordered to enter Kabul after Ghani fled.

Ghani's sudden departure seemingly caught the United States off guard. Blinken later said, "We were in intense conversations with the Afghan government throughout this period of August and into the middle of the month to help organize a peaceful transfer of power." It would have transferred power to the Taliban. "Ghani said to me on the phone that Saturday, 'If the Taliban doesn't agree and engage in good faith, then I will stay and fight to the death.' . . . He fled the country the next day. . . . No notice."[61]

"Ghani went to his residence to take his lunchtime nap, and I with another colleague went to a different building to have our lunch," Bek told us. "Half an hour later, we realized Ghani fled the country through the presidential helicopter. The news of his escape, made to the public, and everything fell apart. Our dreams were crushed and a nation betrayed. The Taliban took over Kabul, and the republic collapsed."

The Afghanistan IG later concluded, "Some cash was taken from the grounds of the palace and loaded onto President Ghani's evacuation helicopters" but "evidence indicates this number did not exceed $1 million."[62] On August 16, Biden indicated that he still bizarrely believed that the Taliban might have been willing to reach a settlement, saying he had urged Ghani in June and July "to seek a political settlement with the Taliban" but that "advice was flatly refused."[63] Mohib later said that the "language used by the Americans" in mid-August was "no longer inclusive" and no longer aimed at a balanced power-sharing agreement, but instead the United States was saying that the goal was only that the Taliban have a "nonmonopoly." Mohib contended, "That basically means a surrender to the Taliban."[64]

BARADAR MEETS MCKENZIE

Zal set up an August 15 meeting in Doha between McKenzie and Baradar. At the meeting, McKenzie displayed two maps, one showing the area between the US Embassy and HKIA where US forces would conduct evacuation efforts, the other with a thirty-kilometer (nineteen-mile) circle drawn around the center of Kabul, with the general warning the Taliban not to enter that zone. McKenzie's information was woefully outdated; the Taliban had not only moved into that zone, it had moved into Kabul.

Baradar told the general that Taliban forces were already inside Kabul, so McKenzie told the Talibs to withdraw. Baradar responded by promising the Taliban didn't intend on interrupting the evacuation, and asked McKenzie if the United States would take responsibility for securing Kabul. McKenzie repeated to Baradar that the US mission was the evacuation only. Baradar then pressed the general again on whether the United States would secure Kabul, and McKenzie simply repeated that his mission was what it was.

Baradar asked what McKenzie thought of the idea of the Taliban taking over the security of Kabul. McKenzie and Zal discussed it, and McKenzie said he had "no opinion" so long as the Talibs didn't interfere with the evacuation.[65] McKenzie testified, "As part of that conversation, he [Baradar] said, 'Why don't you just take security for all of Kabul?' . . . That was not my instruction. And we did not have the resources to undertake that mission." He added, "I did not consider that to be a formal offer, and it was not the reason why I was there, so I did not pursue it."[66] That meant that the Taliban ruled Kabul—and the United States would need to rely on it for security at HKIA.

"You could've taken the offer to the president and asked for more troops to secure Kabul," Congressman Mike Gallagher told the general. "We would've avoided being entirely dependent upon the Taliban and the Haqqani network for security around the airport, which I believe is the original sin which led to the suicide bombing."[67] Congressman Michael McCaul told us that the Taliban offer "was turned down by the White House, which said, in essence, 'Put the Taliban in charge of the evacuation, and importantly, HKIA airport'—which then led to the penetration by the suicide bomber that killed thirteen servicemen and -women."

"MORE QUICKLY THAN WE ANTICIPATED"

On August 16, the day after the fall of Kabul, Biden admitted that the collapse of the Afghan government and the Taliban takeover had happened "more quickly than we anticipated." He asked, "So what's happened? Afghanistan political leaders gave up and fled the country. The Afghan military collapsed, sometimes without trying to fight."[68] Senator Marco Rubio tweeted in response, "This administration was specifically told Afghan forces would surrender faster than our ability to exit. They decided to ignore these warnings."[69] In an interview with George Stephanopoulos just after the fall of Kabul, when asked why he had downplayed in July the chance the Taliban would seize power, Biden asserted that "there was no consensus" in the intelligence community.[70]

"As the president indicated, this unfolded more quickly than we anticipated, including in the intelligence community," Avril Haines said on August 18.

On August 20, Biden was asked why he hadn't properly prepared after he had been warned that the Taliban would be making massive gains at some point. "Well, yeah, at some point. But the point was that although we were in contact with the Taliban and Doha for this whole period of time, that 'some point' wasn't expected to be the total demise of the Afghan National Force, which was 300 [thousand] persons," he said.[71]

The intelligence community quickly defended itself. "Strategically, a rapid Taliban takeover was always a possibility," a senior intelligence official said right after the fall of Kabul.[72] One anonymous US intelligence official said, "Leaders were told by the military it would take no time at all for the Taliban to take everything," but "no one listened."[73]

A US special forces officer said that it was "absolutely true" that the Biden administration had thought it had a lot more time than it did, telling investigators "There was no acknowledgement of the threat on the horizon. The military and civilian thought within the NSC was that the ANDSF was getting beat up but would recover. They were thinking that the ANDSF could hold for at least two years."[74]

Intelligence assessments grew increasingly grimmer in the summer. In mid-June, the US intelligence community concluded that the Afghan government could collapse as soon as six months or up to a year after the US withdrawal.[75] In July, intelligence assessments questioned whether the Afghan military would continue fighting and if Kabul could avoid being taken by the Taliban, warning that Taliban victories on the battlefield could lead to a rapid collapse of Afghan forces.[76] The Pentagon had been making similar predictions for months. Some spy agencies had previously been predicting that the Afghan government could carry on for up to two years after the United States left.[77]

"The trend lines that all of us see today are certainly troubling. The Taliban are making significant military advances; they're probably in the strongest military position that they've been in since 2001," CIA director Burns said on July 22 when asked about estimates that the Afghan government could fall six months after a US withdrawal. "The Afghan government retains significant military capabilities. The big question . . . is whether or not those capabilities can be exercised with the kind of political willpower and unity of leadership that's absolutely essential to resist the Taliban."[78]

On July 30, SIGAR released a report saying that the Afghan news was "bleak" and assessed that the Afghan government was facing an "existential crisis."[79]

Several months before the fall of Kabul, Vasely assessed that "the trajectory of Afghanistan was in a downward spiral and likely not recoverable."[80] A new assessment published on August 3 concluded that Kabul could fall to the Taliban within months or even weeks. Provincial capitals began falling two days later.[81] Kunduz was the first provincial capital to fall, with one US military official later saying "Kunduz was a wake-up call."[82]

The military's assessments on the possible fall of Kabul after the US withdrawal diminished from as soon as six months to three months to weeks as the Taliban advanced.

On August 10, it was reported that the US military had assessed that a collapse could occur within ninety days, while others said that the time frame could be a month.[83] On August 12, it was reported that a new US military analysis warned that Kabul could be isolated within thirty to sixty days and could fall within ninety days.[84] It fell three days later.[85]

On August 17, Sullivan was asked about the US intelligence reports indicating that the Taliban could overwhelm Afghanistan and take the capital within weeks, and he dodged. "I'm not actually familiar with the intelligence assessments you're describing, but I also don't want to get into specific intelligence products."

In late December 2022, Mike McCaul, now the chairman of the House Foreign Affairs Committee, told us, "There was always a disconnect between what the intelligence community and the Pentagon were saying versus the White House and State Department." The IC and Pentagon had a "very grim assessment" that once US airpower was pulled out, Kabul would fall "very rapidly." The State Department "seemed to have rose-colored glasses on through the whole ordeal stating that everything was just fine, it was not going to be chaotic, and it would not happen that fast."

"I've never seen the break, the contrast this stark between the IC and the Pentagon, and the politicos at the White House and State Department. It was very, very different," McCaul said. "I went with the IC's and the Pentagon's interpretation and briefing that this was going to happen faster than State Department had any idea—and they had no capability to plan in advance for the storm that was getting ready to hit." McCaul said that the Biden administration had ignored the bleak assessments by the Pentagon and the intelligence community, and he criticized Zal's claims about the Taliban's intentions.[86]

Zal had repeatedly said that he did not believe that the Afghan government would collapse nor that the Taliban would rapidly take over.[87] He was still insisting even in early August that a Taliban takeover would not happen, saying that such a move would make them "a pariah state which they say they don't want." He added, "When they speak to us the Taliban says there is no military solution."[88] The Taliban was obviously lying—military conquest was its solution to twenty years out of power.

Later, in mid-December, Mohib said that the Afghan government had received "some" information related to the US intelligence assessments. "I remember a security briefing about three or four weeks before the collapse, or perhaps even less than that, in which there was a timeline," he noted. "It was vague. It was not a very clear response, whether they believed that—that would be the fall of Kabul, or that would be the time when the Taliban surround Kabul."[89]

A former high-level US intelligence officer in Afghanistan told us that the CIA analytic prediction in April and May had been that the Afghan government and military would last no more than ninety days absent US troops and advisers. This officer said that some in the CIA had said that the Afghans wouldn't last more than sixty days or even more than thirty days without US support, although that was the minority view. They still failed to predict just how rapidly Kabul would fall, but it was much closer than State ever came. The intel officer also said that the CIA's analytic side had assessed that the likelihood that the Taliban would agree to a power-sharing arrangement with the Afghan government was roughly 5 percent, while the operational side believed that the probability was basically 0 percent.

According to a senior military official, the NSC's position was that "the ANDSF could hold on for at least two years."[90] Krummrich told us that State's predictions had been fantastical, characterizing what they were saying as "The Taliban aren't going to do anything. . . . We're going to be able to hold this and keep our embassy there and have this nice little corridor and maintain operations at HKIA. It's going to be great." Congressman Mike Turner, now the chairman of the House Intelligence Committee, likewise told us, "I believe both the Department of Defense and the intelligence community were much more concerned and cautioning of both withdrawing and the manner of withdrawal.

I also put a lot of blame at the National Security Council. . . . I would not put all the blame on the State Department. I think internally at the White House, the National Security Council deserves and the national security advisor deserves a significant amount of the blame for failing to listen to what the intelligence community and the Department of Defense was clearly saying."

A month after the fall of Kabul, General Milley testified that the intelligence community had "consistently" estimated that the Afghan military "was at risk of fracture and the government could collapse after the departure of US forces at the end of the summer with opinions ranging from weeks, months, or in some cases years after our departure depending on when the intelligence report was written." He contended that the "consensus intelligence view" had estimated an Afghan military fracture and the Taliban takeover of all Afghan provinces except for Kabul "by early to late fall or at the latest December."[91]

That differed starkly from what Blinken later said. "The assessment across the government was that even in worst-case scenarios, as our forces withdrew from Afghanistan, that the Afghanistan government, the Afghanistan security forces, would hold well into the following year," he said in a documentary. "I believed strongly that we were going to have a robust embassy presence in Kabul certainly through the year, well into the next year. Everything that we planned and did was based on that assumption."[92]

Biden advisers said that Biden had "felt let down by his briefers" for not predicting that Kabul would fall as rapidly as it did, but Burns denied that there had been an intelligence failure: "I think we and the intelligence community did an honest, straightforward job of pointing out the frailties—of the Afghan political leadership, especially, but also the Afghan military and the increasing momentum of the Taliban."[93] He added that he had warned that things could "start unraveling pretty quickly" if US troops and contractors were pulled, and that Biden had been briefed on all of that. An anonymous senior White House aide attacked Burns's claims.

Blinken claimed that "the worst case. . . was eighteen months plus." Milley said that the assessments had been grimmer than what Blinken was claiming: "The intelligence I saw predicted months. So we leave the country in August—and in a reasonable, worst-case scenario it's a Thanksgiving, Christmas, January time frame when things fall apart. I think the intelligence was very, very good."[94]

Milley admitted that CENTCOM commander Scott Miller's predictions about when the Afghan government would collapse had been more dire than most—and more accurate. "Scott Miller did say 'hard and fast'—and he also meant that, at least to me and to others, that he meant that to be in the fall, October, November, maybe even December time frame . . . the maybe Thanksgiving . . . likely to be in the October time frame," he said in September. He added that "Miller did, in many, many assessments, say rapid, fast, hard for collapse. He also centered into the October-November time frame as opposed to August." Miller had held the minority view on when Kabul would fall. Milley said, "Nobody called it eleven days in August. There was nobody who did that."[95]

But the collapse of the Army and government had clearly been happening for months. The eleven-day time frame from the fall of the first provincial capital to the fall of Kabul was the culmination of months of Taliban battlefield victories, Afghan military defeats, US force withdrawals, and deals between the Taliban and local Afghan leaders. The warning signs were there throughout 2021, not just in August. The fact that the US government had missed those warning signs meant that the Taliban was back in power.

SIX

NIGHT OF THE ZOMBIES

The security situation melted down quicker than an ice chip in the blazing Afghan heat. Word of capitulation spread through Kabul even before the Russian-made aircraft carrying President Ashraf Ghani had exited Afghan airspace on August 15. Most members of the Afghan forces simply shed their uniforms and withdrew into the surrounding countryside. Of the entire Afghan military, virtually only two units of special forces commandos stayed to fight. They made their way to Hamid Karzai International Airport and asked US officers there how they could help.

Meanwhile, a number of Afghans who had served in the air force burst onto the tarmac of HKIA to commandeer helicopters and fly them north to the safety of Uzbekistan and Tajikistan. But there were far more people than seats, and arguments quickly ensued. Disagreements often became physical, and several supposed compatriots turned their weapons on one another. Also during the mayhem, a group with an Afghan army general hopped into one of the Mi-17 helicopters, only to discover that it couldn't take off. Amid the fighting, apparently no one had noticed that the tank was close to empty. In total, nearly seventy Afghan air force planes and helicopters were flown out of the country by military crews more interested in finding a new homeland than defending their own—against an adversary that totally lacked any form of airpower.[1] At least one of those planes was shot down by the Uzbek authorities reacting to a foreign aircraft entering their nation's airspace unannounced.

The Afghan ground forces didn't exactly cover themselves in glory, either. Hours before initially fleeing the nineteenth-century presidential palace in an Mi-17 helicopter (provided by American taxpayers), Ghani transferred control of the city to Kabul's chief of police, Major General Juma Gul Hemat, an obese bureaucrat with three days' worth of stubble perpetually stuck to his face. Despite his reputation for corruption—or perhaps because of it—he'd managed to fail upward from one provincial police appointment to another before he had been made top cop in Kabul in August 2020. Hemat held his post until Ghani left, but not a second longer. Once his boss was gone, he decided it was time to skip town, too.

That technically left Lieutenant General Afzal Aman in charge. Aman, a bespectacled, stout, bald middle-aged man with a toothbrush mustache, commanded the Afghan army's Kabul garrison. He was the only remaining official with authority over all the security forces in Kabul. But he beat both Ghani and Hemat to the punch, for he had already bolted without notifying anyone. Bottom line, there was not a single soul left in place to coordinate the defense of the capital of more than 4 million inhabitants.

Afghanistan no longer had a government. A night of mayhem was approaching.

THE EMBASSY EVACUATION

Until about two weeks before Kabul fell, State Department officials had categorically refused to consider the possibility of a full-scale evacuation. The US military had tried time and again over the course of four months to convince Chargé d'Affaires Ross Wilson and his staff of the threat, but the diplomats would hear none of it. In the words of a military officer embedded with the embassy, the officials in Kabul had spent most of 2020 and 2021 "constructing a narrative supported by half-truths [and] decoupled from reality."[2]

Now the State Department was in full-on panic mode. Executing an orderly evacuation of the largest US embassy in the world would have required months of meticulous planning under ideal conditions—and the conditions in Kabul on August 15 were about as optimal as blanks in a firefight. For one thing, the embassy had no contingency plan for destroying the tens of thousands of sensitive documents inside its walls. So its staff had started the process only forty-eight hours prior to Ghani's capitulation. An August 13 memo instructing staff to destroy sensitive documents inexplicably stated that a "small consular staff" would remain in Kabul after the Taliban assumed control. In the end, officials left behind reams of material identifying Afghans who had cooperated with the US government, including key informants in the Taliban's ranks. Given all that, it's not surprising that the embassy had never gotten around to establishing an order of priority for evacuation. Most of the diplomats inside the $806 million compound on Great Massoud Road simply had no idea what to do or where to go if the worst—which seemed increasingly likely—occurred.

The result was chaos. US military commanders at HKIA immediately initiated airlift operations once they received the green light from the Biden administration. CH-47 Chinook helicopters touched down at the embassy at roughly 2:00 a.m. local time on August 15. But due to the White House's rigid ceiling on armed assets allowed to remain in country, the US military had only a limited number of Chinooks at its disposal. The State Department had several CH-46 Sea Knight helicopters—the smaller, Vietnam-era predecessor—but the total number of aircraft was still woefully insufficient.

Flight crews were forced to push their aircraft to the hilt. Under normal conditions, the maximum capacity of a Chinook is thirty-three fully equipped troops. But Kabul is more than a mile above sea level, and the thin summer air made carrying heavier loads extremely dangerous. A downed helicopter would have all but doomed the evacuation before it began. Worse, it wasn't clear that the limited forces at HKIA could effectively rescue a downed aircraft without risking significant casualties. Despite these risks, Army aviators stripped their aircraft of nonessential equipment and lifted roughly fifty passengers out of the embassy compound on each flight. Even so, evacuating the nearly two thousand embassy personnel would ultimately require dozens of nonstop round trips over the course of twenty-three hours.

Complicating matters, embassy personnel were scattered across the fifteen-acre complex, and the State Department had no system in place to account for its people. Anxious embassy officials started pushing their colleagues toward the aircraft without keeping track of who had left and who was still on the premises. The newfound urgency did more harm than good. After a few rotations, the officers in charge realized that embassy officials had no way of knowing when the evacuation would be complete. The military leaders at HKIA were forced to corral the embassy personnel who had already arrived and do a head count to figure out how many people were still around.

To ensure that no one was left behind, special forces operatives and troops from the Army's 10th Mountain Division, which first distinguished itself in the Italian Apennines during the Second World War, conducted a door-to-door search of the complex's more than a dozen buildings and annexes, at times kicking in doors and bashing off locks. The search yielded several staffers. According to one of the officers on the ground, the staffers claimed that "they didn't know where to go." He and his men found that explanation unconvincing. Instructions had been blaring over loudspeakers for hours, and as another 10th Mountain officer later told military investigators, embassy officials had been found "intoxicated" and "cowering in [their] rooms."[3]

Getting embassy personnel on board the aircraft presented its own challenges, some of which should have been easily avoidable. Space was at a premium, and with Taliban fighters already freely cruising the streets, the evacuation window was extremely short. Yet several staffers tried to board with multiple suitcases. The air crews were tasked with evacuating several thousand people; they were in no mood to trade lives for luggage. After confirming that the luggage didn't contain sensitive information or equipment, it was thrown onto a pile at the side of the landing zone.

The 10th Mountain still had a second group of stragglers to collect. The embassy employed a few hundred former Gurkha commandos as an outer security force for the sprawling complex. The Nepalese warriors constitute one of the most elite and feared units in the British military and are legendary for their bravery and unflinching discipline. In 2010, a private from the 1st Battalion, Royal Gurkha Rifles regiment was court-martialed for beheading a high-ranking Taliban leader killed in a fierce firefight. The British military declined to pursue charges after learning that the unit had been ordered to return with DNA evidence of the successful mission and needed to leave the kill zone in a hurry to avoid Taliban reinforcements. The young private, using his curved kukri, had followed those orders in their most literal sense.

As the sun was pushing fast toward Koh-e Qrough Mountain in the southwest and the last flights were about to depart, US soldiers conducting their final sweep of the grounds found the Gurkha guards still manning their posts along the embassy walls. One refused to leave his post without first reporting to his superiors. After his phone call went unanswered, he agreed, reluctantly, to evacuate along with everyone else.[4]

After twenty-three hours of continuous operations, US helicopters made their final departure from the embassy at 1:00 a.m. on August 16. The steady chatter of automatic gunfire was beginning to echo in the background.

THE MOB

While 10th Mountain was completing its sweep of the embassy grounds, a sea of humanity began descending upon HKIA. "Afghans heard that

[Ghani] had left the country, and they saw the embassy personnel starting to move north to HKIA," Brigadier General Farrell J. Sullivan later told military investigators. "They saw all this, the [Afghan army] crumbled, and people just started to flood the airfield."[5] The courageous men and women who were at Hamid Karzai International Airport have branded what followed "the Night of the Zombies."

As the night of the fifteenth bled into the morning of the sixteenth, nearly fifteen thousand Afghans pushed through airfield gates abandoned by the Afghan army and onto the tarmac. Only 350 troops stood between the mob that was desperately grasping for life and the airfield's Joint Operations Center (JOC). The JOC is the nerve center of essentially every military operation. It's staffed by a team of soldiers and filled with sensitive equipment, much of it classified, that commanders use to monitor operations and make decisions in real time. At HKIA, the JOC housed secure phone lines for communicating with the Pentagon and the White House, satellite radios for corresponding with other military bases in the Middle East, screens for tracking the locations of friendly and hostile units, and more than a dozen displays with live feeds from every reconnaissance asset the military had in the air. If the JOC were overrun, the entire evacuation would come to a standstill and almost certainly never restart.

Turkish forces were also at HKIA, but due to long-standing ethnic tensions with the Afghans, they remained firmly within their compound at the northernmost end of the airfield. In previous weeks, as the situation had been deteriorating, members of the Afghan security forces had started to pull their weapons on Turkish forces whenever they weren't escorted by Americans. The Turks had opted for the "Alamo plan," and they stuck to it. So they were MIA at the breaking point.

The best US forces could do was secure the JOC and ensure that it didn't get damaged. Whatever else happened, the entire mission hinged on keeping US forces in control of that small sliver of territory. Nearly every soldier and Marine on the airfield was pulled to cordon off the

JOC, standing or kneeling less than an arm's distance apart to prevent the crowd from exploiting a gap in the line. In the mad scramble to form a defensive perimeter, the Marines grabbed whatever nonlethal weapons were in reach. Some carried riot shields; others used tear gas canisters and flash-bang grenades to stun the crowd. Those who had no time to grab anything else used the targeting lasers on their M4s to momentarily blind those who weren't getting the message. Only a handful of people were left inside the JOC to man the phones and the surveillance feeds.

The abounding crowd got to within 200 meters (650 feet) of overrunning the JOC. And it might have done so if not for a fortunate twist of fate. As it moved toward the American-held portion of the airfield, people spotted Air Force C-17s and C-130s on the runways and instead headed toward them, hoping to snag a lift. Still, the situation was untenable, and Admiral Vasely was forced to accept the Taliban's offer to help clear the airfield. It was only the first in a series of events where the US military was placed at the mercy of the Taliban's "goodwill" due to the Biden administration's failure to plan.

The mob inflicted serious damage to critical infrastructure on the airfield during the anarchy. Both air traffic control towers were destroyed, forcing Air Force combat controllers—special operations personnel who hone their craft over ninety-seven weeks of training—to direct air traffic using handheld radios and mathematical formulas sketched on notepads. The combat controllers, supplemented by Marines from the 24th Marine Expeditionary Unit and several airmen scrambled from Saudi Arabia on an hour's notice on August 17, spent the next two weeks manually directing air traffic for more than a hundred flights landing at and taking off from HKIA every day. They conducted the entire operation under a green pop-up canopy tent next to the runway. The White House falsely characterized the use of combat controllers as routine during increases in air traffic volume. It was an attempt to divert attention away from its own incompetence. The White House didn't acknowledge the destruction of the control towers at the time, and it still hasn't.

Even though they faced a crush of people that outnumbered them forty to one, the soldiers and Marines guarding the JOC showed remarkable restraint. They used warning shots and nonlethal tactics only when necessary. When push came to shove, literally, they grappled with members of the crowd instead of opening fire.

Deadly restraint wasn't always an option. A few hours past midnight on August 16, Marines on the southern end of the perimeter observed two armed men with AK-47s moving through the crowd, using civilians for cover. Based on their movements, the Marines knew they were looking for just the right moment to strike. When the gunmen stepped into the open and raised their weapons, the Marines were ready. In a few short bursts, they dropped the attackers without taking any casualties or causing collateral damage.

IT "LOOKED LIKE THE END OF THE WORLD"

While the outnumbered soldiers and Marines at HKIA tried to hang on, the Pentagon was scrambling to send reinforcements to the airfield. That task was complicated by the White House's complete lack of contingency planning. There weren't enough C-17s or C-130s in theater to transport the necessary number of soldiers to Kabul in a few lifts or even in several staggered lifts. To insert desperately needed quick reaction force units, US Air Force crews flew ten-hour round trips from Qatar to Kabul and then immediately collected more soldiers for the next iteration until they were forced to ground for mandatory crew rest. The minute their rest period ended, they started the process all over again.

The military branches don't always play nicely together in high-pressure situations. The shortage of planes led to a "knife fight" between the Marines and the 82nd Airborne Division to get their respective people into the air and into the action. One of the 82nd units arrived at Al Udeid Air Base near Doha, Qatar, and learned that the flight they were supposed to board had already left. In the words of their company commander, "When we got there, we found out the [Marines] took our plane."

Platoons of paratroopers and Marines from various companies arrived piecemeal at HKIA in the dark on the morning of August 16. They were immediately thrown into the fight. They had no firm instructions about what to do when they landed and only a general idea of what they were about to confront.

A battalion from the 504th Parachute Infantry Regiment of the 82nd Airborne Division got there first, landing at 10:00 p.m. on the fifteenth. The history of the regiment is replete with tales of its paratroopers surmounting overwhelming odds. When the men of the 504th learned that Nazi soldiers in the Battle of Sicily had started calling them "the devils in the baggy pants"—referring to their unbloused boots, which distinguished them from other infantrymen at the time—they proudly adopted the moniker.

Over the high-pitched whine of the C-17s still-spinning turbofan engines, the 504th crew chief delivered perhaps the most abbreviated "orientation brief" in US military history. "North is that way," he said, pointing in the general direction of the Joint Operations Center at HKIA. When the cargo ramp dropped, the paratroopers ran off the plane and smack into anarchy. Before they even had a chance to program their radios, they were directed to sprint forward to plug gaps in the perimeter. In particular, they were instructed that the gate on the west side of the airfield was still unmanned and "leaking." That didn't mean much to the 504th paratroopers because they had been at HKIA for only minutes and were still trying to orient themselves. Marines quickly sent runners to guide the paratroopers into their defensive positions.

The first two planeloads of Marine reinforcements from the 2nd Battalion, 1st Marines were only three hours behind. That night, they would live up to their nickname: "The Professionals." One of the C-130s carried 2/1's battalion commander, Lieutenant Colonel Brad Whited, and other members of the battalion headquarters. The second plane was packed with Marines from Echo Company, 2/1's 4th Platoon, and its company commander, first sergeant, and executive officer. The Marines hadn't received anything approximating a briefing about the situation, either. On the flight in, Whited had taken a seat at the front of the plane, directly behind the cockpit. Under the dim cabin lights, he reached out to the pilot over a headset. He wanted to know what his Marines could expect once they hit the ground. The answer: It wouldn't be a picnic.

Over the metallic hum of the engines, the voice on the other side of the headset informed Whited that the runways were surrounded by civilians who had breached the facility, but no one knew how it had happened or whether the Taliban had overrun the airfield. Regardless, it was clear that something had gone very wrong and that the guys on the ground needed help. Whited ordered his Marines to go to "condition one"—bolts forward and rounds in the chamber.

The first wave from 2/1 landed just after 1:00 a.m. on the sixteenth and taxied past the swelling crowd. Whited and a few staff officers immediately made their way toward the JOC to figure out the cause of the catastrophe. Before leaving, he told his Marines to move the aggressive crowd of young Afghan men in their twenties and early thirties off the runway. "We can't have an evacuation if we don't have an airfield!"

The Marines were prepared to fight their way out of Afghanistan. They had dedicated cargo space for mortar tubes and a significant number of rounds. But nobody had warned them that their mission would include serving as HKIA's riot police. They hit the ground without nonlethal weapons, so they, too, were forced to fight rowdy members of the crowd hand to hand. Cracks of rifle fire punctuated the deafening din of Pashtu yells and screams, and tracer rounds pierced the sky above them. The pungent combination of raw sewage and burning rubber from tires lit by the Taliban filled their every breath. The scene, one of the Marine platoon commanders later said, "looked like the end of the world."

THE DENTIST WHO FELL FROM THE SKY

Throughout the morning of the sixteenth, the 82nd paratroopers and the Marines from 2/1 waged a continuous battle with the mob for control of the airfield. Their immediate goal was to keep the runways clear so evacuees could leave and reinforcements could arrive. Above all else, however, they needed to protect the JOC.

By 5:00 a.m., they managed to clear the runways and push the crowd back to the southern end of the airfield. But they hadn't slept in more than twenty-four hours or eaten a meal since they'd arrived, and the physical strain of wrestling with a seemingly endless stream of people was beginning to take its toll. They were also running low on water. Runners from the JOC had staged MREs (Meals, Ready-to-Eat) and packages of bottled water for them several hours before, but those had been devoured by the crowd when they had broken through the line hours earlier. To make matters worse, the mob was increasing in size and strength by the hour. The US troops were locked in a war of attrition, and they held the short end of the stick.

The runways at HKIA run east to west, splitting the airfield in half. The Marines and paratroopers now stood in a staggered line in the southern portion, with an increasingly agitated crowd in front of them, and the runways, the JOC, and hundreds of remaining State Department personnel behind them. By 10:00 a.m., the crowd was exponentially larger than the US force facing it. Holding the line in front of the runways quickly became impossible, short of opening fire on unarmed civilians. The troops had no choice but to fall back and keep themselves between the crowd and the JOC. HKIA's runways were flooded with people once again, this time with twice the volume.

A little over an hour later, a C-17 with the call sign "Reach 855" made its final approach toward HKIA. Reach 855 was loaded with supplies intended for the exhausted units on the ground, including pallets of MREs. The plane touched down at 11:16; however, when it attempted to taxi away, there was nowhere to go. Hundreds of desperate Afghans gave pursuit on the asphalt behind them, and equal numbers sprinted across the grass baked dead by the sun on both sides of the runway.

In less than a minute, Reach 855 was surrounded. The crew radioed the JOC to request help. The command center responded that there weren't enough forces on the ground to escort them to a hangar. Any attempt to secure Reach 855 would require diverting forces from the perimeter around the last remaining square meters of Afghanistan still under American control. Seconds later, the crew received a follow-up message, this time from Admiral Vasely. The message was forthright: Take off ASAP and fly back to Qatar.

At that point, the crew of Reach 855 was more than willing to continue eastward on the runway and take off in the same direction in which it had landed. But that was no longer an option. Hundreds of Afghans had surrounded the C-17 while it was at a standstill on the runway. People in the crowd were latching onto the plane's landing gear and hoisting one another onto its wings. The crew had no good options—continuing forward would require running over civilians, but staying put for more than another few minutes would almost certainly lead to people trying to enter the plane. It asked for assistance a second time.

In response, the commanding officers at HKIA opted for the last tool at their disposal. Two Apache attack helicopters spun up from landing pads next to the JOC. They banked left and headed east—in the direction in which Reach 855 planned to take off—until they were past the plane and the crowd that surrounded it. Once they were several hundred yards past the scene, they made a sharp U-turn and headed back down the runway, staying no more than twenty feet off the ground and using the force of their rotors to try to disperse the crowd on both sides of Reach 855.

The tactic was largely successful, and Reach 855 had a clear stretch of runway to facilitate its escape. It wasn't entirely successful, though. One civilian had already climbed into the wheel well of the plane before the Apaches arrived. At least ten others, most of whom were teenagers or men in their early twenties, ran alongside the C-17 as it gained speed and prepared for liftoff. Several of them clung to Reach 855's landing gear as it took off.

Around noon, Reach 855 began its ascent. The events that happened next were captured on cell phone videos and watched by millions around the world within hours. As the aircraft gained speed, several people fell to the runway and suffered fatal injuries. Two managed to hold on a few minutes longer before plummeting from the sky as the C-17 disappeared in the distance. One of the two was a dentist in his midtwenties named Fada Mohammad.

The night before, Mohammad had excitedly sent his family members Facebook posts saying that the United States would accept any refugee who arrived at Kabul airport. At 8:30 the next morning, he left home without telling his new wife where he was headed. Less than four hours later, he plummeted from the sky and landed on the roof of a house a few miles away.

The other casualty was Zaki Anwari, a seventeen-year-old member of Afghanistan's national youth soccer team. Anwari, who had grown up in a middle-class family, was a standout athlete who dreamed of playing professional sports in the West. On the morning of August 16, he ran to HKIA with several classmates, hoping to find a way to the United States or even Canada. His first encounter with an airplane was the fateful moment he tried to escape on Reach 855.

FLYING BLIND

While everything at HKIA was falling apart, a US Air Force crew with a critical mission was trying to land at the airport. That C-17 was operated by a crew from the New York Air National Guard that had been activated for a relatively routine rotation supporting military activities in South America back in April. The first few months of the rotation had been unremarkable, but on August 13, it had received an emergency mission: Fly a Chinook MH-47 with a crew from the 160th Special Operations Aviation Regiment and nearly two dozen of the Army's best special operators to Kabul.

First, the seven crewmen of Reach 824 from the 105th Airlift Wing had to fly from South America to Qatar to pick up their "cargo." The operators were members of the Army's legendary Delta Force; their mission was straightforward, but exceptionally complicated: they were to locate stranded US citizens across Afghanistan and extract them to HKIA. They made up one of four special operations teams en route to Afghanistan to rescue Americans who couldn't travel to Kabul on their own.

Reach 824's first attempt to land at HKIA hit a wall. It approached Kabul on the night of August 15. There was no air control. Afghan planes were flying unannounced through the airspace on their way out of the country. Thousands of Afghan civilians were on the runways. Taliban small-arms fire was pervasive. The crew had no choice but to abort the mission and return nearly 1,200 miles to Qatar. It made a second attempt the next evening.

If pedigree-obsessed officials at the Pentagon were asked to choose an Air Force crew to execute this mission, with American lives hanging in the balance, the men of Reach 824 probably wouldn't have made the top of their list. On an average day, they lived ordinary lives no different from those of most Americans. Captain Matthew McChesney, the air crew commander and lead pilot, was thirty years old and spent most weeks flying domestic routes for Delta Air Lines. Reach 824's other pilot, Lieutenant Colonel Andrew Townsend, normally worked as a first officer (or "copilot," in layman's terms) on a Boeing 777 for United Airlines. The senior enlisted member of the crew, Technical Sergeant Joseph Caponi, was a stocky Italian American New York Police Department officer assigned to the 120th Precinct on Staten Island. The other crew members included a sheriff's deputy from Putnam County, New York, and a longtime administrative employee at IBM.

But on the night of August 16, they were the perfect crew for the job. The Delta operators on the plane needed to find a way into Afghanistan. Through a combination of ingenuity and sheer grit, McChesney and his crew made it happen.

On their way, they passed roughly a half-dozen other aircraft that had already turned back due to Taliban small-arms fire or an inability to land. The crew still had no real-time intelligence about conditions on the runways, and there was no one to guide them in because the mob had overrun the air control towers. It resorted to initiating informal radio contact with a C-17 that had landed before the airfield was overrun. Reach 824 asked the crew whether a landing was possible under any circumstances. The answer, essentially, was "It's possible, but it won't be easy." They had to wait for a brief window for the airfield to open.

Reach 824 circled HKIA in a tight ten-mile radius for several hours. In the process, the plane was exposed to the antiaircraft fire that had already forced several other planes out of the airspace. As midnight approached, it was running out of fuel and had to adjust course back to Qatar to abort the mission for a second night in a row. On their way out, the crew encountered a KC-10 refueling tanker on its radar and coordinated an impromptu air-to-air refueling operation. At that point, they had already received word that HKIA's refueling capabilities were next to nil, which meant that there was no guarantee that they would have enough fuel to return to Qatar after landing and completing their mission. McChesney asked the refueling tanker to accompany his aircraft to Kabul and top it off one more time before approach.

Reach 824 continued to circle for another hour before receiving word that the runways at HKIA had been cleared. The landing was unorthodox, to say the least. HKIA no longer had working runway lights or a ground crew to guide them in. McChesney flew the C-17 in under cover of darkness, using night vision goggles and communicating with US Air Force special operatives on the ground, who were the de facto air control tower. As Reach 824 made its approach, its left wing was hit with small-arms fire. The final transmission they received before losing radio contact was a warning: "Land at your own risk." The crew was flying blind.

In pitch darkness, McChesney descended onto the first runway he could make out. It was on the commercial side of HKIA, which was temporarily controlled by Taliban fighters amidst the chaos. Fighters in a motley collection of a dozen trucks surrounded the C-17 as soon as it finished taxiing. The crew was able to defuse the situation and cross over to the US side, with the Taliban driving right alongside them all the way. In less than an hour, Reach 824 was back in the air. Ten days later, the crew returned to fly the remains of thirteen fallen US service members out of the country.

The special operators Reach 824 carried went on to successfully evacuate more than eight hundred people. McChesney received the Distinguished Flying Cross with Valor, and five members of his crew received Air Medals with Valor.

CALLING THE HIRED HELP

The soldiers and Marines wouldn't be able to clear the runway of fifteen thousand people and reestablish control of HKIA on their own. The CIA recognized the grave state of affairs and swiftly stepped in. The agency operated its own compound, known as Eagle Base, close to the airfield. It was not only a well-concealed secret but also eminently more defensible; it was surrounded by ten-foot-high, blast-resistant walls and had only a single point of entry.

CIA personnel unilaterally formed an emergency agreement with members of the Afghan National Strike Unit (NSU): 1,300 fighters and 210 vehicles would immediately clear the crowds from the runways.

That was in exchange for the military evacuating the fighters and their families.

The NSU had operated in Afghanistan under a variety of official-sounding names for the better half of two decades. They were CIA-trained and -led paramilitary forces that conducted nighttime raids and other offensive operations against Taliban fighters in volatile religions—even across the Pakistani border—without any of the oversight that normally accompanied military operations. That provided the US government with plausible deniability. The NSU fighters were ruthless and tactically proficient, and their reputation for both attributes preceded them. Make no mistake: most NSU fighters were mercenaries of the purest sort. Uncle Sam was simply the highest bidder for their services. Still, every agency official we spoke to praised their abilities on the battlefield and during the evacuation.

Once the agreement was struck in the early afternoon of August 16, the CIA's once again retooled paramilitary force went to work clearing the airstrip. They started with warning shots and followed with butt strokes to the cranium for those who didn't comply quickly enough. The force also used its trucks to steer parts of the crowd away from the JOC and back toward the gates. The NSU's tactics were brutal but effective. More than two decades of experience had taught civilians that Afghan forces didn't operate under the same constraints as US troops.

US military leaders at HKIA had not been party to the CIA deal, so no one in uniform at first knew that accepting the NSU's help came with the condition of evacuating its members and their families. That suddenly required the military to find seats for an additional thirty thousand people. A cultural difference had been lost in translation. To Afghans, "immediate family" means not just spouses and children but also aunts, uncles, cousins, grandparents, and grandchildren.

Senior military officials have since claimed that the lack of notification carried no practical significance. But the deal later complicated efforts to evacuate US citizens and Afghan SIV applicants. The Biden administration's failure to evacuate all US citizens was baked in once the agreement was made. And although the decision may have been necessary at the time, it was necessary only because the Biden administration had failed to anticipate the obvious strategic consequences of its pullout plan. An after-action report conducted by the U.S. Central Command concluded that "the added responsibility. . . to include a previously unknown 30K NSU personnel" on the evacuation list had overwhelmed the military's airlift abilities.[6]

The CIA's deal with the NSU was one of necessity. If HKIA didn't remain in American hands, there would be no evacuation at all. The truth was that the military had no choice but to execute the CIA's deal once it was made. Failing to do so would have subjected the soldiers and Marines to reprisal attacks from the NSU. General Sullivan told Defense Department investigators that "the risk to not getting the NSU and their families out was that they would turn on us as we approached the end of the evacuation."[7] In all, the NSU and its family members accounted for more than a fourth of the 120,000 people that the Biden administration bragged about evacuating.

"WHAT ARE WE WALKING INTO?"

Due to the shortage of aircraft and flight crews in Central Asia, several Marine platoons were scrambled from Saudi Arabia, spending twelve hours on "layover" at Al Udeid Air Base in Qatar before flying to Kabul. They knew that no rest was in store because the Air Force officers in charge of the flight manifests informed them that their planes would arrive "in the next two hours." Two hours would pass, and the process would repeat itself. The delays—and clear lack of planning—frustrated the Marines no end. On less than twenty-four hours' notice, they had gone from executing training missions in Saudi Arabia to standing on a runway in Qatar, armed to the teeth and ready for combat. Actually getting into Afghanistan as the supposed "quick reaction force," they said, "took forever."

They weren't the only reinforcements forced to hurry up and wait. A company of paratroopers from 2nd Brigade, 82nd Airborne Division flew twelve hours from Fort Bragg, North Carolina, only to find itself stranded in Qatar alongside Marines, waiting as events unfolded.

In the early-morning hours of the sixteenth, before they boarded their flight from Saudi Arabia to Qatar, the noncommissioned officers of the three remaining platoons in Echo Company gathered in a command room that was off limits to anyone without a security clearance. Huddled in front of a computer screen, they watched live drone footage of their buddies in 4th Platoon wrestling hand to hand with a crowd of several thousand people only seconds after landing. That was the last information they received about conditions on the ground at HKIA before they landed.

The Marines waiting at Camp Arifjan in Kuwait to catch a flight to Kabul were given no intelligence updates about the situation on the ground. They resorted to using social media on their phones. "We were on all the random Instagram pages that were posting pictures and videos and seeing news outlets posting pictures of people falling off the planes and stuff," one of the Marines in the last wave told us. "We're looking for pictures of our boys and just kinda sitting there waiting to get over there. We were just thinking, what are we walking into?"

After watching the scenes on the airfield, the commanders of the three weapons platoons "tactically acquired" (i.e., borrowed without asking) several whiteboards from nearby buildings so they could brief their Marines about the tactics the platoons would use to maintain security against a swarm closing in on them from all directions.

At roughly 4:00 p.m. on the sixteenth, their transportation finally arrived. It was parked next to one of the C-17s that had taken off from HKIA earlier that day with Afghans clinging to its wings and landing gear. Parts of some of those men and women were still caked on the landing gear. The body of another Afghan civilian was stuck in one of the wheel wells. The Marines had watched videos of the plane taking off from HKIA on social media only hours earlier. Now they watched the crew wipe blood off its fuselage while they lined up to board the aircraft next door.

The last platoons from Echo Company arrived in the early hours of August 17. No one told them that the airfield had been cleared in the meantime. "We sprinted off the plane thinking they had us surrounded in a three-sixty," a squad leader in one of the platoons said to us. A few of the Marines got down on their stomachs in the "prone" position. "Then our first sergeant on the tarmac starts screaming at us, 'Hey dickheads, get over here. You're fine.' And then we realized, 'Oh, okay, we're all good.'"

The "Night of the Zombies" might have been over, but the horror would continue.

SEVEN

CHAOS AT THE GATES

As of August 17, the official line of both the White House and the top military brass was that despite the chaotic airport scenes broadcast around the globe, the United States would stand by its commitment to ensure that all US citizens made it home. National Security Advisor Jake Sullivan tweeted his personal reassurance the evening of the seventeenth: "When I was asked about whether we're going to get all Americans out of Afghanistan I said 'that's what we intend to do' and that's exactly what we'll do, and are accomplishing right now with HKIA reopened and operational, thanks to the incredible work of our troops and diplomats."[1]

In less than twenty-four hours, however, that message was contradicted by the US Embassy in Kabul: "New warning from U.S. Embassy Kabul: The United States government 'cannot ensure safe passage' to the airport in Kabul for evacuation."[2] With the airport finally cleared, attention turned to continuing the evacuations. The various units charged with executing the operation arrived piecemeal, whenever a plane became available. The remaining members of 2/1's Shock Trauma Platoon—a medical platoon consisting of two emergency physicians, two physician assistants, three nurses, and fifteen corpsmen—showed up early in the morning on the seventeenth.

Later that morning, General McKenzie departed Doha for Kabul. It was his second attempt. The CENTCOM commander had made his first try the night before, after wrapping up his meetings with Taliban leaders to coordinate security arrangements for the airport. His plane had been forced to turn around, unable to land in Kabul, when the crowds had thronged the airport tarmac. Senior Taliban leaders were only hours behind McKenzie. They were given a private flight to Kandahar by the Qatari air force.

Later that afternoon, Delta Company, 2/501 PIR (Parachute Infantry Regiment) touched down at the airfield. Like the other incoming units, they'd received no intelligence updates about what they were walking into (Air Force C-17s aren't exactly well known for their in-flight Wi-Fi packages). The last thing they'd heard before taking off was that the airfield was a disaster zone. But that was no longer the situation on the ground. A Delta Company platoon leader described the contradiction to us: "You get off expecting to deal with massive people and then you get off, and it's nighttime but it's calm, it's quiet. There's nothing. You look out, and it looks like there's nothing wrong here at all. Like, our adrenaline's rushing and we're expecting a fight."

On August 18, 82nd Headquarters officials, including Major General Christopher Donahue, and 1/8 Marines arrived at HKIA. Donahue went to work, immediately surveying the airport perimeter. Also arriving with the 82nd was former ambassador to Afghanistan John Bass, who was tasked with overseeing the evacuation operations. The delineation of authority between former ambassador Bass and Chargé d'Affaires Wilson, however, was never specified, leading to persistent confusion among the military leaders, who were caught in the middle throughout the evacuation.

At roughly the same time, an Army Psychological Operations (PSYOP) team, including Staff Sergeant Ryan Christian Knauss, departed for HKIA from Joint Base Charleston, South Carolina. Army

Special Operations Command ("USASOC") could see the train wreck about to occur, even if the Biden administration preferred to shield its eyes, and the PYSOP team prepared accordingly. The team leader later recounted, "We knew it [the deployment] was happening on August 10." Even so, the aircraft shortage inhibited the team's ability to get where they needed to be. After sleeping at their unit headquarters at Fort Bragg for several days while trying to catch a flight, the team drove to Charleston and secured seats on an outbound plane on August 18 and arrived at HKIA the following day.

HERCULES TO THE RESCUE

A few hours before midnight on the eighteenth, a C-130J Super Hercules operated by the special operations wing of the Royal Air Force, known as 47 Squadron, took off from a military airport near Dubai and turned off its radar identifier.[3] The Hercules was carrying a team of elite SAS operators, and its destination was a remote strip of desert in Kandahar, Afghanistan, just over two hours away. Waiting for them were twenty fellow SAS troops who had been trapped for five days after the province had fallen to the Taliban.[4]

The stranded commandos had been assisting the Afghan military's monthlong defense against a sustained Taliban offensive that had begun on July 9. By August 12, the Taliban had taken the city and begun to encircle the airfield, where the Afghan army was making its final stand. Staying put and subjecting themselves to a prolonged Taliban siege would have been nothing short of a suicide mission. But making an overland journey through hostile territory halfway across the country to Kabul would have been equally foolish. The SAS troops' only option was to get to a concealed location and use long-range communications to request an exfiltration. They made their way to a flat, deserted area, hunkered down, and waited for help.

After five days of waiting, help was finally on its way. In pitch darkness in the middle of the desert, the special operations pilots touched down using night vision goggles and infrared signals from the men on the ground to guide them in. Within minutes, they were back in the air. The crew and its cargo arrived safely in Dubai in the early-morning hours of the nineteenth.[5]

"IF YOU CAN HOT-WIRE IT, IT'S YOURS."

HKIA was littered with vehicles of all types that had been abandoned by Afghan forces when they had fled the airfield, but almost none of them had keys. The units on the ground had to improvise. The military is a cross section of society, and as any combat arms officer will tell you, every company has a few people with some street skills. The Marine and 82nd Airborne units were no exception. Across every branch of service, every battalion, and every company, the story was the same: officers asked NCOs to figure out transportation, and the NCOs found guys in their ranks who knew how to hot-wire vehicles and put them to work. An 82nd platoon leader nonchalantly remarked to us, "We had some dudes that were pretty experienced in those extracurricular activities, so we were able to procure some vehicles." An NCO from a different 82nd company was a bit blunter: "That's how we got shit."

After getting a vehicle running, each unit immediately tagged it with spray paint so other units knew not to commandeer it for themselves. The markings were usually what one would expect from combat arms troops in a combat zone, things such as "2/1 FUCK YOU."[6] A squad leader from 2/1 described the situation to us as "pretty much a free-for-all. Every unit out there would steal a car, and then they'd tag it with spray paint so that everybody knew it was theirs. If you didn't tag a vehicle with anything, then it would probably get stolen by another unit." A platoon sergeant from the 2nd Battalion, 501st Parachute Infantry Regiment of the 82nd Airborne echoed the sentiment: "When we got there, man, it's like 'If you can hot-wire it, it's yours.' People were stealing all sorts of cars and light trucks and stuff."

The Marines from 2/1 secured an up-armored Chevy Tahoe from the early 2000s, several flatbed trucks and all-terrain gators, a stripped-down ambulance, a white baggage truck they nicknamed "Casper," and even a large blue school bus that they affectionately nicknamed "Big Blue."[7] Alpha Company, 2/501 of the 82nd, made their way to the small fire station on the airport and hot-wired two fire engines. They gave one of the fire trucks to the Marines at one of the gates to use for crowd control a few days later but continued to use the other—which they named "Clifford"—for the remainder of their deployment. The 82nd troopers from the 1st Battalion, 504th PIR were not about to be outdone. One of their platoons chanced upon a Mercedes G-Class SUV, which retails for $140,000 brand new.[8] Another traded a group of fleeing Afghan National Army soldiers two cans of dip for the keys to an old Toyota Land Cruiser outfitted with a Soviet-era antiaircraft gun.[9]

A few vehicles acquired by US forces hadn't exactly been "abandoned" by their previous owners. Several Marines from Weapons Company, 2/1, were "tasked to find more vehicles," but their area of operations (and the rest of HKIA under US control) had already been stripped clean.[10] After a few hours of searching, they arrived at the small section controlled by the Turkish military at the northern end of the airfield. The Turks were largely staying inside their compound until evacuation day, but they had a small motor pool with several vehicles. The Marines decided to put one of them to better use. They quickly settled on an airport passenger van. One member of the Marine search party was "proficient in hot-wiring" and quickly got to work, while the rest of the crew kept watch.[11] They peeled out of the Turkish motor pool a few minutes later and scrubbed all of the Turkish markings off the vehicle as soon as they got it back to home base. For the rest of the evacuation, they used it to shuttle to and from Abbey Gate.[12]

COVID FIRST—EVEN DURING A WAR

The Biden administration's covid obsession interfered with the execution of the evacuation, just as it had with SIV applicants' evacuation planning. The administration's covid vaccination requirements deprived critical units of key personnel. The problem was especially acute for the Marines in 2/1. From April to October 2021, the battalion rotated in as the combat arms unit of the Special Purpose Marine Air-Ground Task Force—Crisis Response—Central Command (SPMAGTF-CR-CC). In classic military fashion, the task force has an eleven-word name but a straightforward mission: part of the battalion safeguards embassies in the region, and the other part serves as the regionwide "Oh, shit!" response team. Because the unit is tasked with securing embassies, however, the Marines must abide by the State Department's rules. In early 2021, a CENTCOM report noted that military contractors in Afghanistan were largely focused on covid response instead of operational planning.

The State Department's covid rules from fall 2020 to summer 2021 were asinine. When the Marines from 2/1 showed up in Baghdad, their outgoing counterparts from 2nd Battalion, 5th Marines—who were also based at Camp Pendleton in southern California—warned them that "the diplomats are fucking stupid." One of the officers from 2/5 told us, among other things, that embassy officials had required them to wear disposable masks whenever they left their barracks—including when they were in full kit, manning their posts outside the embassy in Baghdad's sweltering summer heat. The masks quickly caused their eye protection to fog up, making it nearly impossible to see. Nevertheless, embassy employees were quick to reprimand any Marine who tried to sneak a few minutes without a pointless face cover while standing alone outside in the blazing sun.

The State Department also required anyone who might have been exposed to covid to quarantine for two weeks, including the Marines and members of the embassy's diplomatic security staff. Needless to say, the men and women of 2/5 were not about to short staff their guard shifts by shutting perfectly healthy Marines into their rooms for two weeks because they might have encountered someone who later tested positive. When pressed to do "contact tracing" by embassy staff, the NCOs in 2/5 simply asked (or, more accurately, told) their Marines, "No one's getting sick, right?"

From a combat readiness standpoint, however, the State Department's most damaging rule was its vaccine mandate, which it applied as stringently to Marines as it did to its own staff. The rule's only accomplishment was to deprive various Marine QRF units in Kabul of critical manpower and experience when it mattered most. For example, the squad leader and both team leaders of one of the squads in Echo Company, 2/1 were not deployed because they were unvaccinated. A corporal became the acting squad leader and borrowed a rifleman from another squad to carry one of their automatic weapons. Likewise, a member of Ghost Company did not deploy "since he was unvaccinated," we were told.[13] He sat in the classified vault back in Jordan, monitoring intelligence reports, watching drone feeds, and attempting to relay them to Kabul in real time.[14]

Nearly every service member we spoke to mentioned the absurdity of the State Department's approach to a combat evacuation. The mission was exhausting enough without their having to cover unfilled positions. One Marine dryly noted, "There were greater threats to life at the airfield than covid." Others emphasized that the mandate was pointless in any event because their mission required them to interact with thousands of unvaccinated Afghans on a daily basis.

Unnecessary personnel shortages owing to nonsensical covid requirements were a common problem across nearly every unit—units that were there to clean up the Biden administration's mess. The surgeon attached to one of the medical units at the airfield, for example, could not deploy because he, too, was unvaccinated. His unit had to use a lesser-trained individual in his place. In official terms, the surgeon would "support [the mission] from Bahrain."[15] There was no clear explanation why the unvaccinated surgeon had been considered medically fit to deploy to Bahrain but not to accompany his unit to Kabul months later.

Because the administration's vaccine mandate didn't formally go into effect until August 24, the 82nd Airborne made an eleventh-hour decision to ignore it. Combat effectiveness was the most important consideration, and it simply made no sense to leave some of their best soldiers behind. Even then, the uncertainty imposed by the mandate actively disrupted critical preparations at both the company and platoon levels. One of the platoons in Alpha Company 2/504 rearranged its organizational structure at least three times in the week before they went wheels up for Kabul, because the list of deployable paratroopers was constantly shifting.

A soldier in the platoon said, "We didn't know who was going or not—and, like, this is while we had already been called up and were packing our stuff. I became a squad leader for a little while as we were deploying, because somehow, I was the next man up."[16] A platoon leader in his sister company echoed those thoughts: "Once we knew our unvaxxed guys were coming, I was like 'Okay, perfect. Now we have all the key people back where they need them.' But at first it was kind of like 'Great, now we have to piecemeal together some squads and teams based on what we think is happening.'" Less than forty-eight hours before takeoff, they were still reshuffling, making it impossible to assign tasks to specific soldiers or to conduct rehearsals as cohesive units.

The first soldier added, "It seems pretty clear to me that making those decisions because of a fucking covid vaccine directly impacted the lives of people on the ground. I mean, that's an easy connection to make."

GET "ASSES IN SEATS"

During the first forty-eight hours of the evacuation, the troops at HKIA were under strict orders to admit only American citizens, permanent residents, former Afghan interpreters, and government employees who qualified for the Special Immigrant Visa (SIV) program. Identifying those individuals and pulling them through the throngs of bodies at the gates was difficult, but the extraction teams were making steady progress. Then, in the early evening Kabul time on August 18, Biden threw another wrench into the works.

Back in DC, public pressure on the administration was building by the hour. The media was asking the administration for daily updates about the number of evacuees, and the White House was desperate to show that it was doing something—anything—productive. So it opted to simply inflate its "success rate" by bringing vast numbers of people onto the airfield and claiming to have executed one of the most audacious airlift operations in history.

On a call with Chargé d'Affaires Wilson, senior Pentagon and State Department officials in DC, General Sullivan, and Major General Chris Donahue, newly arrived in Afghanistan, Biden complained that the evacuation was moving too slowly and ordered the military to "open the gates" and get "asses in seats."[17] General Sullivan later said that the administration simply "didn't understand the massive human compacting that was occurring outside these gates as 10,000 people were massed outside." The embassy's deputy chief of mission, Ian McCary, had no firsthand knowledge about the situation at the gates, either, but was eager to please. He responded to the White House's demands by assuring Biden that the evacuation force could accomplish the task. Military leaders on the ground who participated in the call later stated that McCary didn't "understand the human [element] compacting at [the] gates."[18]

During the same meeting, Biden ordered the military to start sharing intelligence with the Taliban, so they could "coordinate" security together. In response, the military gave the Taliban eleven folders of detailed information about potential threats to the airfield.[19]

Immediately afterward, the consul general in Afghanistan, Gregory Floyd, who had been in the country for only a month, emailed the State Department's team of consular officers and embassy officials in the country and relayed the specifics of Biden's instructions:

Team,

President Biden phoned Ambassador Wilson with the following directive about who to clear to board evacuation flights:

1. Anyone with a valid form of ID should be given permission to go on a plane if that person plausibly falls into the categories we will evacuate: U.S. citizens and LPRs plus their immediate families, LES plus their immediate families, those entitled to an SIV, and Afghans at risk.

2. Families including women and children should be allowed through and held to fill out planes.

3. Total inflow to the U.S. must exceed the number of seats available. Err on the side of excess.*

This guidance provides clear discretion and direction to fill seats and to provide special consideration for women and children when we have seats. I expect that C17 flight volume will increase.[20]

At 7:00 that evening, Donahue gathered senior commanders and staff at the airfield and relayed the same instructions.[21] Suddenly, the troops manning the gates were required to admit any group who arrived at the gates and presented themselves as a "family" as well as any other Afghan who "plausibly" claimed to be "at risk."

The consequences were predictable to anyone with common sense—a quality that was consistently absent on Pennsylvania Avenue throughout the evacuation. The instruction created perverse incentives for kidnapping, human trafficking, and other crimes that would enable ineligible evacuees to gain access by pretending to be family units. Moreover, in a city recently overrun by an army whose members resembled medieval barbarians, practically *everyone* could "plausibly" claim to be "at risk" in one way or another.

At 1:00 the next morning, Ghost Company from the 2nd Battalion, 1st Marines landed at the airfield at HKIA. They were accompanied by two platoons from their sister unit Fox Company. (Fox's company leadership and one of its platoons remained in Baghdad to secure the US Embassy there.) Living conditions for the reinforcements who arrived at HKIA were ad hoc, to put it mildly. Because the administration had repeatedly refused to acknowledge the possibility of the Afghan government's collapse, there were almost no resources on the ground for the units who arrived at HKIA.

Over the previous two days (August 16 to 17), the NSU and additional forces flown to HKIA had consumed the logistical reserve of food. That led to rationing on the eighteenth and several days afterward. As late as August 21, the airport manager asked outside veterans groups bringing their own aircraft to bring food and water because supplies were running low. A member of a vets group relayed the following request to their contacts: "[We've] been asked by the airfield manager to please bring in whatever we can. . . . If possible, [incoming flights] should bring water/food for while they are there. Situation is getting desperate." The troops quickly sized up the situation. An 82nd platoon leader told us, "Those three days was the toughest, because . . . we were probably another two days away from serious water rationing, serious food rationing . . . not that anyone was going hungry, but you had to start being like 'Hey, we need to consolidate all the food that guys have, because we can't have anyone eating more than just what is absolutely necessary.' You don't like rationing water bottles, but we were going to run out otherwise. That was really the theme for those three days."[22]

There wasn't even an area where the troops could get a few minutes of shut-eye. After two hours, the Marines of Ghost Company ended up sleeping in a room cluttered with gym equipment on the north side of the airfield. They quickly ran out of floor space. Noncommissioned officers and platoon commanders gave up coveted spots on the floor to their junior enlisted Marines and instead slept on the ramps of treadmills. Company leadership got very little rest that first night, spending most of it reviewing the layout of the airfield and trying to plan for what was to come

Twelve minutes after Ghost Company landed in Kabul and one hour and forty-eight minutes before they bedded down on treadmills, the White House released a video from Principal Deputy National Security Advisor Jon Finer. Without a hint of irony or self-awareness, the number two official on the National Security Council claimed that the "mission" to "provide security and stability at the international airport in Kabul" had been "accomplished in large part because we planned for it."[23] He added, "President Biden ordered the prepositioning of US forces in the region and deployed those forces in recent days to ensure that stability and security could be brought to the airport."[24] Nothing could have been farther from the truth.

At first light, Ghost Company was assembled outside, in full kit, ready to start their mission. Because they had no vehicles, they were forced to engage in the now-ritual act of hot-wiring their transportation. One of their platoon sergeants chalked the need for doing so up "to a lack of planning."[25] They arrived at Abbey Gate at 8:00 a.m. and linked up with UK paratroopers and a smattering of other foreign forces securing the inner corridor of the gate. A set of heavy steel doors separated them from a throng of countless Afghan civilians filling the gate's outer corridor on the other side.[26]

The situation was untenable. The Marines and pararescue airmen needed to push the crowd back from the gate to create enough distance to give them a chance to begin processing valid evacuees. The senior leaders from each unit congregated to devise a course of action. The group, which consisted of Ghost Company commander Geoff Ball, a wiry company commander from the United Kingdom's Parachute Regiment, officers from the US Air Force's elite 71st Rescue Squadron, and several Marine NCOs, settled on a plan: as soon as they opened the gates, successive squads of Marines, airmen, and British paratroopers standing in close formation would advance and force the crowd back down the outer corridor.

The mob had different ideas. The gates swung open, and the Marines and British paratroopers were instantly greeted by a violent mob clawing and shoving them in an all-out attempt to break through the perimeter. According to the director of operations for the Air Force rescue squadron, the resistance came "Not from deserving interpreters and their families trying to escape the Taliban, but from a large group of military aged males that didn't speak English." He had "no doubt" that none of them had assisted the United States or their fellow countrymen in the previous two decades of war against the Taliban. The group vastly outnumbered the Marines and Brits who were trying to push them back without using lethal force. The first wave was quickly engulfed. Second and third waves of reinforcements quickly followed, but the scene was already too chaotic to allow for the disciplined "Roman Legion"–style operation they'd planned. Some of the Marines and airmen were able to subdue the more violent members of the crowd with flex-cuffs, but others were dragged into the fray away from the rest of their squads. An Air Force pararescueman (PJ) who was separated from the team drew his SIG Sauer 9-millimeter pistol and started firing in the air to create enough physical separation to allow him to fall back to the gates.[27]

In a last-ditch maneuver, a final wave of Marines and Brits from the United Kingdom's 2nd Parachute Battalion formed a wedge and pushed headlong into the crowd, but the mob simply folded around them as soon as they passed. An Air Force officer from the 71st jumped into the crowd to try to help and was immediately greeted with a punch to the face. The squads of Marines and paratroopers attempted to fall back but found themselves trapped between the mass of bodies and the safety afforded by the gates. The crush of the crowd was enough to push the air from the lungs of civilians in street clothes, but the pressure on each side of the bulletproof plates in the troops' body armor compounded the effect. Several Marines and airmen later remarked that they had thought they were about to die.

Unsurprisingly, the group of unworthy young males' strategy of beating US troops until they were allowed to go to the United States proved counterproductive for all involved. As the situation increasingly got out of hand, the US forces who remained at the entrance of Abbey Gate had no choice but to deploy every available nonlethal measure at their disposal. They launched flash-bangs into the crowd and began firing warning shots over their heads. The munitions gave the stranded Marines and airmen just enough time to fall back to the rest of the troops at the front, but the crowd kept coming. In response, the airmen and Marines began to launch canisters of CS gas en masse to force the crowd to fall back, even though they knew that a decent percentage of the civilians in front of them weren't among the troublemakers. The choking effects of the gas suppressed the crowd long enough for all US and allied forces to regroup at the gates and seal them off once again.

A platoon sergeant from Ghost Company described the events as "the most desperate moment I saw. The only thing I can compare it to was a zombie movie." He added, "The pushing was so intense that there were NCOs that didn't want to do it again. Marines would get pulled into the crowd by themselves, people would reach through the crowd and grab Marines' weapons. I saw people try to grab a Marine's weapon and shoot it into the crowd."[28]

Still, the gate needed to be cleared. As night fell, Ghost Company began clearing operations in conjunction with the Brits. Because it was nearly impossible for the crowd to move in one direction or another, they let roughly three hundred people through the gate and corralled them in the interior to try to create some breathing room on the outside.[29] Then the allied forces stood shoulder to shoulder, making a slow advance on the crowd, the squad leaders at the very front alongside their men. The efforts were painstaking, and progress was slow.

By dawn on the twentieth, Ghost Company was finally able to open the gate and begin processing evacuees in an orderly manner. After nearly eight hours of continuous effort, they'd pushed the crowd far enough down the outer corridor to give them room to operate. But there was no rest for the weary. They had, at best, a week and a half to evacuate tens of thousands of people. Exhausted, hungry, and soaked in sweat, the Marines immediately initiated screening procedures.

Abbey Gate wasn't an outlier. The same day, stampedes had occurred outside North Gate and East Gate, too. More than a dozen women and children had been trampled to death. When possible, medics retrieved the bodies and stored them in the morgue on HKIA until local Red Crescent officials could retrieve them. Still, the crowds continued to swell as word spread that the United States was "accepting everyone," and they became virtually impossible to navigate. Stuck behind them were the thousands of US citizens and SIV applicants that the military units were there to evacuate.

BIDEN POLICY: PRIVILEGING THE WRONG PEOPLE

Biden's order afforded a distinct advantage to one demographic: aggressive young males who had no relationship with the US government—or to anyone else in the crowd, for that matter. They were stronger than the women, children, and elderly, and they were "unencumbered" by responsibilities to bring others along with them. They were able to shove their way to the front and frequently slipped through the gates by blending in with family units. "At the front it was all [military-age males]. The families were on the far side of the canal," a Ghost Company squad leader recalled.[30] Some officers noted that among the single males who had managed to push through the crowds and enter the airfield were former Afghan soldiers who had simply shed their uniforms. Another officer at Abbey Gate bitterly remarked, "If these guys fought the Taliban half as hard as they are fighting us to leave, we wouldn't even be in this mess."[31]

A State Department consular officer on the ground who served as State's liaison to the military estimated that "less than 30 percent were of legitimate U.S. connection."[32] A platoon sergeant from the 82nd Airborne, whose platoon was tasked with internal security, echoed the sentiment: "The process of vetting people was almost non-existent. We felt like a ton of single military-aged males probably had no connection to the United States." A Marine at Abbey Gate spoke to us in frustrated agreement: "I couldn't tell you why a lot of the single males were getting in. That was a State Department decision."

The young single males were problematic in other ways, besides sliding through without credentials. One Marine contrasted the resiliency and good spirits of the children, compared to the aggressive young males, who took more than they gave: "It was the single male populace that was the problem to deal with. . . . The single males pissed me off everywhere we went. I'm sure you understand. At the terminals, the single males were stealing food from little kids or complaining about not having the stuff we were handing out to women and children. We had a very limited amount of blankets and stuff. Single males would try to steal them from kids or women. The kids were always really in decent spirits for the most part. It blew my mind that rounds flying over little kids' heads every now and then didn't seem to bother them."

The behavior of some older men, likewise unaffiliated with the US government, was even more hideous. U.S. Customs and Border Protection catalogued numerous instances where older men "purchased" young girls to pass off as their "wives" and gain entry to HKIA and a ticket to the United States.[33] The report, issued on August 27, 2021, and titled "Afghanistan Task Force SitRep No. 63," stated that "Afghan girls at a transit site in Abu Dhabi have alleged they have been raped by older men they were forced to marry to escape Afghanistan."[34] A US government official familiar with the issue described the number of older men who used the tactic as "not a small number,"[35] and Secretary of State Blinken later admitted under oath that he was aware of a "handful" of such instances.[36] Sickeningly, at least a few of the men identified several girls as their "wives" when questioned by authorities.[37]

The poor vetting was a direct result of the massive pressure the White House placed on military officials to increase evacuee numbers. A State Department consular officer later recalled, "There was a push by the executive branch to get the flow started. Doing the right processing was too slow, so the quality of intake dropped because we were barely checking paperwork."[38] Roughly a dozen individuals, ranging from the generals in charge of the evacuation to State Department consular officers and company-level officers, reported constant pressure from the White House to increase the total evacuee numbers at virtually any cost. Each described the administration's motivations in his own terms, but every description shared a common theme: the decision was reckless, dangerous, and counterproductive.

The most charitable interpretation was that the White House was staffed by naive politicos who had grown up watching *The West Wing* and had zero knowledge of how complex military operations played out in real life. The darker—and prevailing—view was that the administration simply didn't care about anything other than the evacuee numbers it could tout at its daily press conferences to rebut the mounting accusations about its incompetence. Numbers were numbers, and the most important consideration was whether a press secretary could describe the airlift as a "historic effort" in numerical terms, real-world outcomes notwithstanding.[39] Admiral Vasely later told investigators that "the flood gates were open" once Biden issued his directive.[40]

Biden's directive not only led to stampedes, vetting issues, and child trafficking but also jeopardized the safety of the troops and worthy evacuees inside the wire. Suddenly, tens of thousands of unvetted civilians, many of them military-age males, were inside the wire and demanding to board flights immediately. The forces on HKIA simply weren't equipped for the situation. Things quickly—and repeatedly—got out of hand, culminating in a six-hour-long riot at one of the staging areas, with many evacuees throwing rocks and swinging two-by-fours at the troops trying to get them under control. A separate riot broke out at the passenger terminal, with evacuees fighting over access to departing flights.[41] Marines quickly nicknamed the holding area "the thunder dome" due to the frequent unrest.[42]

By August 20, barely thirty-six hours after Biden's directive, the refugee capacity at HKIA was stretched beyond its limits. Military leaders were forced to temporarily close the gates while the unvetted thousands were evacuated (or in some instances cleared from the airfield for posing security risks). "Priorities shifted to internal support of riot control, riot prevention, and crowd subduing as the crowds inside were also large and frustrated."[43] Except for a few isolated cases, nobody—including US citizens, UK citizens, and former interpreters—was able to enter. The resulting delay ultimately led to the airfield commanders' decision to keep Abbey Gate open for as long as possible, despite highly reliable intelligence forecasting an impending attack, so that as many US citizens and other Westerners (UK citizens in particular) as possible could be evacuated.

Officers on the ground stated that the White House directive had "set the stage"[44] for the suicide attack on the twenty-sixth by "massively" increasing the military's workload without helping to accomplish the mission they'd been given: namely, to rescue US citizens and designated allies and get all US forces out of the country safely.

If Biden's decision to close Bagram was the original sin of the withdrawal plan, his panicked, reflexive order to open the gates was the original sin of the evacuation itself.

EIGHT

SEEING THINGS THAT NO PERSON SHOULD HAVE TO SEE

Before the Marines arrived at Abbey Gate, their battalion chaplain, Father Dan Schwartz, tried his best to prepare them for what they would experience. He told them that they "were going to see things that no person should have to see" and that their "morals would be tested" continuously.[1] No amount of preparation could have sufficed, however. As a senior Marine leader on the ground later reflected, "You can't really train people to see what they saw."[2] Struggling to describe their experiences, several soldiers and Marines simply told us that Kabul in August 2021 had been far worse than words could capture.

THE TALIBAN
The security situation confronting US troops at the airfield gates was volatile and unprecedented. Throughout the evacuation, the men and women defending HKIA had front-row seats to the Taliban's gruesome violence against innocent men, women, and children. Worse, their hands were tied: they were forbidden from doing anything to stop it. The administration described the Taliban as a partner in its evacuation efforts, but US forces at the company and platoon level saw dozens of examples each day proving that that wasn't the case.

Tasked with the "outer security" surrounding the entire installation, the Taliban set up checkpoints on the major avenues leading to the airfield and stationed men outside the gate, a few hundred yards or less from the Americans just inside. Taliban fighters stood guard on rooftops and walls overlooking the airport, peering down at the Marines who were attempting to control the crowds. They likewise manned positions atop shipping containers that Marines had placed at the entrance to the outer corridor of Abbey Gate. Placing the shipping containers served a dual purpose: to funnel evacuees toward Abbey Gate and to block vehicle traffic to the gate, a necessary precaution to reduce the risk of suicide car bombs.

The Taliban's proximity created an eerie and unpredictable vibe. The Taliban fighters videotaped the Marines' movements and radioed updates to their superiors. Some tried to provoke incidents by unpredictably raising their weapons toward the Marines for brief moments before returning them to the "low-ready" position. The tension was unrelenting. And in the chaos outside the gates, the Taliban knew that they held the upper hand. One Marine recalled, "Gunfire was a constant thing. Never thought I'd get used to hearing it, but I did. What bugged me was watching the Taliban shoot unarmed civilians, and I couldn't do anything about it. I knew on my first deployment that we encountered the Taliban . . . but seeing them in Kabul, knowing it was them was unreal to me."[3]

The Taliban guarded one of the airfield's four major gates, South Gate, which was kept closed throughout the evacuation. The Taliban commander at South Gate was a member of the Haqqani Network and had a visceral hatred of Westerners.[4] During a "security planning" meeting with Admiral Vasely a few days into the evacuation, he openly taunted the Americans, accusing all US military officers, Vasely included, of being liars.[5] On the US side of South Gate, National Strike Unit (NSU) fighters faced off with the Taliban units. Both the NSU and the Taliban had inflicted battlefield losses and unspeakable atrocities upon each other for more than a decade. Now they stood half a football field length apart in an uneasy truce, separated only by the chain-link fence marking HKIA's boundaries. Reenacting their previous battles in the open would only lead to mass casualties and—if they survived—potential execution by their superiors. So, no longer able to shoot at each other, the NSU and the Taliban resorted to hurling insults back and forth in the limited English both sides knew: "pedophiles," "goat fuckers," "pussies." US troops stoically stood nearby.

THE GATES

The Marines assumed general responsibility for securing the three remaining main gates, Abbey Gate, North Gate, and East Gate. Abbey Gate was covered by the Marines from 2/1. The Marines from 1/8 took North Gate and split the responsibility for East Gate with a company of 82nd paratroopers from 1/504. In addition to gate security, the Marines from 2/1 and 1/8 were jointly responsible for evacuee processing and safety at all three of HKIA's main gates, while soldiers from the 82nd Airborne and 10th Mountain divisions handled perimeter security between the gates and interior security on the airport footprint. Adjacent to the Marines on the south side, several companies from 2/501 secured the fence line from the center of the airfield toward the east, an area that included the former civilian terminal of the airport. The battalion's Alpha Company positioned itself across a broad swath of land dotted with hangars housing abandoned or disabled civilian aircraft. They called the area "the Boneyard" and set up a company command center inside one of the abandoned planes. To their right, 1/504 secured the other half of HKIA's southern perimeter. Directly to their rear, on the other side of the airfield, several platoons from 2/504 guarded the north side of HKIA.

The Shock Trauma Platoon set up operations in a building halfway between East Gate and Abbey Gate. They used an up-armored Toyota

Land Cruiser as a makeshift ambulance, shuttling the injured from entry points to emergency care. Until the bombing, they treated mainly Afghans and US civilians suffering physical injuries or heat exhaustion due to the chaos outside the gates.

Officially, evacuees could access the airport only through one of three gates. CIA teams and special operations units, however, used two clandestine portals to evacuate Americans and high-priority Afghans off the books. SEAL Team Six brought their Afghan allies inside the wire through their own "gate"—a small, nondescript doorway on the southwest side of the airfield, about halfway down the single runway that split HKIA in half and away from most of the commotion.[6] The CIA entrance, known as "Black Gate" (among several other names), was almost directly to the north, on the other side of the airfield. It was barely more than a hole in the fence and conveniently positioned near multiple avenues of approach from both Afghan residential areas and the agency's Eagle Base. A gas station across the street served as a rendezvous point where NSU fighters under the agency's control would meet evacuees and spirit them to safety. The Taliban were completely unaware of the gate's existence, and its precise location was so closely guarded that some members of partner intelligence agencies didn't know where it was. We reviewed multiple Signal messages from US government officials asking well-connected members of veteran evacuation networks how to send people to Black Gate.

When conditions on the ground made linkups at the gas station too risky, NSU personnel met evacuees wherever they were sheltering in place inside the city and took them directly to Eagle Base. Agency officials then transported them to HKIA using Russian-made Mi-17 helicopters—the most common aircraft in the region and the least likely to attract unwanted attention—that were listed in flight logs as commercially owned aircraft because they were registered to a CIA shell company. The CIA operatives pinned a large poster board to the wall of their Kabul operations center, with LIVES SAVED, KABUL AFG, AUGUST

2021 written at the top in block letters. In the space below, they used tally marks to record the number of men and women they'd brought to safety. By August 27, there were more than 1,970 tally marks on the board.

ABBEY GATE: DEAD BABIES

The Marines at Abbey Gate had a clear view of the atrocities unfolding in front of their eyes. Some they could try to prevent, but more often they were powerless to intervene. Sometimes they came face-to-face with human suffering resulting from violence occurring just out of sight, when they were approached by traumatized civilians covered in blood, sobbing women who had been raped, or newly orphaned children in shock.

Unsurprisingly, the deaths of children were the most difficult to witness. Horrific images seared themselves into the memories of brave young service members, haunting their sleep and breaking their hearts. Several Marines at Abbey Gate described shocking scenes of infants being knocked out of their mothers' hands and trampled to death before their eyes, too fast for the Marines to intervene. On several occasions, the mother was unable to push back through the surging crowd to recover her lifeless child or was knocked to the ground and trampled herself. Sometimes the losses flowed in the other direction: parents were trampled to death, slowly pressed into the razor wire in front of the walls, or simply died of heatstroke in front of their children. Chaos, brutality, and death were daily fare at the gates. Too often, the Marines could only watch in horror scenes they would never forget.

At 2:00 a.m. on August 22, Echo Company relieved Ghost Company at Abbey Gate. Relief was overdue. The Ghost Company Marines were nearly delirious from fatigue. Some of them had gotten only three hours of sleep over the previous three days[7] and slept for eighteen hours straight once their shift mercifully ended.

Father Schwartz's earlier warning to Ghost Company—that they "were going to see things that no person should have to see"—had certainly been borne out. Now the chaplain's warning to Echo, preparing for their turn at Abbey Gate, was even more blunt. A squad leader from Echo recalled that moment: "Before our first couple days at Abbey Gate, the chaplain said, 'you're guaranteed at least one or two dead babies a day.' At the time, I didn't know what he meant." But it didn't take long to understand. "I saw a dead kid in the canal the first night I was there," continued the squad leader, before his voice trailed off. "He was just kind of floating around."

Tragedies arose each day in uniquely awful ways. One of the Marines at Abbey Gate recalled instances when he and others had searched a bag carried by a woman entering the airfield and made the stomach-churning discovery that there was "a dead baby inside." Desperate to protect their little ones from being knocked out of their hands and trampled under the crowd, the women had tucked their babies inside backpacks or garment bags strapped to their bodies and cracked the zippers open slightly to try to provide some air. Only after fighting their way through the crushing crowds and submitting to the search process did they discover that their children had suffocated. Other times, a woman tried to throw an infant or toddler over the fence but misjudged the distance, and the child landed in the stack of razor wire on the wall's exterior. Trying to hide the emotion in his voice, one Marine initially described the events in detached terms: "There would be dead kids here and there." Moments later, he exhaled deeply and acknowledged that the experience had been singularly horrific, no matter how many times it had occurred.

NORTH GATE: PERSISTENT VIOLENCE

The dynamics at North Gate were different; the situation was equally chaotic but even more violent. The crowd was aggressive from the minute it gathered outside the gate on the night of the sixteenth, after US and allied forces restored control of the airport. Hundreds of military-age Afghan males without valid paperwork pushed and shoved their way to the front entrances. Relentlessly aggressive, they advanced to within a few feet of the men and women of 1/8 and berated the Marines for not letting them in. The Marines from 1/8 were fed up. They responded in kind, yelling at them to step back. The young, single men typically refused to listen. The only communications they respected came in the form of flash-bangs, batons, and the occasional warning shot. Some Afghans intentionally injured themselves on the concertina wire outside the gate, hoping to be let in. Still, the Marines' options outside of lethal force were slim. Although they had acquired a precious few riot control tools by bashing the locks off storage containers on the airfield, those offered minimal leverage against the seething crowds.

The NSU operated its own entrance only a few dozen yards to the left of the Marines manning North Gate, and the crowd outside spanned both entrances. The Afghan militiamen operated with far less restraint than the adjacent Marines, however. As one Marine described it, the NSU simply went from zero to eighty when military-age males refused to comply with their commands, "firing rounds in the air, at people's feet, or at people to crowd control." Those "warning shots" frequently hit other people in the crowd, some barely in the vicinity of the intended targets. "Every few hours, we would have to take in a gunshot wound for treatment until RADM Vasely ordered [us] to stop treating noncompliant military aged males."[8] If members of the crowd were too close for effective warning shots or were accompanied by women or children, the NSU kept them at bay by whipping them until they retreated.[9]

For the right price, however, the NSU were willing to overlook admission requirements. They frequently solicited bribes to allow in-eligible people inside the wire. At times, the going rate reached $5,000 per person—several times greater than the country's annual per capita income.[10] Many of those offering cash for passage were members of Kabul's upper middle class, but there was no way to be sure of their intentions. Everyone knew that the influx of unvetted, unknown individuals increased the chances of an insider attack on the airfield.[11]

EAST GATE: PUSHED TO THE BRINK

It required considerable ingenuity to secure the East Gate. The gate was surrounded by low fences that could easily be breached or overrun by a crowd half the size of the one now outside it. The paratroopers from B Company 2/501 and the combined antiarmor team (CAAT) from the 1/8 Marines' weapons company used a hot-wired fire truck and two flatbed cargo trucks to pin the gates closed to prevent the mob from pushing them open. The troops clambered aboard the parked vehicles. Standing on top of the trucks offered a sweeping view of the crowds below. Razor wire was hastily strung along the top of the walls to their left and right by engineers after the mob started climbing the walls during the initial days of the evacuation.

The gate stayed shut unless a specific family or evacuee needed to be brought in. The troops would crack the gates open long enough to verify the identities of the evacuees and bring them inside. Then they would immediately seal the entrance. Even then, the crowd routinely rushed the entryway. The troops had no choice but to throw flash-bangs into the throng to stun them, counting on the red smoke to disorient people and keep them from converging onto the gate. The evacuees who made it through often needed immediate medical treatment for injuries inflicted at Taliban checkpoints or by the brutal jockeying amid the press of bodies in the crowd. Other evacuees collapsed from heat exhaustion, as the hours of standing outside in the punishing temperatures without food or water for days on end took their toll.

After several days, military leaders decided that the effort needed to keep East Gate open didn't justify the meager results. Moreover, the Taliban commander at the gate openly refused to comply with US requests. He "basically told the company commander to shut the gate down around the twenty-fourth," recounted one Marine, "because he wasn't going to cooperate."[12]

PROTECTING THE VULNERABLE

The Americans at the gates tried their best to protect the vulnerable, often at great risk to their own safety. An Air Force PJ from the 58th Expeditionary Rescue Squadron charged into a stampede and carried four children to safety after their parents were trampled before their eyes.[13] Navy corpsmen had Marines hold their ankles while they leaned headfirst into the crowd to pull up women and infants who were struggling to breathe.[14] Almost every service member we spoke to shared multiple stories about the selfless actions of those who had served alongside them.

The Marines at Abbey Gate turned one of the comfort areas on the eastern end of the airfield into a makeshift orphanage for children whose parents had been killed in the chaos outside the gates. But they didn't just create a refuge; many of them visited the children repeatedly, bringing them candy from their MREs and taking pictures with them (a crowd favorite). In one instance, a Ghost Company platoon sergeant detoured to the area just to check on the children, and a little girl repeatedly cried out to him in Pashtu. He didn't understand what she was saying until a translator relayed the message: "Thank you for being kind."[15] Touched, he frequented the orphanage in the days that followed to make sure she made it on a flight out of the country.[16]

The airfield had all kinds of supplies, but diapers and baby formula were not among them. No one had planned to take care of orphaned infants. But the ingenuity of the American war fighter prevailed over such obstacles. Troops worked their local contacts outside the wire to acquire basic necessities for the children. Even a few minutes spent with the children brought joy to an otherwise dark place, sustaining the troops in heart, mind, and soul. In a poignant example, just days before she would lose her life to the suicide bomber at the gate, Marine

Sergeant Nicole Gee posted a photo on Instagram, showing herself tenderly holding an Afghan infant, looking pensively at the child sleeping in her arms. She captioned the photo simply, "I love my job."[17]

"WAIT, THAT'S FUCKED UP."

The American men and women holding the line took immense satisfaction in rescuing the vulnerable, but they had an equally strong distaste for the cowardly, specifically some of the men attempting to come through the wire, many of whom were no older than they were. Service members at the gates recounted several occasions when they had handed out water bottles to help the crowd survive the punishing heat, only to watch the men guzzle the water without sharing any with their wives and children. "You'd see a male take water and let their kids sit there dying," one said.

Worse yet, some of the men abandoned their families altogether in a bid to start fresh in the West. An officer on the ground described how "the men would rush through" the gates when an opportunity presented itself, leaving their wives and children behind to navigate the violence of the crowd and the stifling heat—and usually their future lives under the Taliban—all alone. The cowardly acts often placed the Marines at the gates in a stomach-churning, no-win position: abandoned women and children would arrive at the gates and tell the Marines that their husbands or fathers had passed through without them. But the women had no paperwork, and allowing anyone with a sympathetic story to proceed would effectively have resumed the unworkable "family unit" standard President Biden had ordered at the beginning of the evacuation. Describing the scene, another officer simply said, "Emotionally, it was tough."[18]

It was more than "tough"; it was enraging. Several members of an 82nd Airborne platoon recounted incidents when Afghan fence jumpers had cited their decision to abandon their families as the reason why the paratroopers should let them stay. The platoon witnessed three men in their late twenties or early thirties attempting to jump the fence on the south side of the airfield. They corralled the interlopers and were immediately greeted with an ill-considered sob story. The spokesperson for the would-be stowaways protested, "Hey, man, we abandoned our families, we took a huge risk to come here." That excuse was dead on arrival.

One of the paratroopers blurted out, "Wait, did he really fucking say that? Holy shit, he left his family to the Taliban to try and sneak out of here himself." The platoon sergeant thought he must have misheard the answer, so he tried to clarify: "What do you mean, you abandoned your family?" The man replied, "We left our—you know—I left my wife, I left my kids, I left my family to try and escape. I took a huge risk to come here." The platoon sergeant's response was relatively measured: "Well, it sounds like you shouldn't have done that." One of the platoon's team leaders was more acidic: "Dude, I don't give a fuck. You're not getting into this airport if you're leaving your family behind. That doesn't make me sympathetic to you. That makes me want to toss your ass over the fence and personally give you to the Taliban."

Summarizing the platoon's reaction, one of the men said, "As Americans, we were all like 'Wait, that's fucked up.'" Needless to say, those suddenly solo men were not escorted to the flight line as they'd hoped. Several paratroopers described the episode as a turning point in their interactions with the local population. "At this point, we were still pretty sympathetic. But that was kind of the tipping point. That's where our sympathy for people dwindled relatively fast," one said. From there on out, they viewed claims from anyone without a documented connection to the United States with a jaundiced eye.

"FORCED TO PLAY GOD"

According to a senior leader in charge of the evacuation efforts, the young soldiers and Marines at the gates "were forced to play God by identifying who would be allowed into the airfield." The State Department had informed SIV applicants that their "immediate families" were eligible to leave with them. But there was one problem: it had never specified the parameters of the term "immediate families." The State Department's definition of "family" included only spouses and children under twenty-one. In Afghan society, "family" means something far different. As a result, Afghan SIV applicants spent hours and even days traveling to the gates with their parents, siblings, and other family members in tow, only to learn that most of them were ineligible.

The Marines standing post, many of them barely twenty years old, were forced to issue a harrowing order to Afghan SIV applicants: You have two minutes to choose: either you can abandon your parents, siblings, and adult children, or you can all remain in Afghanistan together.

A Marine corporal who was part of the process described how watching "families getting split up" just "wore on a lot of people over time." The families' anguished reactions cut them to the core. He added, "How I can tell somebody that's extremely desperate, 'Hey, you have to walk over there and go back out into Kabul, where you think you're going to get killed'?" When eligible evacuees chose to take their wives and children to safety and leave their extended families behind, the stranded family members often refused to move, no matter how many times the Marines asked them to do so. "Every now and then, we'd say, 'Hey, we can't take you,' and you'd have a dude come up and scream at you and be like 'You're sentencing me to death.' We had guys grab a rifle and just put the muzzle to their head and say, 'Just shoot me now, then.'" The Marines were forced to physically drag many of these Afghans off the gates, which only compounded their feelings of guilt.

Each shift depleted them physically, emotionally, and spiritually. As one officer recalled, "We had a few Marines who were very religious and it was very challenging for them to separate the job they had to do and their personal morals."[19] They could not save everyone, not even close. Through no fault of their own, the Marines at the gates were thrust into the position of playing God, being arbiters of which families, or which family members, would survive and which would be subjected to the brutality of the Taliban. They'd always believed that the purpose of their profession was to protect the vulnerable and destroy the venomous. Now they had to sort innocent family members and decide which ones would live and which would likely die. That obligation had been forced upon them by the highest levels of government, including the White House. The Marines didn't deserve it, but they had no choice but to endure it. Being forced to make impossible choices inflicted deep interior wounds on the men and women holding the line. Some Marines at Abbey Gate spent their fifteen-minute rest periods in the solitude afforded by the base of the sniper tower, where their tears flowed freely.

Even when families weren't involved, the difficulty of separating imposters from legitimate evacuees only heightened the moral confusion. Many SIV applicants had burned their documents lest the Taliban find them and use them as pretexts for summary execution. That decision was sensible, but it left those men and their families in limbo. Unless someone had proper documentation—or a trustworthy military contact who could vouch for their identity *and* provide identifying information to confirm that the individual at the gates was the same person they were vouching for—the Marines had no choice but to turn them away. Practically speaking, admitting people based on verbal assurances alone would have meant admitting the entire crowd. And as Biden's since-rescinded directive to admit every "family unit" had made painfully clear, that outcome was plainly not feasible.

But for those turned away, death was often inescapable. Several times each day, Marines would refuse entry to people who lacked proper paperwork, only to see them executed by the Taliban minutes later. Similar scenarios played out around the HKIA perimeter. When they could, troops developed their own methods of discouraging Taliban cruelty. One young soldier described how he and other members of his platoon would shoot over the Taliban fighters' heads when they saw them preparing to execute someone. He added, "Guys were just shooting over to try to do *anything* to get them to stop . . . just to get them to get the hell out of there. I mean, that was just like an every-night occurrence."

One afternoon, three Afghan male teens sprinted up to the chain-link fence marking the airfield's southern perimeter, grabbed hold of it, and begged to be let in. The soldiers of the 82nd who were guarding the area responded, "Hey, you guys can't come in here. If you want to come in, go find a gate and show your documentation." The three panicked boys started pleading "No, the Taliban are about to kill us. How can you let them kill us?" The senior enlisted leader of the Americans, a seasoned NCO with nearly a decade of service, told us that his men had wanted to help, "but we couldn't just let them jump the fence." Right then, the Taliban saw the teens. In seconds, several armed fighters wrestled them off the fence and took them away. The senior enlisted leader sounded stoic. "Like, they just walked them away, and we were on the other side of the fence, and we all knew what was about to happen. The whole time, these kids kept saying 'They're about to kill us.'" After a moment's reflection, he quietly added, "Morally, that's still really tough to deal with."

Company and battalion commanders tried to keep the Marines' spirits up by sending them to the flight line to see the tangible benefits of their efforts. After rotating off gate duty, units often spent hours watching and interacting with families boarding planes to safety.

They needed to see that this wasn't all for nothing.

THE STATE DEPARTMENT: BUNGLED MESSAGES AND BROKEN TRUST

General George Patton apocryphally declared, "Lead me, follow me, or get out of my way." Even though long-standing doctrine technically placed the State Department in charge of the evacuation, State neither led, followed, nor got out of the way. If the bureaucrats and political appointees at Foggy Bottom excelled at one task during the two-week evacuation, it was finding novel ways to screw things up. An aide to General Sullivan put the problem plainly: "It's difficult to work with [State] when they don't really know what to do."[20]

State's most fundamental error was failing to convey accurate information to evacuees. Even though the agency took charge of the evacuation, it consistently disseminated incorrect—and counterproductive—guidance about the most basic facts. It provided inaccurate information about who was eligible to leave the country, where evacuees should go, and which documents they should bring. A senior Marine officer on the ground described the State Department's bungled communications in stark terms: State "did not get one message right" in its directions to potential evacuees.[21]

It wasn't for lack of trying. The generals on the ground at HKIA held daily meetings with Chargé d'Affaires Wilson, Ambassador Bass, and other State Department officials to coordinate messaging and clarify which gates would be open to US citizens and SIV applicants. According to an officer present at the discussions, the State Department always confirmed the agreed-upon times and locations, yet "every message they sent out was in error in some way." He found their level of incompetence mystifying.[22]

It was worse than mystifying; it was dangerous. The military was forced to make corrections on the fly or play cleanup. In one instance, the Army PSYOP team on the ground refused to disseminate a State Department message that they believed would heighten the risk of human trafficking or at the very least create insurmountable difficulties for the Marines at the gates trying to distinguish, in a matter of minutes, real evacuees from opportunists. A PSYOP soldier explained that they "decided not to disseminate" a State message telling "civilians to approach service members if they had concerns about a missing family member." We already had problems with child theft and there was no shortage of people asking to be prioritized because of family members, so we decided it was better not to use that messaging." He diplomatically described the State Department's "messaging" as "a little broken."[23]

Factual inaccuracies and cultural cluelessness were just the beginning, however. From the get-go, almost everyone in the crowd outside the gates waved a piece of paper of some sort to get the Marines' attention. It might be a certificate showing they had completed a cultural course provided by the State Department to the public, a photocopy of a letter of appreciation from a government official years prior, or some other link to the Americans. Most of the papers were likely fraudulent. It was impossible to tell. But even those that were authentic usually didn't meet the required standard for evacuation to the United States. Nevertheless, the continued lack of clarity from on high complicated the military's efforts to distinguish legitimate evacuees from opportunists or worse.

One hallmark of leadership is recognizing, and swiftly correcting, poor decisions. In a dangerous situation, this is critical. But as the evacuation mission teetered on the precipice of disaster, the State Department made things worse. On August 21, State sent a form letter to thousands of SIV applicants. It was like tossing a match into a gas can: the situation exploded. The letter purported to guarantee the recipients access to HKIA by simply presenting the form letter to military guards outside the airport. The sheer stupidity of such a move should have been obvious, even to faraway State bureaucrats. The admission letter, though addressed to a particular person, was generic and contained no protections against duplication. Not surprisingly (except, perhaps, to the clueless functionaries who issued it), the form letter was quickly forwarded by text and email to thousands of ineligible individuals. Would-be evacuees who had a phone but no connection to the United States began air-dropping the form letter to one another outside the gates. The letter quickly became worthless to the initial recipients and anyone else who tried to use it. At Abbey Gate, within a matter of hours, six different people tried to gain entry by presenting a form letter addressed to the same individual. The platoon sergeant overseeing evacuee admissions at Abbey Gate quickly caught on, but it was an unforced error that military officials later said "created its own risk" to American troops at the gates by unnecessarily complicating their efforts to distinguish worthy evacuees from security threats.[24] Worse, that risk was created by the very people who were supposed to set the rules for an orderly, safe evacuation of American citizens and US allies.

State's internal communications with the units manning the gates were no more reliable. Admiral Vasely later stated that the military leadership had had to make "a daily decision" about whom to prioritize, "based on State's changing priorities."[25] Another officer characterized State's instructions as "constantly changing."[26] Members of the Biden administration privately admitted to us that State had no prepared strategy for tracking or processing stranded Americans. A Biden State Department official who participated in the evacuation efforts vented that "It just never really looked like there was a plan," even though the evacuation had become increasingly foreseeable over the previous months. The ever-changing guidance put the Marines into a gut-wrenching position. They were forced to escort people out of HKIA minutes or hours after admitting them and telling them they'd been approved for evacuation. Even a State Department official admitted, "I felt like it was very ad hoc. I never even got a list of criteria." The shifting guidance also required the Marines at the gate to give conflicting directives to members of the crowd, often within a matter of hours, further agitating the desperate, angry people outside the gates.[27] "For every legitimate evacuee, there were thousands of illegitimate people trying to get into HKIA. We had such pressure to get as many people into HKIA as possible. There was a lot of outside messaging to the Afghans that almost anyone would be evacuated. This made perimeter security tough."[28] This bureaucratic bungling damaged the trust between the troops and the diplomats charged with organizing the evacuation. As one Marine summed it up, "The State Department really pissed us off."

Ironically, even the Taliban expressed frustration with State's un-predictable messaging shifts. Though they pretended to cooperate with the US government's evacuation plans during the first days after the collapse of the Afghan government, Taliban commanders at checkpoints outside the airfield frequently told military leaders that they couldn't keep track of whom they were supposed to let in.

DIPLOMATS: PUNCHING A TIME CLOCK IN A WAR ZONE

The State Department's inaccurate and ever-changing directives were only half the problem, however. Consular officials often failed to show up to the gates to process evacuees—even though that was their job. General McKenzie later acknowledged that the wait for consular officials had created significant delays. "What you've got is a capacity problem. You've got to process all these people. It took a while, frankly, for our consular officials to get there in the numbers needed to handle the press of people that were outside."[29]

When the bureaucrats did show, according to troops on the ground, they usually remained at their posts only until their shifts were technically over, *even if no one arrived to relieve them.* It is impossible to punch a time clock in a war zone. But apparently no one had told the bureaucrats to stay on the job. The service members guarding the gates and trying to evacuate Americans and SIV applicants often worked more than twelve hours in a row under a broiling sun, with little temperature relief at night. The air was foul, the situation fraught, and the dangers real, but not one of them would have considered leaving their post until relieved.

The State Department officials, however, treated their duties like shift work at the local DMV. They arrived for their four-hour shift, punched in, and then left as soon as the clock struck the magic hour, evacuees be damned.[30] And the Marines bore the brunt of the bureaucratic indifference. A Marine working the gates at the time bluntly stated the consequences of State's time clock mentality: "We can't process people if the State Department's not there." And unlike applicants at the local DMV, when the doors closed in their faces, desperate would-be evacuees couldn't always "come back later."

Incredibly, State Department officials sometimes went to the gates to tell the troops that they weren't doing enough. Their arrogance was astounding. On the evening of August 24, for example, two consular officials showed up at the search pit at Abbey Gate and "complained that everything was moving too slow."[31] After registering their dissatisfaction, they departed about an hour later. A sergeant from Echo Company recounted a similar incident when consular agents had left Abbey Gate on the night of the twenty-second and returned the morning of the twenty-third with a "better idea" about how the Marines could speed up the screening process. The Marines had spent the whole night pulling men and women from the stinking canal, "loading them into the queue and waiting for DOS [the State Department] to come back out." For the sleep-deprived Marines, "Only quick naps and cigarettes [kept them] awake." They were sick of it. And the posturing of the bureaucrats was hard to swallow. In answer to the consular agents' "better idea," the sergeant replied, "Ma'am, my Marines have been at this post for 36 hours. You've been here for 5 minutes this morning. Please tell me what more my Marines can do for you. And then, I'll tell you that there is so much more DOS can do here. After all, ma'am, this is your operation."[32]

The diplomats, according to military officers, were afraid of the crowds. The situation was dangerous, dirty, and tense—but so was all of Kabul, for that matter. When they deigned to show up—to instruct the Marines whom to admit for processing—each diplomat was flanked by two armed members of the State Department's Diplomatic Security Service.[33] One of the Marine platoon sergeants working the gates recalled an incident when a risk-averse consular officer "wouldn't come within 50 meters of the gate." He added that the "bottom line is these guys wouldn't interact with the Afghans unless they were away from the line."[34] The lack of cooperation made a difficult evacuation nearly impossible at times.

The American public never heard a whisper from the administration about those problems. After all, the difficulties were of State's own making. Despite those colossal failures, Wilson and others continued to publicly present the State Department's efforts as successful. On the evening of August 22, for example, Wilson tweeted a picture of himself with State employees, announcing that he was "proud of the work" the embassy team was "doing to assist U.S. Citizens and Afghans as part of our historic relocation effort."[35] An hour later, he tweeted a picture of himself waving to a line of evacuees preparing to board a plane, and commented, "This morning I was able to wish American citizens well and ensure their safe departure from #Afghanistan. Thank you to our @DeptofDefense colleagues for their support and assistance."[36] And on August 30, when General McKenzie and State Department spokesman John Kirby announced the end of the evacuation, General McKenzie lauded the diplomats, as if everything had gone according to plan: "Our diplomats have also been with us in Kabul from the beginning, and their work in processing over 120,000 people stands right beside that of their military partners. We were a team on the ground."[37] The troops saw right through the posturing. Unfortunately, the American people knew little else but the official media narrative.

DITHERING, DOUBT, AND DISINFORMATION IN DC

President Biden apparently—though briefly—considered keeping his promise to leave troops in Afghanistan until every stranded US citizen had been rescued. On August 18, he sat down for an interview with George Stephanopoulos, the former Clinton aide turned ABC news anchor. Interviews with Stephanopoulos are widely understood as being the preferred way for left-wing politicians in crisis to rehab their image. But Biden's failure in Afghanistan was so glaring that even the palace scribes struggled to gloss it over.

The interview began on a defensive note. When Stephanopoulos cornered Biden on the obvious inconsistency between his reassurances earlier in the summer and the disaster unfolding in prime time, Biden was defiant. Stephanopoulos: "Back in July, you said a Taliban takeover was highly unlikely. Was the intelligence wrong, or did you downplay it?" Biden: "There was no consensus when you go back and look at the intelligence reports. . . . The idea that the Taliban would take over was premised on the notion that somehow the 300,000 troops we have trained and equipped would just collapse. I don't think anyone anticipated that." He deflected again when Stephanopoulos asked the straightforward question "When you look at what's happened . . . was it a failure of intelligence, planning, execution, or judgment?"

But when Stephanopoulos pressed the president on reports that his "top military advisers had warned against withdrawing on this timeline, they wanted you to keep about twenty-five hundred troops," Biden got visibly agitated. "No, they didn't," he countered. "It was split. That wasn't true." Stephanopoulos doubled down: "They didn't tell you that they wanted troops to stay?" Biden's response was garbled and guarded. "No, not in terms of whether we were going to get out in a time frame all troops. They didn't argue against that." Stephanopoulos pressed again, "Your military advisers did not tell you that we should just keep twenty-five hundred troops, it's been a stable situation for the last several years?" Biden: "No. No one said that to me that I can recall."[38]

In fact, Biden glossed over the mess his administration had created, saying, "No one's being killed right now . . . we're going to get those people out . . . the idea that somehow there's a way to have gotten out without chaos ensuing, I don't know how that happens." For the administration, chaos was "priced into" the decision.[39] As the facts now show, the Biden administration not only "didn't know" how to prevent chaos, it blundered along until, just days after that fateful interview, "chaos" became "catastrophe."

In perhaps their most crucial exchange, Stephanopoulos asked Biden, "Are you committed to making sure that the troops stay until every American who wants to be out is out?"[40] On national television, the president's answer was an unequivocal "Yes." "Yes . . . the commitment holds to get everyone out. . . . if there's American citizens left, we're going to stay until we get them all out."[41] That "commitment" proved to be little more than a fleeting sentiment.

On August 21, US military leaders at HKIA floated the idea to their Taliban counterparts that US forces might stay past the thirty-first if the evacuation of US citizens hadn't been completed. The Taliban communicated with their feet and immediately abandoned their posts outside the airfield to convey their disapproval.

Twenty-four hours later, the question became more urgent. By then, Admiral Vasely had concluded that the military simply could not evacuate every American before the thirty-first.[42] That reality wouldn't play well with the public, however, so the administration simply acted as though it didn't exist. The next day, Jake Sullivan continued to claim that "we have time between now and the 31st to get out every American who wants to get out."[43] The administration's failure to plan for full evacuation, coupled with Biden's previous order for the unrestricted entry of every "family unit" at the gates, rendered the complete evacuation of US citizens a logistical impossibility on the president's timeline. There was no way around it: getting every US citizen to safety would require a military presence beyond August 31. Over the next few days, the Biden administration deliberated—or, some might say, dithered—about what to do next.

THE TALIBAN CALLS THE SHOTS—LITERALLY

On August 23, Admiral Vasely and CIA director William Burns hosted senior Taliban leaders, including Abdul Ghani Baradar, at HKIA and broached the possibility of US forces "needing a few extra days" to evacuate the remaining Americans.[44] The Taliban told them in no uncertain terms, "You won't stay past the 31st" and warned that "there would be consequences" if they did.[45] Taliban leaders repeatedly invoked Biden's July 8 speech promising to withdraw by the end of August and accused military leaders of double-crossing them.[46] In what could not possibly have been a coincidence, Taliban forces began transporting mortar tubes to outside the North and East gates of the airfield, in full view of US forces, just hours after the meeting concluded.[47] The Taliban's message was unmistakable: If you're not gone by August 31, we will attack you. The United States' commander in chief folded in the face of the Taliban's intransigence.

The White House had no stomach for a fight, even if capitulation meant abandoning US citizens. The administration pivoted swiftly, conducting a bipartisan congressional briefing and announcing its decision to leave the country *before* the thirty-first. Immediately after the briefing ended, one of the individuals present texted colleagues, "Congressional briefing just completed. Administration just doubled down on 8/31 exit despite strong bipartisan push back. No one appears in charge." Biden then publicly reaffirmed his commitment to withdraw all US forces from Afghanistan by August 31.[48] The announcement included a caveat that he had ordered military leaders to create "contingency plans" to maintain a military presence if total retreat proved to be impossible. As subsequent events made painfully clear, however, there was no backup plan he would accept. On August 24, the same day Biden reaffirmed his commitment to a total withdrawal by August 31, White House press secretary Jen Psaki scolded reporters for suggesting that the fixed withdrawal date might leave Americans "stranded": "First of all, I think it's irresponsible to say Americans are stranded. They are not."[49] She doubled down the next day, arguing "I would not say that [the evacuation] is anything but a success."[50] Thousands of US citizens attempting to survive the mayhem in Kabul certainly would have begged to differ.

On August 25—just days after he'd been briefed that US citizens would be stranded in Afghanistan if the military left by the thirty-first— Biden made light of that inevitability, never letting on that he knew his withdrawal plans would cause the abandonment of US citizens. At a press conference with executives from Silicon Valley about cybersecurity, a reporter shouted the question "If Americans are still in Afghanistan after the deadline, what will you do?" The White House cut the audio feed immediately, but Biden's remarks were still audible to those nearby. He smirked and sarcastically replied to the reporter, "You'll be the first person I call."[51]

Biden's feeble response to pressure by a third-rate Islamist militia placed the White House press office into a difficult position. Administration lackeys couldn't pretend that the president was taking the fight to the enemy, because the entire world was witnessing the opposite. At the same time, they also couldn't acknowledge that a US president had knowingly decided to abandon thousands of US civilians to enemy forces for the first time in history. The only recourse was to lie. And lie they did.

CALL IN THE HOUNDS

While the troops dealt with the gates, the generals at the command center faced chaos of a different nature. After ignoring the generals' warnings for months, the Biden administration now wouldn't leave them alone, even as they attempted to navigate a borderline impossible situation of the administration's making. The sheer volume of requests nearly crashed the communication systems at the airfield. Details that emerged months later documented the sudden avalanche of evacuation requests from high-powered people, including the White House and the NSA's Jake Sullivan. For example, "BGEN [Brigadier General] Sullivan was receiving calls from the White House and a lot of the requests were not AMCITs [American citizens]."[52] Admiral Vasely spent up to ten hours a day fielding phone from Biden, Vice President Harris, Lloyd Austin, and General Milley. First Lady Jill Biden reached out to Admiral Vasely as well, asking him to prioritize specific individuals.

An aide told Army investigators, "Much of [Vasely's] time was consumed by these daily phone calls."[53] Cabinet officials relentlessly pressured Vasely to maximize the number of people the military brought through the gates. "The constant theme on POTUS calls was 'How do we get more people out?'"[54] (Curiously, the administration officials did not seem particularly concerned about *who* the military was bringing through the gates.)

On top of the incessant, ever-shifting demands and questions from DC, the generals were flooded with requests via private calls, text messages, and emails from an array of special-interest groups. According to later testimony, representatives of Pope Francis contacted Brigadier General Sullivan,[55] and Bush Institute employees working out of Dallas were "steamrolling" to get 120 people through the gates.[56] Government officials had shared the phone numbers and email addresses of the officers at the command center with a small circle of individuals, working under the assumption that the information would stay closely held. Several days into the crisis, however, the generals' contact information had been widely circulated and was available to essentially anyone with skin in the game. Even their personal contact information was distributed far and wide, so that the generals' wives and friends started getting calls. In total, they received more than four thousand requests in less than two weeks.[57] Of that number, approximately one-quarter were for US citizens and the rest for Afghans.[58]

Even PETA obtained Vasely's direct line and petitioned him to evacuate "at-risk" animals. As Vasely later related to investigators, "4,000 separate requests came in, and the team recovered over 8,000 people, but it was mostly Afghans from special interests [rather than AMCITs], and even included dogs."[59] Vasely's reference to dogs was no exaggeration. The animal rights activist Paul "Pen" Farthing launched a public effort to airlift hundreds of stray dogs and cats out of the country before the Taliban took over. He had started a foundation to care for Afghan animals after he had deployed to Afghanistan as a Royal Marines sergeant in 2006. British defense secretary Ben Wallace initially rejected Farthing's public requests, stating that he would not "prioritize pets over people." But after Farthing's campaign gained support from celebrities such as Ricky Gervais and Judi Dench, the British military relented and brought the dogs and cats through the gates. The fiasco consumed resources and hampered coalition efforts to extract Western citizens and Afghan allies.

US SPECIAL OPERATIONS FORCES: OUTSIDE THE WIRE

As the evacuation deadline approached and the political pressure ramped up to new levels, US special operations forces (SOF) were already working overtime to rescue US citizens at risk of being stranded, as well as Afghan partners for whom being left behind would be a certain death sentence. As General McKenzie reported on August 30 when he announced the official end of the United States' military presence in Afghanistan and the final evacuation results, "US special-operations forces reached out to help bring in more than 1,064 American citizens and 2,017 SIVs, or Afghans at risk, and 127 third-country nationals, all via phone calls, vectors, and escorting."[60]

As a summary, that's all true. And many details can never be shared due to operational security concerns, but the few details we can share help sketch the range of missions they undertook and help bring those efforts into focus. On August 20, for example, Army special forces conducted an airlift mission outside the wire to rescue twenty US citizens. On the ground, 1st Platoon, 2nd Marine Reconnaissance Battalion conducted a wide array of snatch-and-grab operations every day. The names of their rescue operations perfectly captured the gallows humor that emerges under stressful circumstances in virtually every military unit. Between August 19 and 24, they saved 1,426 people in a series of operations labeled "Nun Run," "Ladder Time," "Terp Pull," and "Shits Creek," among other things.

THE THREAT BUILDS

By August 24, security around the gates had become increasingly precarious. ISIS-K personnel were in Kabul, and they were gunning for the Americans. Intelligence picked up a significant increase in traffic concerning ISIS-K threats, warning that an attack was imminent in less than twenty-four hours, most likely by a suicide bomber.

At 4:00 p.m. on August 25, Ghost Company relieved Echo Company at Abbey Gate. Taking charge, Ghost Company's commander, Captain Geoff Ball, sent messages of an "imminent" IED threat to the company. As day faded into night, the tension reached new levels. By 8:00 p.m., the crowd at Abbey Gate had begun to swell—and the larger the crowd, the greater the risk of a suicide bomber going undetected. That evening, the State Department officials left Abbey Gate, ending their case processing for the night to be resumed the next day.

At 10:00 p.m., Captain Ball again messaged company leadership, warning about "SVEST threat" to the company. "SVEST" is shorthand for the threat of a suicide vest, worn by an enemy willing to die in order to bring death to Americans. According to the chat logs, the message read, "Legitimate SVEST threat on Abbey from [Battalion Headquarters]" Shortly thereafter, Captain Ball issued an order for the company to move its position back 150 meters (500 feet) toward Abbey Gate. The move was a practical one, designed to ensure a more direct route for casualty collection in the awful event of an attack.

At 11:00 p.m., Ghost Company began reducing its posture around Abbey Gate, a protective measure for the troops. Just a half hour later, at 11:30 p.m., Captain Ball ordered his Marines to take a knee behind the "Jersey walls" (concrete barriers normally used as highway dividers in America) separating them from the crowd in and around the canal, to mitigate the increasing threat. The Marines did as commanded, largely holding that position until the next morning.[61]

NINE

ANSWERING THE CALL

O n August 13, a former special forces interpreter named Abdul and his family frantically packed their belongings in a village in Kandahar. Abdul was in his early forties, but a dozen years of hard living and firefights alongside the Green Beret teams who rotated through the country every six months had added more than a decade to his appearance. The family sorted their belongings, keeping heirlooms and the few valuables they had for their next chapter of life and leaving everything else behind. But Abdul's most valuable cargo was his wife of twenty-four years, Muhafiza, and their seven children. Their youngest, Hela, had large brown eyes and was only two months from her third birthday. The Taliban had conquered the surrounding area and were already moving from house to house to find "collaborators" who had worked with the Americans. They had only a few hours to escape.

The Taliban got there first. A pickup truck of fighters arrived outside the home and burst inside. They ransacked the small house for any evidence of Abdul's connection to US forces but found nothing. Abdul had burned his visa documents and photographs with US troops the moment the Taliban had entered his village. He kept digital copies on a thumb drive hidden beneath his clothes. With no evidence to prove his "disloyalty," the Taliban told Abdul that they knew that he'd worked with Americans and would be back with witnesses to prove it.

At that point, interpreters across the country were being executed by the Taliban. But the executions usually weren't swift. Sometimes the men were placed on top of street guardrails with nooses around their necks. In other instances, they were forced to stand in the back of Taliban pickup trucks with a noose connected to a crane above them. The outcome, however, was always the same: the men were frequently tortured, and their wives and daughters were raped in front of their eyes. Only after the Taliban castrated them to take the last ounce of their manhood were they finally hung and left in public view as a warning to others.

The minute the fighters left, Abdul packed his family into the back of a flatbed truck driven by a relative and headed for Kabul. They finally arrived in Kabul on the night of August 14, just hours before the Taliban got there. They sheltered in a single room at the back of a friend's house for days, while Abdul sent Facebook and WhatsApp messages to every American he'd served alongside. The message was simple: "We are in Kabul, and we will die if we don't get out. Please help my family."

Thankfully, one of his friends answered his message, connecting him with operators inside HKIA. Abdul and his family were spirited away by an extraction team and brought inside the wire at 2:00 a.m. on August 20.

At the same time, another former interpreter, "Sayyid," was making an equally desperate journey to Kabul with his wife and two young children. Unlike Abdul, he had no vehicle, no support system—and no legs. He had become a double amputee several years before, when the military vehicle he was riding in had struck a roadside IED. The force of the blast had ripped off his legs above the knee. In Afghanistan, a crippling physical disability is tantamount to a life sentence of poverty. The Afghan government had few rehab programs for people like Sayyid, and its health care for wounded veterans would make a US VA hospital look like the Mayo Clinic. But Sayyid was one of the fortunate ones, to the extent that the term can be applied to an Afghan father in his late twenties with two children and no legs: an Austin-based medical company had donated a set of prosthetic legs to him after receiving an appeal from the men who had served with him.

Now his "luck" seemed to be running out. The Taliban were approaching his village, and, unlike other former interpreters, Sayyid lacked even the thin reed of plausible deniability that he'd worked for Americans. His prosthetics gave him away immediately. So he did the only thing a man in his position could: he started walking. Wife and children in tow, he spent three days walking over uneven terrain on his prosthetic legs.

Sayyid and his family were met by representatives of a veteran-led evacuation network, who brought them to safety. Once inside the wire, he donned an orange T-shirt bearing the logo of the American company that had donated his prosthetics and took a picture of himself and his family. They now live in Massachusetts.

Shocking as they are, Sayyid and Abdul's stories are not unique. Thousands of Afghan interpreters and former US government employees made similar treks in the days immediately before and after Kabul fell. All of them made the journey because they shared an unshakable belief that the United States, the most powerful country on Earth, would keep its promise to grant them new lives in exchange for their years of service. Some of them were rewarded for their hope, but most ended up physically and emotionally shattered—and bitterly disappointed.

FALSE PROMISES

On July 8, Biden announced his decision to accelerate his withdrawal deadline from September 11 to August 31. As part of the announcement, he promised to evacuate every Afghan eligible for a Special Immigrant Visa (SIV): "Our message to [you] is clear: There is a home for you in the United States if you so choose, and we will stand with you just as you stood with us." In the same breath, the president claimed that "fewer than half" of SIV applicants had chosen to leave and that "the other half believe they want to stay."[1] Later that afternoon, State Department spokesman Ned Price echoed Biden's promise and claimed that the administration was "preparing for any number of contingencies" to ensure that our Afghan allies would be evacuated.[2] Neither statement was remotely true. Nevertheless, they became the administration's core talking points whenever the topic of Afghanistan arose during the summer of 2021.

In reality, the State Department had no concrete plan for evacuating the tens of thousands of Afghans who had risked their lives alongside those of US forces. The bureaucrats at Foggy Bottom still hadn't processed half of their applications, and there were no signs that they planned to fix the backlog. Moreover, the administration couldn't agree on whether it was even *planning* an evacuation. On May 26, General Milley told reporters that plans to evacuate SIV applicants and allies were "being developed very, very rapidly."[3] Later that day, a National Security Council spokesperson said the exact opposite: "I can tell you that we have no plans for evacuations at this time."[4]

A few days later, Guam's governor, Lou Guerrero, offered the island as a temporary processing location for SIV applicants while their paperwork was being verified,[5] but the administration rejected that option without providing any public justification for its decision. Senator Richard Blumenthal, a Democrat from Connecticut, later remarked, "I remember our expressing the sense very directly that there had to be an evacuation, beginning right then, of thousands of our Afghan partners to Guam. The response basically was 'We're on it. Don't worry. We know what we're doing.'"[6] White House officials did not, in fact, know what they were doing.

Domestic political considerations came first. The White House was concerned that announcing a large-scale evacuation of Afghan interpreters to US soil—even if just to an island territory in the Pacific—would invite unhelpful comparisons to the crisis at the southern US border and create unnecessary headaches while the administration was trying to pass a trillion-dollar infrastructure bill.[7] Months before the collapse, a senior administration official had lectured the *Atlantic*'s George Packer, "Remember, this kind of crisis was coming at the worst possible time. In the spring there was wall-to-wall coverage of the border—'Who are these people coming into our country?'—and at the same time we're contemplating bringing in tens of thousands of Afghans." The official added, "I feel passionately about it, but politically it could be risky."[8]

Political considerations aside, the administration's complacency also flowed from its basic ignorance about Afghanistan. Some White House decision makers didn't seem to even know where the vast majority of SIV applicants lived. Packer recalled, "In mid-June, I asked another senior administration official about Afghans who lived outside Kabul and were quickly losing any exit route, he replied, 'The vast majority of SIV applicants, based on the work that could be done on this, are in or around Kabul.' This was untrue."[9]

At bottom, the White House had no plan to evacuate SIVs and showed little urgency about their fate. The National Security Council held a deputies' meeting on Afghanistan once a week, and the topic came up from time to time in cabinet meetings run by Jake Sullivan,[10] but all available evidence shows that the administration's approach to the SIV issue never progressed beyond highly general discussions and an agreement that somebody should do something down the road.

The lethargy on Pennsylvania Avenue wasn't due to a lack of urging. By July, a broad bipartisan coalition of veterans' groups, religious organizations, and humanitarian outfits had already spent months shouting about the emerging danger to anyone in Washington who would listen. They warned that the administration's charted course would abandon tens of thousands of US allies to torture, rape, and execution. If the administration wished to avoid that outcome, planning needed to start yesterday. The loose network, called Evacuate Our Allies, scored a few meetings with White House officials, but little to nothing came of them.[11]

Complicating the issue, Chargé d'Affaires Wilson had locked down the embassy a week or two before, suspending all visa processing. Even if a plan existed, the embassy wouldn't have executed it. The entire embassy was teleworking. Applicants with interview appointments—the final step before receiving visa approval—suddenly found them canceled without notice. Many had traveled for days to get to the capital for their appointments. By the time the appointments were rescheduled, their hometowns had already been taken over by the Taliban, and they were behind enemy lines. An officer who served with the U.S. Army Special Operations Command summarized the problem: "So as the President makes his announcement about getting special visa requirements in July, the embassy was entirely unresponsive. They couldn't see reality for what it was. They were entirely unhelpful or unresponsive [at] the time."[12]

On July 14, the administration finally announced Operation Allies Refuge to facilitate the evacuation of SIV applicants but didn't facilitate the first flight of SIV applicants until July 30, sixteen days before the capital fell. The maiden flight was operated by Qatar Airways and took just 221 SIV applicants and their family members to Fort Lee, Virginia.

TRUE PROMISES

Now that Kabul was controlled by the Taliban, the United States no longer had a functional embassy to facilitate evacuations, and tens of thousands of people were stranded.

After days passed without any meaningful action from the White House, many veterans decided that they would step into the void to keep their nation's promises. Loosely organized rescue coalitions emerged almost overnight. Some of those efforts were public and played out over social media; others wouldn't be revealed until months later. But they all shared a common goal: getting out as many allies from in and near Kabul as possible.

We spoke with dozens of people who were involved in the efforts; most emphatically asked that they not be named. Not because they're still working in sensitive positions—the majority are retired—but because they eschew receiving any sort of public recognition for their actions. For them it was a matter of duty; they did what they could with the tools at their disposal. For many, the final mission was a useful distraction from the psychological pain of seeing twenty years of sacrifices cavalierly tossed aside. They had given the best years of their lives to training and fighting in harsh conditions, burying friends, and enduring long periods of separation from loved ones while trying to keep their families together. In an instant, all those efforts were erased. They tried to channel their anger and anguish into doing something productive.

A former special operator who was part of the effort explained, "There were a lot of people that had skin in the game. It was a conglomeration of intelligence community people, special operations guys, a lot of retired folks, and then a lot of folks with deep pockets and serious political connections. They just felt that moral draw to get in there and do something about it." From August 17 to 30, he went to his day job and then stayed up most of the night at his kitchen table to coordinate efforts during daylight hours in Afghanistan. "Watching the country fail on the biggest geopolitical stage was not acceptable for us, and definitely not acceptable for those people that we had built personal bonds with," he added.

The grassroots efforts were as broad and diverse as the men and women running them, and some were more formal than others. A few had members who returned to Afghanistan and executed missions on the ground, but most operated remotely, leveraging contacts and facilitating snatch-and-grabs with troops at the gates. They scoured commercial satellite platforms to identify the locations of Taliban checkpoints and provide interpreters with back routes to the airport in almost real time. The technique was particularly useful in the first few days of the operation, because most of the Taliban fighters were from rural areas and were not familiar with the city yet.

A former Green Beret who worked on the evacuation efforts broadly characterized the various private evacuation groups as "blue-collar" and "white-collar" efforts. The "white-collar" crowd were mainly former senior officials who had worked in DC or the private sector and had high-level connections to make sure things got done. The "blue-collar" side of the operation was run by former service members who had no political connections but just knew how "to make shit happen." "Some of them were just awesome Green Berets that retired in Clarksville or somewhere else and had a knife-making business or something, but they knew how to build a network."

The sum of those efforts was often referred to as "digital Dunkirk," a reference to a British citizen–based effort to evacuate troops stranded in that town during World War II. One key difference between the original Dunkirk and its "digital" counterpart, however, was the government's role. The British government organized the original Dunkirk effort, commandeering civilian vessels and impressing citizens into service. By contrast, the veteran-led evacuations in Kabul were neither initiated nor led by the government. In many cases, the efforts succeeded despite the White House's and State Department's actions. One of the most prominent groups was Operation Pineapple Express, run by a collection of former Green Berets and intelligence operatives, many of whom flew back into Afghanistan to execute the mission. Another effort was Team America, led by Joe Saboe, a former Army infantry officer based in Denver.[13] A third was Allied Airlift 21, run by retired colonel Mike Jason, who had served as an Army battalion commander in northern Afghanistan.

Other groups didn't have formal names and operated under the radar but were no less effective. One group in particular—a network of former national security pros, including several who had worked in either the Trump or George W. Bush administrations—single-handedly saved hundreds, if not thousands, of allies who would have been stranded otherwise. It included active duty intelligence officers moonlighting to get people out, former assistant secretaries of defense, a few former "direct action" intelligence operatives with experience on the ground in Afghanistan, a retired special forces general, a State Department appointee who was fed up with State Department incompetence, and several veterans who had served in-country. Some traveled back to Afghanistan and worked on the ground; others coordinated efforts remotely. It was a perfect blend of the "blue-collar" and "white-collar" approaches. Records of their coordination efforts, which we reviewed, reflect an array of deep international networks built over years in service. The following exchange is typical.

> *Person 1:* If you guys can get to Pak [Pakistan], I think my network
>   can take from there.
> *Person 2:* I want to catch a lift.
> *Person 3:* I can do it from Uzb [Uzbekistan] as well.

In short, the full campaign was an awe-inspiring display of self-sacrifice on behalf of friends and strangers alike.

BY ANY MEANS NECESSARY

While State Department and White House personnel labored to hack through red tape, the veteran-led groups drew on every resource at their disposal. Many of the groups worked day and night, coordinating directly with Marines at the gates to get SIV applicants and US citizens to safety. The most common tactic was for a prospective evacuee to write a call sign, such as PALE RIDER 2 or WARHAMMER 6, on a piece of paper and hold it above the crowd. As soon as they spotted the sign, the Marines would jump into the crowd and pull the evacuees and their family members to safety.

When other members of the crowd caught on and started mimicking the signs, the Marines and veterans' groups were forced to shift tactics. Most of the time, they simply shuffled the call signs that evacuees were expected to use, but on certain occasions they asked evacuees and their families to identify themselves through alternate means, such as holding up a bright-colored umbrella. The groups also used prearranged code words for evacuees who were able to get close enough to the gates. Usually, the codes involved some variation of the name of a commanding officer or senior enlisted Marine in charge of gate operations at the time, like "Captain Bobby" or "Gunny Tate." On other occasions, the Marines used a classic challenge-and-password approach: they would say the name of an American city, and the evacuee would respond with the name of a prominent sports team associated with it. (During the Battle of the Bulge in World War II, American GIs used similar tactics to identify Nazi infiltrators wearing US uniforms— they asked various questions about baseball that the average young American would have been familiar with but would have been utterly foreign to the Germans.)

The veterans' groups disguised interpreters as journalists so they could fill empty seats on flights chartered by foreign media organizations. They leveraged private sector connections to place SIV applicants on private jets owned by Eastern European oligarchs with business interests in Afghanistan. They even turned to asking allied governments for support: backbench members of the UK Parliament, retired Polish generals, and Dutch politicians, whoever could make things happen. On August 23, in a particularly damning episode for the Biden administration, they even relied on French special forces units to accomplish what the Biden administration either could not or would not do. In one instance, the French forces met a stranded family of six outside the wire "and brought them onto HKIA French Camp." In another, French special operators linked up with a group stranded at a local hotel and escorted them through North Gate.

As time drew short, they even resorted to openly leveraging media connections to coerce the lethargic but press-conscious administration to take active steps to help specific US citizens stuck outside the wire.

One group, for example, had spent a number of days trying to shepherd two buses with more than forty US citizens through the gates, only to have the Taliban turn them back each time. In an August 25 missive about the stranded Americans, a former National Security Council official informed colleagues, "I told a WSJ reporter who is talking to USG inside the airport that buses full of AMCITs aren't making it in. He says he'll be willing to tell his USG [contacts] about our buses that need help if we provide locations/descriptions." She added, "It sounds bad to pull in press help, but USG reacts to them. If he passes this on and they ignore, it's a story." That time, the buses made it through.

BEATINGS OUTSIDE THE GATES

As word spread that the veterans groups were able to push Afghans and US citizens through the gates, they became inundated with calls from around the world. Everyone had a former interpreter or a friend of a friend they wanted to save. The stream of requests from vulnerable people who would be left behind without assistance was unending. Throughout the day, the groups received texts and Signal messages such as "68-year-old US Citizen in Kabul looking for assistance getting out. PIN to follow." As soon as they got one person across the finish line, they turned to the next.

The stories from the ground were horrific, but they only added to the groups' sense of urgency. Afghan officials at the Ministry of the Interior fled without destroying detailed personnel records for most Afghan government employees, including interpreters. The records included their cell phone numbers. While they sheltered in place or moved between safe houses to evade capture and execution, interpreters received taunting text messages from the Taliban search teams hunting them down: "We know where you are, and we're coming to kill you." The psychological torture heightened the extreme stress and paranoia many already felt. Until they were safely inside the airport, they knew they could die at any minute; it was only a matter of time.

One stranded interpreter who had worked for the US intelligence community was hiding in the back room of a friend's ground-level apartment when he heard shouting and screaming in the unit next door. Then a series of rapid-fire shots. Then another. And another. One series for each member of the family. From the back corner of the room, he recorded the sounds of the executions on his cell phone. Mercifully, the Taliban who had tracked down the unfortunate family hiding next door were unaware that another wanted man was only yards away. After they left, the interpreter sent the video to a former national security official who was trying to arrange his rescue. The implication was clear: time is running out.

The groups already faced the herculean task of guiding people they'd never met through dense crowds seven thousand miles away, but the Taliban made things infinitely more difficult. A consular official later described "trying to find someone at the gate" as "hectic, like trying to find your wife at Disney Land."[14] The comparison would be apt if Disneyland were filled with marauding terrorists beating people at will. After the evacuation, the White House tried to cast the Taliban as "businesslike and professional."[15] In reality, they were anything but. Taliban fighters routinely blocked US citizens' paths to the airport and in some instances even confiscated their passports to make it more difficult for them to leave. Many Americans used their savings to bribe Taliban fighters to grant them passage. Texts from desperate Americans to the US-based vets supporting them often included statements such as "Currently awaiting cost to get to next checkpoint" and "Will update cost and forward progress."

US citizens who did make it past Taliban checkpoints were often brutally beaten with fists and wooden rods, sometimes sexually assaulted first. An American couple filmed the aftermath of one such episode outside North Gate and sent it to the veteran group assisting them so the stateside operatives could see what they were up against. The video shows men and women staggering away from the scene, their faces covered in blood. A lifeless body lies on the ground as gunshots continue to ring out in the background. The Afghan journalist Ziar Khan told us that on the nineteenth, he had witnessed UK citizens being beaten outside Abbey Gate and having their passports ripped away. Biden continued to ignore the mounting evidence of those and other atrocities, however. Less than twenty-four hours later, he repeatedly claimed during a White House press conference that no Americans or other Westerners had been blocked from accessing the airport. The military quickly walked back that statement.

Taliban units appeared to take special pleasure in beating American women. Chat logs from August 25 depict a harrowing back-and-forth between an American legal permanent resident from California and former intelligence community operatives desperately trying to redirect assets on the ground to rescue her from the Taliban: "We have a US legal permanent resident near [the Ministry of Interior] who was beaten pretty badly by the Taliban. Is there anyone in that vicinity that could possibly grab them?" After getting additional information from one of the woman's colleagues, one of the former operatives sent a follow-up message with even greater urgency: "She's being assaulted currently. California driver's license. Let me know if anyone needs coordinates." The former operatives, who provided the logs on the condition that they remain anonymous, were eventually able to get the woman to safety— but not before she suffered a savage assault simply because she was an American woman and the Taliban knew it could act with impunity. Even families with infants were not spared. An American couple with a four-month-old baby were forced to return home and shelter in place on the night of August 24 after being beat up at a Taliban checkpoint and denied passage, according to real-time messages sent from the couple to veterans groups working on their escape.

There is no evidence that the Biden administration intervened with Taliban commanders to stop those types of incidents. Much to the contrary, the administration repeatedly praised the Taliban as being a cooperative security partner throughout the evacuation. The White House was virtually silent about anything that might disrupt its preferred narrative, which was that Kabul had fallen in an orderly manner and no US citizens or permanent residents were in danger. On August 23, the State Department and Pentagon briefed members of Congress on the ongoing evacuation efforts and claimed that everything was going "smoothly" and that the Taliban was "allowing people through" to the gates. After hearing about the details of the briefing, a member of one of the veteran groups replied, "Excuse my language . . . fuck off."

There is overwhelming evidence that this narrative is false, but the administration and its lackeys have stuck to it. Even now, the scale of the Taliban's brutality against Americans stranded by the Biden administration has remained hidden from the American people. In at least one instance, the Taliban did not "limit" themselves to simply assaulting Americans. In the second week of August, "Ahmad," a legal permanent resident in Texas, had seen enough. He could read the handwriting on the wall and knew that the government was about to collapse. Ahmad had served as an interpreter for the CIA and special forces in Afghanistan for several years before applying for a visa and eventually legal permanent residence. Because he was a green card holder and not a citizen, however, his wife and children couldn't join him in the United States until he satisfied the statutory requirement of five years of continuous residence. Now, they were about to be stranded in Afghanistan under Taliban rule.

Disregarding the bounty on his head, Ahmad purchased a ticket on one of the last commercial flights to Kabul only days before the city collapsed, to make sure his family would escape. He knew he couldn't take them to the United States yet, but at the very least, he felt, he could get them to a safe third country. The Taliban had other ideas. They recognized him as a former American "collaborator," shot him in the face and the shoulder, and left him for dead. The desperate mob simply stepped over his body and continued to surge toward the entrance to

HKIA. But Ahmad did not die. He was evacuated and given medical care by local Afghans affiliated with one of the veteran-led evacuation networks. The group repeatedly contacted the State Department and the Pentagon to inform them that an American permanent resident had been grievously wounded and needed immediate assistance. Their pleas were met with only automated responses. Months later, when he was well enough to travel, Ahmad was finally evacuated to a safe house in a neighboring country by the veterans' network (which will remain unnamed to protect its ongoing efforts in the country). Because his family's immigration status remains in limbo, he still hadn't returned to the United States when this book was finished.

On the whole, navigating the gates was an even more brutal experience for Afghans. Accounts of Afghan SIV applicants and their families being beaten are ubiquitous and too numerous to recount. The Taliban lashed them with canes and dumped sewage on them, jeering "Your owners have left you behind" and "Your Western masters have abandoned you." A group of Afghan Christians, mostly women and children, who had seats on a charter flight out of the country were forced to turn back after learning that Taliban fighters had chosen several teenage girls in the group to be taken as "brides" of local commanders. When the evacuation ended, they were still in a Kabul safe house.

In a particularly heartbreaking episode, an Afghan family of four who had been approved for evacuation to Spain spent thirteen hours trying to slip past Taliban checkpoints. (We are withholding their names because they are still stuck in the country and at serious risk of reprisals.) The husband and wife and their two sons—two and seven years old, respectively—were intercepted and forced to sit in a puddle of sewage next to the checkpoint. Whenever the Taliban fighters seemed distracted by their phones or internal conversations, the family tried to quietly scooch forward to get close enough to the crowd to make a break for it. Each time, they were discovered, and the militants at the checkpoint held the husband at gunpoint while lashing his wife. After an hour or two, they pretended to give up and head home. As soon as they were out of sight, they made a beeline for a different gate, but the result was the same: no passage, more humiliation, more beatings.

The night before, their seven-year-old had been "jumping up and down preparing his bags and selecting his drawings" to take with him. Now he begged his parents to go back home. "I will tell Taliban to take two of my toy cars if they don't hurt my father and mother." The woman's preexisting back injury had been fully inflamed by the beatings, and she was having difficulty standing. She, too, wanted to return home. With no foreseeable way to access the gates and present their paperwork, the family went back to their Kabul apartment. The mother and children were understandably traumatized by the ordeal and refused to return to the gates the next morning. In an email to his handlers later that night, the man informed them of the family's decision to stay put for the moment, come what may:

> My hands are shaking, my eyes are hardly seeing the screen, tears are just rolling down. My children and the other thousands of children and women don't deserve this. My wife was hit so many times and I could only beg Mullah Sahib [an Afghan term for a religious leader in charge], "Please don't hit her, she is sick." One has to live the moment where your family is flogged and you have nothing in the world you can do, feeling to become a lesser person. That moment of helplessness will live with me forever.

THE GOVERNMENT ASKS PRIVATE CITIZENS FOR HELP

The administration's utter failure to plan for the inevitable evacuation meant that it had barely enough resources to focus on getting (some) US citizens out of the country. If the government was the only actor calling the shots—normally standard procedure in war zones, to say the least—then the tens of thousands of Afghan allies who had risked their lives based on years-long US promises of loyalty would be on their own. Seth Krummrich told us that US special forces had had just enough capacity to rescue Americans stranded across the country, but evacuating SIV applicants was simply beyond their bandwidth. So they had to rely on the veterans' groups. The ad hoc reliance on veteran-led groups was necessary "because there was not a plan or procedure in place to move our allies out of the country."

For several days after the Taliban took over, State continued to operate as if no emergency existed, charging US citizens $2,000 or more for their flights out of the country, as it would under normal conditions. Krummrich ripped into Blinken and the State Department as "criminally incompetent." The total lack of established procedures, he continued, was because "the plan that Blinken and Biden agreed to was unicorn thinking." The administration's decision makers had theorized a best-case scenario and organized everything around that outcome, without considering whether things might turn out differently. "Blinken was not going to sit there in front of the President and be like 'Well, you know, the State Department is totally backed up by three to five years on all of our pieces right now. If we have to surge 100,000 visas in three months, we can handle it, boss.' That conversation never came up, so there was no system in place."

On August 24, Krummrich sent a Signal message to one of the vet groups, asking for assistance extracting the family of a former special forces interpreter. The family had been to the gates several times over the previous few days but couldn't make it through. He added, "US SOF in-theatre asking for assistance to get them onto HKIA as they are currently overstretched by AMCIT [American citizen] extractions." A subsequent request for help from special operations officers read similarly: "Team, looking for help moving two interpreters (+1 wife) and an ANA brigadier general + wife and 3 sons. They worked closely with SF ODA 0321 and the USMC during the heavy Helmand fighting. They all are being actively hunted by the Taliban. Forced to flee their homes, they are at the Serena hotel when they are not at the East Gate trying to get in."

SOCCENT's request was unique in that it came from a military unit tasked with evacuating people. Otherwise, it was downright ordinary. By now, numerous government agencies had reached out to privately run evacuation networks for assistance in evacuating their people. On August 22, Treasury Department officials asked the same network to rescue seventy-five employees and family members of the Afghan National Bank. A few State Department officials who actually cared about the bottom-line mission instead of their own reputations likewise asked for assistance. The Defense Intelligence Agency's entire rescue mission for the first several days of the evacuation was quarterbacked not by central headquarters or the agency's operations division but by a disparate group of individual agents who took the initiative and created their own operations center out of a DIA field office in San Antonio, Texas. And government officials of all stripes frequently reached out to ask for phone numbers or email addresses of military officers on the ground.

The groups also cleaned up the federal government's messes even when it didn't ask for help. On August 18, the State Department emailed a former Afghan interpreter—now a US citizen—instructing him to take his family to the gate for admission.[16] Like Ahmad, the man had returned to Afghanistan from Texas a few days before to secure his family. They successfully navigated the crowds and were admitted into HKIA. But after four days of waiting—and watching subsequent arrivals board evacuation flights—the family was told that only the father had permission to leave because he was the only US citizen in the group. They were then ejected from the airfield, back into the mayhem outside. The decision was made despite the fact that the email the family had received from the State Department on August 18 had expressly stated that "A non-citizen spouse or unmarried children (under age 21) of a U.S. citizen or LPR may accompany" a US citizen or permanent resident as long as he or she had documents validating their familial relationship.[17] The family was later brought back inside the gates and escorted to a flight by special forces veterans who were part of Operation Pineapple Express.[18]

TURF WARS

Even while drowning in a crisis, bureaucrats were territorial as ever. The State Department deemed the NEO to be exclusively its operation, and it guarded it jealously. On August 22, the veteran-led organization No One Left Behind brought a group of roughly five hundred Afghan SIV applicants and long-term applicants through the gates. The men had been carefully chosen because they were particularly at risk from Taliban reprisals due to their relationships with the US military. After they had safely made it onto the airfield, State Department officials booted the entire group out, purportedly because of paperwork discrepancies. The vast majority never made it back to HKIA.[19]

During the evacuation and even afterward, several veteran-run organizations significantly scaled back their activities because of threats that the Biden administration would prosecute them for "providing material support to terrorists." In back-channel conversations, State Department employees warned that paying guides to sneak people out of the country or border guards to look the other way likely violated the law. The pressure campaign was morally grotesque, but in one sense, it was not unprecedented. During the Obama administration, National Security Council and State Department officials had used similar threats to keep the families of ISIS-K hostages from paying their ransoms. In the end, the majority of Afghan SIV applicants were left behind.

As briefly mentioned above, the extraction efforts of the Defense Intelligence Agency (DIA) were run largely by a rogue group of agents operating with the agency's knowledge and informal blessing. That lasted for the first week. Then the DIA's head of operations, Mark Mullen, inexplicably shut them down. He issued a cease-and-desist directive to all DIA agents involved in ad hoc evacuation efforts. The order was accompanied by commentary that the Directorate for Operations was fully capable of rescuing DIA assets on its own and that all requests should be routed to the central office in DC from then on. We reviewed internal DIA messages confirming both facts.

For days before the directive came down, the ad hoc DIA cell had been arranging the evacuation of roughly fifty former assets and local national DIA contractors to be airlifted from the CIA's Eagle Base to HKIA. The operation was complex and had required extensive planning in an environment in which conditions on the ground shifted by the hour. Part one was finding a way to get the evacuees from multiple safe houses to Eagle Base. The group had a combined several decades of experience in Afghanistan and knew how to solve that one: they found "a guy who knew a guy" and had him trade several vehicles to an ideologically flexible Taliban checkpoint commander to let their people pass. Step two was arranging an airlift from Eagle Base, which they accomplished through their long-standing relationship with a CIA official on the ground.

When the stand-down order came on August 25, the fifty or so people were already inside Eagle Base, waiting for helicopters to take them out. Mullen apparently wasn't satisfied with scuttling future operations, however; he wanted his staff to take this one from the top, too, even though it was already on the one-yard line. He contacted a peer at CIA headquarters in Langley, Virginia, and demanded that the airlift be scrapped and responsibility for the DIA assets be given to his office alone. One of the DIA officials involved—a career national security professional who had deployed to Afghanistan multiple times and seen combat—said that Mullen "was concerned" that the ad hoc working group "was making him look bad, like he wasn't in control of getting our people out." The fifty souls who were waiting for their flights to arrive didn't care who got credit for their evacuation; they just wanted to get to safety. Back in DC, however, the credit was the most important part, so the evacuation was put on hold.

The group never made it out.

DANCING WHILE KABUL BURNS

Members of Congress on both sides of the aisle recognized the gravity of the situation and attempted to use their influence to save the vulnerable. Individual Democrats and Republicans alike tried to help as much as they could. The attention a congressman or senator devoted to the issue, however, usually had an inverse relationship to the number of years he or she had spent in office. The longer a politician's tenure, the less likely he or she was to burn the midnight oil to make sure that Americans and allies got home safely. Many high-ranking members simply had other priorities and weren't shy about flaunting them.

But as others worked their fingers to the bone, House Speaker Nancy Pelosi hosted a fundraising lunch in Napa Valley on August 21 that cost attendees a cool $29,000 per plate.[20] Later that evening, Senate Majority Leader Chuck Schumer danced backstage with talk show host Stephen Colbert at an outdoor concert in New York City titled "We Love NYC."[21] While the speaker and majority leader were living it up, seemingly unconcerned about the plight of their fellow Americans and constituents, staffers for Senator Tom Cotton of Arkansas spoke on the phone with a stranded US citizen named Haroon (who normally lived in Colorado) and coordinated his evacuation.[22]

TEN

KNOWN WOLF

A t 2:45 a.m. on August 26, Sergeant Tyler Vargas-Andrews sat in the tower overlooking Abbey Gate. Vargas-Andrews and other members of his sniper team, Reaper 2, were providing overwatch while their fellow Marines continued to pull Americans and Afghan allies from the canal in a last-ditch attempt to save as many people as possible. A new message appeared in the unit's classified chat log: "Intel confirms IED attack imminent."

Over the last forty-eight hours, the threat stream had grown increasingly ominous. The tone of the reports had switched from "if" to "when." The longer the Marines stayed at the gate, the greater the chance of catastrophic loss of life. But the mission wasn't done yet. US forces had originally planned to close Abbey Gate on the evening of the twenty-sixth, but the British government hadn't finished evacuating all of its citizens and had successfully lobbied for more time. Plus there were still thousands of stranded Americans and SIV applicants to save.

A source provided us with evidence of contemporaneous intelligence-community assessments indicating that Taliban officials were likely flooding intelligence-sharing channels with supposed warnings about threats at other gates to funnel the crowd toward Abbey Gate.

Abbey Gate would stay open, even though it almost certainly meant US casualties. For the next fifteen hours, the Marines tried to thread

174

the needle, protecting themselves as much as they could and still saving as many people as possible. All the while, they knew that death could come at any moment.

Still, the knowledge of a forthcoming attack loomed large in their minds. In the days prior, junior Marines had been allowed to take their helmets off for a few seconds at a time to wipe their brows and get some relief from the oppressive heat. Now NCOs yelled at any Marine who so much as unbuckled the strap on his Kevlar. Ghost Company's commander, Captain Geoff Ball, policed the line, spot-checking for Marines who were congregating too close together or who weren't taking sufficient cover.

Thirty minutes later, Captain Ball received another message: "Imminent SVEST [suicide vest] threat headed to Abbey." Ball ordered his Marines to seek cover and take a knee to minimize their exposure to a potential blast. They spent most of the night in that posture.

GUARDING AGAINST THE INEVITABLE

Ghost was stretched from the inner gate all the way down the canal. Ball knew an attack was likely to occur, but it was unclear which part of his formation it would strike. A bombing targeting the Marines at the very front of the canal—150 meters (500 feet) away from the entrance to HKIA—would make casualty evacuation extremely difficult. Carrying a Marine with sixty pounds of equipment for at least a few football fields is a tall ask in the best of circumstances, and doing it while navigating a panicked crowd would be even harder. Weighing the pros and cons, Ball ultimately decided to collapse his forces back to the gate to shorten the evacuation time if the forecasted attack occurred.

By 7:30 a.m., Ghost had successfully fallen back 150 meters and manned positions on the wall of the canal to keep the crowd from forcing its way into the outer gate. An angry mob followed them all the way back. Over the previous twenty-four hours, the crowd's mood had progressed "from desperate to aggressive."[1] In a repeat of their first day at the gate, Ghost Company Marines were forced to fight hand to hand with desperate and increasingly violent masses of local nationals. Nevertheless, they continued to actively search for US citizens and specific Afghan allies among the crowd.

While scanning for an American man whose wife had already been admitted to the airfield, an officer with the 24th Marine Expeditionary Unit who was tasked with force protection spotted an Afghan mother and her daughter—a one- or two-year-old girl wearing a red dress—frantically trying to find an opening in the crowd to avoid being trampled. He tried to keep tabs on the pair while searching for the American man and enlisted an Afghan couple near the wall to assist in the effort. The mom and daughter continued to pop into and out of sight amid the sea of bodies. The officer jumped down from the wall into the space directly behind the Ghost Company Marines, who were now actively fighting with the crowd attempting to storm the gates, and passed CS spray forward to Captain Ball, who was toward the front. One of the men from 2/1 tried to pull a flash-bang grenade in the middle of the melee to stun the surging crowd, but the pin became dislodged before he could drop it. The device detonated, "blowing off pieces of his hand."[2] Another Marine from his unit carried him away from the fight.

Amid the chaos, the officer continued to try to rescue the toddler and her mom. He later told investigators, "I couldn't leave the little girl in the red dress and her mother."[3] Eventually, a few Marines at the front located the pair. They pulled the mother to safety and handed the girl to the officer, who carried her away from the fracas in his arms. When they were all safely away from the stampede, the mother became distraught and tried to run back into it—she and her daughter had become separated from her husband (a man "in a pink shirt") earlier in the day, and she'd been trying to find him.

Harrowing as it was, the ordeal was far from an isolated incident. Once the Marines reestablished control, their orders were to stay out of the crowd; the threat of a suicide attack was too high and too credible to justify the risk. Nevertheless, corpsmen jumped into the crowd on several occasions to save pregnant women who'd passed out in the heat and otherwise would have been crushed to death.

PREPARING FOR THE INEVITABLE

As the day progressed, it became clear that senior leadership was preparing for the worst. At 11:30 a.m., Admiral Vasely ordered every medical unit on the airfield to prepare for an imminent attack and to expect a potential mass casualty (MASCAL) situation. Runners woke up the doctors and medics who had bedded down after completing the night shift a few hours before. Over the next hour and a half, the threat reporting intensified. By 1:30 p.m., every medical and surgical team on the airfield was standing by at full readiness.

While the medical units spun up, Captain Ball passed along yet another classified alert to his Marines. This time the intel was more specific: the Marines should prepare for an ISIS suicide bombing and be on the lookout for a cameraman to dismount from a motorcycle at the marketplace where the outer gate ended and the Taliban-controlled portion of the city began.

Ball stayed at the front with his Marines and directed his first sergeant and all corpsmen to fall back to the outermost portion of the gate. If an explosion occurred, the company couldn't afford to have both of its senior leaders and all its medical personnel in the kill zone together.

In addition to the massive crowds and unfavorable terrain, the military's ability to scan for threats had been compromised by the administration's failure to plan for the inevitable. Before Kabul fell, the staff at the HKIA Joint Operations Center had used sixty different infrared camera systems to monitor the airfield security. (Rapid Aerostat Initial Deployment [RAID] system cameras had been a fixture of US bases in the Middle East since 2005.) Because the civilian contractors who managed the cameras had been first in line for evacuation, however, no one was left to perform basic troubleshooting or maintenance functions on the systems. By August 26, only three of the cameras on the airfield were still functioning. Moreover, the control systems of the airfield's two other static surveillance assets had been located within the embassy compound, and troops had been forced to destroy them during the ad hoc evacuation mission on August 15 and 16.

PERMISSION DENIED

The military officials weren't totally blind. The previous night, military commanders at HKIA had received an intelligence briefing containing a description of the likely suicide bomber who was expected to attack on the twenty-sixth. Contrary to the post hoc assertions by Army Brigadier General Lance Curtis at the Department of Defense press conference in February 2022, announcing the results of the Pentagon's internal investigation, the threat stream was not vague or nonspecific. The intelligence assessment contained a detailed profile of the suspected attacker, and the intelligence community was aware that the individual had already completed his "exit interview" with the ISIS media wing (which would publish his final testimony once the attack was complete, per its standard operating procedure).

The Marines of Reaper 2 were told to look for an Afghan man with a shaved head and close-cropped beard, dressed in all black. They were also told that it was highly likely that the suspect would be carrying a backpack with three yellow arrows stitched on the exterior. Several other Marines confirmed that they had been given the same threat description.

Before the bombing on the twenty-sixth, the Reaper 2 sniper team spotted a suspicious individual whose appearance matched the description of the bomber nearly verbatim. The man was toward the back of the ground and trying to maneuver forward, but his route didn't seem to be oriented toward the entrance to the gate itself. That report is consistent with sworn statements submitted by members of Ghost

Company's third platoon, which received the same suspect profile and whose members stated that they had achieved positive identification for the threat and reported it to higher headquarters. Vargas-Andrews requested permission to engage the suspect several times, but his requests were not granted.

Vargas-Andrews said that he and two other US service members spotted a man who "fit the description" of the suspected bomber "exactly" between noon and 1:00 p.m. The suspected bomber was with an older man who "seemingly coached the bomber" as the suspected bomber "consistently and nervously looking up at our position through the crowd." Vargas-Andrews said that "I requested engagement authority" but that he was specifically told, "Do not engage." The Marine sniper said that "psychological operations individuals" then "came to our tower immediately and confirmed the suspect met the suicide bomber description." Vargas-Andrews said Lieutenant Colonel Brad Whitehead then arrived to review the evidence, and that "we asked him if we could shoot." The Marine said the battalion commander told him, "I don't know." Vargas-Andrews said that "we received no update and never got our answer" and that "eventually the individual disappeared." The Marine added: "To this day, we believe he was the suicide bomber. . . . Plain and simple, we were ignored."[4]

Supporting exhibits from the Pentagon's Abbey Gate investigation appear to confirm Vargas-Andrews's account. Exhibit 184 of the report—which was fully redacted—is labeled "Man Identified Shortly Before the Attack." Another fully redacted exhibit says, "Man identified by Recon as suspected accomplice." The next exhibit is a picture of Vargas-Andrews and another member of Reaper 2 photographing the crowd with a telescopic lens from the sniper tower.

Vargas-Andrews's account is nearly identical to the account provided by another Marine who was also present. Tristan Hirsch, who was assigned to Echo Company, has repeatedly stated that the Marines at Abbey Gate "knew about [the assassin] two days prior to the attack."

He added, "We knew what he looked like. The CIA let us know. He looked exactly as they'd described him." Perhaps most significantly, he reported, "a friend of mine who was a sniper racked back his rifle and was ready to kill the guy," but permission was denied.[5]

COUNTDOWN

By 4:00 p.m., Ghost Company's 4th Platoon was exhausted from constantly battling the crowd. Captain Ball directed 1st Platoon to relieve them an hour ahead of schedule. As the daylight faded, so too did the crowd's chances of getting inside the wire. And they knew it. Word leaked to the local population that US forces would be closing the gate for good that night or the next morning, and the crowd sensed that time was running out, for all practical purposes. The anxiety created a vicious cycle. The more desperate the people outside the gates felt, the more forceful they became. The resulting panic only reinforced other would-be evacuees' belief that their final window of opportunity was about to close.

Military doctrine normally dictates that forces spread out to avoid clustering a significant number of personnel within a single blast radius, but the size and violence of the crowd made that impossible. The Marines needed to stay shoulder to shoulder to prevent individual Marines from being swarmed and to keep members of the crowd from exploiting gaps in the line. They stood on the US side of the canal, three rows deep. Among the first row of Marines, standing on the elevated curb at the edge of the canal, were Corporal Daegan Page, Lance Corporal Dylan Merola, and Lance Corporal Rylee McCollum. Their platoon sergeant, Staff Sergeant Jonathan Eby, stood in the middle of the three. Corporal Hunter Lopez stood a few places down, manning their left flank. In the two rows backing them up were Sergeant Nicole Gee and Sergeant Johanny Rosario Pichardo, both of whom were members of the Female Engagement Team attached to the platoon.

The PSYOP team, including Army Staff Sergeant Ryan Knauss, was blasting prerecorded messages to the crowd from a loudspeaker next to their truck, about 15 meters (50 feet) back from the crowd. The prerecorded loop directed Afghans to disperse if they didn't have one of several types of documents approved for entry. Virtually no one listened, and on the few occasions when a member of the crowd actually left, someone else immediately took his or her place. The team had no interpreter, however, so prerecorded messages were the best they could do.

By 5:20 p.m., things were getting increasingly out of control. The dense mob of bodies slowly surged forward, as if it were a living organism. The men and women waving pieces of paper at the front were there one moment and then simply folded under and subsumed by the blob the next. The otherworldly chorus of high-pitched cries for help from people suffocating in place increased in direct proportion to the forward movement of the masses. Still, the Marines continued scanning for legitimate evacuees and pulling them over the wall in ones and twos.

An Afghan civilian and his wife and children were among the lucky souls who were pulled out of the canal at the very end. As the family moved down the gate corridor onto the airfield, a Marine PSYOP officer observed that the man spoke perfect English in addition to Pashtu and gently pressed him into service. "Just give me ten minutes. Just help me for ten minutes, and I'll bring you back to your family." The man was understandably hesitant to leave his family once they'd finally made it inside together, but he reluctantly agreed to speak to the crowd. At 5:25 p.m., he took the microphone next to the PSYOP truck, and the officer set a timer for ten minutes. He implored the crowd to stop pressing: "Stop pushing." "Please calm down and give some space." "You are hurting women and children!" No one paid any attention.

While the impromptu interpreter spoke, Marines at the front saw a man suffering from heatstroke and hoisted him over the wall. They dragged him to the concrete Jersey barriers several feet away from the ledge and yelled for a corpsman. Without hesitation, twenty-two-year-old Corpsman Third Class Maxton Soviak from Berlin Heights, Ohio, sprinted forward from his protected position at the rear of the outer

corridor to render aid. At the same time, Sergeant Vargas-Andrews—
fresh off his overnight shift but volunteering to help—linked up with
an interpreter in the canal and prepared to guide him to the gate. But
the man wasn't ready just yet; he needed to find his father, who was
somewhere back in the crowd. Vargas-Andrews waited in the canal.

At 5:35, the PSYOP officer's timer dinged. The ten minutes were up.
The helpful civilian apologized for the lack of success. "I did my best."
True to his word, the officer began to escort the man back through the
gate to reunite with his family.

At 5:36, an ISIS suicide bomber—Abdul Rahman al-Logari—stood
at the top of the wall on the other side of the canal, directly across from
the assembled Marines, and detonated a twenty-pound vest packed with
hundreds of 5-millimeter ball bearings.

CHAOS

Page, Eby, McCollum, and Merola were only three meters from the
blast. The sheer force of the explosion left even those who avoided
direct injuries temporarily dazed, and the pressure knocked most if
not all of them off their feet. Ball bearings and shrapnel punctured the
CS canisters on the Marines' kits, releasing clouds of tear gas into the
air. To make matters worse, the wind was blowing from east to west,
pushing the gas down the outer corridor of the gate toward the entrance
that reinforcements needed to use. The sound of gunfire erupted all
around and reverberated from the surrounding buildings.

The other members of Ghost Company flooded the area. Some
squads treated the wounded, while others took up security positions
using the Jersey barriers and the PSYOP truck as cover. The 82nd paratroopers heard and felt the blast from several hundred meters to the
west and immediately dispatched medics to the scene. The Air Force
PJs, experts in treating casualties, converged on Abbey Gate as well.
Crucially, the Marine Shock Trauma Platoon seamlessly established a
casualty collection point to stabilize the most critical casualties. The

platoon, which drilled relentlessly on mass casualty situations in its spare time under the tutelage of its chief medical warrant officer, despite instructions from Washington to focus on covid mitigation, saved the lives of two Marines who would have bled to death if they had had to make the longer drive to the Role 2 hospital across the airfield instead of getting immediate treatment.

In what had already become a common theme throughout the evacuation, the Marines, soldiers, and airmen responding to the attack were forced to improvise with whatever resources they had. Some Marines raced down the airfield carrying two of their wounded in a gator utility vehicle with a flat bed. The men in the back were heavily bandaged but still "in pretty bad shape and screaming," according to one of the Marines present. Others evacuated casualties on riot shields, which are only four feet long. Sergeant Charles Schilling used a pair of bolt cutters that Vargas-Andrews had "commandeered" several days prior to cut a hole in a fence and shorten the casualty evacuation distance by 20 meters (65 feet). When lives are on the line, every extra second matters.

Heroism, however, wasn't in short supply. Then Corporal (and now Sergeant) Wyatt Wilson was in the third row of Marines overwatching the canal when the bomber triggered his device 10 meters (33 feet) away. According to the citation for his Bronze Star with Valor, the blast "threw him into the air as it sprayed shrapnel throughout his body." A ball bearing ripped through his jaw. Despite those injuries, his first reaction was to try to save Corporal Kelsee Lainhart, a member of the Female Engagement Team who lay next to him, paralyzed from the chest down. Wilson dragged her back toward the gate until he began to pass out due to loss of blood. Even then, he "passed [her] to an uninjured Marine and refused medical treatment for his own life-threatening wounds."[6] Wilson's own life was saved by a medical officer who performed CPR on him until he stabilized. In the weeks afterward, he communicated with friends and family by writing on a whiteboard.

Wilson's extraordinary actions were consistent with those of other 2/1 Marines he served alongside. One of 1st Platoon's squad leaders, Sergeant Jonathan Painter, absorbed a direct shrapnel hit to the helmet. Other fragments sliced his face. But he coordinated with Eby—who himself was wounded—to evacuate the Marines under his care. The battalion's operations officer was also wounded, but he waved away junior Marines trying to treat him, telling them to "take care of the guys" instead. Lance Corporal Michael Gretzon was among the Marines pulling security after the attack. Unlike the others, however, he was bleeding from a shrapnel wound to his arm. In a social media post praising Gretzon's actions, Eby recounted how Gretzon had "simply switched his weapon to his other hand and got on security, scanning rooftops and barriers deeper for a cameraman or to prepare for a follow-on attack" and ignoring encouragement from other Marines to head to the casualty collection point.[7]

Eight of the thirteen Americans killed in action had already expired when they were taken to the Role 2 hospital. The other five had life-ending injuries and died within two hours of arriving. For hours after the attack, the public announcement systems on the airfield requested anyone with O negative blood to report to the Role 2 hospital to donate to the wounded. The attack was the military equivalent of a sucker punch to the face of a distracted opponent, but no one at HKIA lost the will to fight back. One of the Marines at the Role 2 hospital, "loopy on meds," attempted to leave the field hospital and return to his post wearing nothing but a hospital shirt and boxers. When he was intercepted by other members of his unit, he kept insisting that he "wanted to get back to work." His fellow Marines "told him to sit down and let [them] find him some pants."[8]

After all American casualties had been treated, the remaining troops at Abbey Gate escorted nearly eighty children who had been orphaned by the attack to the makeshift orphanage in one of the comfort areas. They cared for the children until UN officials arrived to take custody of them.

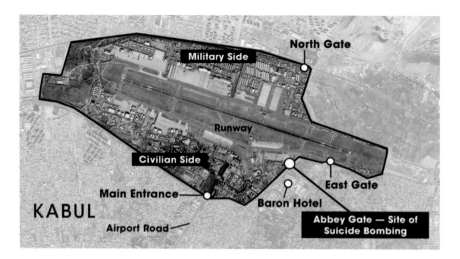

Above: Overview of Hamid Karzai International Airport (HKIA) and the main entrances used for the evacuation. (NASA/Timothy Shaner) *Below:* Paratroopers from Alpha Company, 2/501 Parachute Infantry Regiment, 82nd Airborne Division, posing with a fire engine ("Clifford") they hot-wired and used as transportation around HKIA. (OAR Foundation)

Right: Staff Sergeant Taylor Hoover (left) conducting a patrol during his first of three deployments to Afghanistan. Nicknamed "Hoova" by his fellow Marines during that deployment, he served as the point man on every mission, scanning the ground ahead for improvised explosive devices. (Darin Hoover)

Top: Evacuees waiting on the flight line. (OAR Foundation) *Above:* Lance Corporal Kareem Nikoui entertaining a young Afghan evacuee at the staging area. (Shana Chappell) *Below:* Lance Corporal Kareem Nikoui (second from right) with fellow Ghost Company Marines during a moment of downtime. (Shana Chappell)

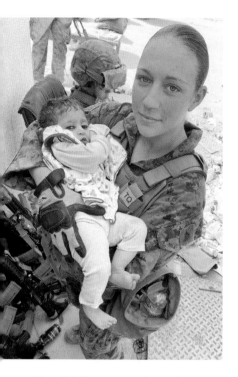

All good here mom, I love you

Above left: Sergeant Nicole Gee during one of the many times she comforted babies orphaned or passed to the Marines at the gate by desperate mothers. (Christy Shamblin) *Above right:* Army Staff Sergeant Ryan Christian Knauss's final message to his mother, Paula Knauss Selph, sent from HKIA just two days before the deadly suicide bombing. (Paula Knauss Selph) *Below:* A banner that hung inside the CIA compound in Kabul, tallying the number of people rescued by agency personnel since the evacuation began. (Anonymous)

Left: A view of the crowd outside North Gate from a Marine sniper's overwatch position. (Anonymous)
Above : The photo taken by "Amir" of the placard he painted with his designated call sign and held aloft to signal troops manning Abbey Gate.
Below: The photo taken by "Amir" and relayed to handlers roughly a minute before the suicide attack at Abbey Gate.

Above left: Army Staff Sergeant Ryan Christian Knauss. (8th Psychological Operations Group)
Above right: Marine Corporal Daegan W. Page. (US Marine Corps) *Below:* Marine Corporal
Dylan Crawshaw (center) from Echo Company, 2/1, visiting an Afghan family he
assisted at HKIA at their new home in the United States. (Marine Corporal Dylan Crawshaw)

Above: Lance Corporal Schmitz with a platoonmate in a rare moment of rest after gate operations. (Suzanne Schmitz) *Left above:* Marine Sergeant Johanny Rosario Pichardo. (US Marine Corps) *Left center:* Marine Lance Corporal David L. Espinoza. (US Marine Corps) *Left below:* Marines from 2/1 doing their utmost to ensure that the Taliban would not take over a pristine airfield. Senior leaders at HKIA bristled at the Marines' "inappropriate" behavior and forced several platoons to clean the area before US forces abandoned it to the Taliban. (OAR Foundation) *Below:* Two 82nd Airborne Division paratroopers posing with one of the first aid mannequins US troops placed in guard towers to conceal their lack of manpower during the final stages of the evacuation. (OARFoundation)

Top left: Marine Corporal Hunter Lopez. (US Marine Corps) *Top right:* Marine Lance Corporal Dylan R. Merola. (US Marine Corps) *Above:* The Marines of 2nd Platoon, Echo Company, 2/1, posing for a platoon picture at the end of their deployment. (OAR Foundation) *Below left:* Marine Lance Corporal Rylee McCollum. (US Marine Corps) *Below right:* Navy Hospital Corpsman Maxton W. Soviak. (US Navy)

Top: Marine Corps Corporal Humberto A. Sanchez. (US Marine Corps) *Above:* 2/1 Marines standing between the crowd and Abbey Gate. (OAR Foundation) *Left:* ISIS-K suicide bomber Abdul Rahman al-Logari. Logari was captured by the CIA in 2017 but escaped when the Taliban overran Bagram Air Base. Several days later, he murdered thirteen Americans. Western intelligence agencies have unanimously confirmed that Logari was the Abbey Gate bomber, but the Biden administration has refused to acknowledge his identity.

THE THIRD DEADLIEST DAY

The Abbey Gate bombing was the third deadliest day for US forces during the entire two-decade war, ranking just behind two notorious Chinook helicopter shoot-downs by the Taliban: one in August 2011, which killed all thirty US troops and all eight Afghans on board, and the other in June 2005, which killed eight SEALs and eight Army Night Stalkers. The bombing at HKIA— and the deaths of the thirteen—did not have to happen.

HE WHO SHALL NOT BE NAMED

The direct through line from the United States' abandonment of Bagram to the Taliban's freeing of terrorist prisoners there to the United States' reliance on Haqqani Taliban security outside HKIA to the Abbey Gate bombing is clear. Even though the Biden administration has steadfastly refused to do so, Admiral Vasely acknowledged the direct line between the Taliban's capture of Bagram, Logari's subsequent release, and the Abbey Gate attack. A month after the withdrawal, he remarked that "bringing in an individual who had been in prison to execute an attack is pretty telling of [ISIS-K's] capability."[9]

The Biden administration has pointedly refused to say Abdul Rahman al-Logari's name because of this embarrassing reality. It is, to our knowledge, the only terrorist attack in which the government has known the perpetrator's name but refused to share it with the public. US officials who insisted on anonymity confirmed to us that the United States has determined that the bomber was Logari, but the Biden administration has repeatedly refused to publicly name him. We obtained a photo of Logari from alternate sources and showed it to a number of special operations officials who had been present at HKIA throughout the evacuation and received regular threat updates. Each confirmed that it was Logari.

Not only is Logari's identity known, but he actually had a long history with the United States—including time spent in CIA custody. Still, on the six-month[10] and one-year[11] anniversaries of the bombing, the Biden administration refused to name Logari. A senior defense official said that "due to sensitivities surrounding ongoing counterterrorism operations, we are unable to confirm the identity."[12] When asked in February 2022 whether it was true the identity of the bomber was known in advance of the attack, Curtis deflected: "There is a separate investigation that is being conducted by the FBI that is taking a look at that."[13]

In February 2022, the State Department's Rewards for Justice program offered a $10 million reward for information on the ISIS terrorist leader Shahab al-Muhajir and another $10 million for the arrest of "terrorists responsible for the attack" at HKIA. State wouldn't say whether its refusal to publicly identify the bomber would hinder finding those responsible for the attack.

In January 2022, Biden administration officials selectively leaked that they had "pieced together a profile" of the ISIS-K cell responsible for the attack and strongly suggested that the members of that cell would be the administration's first targets of retaliatory drone strikes in Afghanistan.[14] More than a year later, those drone strikes have never materialized.

LOCATION KNOWN

Bombshell declassified and partially-redacted CENTCOM records show that the US military was aware of ISIS-K's location in Kabul prior to the bombing on August 26—but the military brass rejected calls from US service members to conduct a preventive strike.[15] The green light was given only after a bombing had killed thirteen Americans and crippled several others. A Pentagon investigation of the bombing revealed that military intelligence officers had known that ISIS-K was staging in a hotel two to three kilometers (one to one and a half miles) west of HKIA and that General Chris Donahue had asked the Taliban to conduct an assault on that location on the night before the bombing—but the Taliban had never done it. The botched August 29 US air strike and the rocket attack by ISIS-K on August 30 occurred in roughly the same area in which ISIS was believed to have been located before the HKIA bombing, according to a service member interviewed for the Pentagon's Abbey Gate Report. CENTCOM documents show that ISIS-K had used the same area to facilitate other Kabul attacks in 2020.

A US military officer with target engagement authority in Afghanistan stated that intelligence reports from August 18 to 20 had indicated that ISIS-K intended to attack the US forces at HKIA. On August 19, the "threat level spiked and ISIS-K began moving forces to hit HKIA."[16] From August 20 to 23, they homed in on the threat and initiated "a targeting effort focused on ISIS-K threats leading into Kabul." The strike unit was "authorized to look at ISIS-K targets" but had to submit detailed proposals for permission to engage. Before the Abbey Gate bombing, Vasely and Donahue had "both determined conducting a strike was infeasible due to the negative response" from the Taliban. This indicates that the commander of U.S. Forces Afghanistan–Forward and the commander of the 82nd Airborne Division had both rejected efforts to conduct a strike against ISIS-K before the HKIA bombing, due to how the Taliban might respond.

The officer also said, "Once fixed, we sought permission through [U.S. Forces Afghanistan–Forward] to commander of CENTCOM." The CENTCOM commander was General McKenzie. Notably, McKenzie testified under oath in September 2021 that it was "not true" that US forces in Afghanistan had had an ISIS-K cell under surveillance prior to the Abbey Gate bombing or that military forces could have struck the ISIS-K group but hadn't been given the authority to strike. At no time did he mention the US military's declining to strike ISIS-K ahead of the Abbey Gate bombing because of the worries of Pentagon leaders about how the Taliban would react. He did say that the bombing had not been the result of "any lack of attention" on the part of the U.S. in "trying to find those cells." The general claimed, "We did find a number and we did . . . enable and stop those attacks from occurring."[17]

Those allegations are consistent with military leaders' public statements at the time. On August 22, Jake Sullivan had claimed that the ISIS-K threat to HKIA was "something we're focused on with every tool in our arsenal" and that "we'll do everything that we can as long as we're on the ground to keep that from happening."[18] But the United States never conducted any strikes against ISIS-K until after the Abbey Gate bombing.

LETHAL THREAT

In short, all available information indicates that US officials knew that an ISIS-K attack was coming and that the military and the CIA had been tracking a potential ISIS attack on the airport since August 19. The next day, Biden went out of his way to specify that there would be consequences for the Taliban if there was an attack on US forces or a disruption of US evacuation operations. The president specifically mentioned a threat from ISIS-K and from ISIS-K terrorists released during the nearby prison breaks from particular nearby prisons.

Top Biden officials later detailed the seriousness of the ISIS-K warnings. White House chief of staff Ron Klain recalled that "the thing we thought about every day was: Would Americans wind up giving their lives in service of that mission?" He added, "We knew there were terrorists in Kabul. We knew there were terrorists trying to kill Americans."[19] Blinken went even farther: "We had incredible intelligence about attacks by ISIS-K that were in the offing. Of course, we didn't have the specificity, but honestly, this was like a slow-motion nightmare. You know it's happening, but you can't do anything about it."[20] There were, of course, things Blinken and Biden could have done about it—they just didn't. On August 24, Biden once again warned that "ISIS-K is seeking to target the airport."[21] Twenty-four hours later, Blinken also cautioned about "the very real possibility of an ISIS attack."[22] US defense officials likewise alerted the government to a "very specific threat stream" indicating that ISIS-K was planning to attack HKIA, and later that night, the embassy advised US citizens to avoid the airfield gates.

Allied nations also publicized the threat. The British Foreign Office warned of "an ongoing and high threat of terrorist attack" at the airfield,[23] and Australia's Department of Foreign Affairs and Trade likewise observed a "very high threat of a terrorist attack."[24] Just hours before the bombing, British armed forces minister James Heappey stressed that "the threat is credible, it is imminent, it is lethal." He pointed out that the packed crowds offered "the Islamic State a target that is unimaginable."[25]

By "12–24 hours prior" to the bombing, intelligence officials "were certain the attack was coming." A senior military intelligence analyst later told investigators, "On 26 AUG, I knew the attack would happen" that day. He said "Intel reporting indicated ISIS-K was moving the bomber into place at 1630 on 26AUG." The same official said that he had "shared intelligence about the pending attack" with allied nations during a regularly scheduled coordination meeting on the airfield at 4:30 p.m. on the twenty-sixth. The briefing's purpose was to ensure that "everyone was aware, and knew it was happening." The official added that the intelligence community had "assessed it would be Abbey Gate due to the number of people there."[26]

Pentagon testimony also revealed that "the Taliban were tasked to screen for the specific threat."[27] In the twenty-four hours leading up to the attack, everyone on the line knew to look for a man dressed all in black with a shaved head. The intelligence was deathly accurate. The bombing occurred close to the projected hour, and it was later revealed by the Pentagon that Logari had, in fact, been clad in black.

The threat from ISIS-K did not emerge out of the blue, and ISIS-K suicide bombings in Kabul had become a regular fixture of life in Kabul in 2020 and 2021. Many of those attacks had been high profile and caused significant loss of life. For that reason alone, the administration should have known better than to choose HKIA—a small, encircled airfield in the middle of a city with several high-speed avenues of approach—as its preferred base for executing a civilian evacuation. In the first four months of 2021 alone, ISIS-K conducted at least seventy-seven attacks—a sharp increase from the twenty-one attacks it had conducted during the same period in 2020.[28] A few months prior to the Biden administration's decision to base any evacuation out of Kabul, a US intelligence official assessed that ISIS-K "maintains a steady operational tempo and probably retains the ability to conduct attacks in Kabul and other urban centers."[29] ISIS-K's sleeper cells were active "particularly in Kabul, where the current commander and his overall ISIL-K deputy are based," and ISIS-K had claimed responsibility for "many recent high-profile attacks" in Kabul.[30]

JAILBREAK

ISIS-K bomber Abdul Rahman al-Logari was sprung from the Parwan Detention Facility at Bagram by the Taliban as Kabul fell; the match was struck, and the fuse was lit. Logari was one of more than 1,800 ISIS-K fighters and nearly three dozen al-Qaeda terrorists released from Parwan and Pul-e-Charkhi Prison. Taliban spokesman Zabihullah Mujahid said on August 15, "The most important prison at Bagram Airfield was also captured. The latest info shows all the prisoners have been transferred to a sheltered place."[31] In fact, the Taliban had freed almost every prisoner. On August 16, Kirby claimed that he was ignorant of what had happened to the prisoners at Bagram. A week and a half later, he admitted that the prisoners had been released, but still claimed that he didn't know the exact number of ISIS-K fighters released. The number, he acknowledged, was "in the thousands."[32]

ISIS-K CLAIMS CREDIT

ISIS-K claimed credit for the attack and named Logari within hours as the terrorist who had carried out the "martyrdom operation" at the Kabul airport, with ISIS's Amaq News Agency recounting the terrorist group's narrative. ISIS-K said that Logari was able to get within 5 meters of U.S. troops as they led the evacuation.[33]

The Pentagon's Abbey Gate investigation did not conclude how Logari had made it past the Taliban security, through the packed crowd, and up to the Marines, though it claimed he had "likely" used an alternate avenue to bypass the Taliban checkpoints. "This was not preventable," Army Brigadier General Lance Curtis insisted in February 2022.[34]

US officials said that Logari was a former engineering student who had been recruited by ISIS-K years prior. The CIA had warned Indian intelligence in 2017 that Logari was planning an attack in New Delhi, and India's Research and Analysis Wing had captured him and handed him over to the CIA in September 2017. Logari then spent time at both Pul-e-Charkhi Prison and Parwan Detention Center before being freed by the Talibs.

Indian intelligence sources stated that Logari had been incarcerated at Bagram for four years before getting sprung from jail.[35] The ISIS-K plot that India disrupted—planned suicide bombings in New Delhi and other Indian cities—had likely been planned at the behest of Pakistan's Inter-Services Intelligence (ISI).[36] The Indians handed him over to the CIA and NDS to be questioned, during which Logari allegedly gave up information that led to successful drone strikes against numerous ISIS leaders.

ISIS-K released a photo allegedly of Logari wearing a black mask and black suicide vest with a tan robe, holding up a rifle in one hand and one finger of the other hand, symbolizing victory, with the black ISIS flag displayed behind him. The front page of the Islamic State's *Al-Naba* weekly newsletter in September 2021 featured photos of twelve of the thirteen US service members killed, blurring out the faces of the female service members. Another graphic included Biden closing his eyes and bowing his head during a postbombing White House press conference juxtaposed with a picture from the dignified transfer of the coffins at Dover Air Force Base. ISIS-K wrote of its alleged "fight of monotheism in Kabul" and said that Logari had escaped "when the former [Afghan] government forces fled" from Bagram—but made no mention of the Taliban's role in freeing him. The terrorist group was thrilled that its "blessed attack" had resulted in the "greatest human loss" for US forces in Afghanistan in a decade.[37]

ISIS-K falsely claimed that the only people killed had been US troops and Taliban. There is no evidence that the attack had killed any Taliban, and nearly two hundred Afghan civilians were also killed (apparently an inconvenient fact for ISIS). Even the Taliban immediately denied that any of its fighters had been killed.

In September 2021, as the Islamic State made its enmity toward India clear, its Indian magazine, *Sawt al-Hind*, confirmed that the airport bomber had previously been captured in New Delhi. ISIS-K released more alleged details of Logari's biography in its *Voice of Khorasan* magazine in February 2022, saying that the terrorist had been born to a wealthy family in Afghanistan's Logar province in 1996. When Logari had been undergoing terrorist training in Afghanistan, he had specialized in explosives, "developed an interest" in suicide operations, and been picked for an operation. The terrorist group said that as he had awaited his mission, he had helped fellow suicide bombers write their "wills" and delivered the wills to their families. After being freed from Parwan, ISIS-K said, Logari had "directly requested to be given a mission" to conduct a suicide attack at HKIA.

HAQQANIS AT THE GATE

The Haqqani Network, which had long had a secret working relationship with ISIS-K, were in charge of security at HKIA. Khalil Haqqani, who had been sanctioned by the United Nations more than a decade before due to his long-standing ties with al-Qaeda and Osama bin Laden, had been made head of security for Kabul after the Taliban took it over.

Sirajuddin Haqqani, the leader of the Haqqani Network and the "deputy emir" of the Taliban, is also a card-carrying member of

al-Qaeda's global leadership, and he has claimed responsibility for numerous suicide bombings in Kabul, including the 2018 attack on the
Kabul Inter-Continental Hotel that killed forty people, including more
than a dozen foreigners. Beyond Sirajuddin's rise to Taliban minister of
the interior, Haqqanis filled dozens of other key Taliban government
security posts.

On August 22, Jake Sullivan admitted, "The Taliban, obviously, to
a considerable extent, are integrated with the Haqqani network. Our
effort is with the Taliban military commanders currently in charge of
security in Kabul."[38] Those were the Haqqanis. The State Department
repeatedly insisted that the Taliban and the Haqqani Network were
somehow separate entities and argued that the United States' providing
information to the former did not mean it was doing the same with
the latter—an obvious falsehood. General McKenzie later admitted, in
September 2021, that Badri 313 units (the Taliban's suicide squads) had
been part of the forces providing security at Kabul airport.

Mohammad Salim Saad, who helped lead the Badri 313 unit stationed outside the Kabul airport, said, "The troops that are stationed
here are the suicide unit of the Badri 313."[39] In some instances, the
Badri units, dressed in US-made military gear, were patrolling the
same airport parking lots as the Marines were, with only a bit of razor
wire separating the two.

The Taliban said immediately after the bombing that it had not
considered it its responsibility to make sure that ISIS-K did not conduct such an attack against the Americans. "Just because we have an
agreement not to attack the Americans until they complete their pullout
doesn't mean that we have cooperation with them or provide security
for them," Taliban official Inamullah Habibi Samangani said.[40]

The Taliban quickly attempted to shift responsibility for the successful suicide bombing to the United States, saying the night of the
bombing that it had "warned the foreign forces the repercussions of
the large gathering at Kabul airport."[41] Taliban spokesman Zabihullah

Mujahid had previously dismissed reports of possible ISIS-K attacks, wrongly claiming that "it's not correct."[42]

"NO EVIDENCE" OF "COLLUSION"

The day of the bombing, Biden officials quickly denied that there had been collusion between the Taliban and ISIS-K and defended the United States' decision to coordinate with the Talibs on airport security. Biden claimed that he had seen "no evidence" of "collusion between the Taliban and ISIS in carrying out what happened today."[43] Jen Psaki insisted that the United States did not have any information on Taliban involvement, adding "I'm not trying to sugarcoat what we think of the Taliban." But she announced that "because of coordination with the Taliban, we've been able to evacuate more than 104,000 people, save 104,000 lives—and that coordination is necessary."[44]

McKenzie said that the United States would continue to ask the Taliban to assist with security, saying he hadn't seen evidence that the Taliban had let the attack occur. He repeatedly defended working with the Taliban, noting that the United States had been sharing "versions" of its intelligence with the Taliban "so that they can actually do some searching out there for us." He said that the Talibs had helped stop attacks against the United States, but he did admit that the bomber's managing to make it past the Taliban perimeter all the way up to Abbey Gate meant that Taliban security must, at minimum, have failed.[45]

McKenzie said, "I don't think it was anything to convince me that they [the Taliban] let it [the bombing] happen." He insisted that the Taliban had a "common purpose" with the United States in the evacuation: "As long as we've kept that common purpose aligned, they've been useful to work with. They've cut some of our security concerns down. And they've been useful to work with going forward." He did not bring up the common purpose that the Taliban and ISIS-K had: killing Americans. The next month, he said that it was "possible" that the Taliban had let the ISIS-K bomber through "on purpose." But, he insisted, "The body of intelligence indicates that is not in fact what happened."[46]

In February 2022, Army Brigadier General Lance Curtis claimed, "We don't have any evidence through the course of our investigation that leads us to believe the Taliban knew about this attack."[47] Marine Colonel C. J. Douglas contended that "very quickly, Marines determined the Taliban were neither involved nor threatening U.S. personnel."[48] In fact, many people on the ground immediately suspected that collusion had occurred. One member of the 24th Marine Expeditionary Unit said the Taliban leadership outside HKIA was fragmented, telling investigators that "there was some reporting of lower-level Taliban moving over to ISIS-K when the Taliban started working with the Americans," noting that "it presented an ideological issue for them."[49]

A HISTORY OF COLLUSION

Contrary to the claims by Biden and his team, there was a long history of collusion between ISIS-K and the Haqqanis, especially in Kabul.

An Indian journalist, Praveen Swami, tweeted the day of the bombing: "ISIS-K's biggest grouping had a very cosy relationship with the Haqqani Network, architects of many suicide bombings and now rulers of Kabul, as well as Pakistan's ISI."[50] In May 2020, the United Nations said that ISIS-K "remains capable of mounting attacks in various parts of the country"—including in Kabul—and that some of the ISIS-K attacks might have arisen via "tactical accommodation" with the Haqqani Network.[51] The UN monitoring team viewed communication intercepts in the wake of attacks claimed by ISIS-K that were traceable to known members of the Haqqani Network.

"At the very least, I think there was deconfliction," Edmund Fitton-Brown, the former head of the UN Analytical Support and Sanctions Monitoring Team, told us. "At the very least, I think there were Haqqani

Network–inspired or –facilitated attacks, which ISIL-K were allowed to take credit for."

In June 2021, the UN team stated, "Authorized movement of personnel with a tacit understanding that both groups benefit from certain joint venture attacks is likely. . . . One Member State has suggested certain attacks can be denied by the Taliban and claimed by ISIL-K, with it being unclear whether these attacks were purely orchestrated by the Haqqani Network, or were joint ventures making use of ISIL-K operatives."[52]

Dr. Antonio Giustozzi, a visiting professor at King's College London and a senior research fellow at the Royal United Services Institute, wrote in *The Islamic State in Khorasan: Afghanistan, Pakistan, and the New Central Asian Jihad* about Sirajuddin Haqqani's close relations with ISIS-K. He said that the Azizullah Haqqani Group had been formed by sympathizers of the Islamic State in Waziristan, then become one of the component groups of ISIS-K in 2014. ISIS-K's ranks soon began to be filled out by thousands of Haqqani fighters and Taliban defectors in Afghanistan. The book also laid out Pakistani intelligence's efforts to cultivate ISIS-K. The Haqqanis, who were also close to the ISI, took steps toward working with ISIS-K in 2016 and 2017. Sirajuddin was personally involved in those efforts. When the group's military shura of ISIS-K chose Aslam Farooqi, a former Lashkar-e-Taiba commander, to be the new so-called governor of Khorasan in 2017, the book said, an ISIS-K source indicated that the choice had been the result of contacts with Pakistani ISI. Farooqi was arrested in Kandahar by the NDS following a March 2020 deadly attack against a Sikh temple in Kabul, and he admitted that ISIS-K was cooperating with the Haqqani Network. Farooqi was also freed from prison by the Taliban in August 2021, though he was killed in 2022.

Giustozzi added that "Haqqani network sources indicated in 2017 that Sirajuddin Haqqani was using his former commanders inside the

Azizullah Haqqani group as a lobby to influence IS-K towards dropping its jihad aims" against Pakistan and China.[53]

"There has, in fact, been a tactical and strategic convergence between the Islamic State-Khorasan and the Haqqanis," Sajjan M. Gohel, the international security director at the London-based Asia-Pacific Foundation, wrote in a story published hours after the ISIS-K attack at HKIA. He noted that "several major attacks between 2019 and 2021 involved collaboration between IS-K, the Taliban's Haqqani network, and other terror groups."[54]

Masoud Andarabi, Afghan minister of the interior from 2019 to 2021, argued in 2020 that "when their [Taliban and Haqqani] terrorist activities do not suit them politically, they rebrand it under" ISIS-K instead.[55] Afghan officials said in 2020 that ISIS-K fighters processed with fingerprint checks and eye scans often pop up in Afghan databases as connected to the Haqqani Network or to prior Haqqani attacks. The Taliban said that those claims were "rumors to muddy the public perception."[56] Amrullah Saleh, a former vice president of Afghanistan, has long contended that the Taliban and ISIS-K were closely linked.

In 2020, the United Nations said that some countries had noted that most ISIS-K attacks had included "involvement, facilitation, or the provision of technical assistance" by the Haqqanis and that ISIS-K "lacked the capability to launch complex attacks in Kabul on its own" without Haqqani help.[57] In June 2021, the UN sanctions monitoring team said that some countries "have reported tactical or commander-level collaboration between ISIL-K and the Haqqani Network." After the fall of Kabul, Hamdullah Mohib also said that the Haqqanis and ISIS-K had worked closely on numerous attacks.

In 2022, the UN's monitoring team stated that some people in the Haqqani Network believed that the alliance of convenience with ISIS-K might have outlived its usefulness now that the Taliban ruled Afghanistan.

THE "URBAN LION" OF KABUL

In 2020, Sanaullah Ghafari, also known as Shahab al-Muhajir, became the new head of ISIS-K. Andarabi tweeted in August 2020 that Muhajir was a "Haqqani member," too. Muhajir had deep Haqqani ties—and specialized in attacks in Kabul.

In February 2021, the United Nations said that "under al-Muhajir's leadership, and based on his expertise, ISIL-K will continue to undertake terrorist attacks, predominantly in Kabul." It assessed that the group remained a threat, including because of Muhajir. One UN nation said that Muhajir was "previously a mid-level commander in the Haqqani Network" and continued to cooperate with the Haqqanis.[58] Muhajir was "widely accepted to have been himself a former member of the Haqqani Network," Fitton-Brown told us.

In June 2021, one UN country said that Muhajir's ongoing relationship with the Haqqanis provided ISIS-K with "key expertise and access to [attack] networks."[59]

In January 2022, an article published in West Point's Combating Terrorism Center's journal, *CTC Sentinel*, said that Muhajir had joined "Taliban factions affiliated with the Haqqani network" and "had close links to the Haqqani network's senior commanders, Taj Mir Jawad and Qari Baryal, who ran terrorist networks in the capital."[60] In September 2021, Taj Mir Jawad had been named deputy chief of intelligence for the Taliban. In November 2021, Qari Baryal had been named governor of Kabul province by the Taliban. In January 2023, Jawad bragged about directing suicide attacks in Kabul that had killed hundreds of civilians. This all means that not only was Muhajir closely linked to the Haqqani Network generally, he was closely linked to two men who had led attack networks in Kabul and gone on to hold key roles in the Taliban government.

The ISIS announcement of the appointment of Muhajir called him one of the "urban lions" of ISIS-K in Kabul. In June 2021, the UN noted that "prior to being appointed Emir, al-Muhajir served as ISIL-K chief planner for high-profile attacks in Kabul."[61] In 2022, West Point analysts said that ISIS-K credited Muhajir for the group's resurgence after its low point in 2019, including because of his extensive recruitment networks in Kabul.

In November 2021, Blinken announced that the State Department was sanctioning the "current overall emir" of ISIS-K: Muhajir. He said that Muhajir was "responsible for approving all ISIS-K operations throughout Afghanistan and arranging funding to conduct operations."[62] Presumably that would include the ISIS-K suicide bombing at the HKIA, as the Haqqanis had provided security there. Unmentioned by Blinken was Muhajir's past leadership role in the Haqqani Network. He remains at large.

THE CASE FOR COLLUSION

Throughout August, Biden repeatedly called the Taliban and ISIS-K "sworn enemies," but the situation was vastly more complicated. Though the Taliban and ISIS-K were often at each other's throats, the Haqqanis frequently collaborated with ISIS-K on carrying out attacks, especially in Kabul.

A Tajik Afghan American interpreter named Gulam who had worked for several US generals in Afghanistan and who was on the ground at HKIA was interviewed during the Pentagon's investigation and repeatedly raised the possibility that the attack had happened through collusion between Haqqanis and ISIS-K. The summary of his thoughts was that "the Taliban downplayed the threat, overestimated their abilities, had no command and control, and local Taliban may have been willing to work with ISIS-K.

"It must have been very difficult. It's possible the attack was an insider job and the Taliban brought him closer. The Taliban at that gate were more hostile," he said when discussing how Logari had made it all the way up to the Marines. "I believe the other factor that may have led to the attack is conspiring with the Taliban. The Taliban commander at Abbey Gate was a Haqqani, he was very uncooperative. . . . The

Haqqani Taliban commander at Abbey Gate was uncooperative and that subordinate Taliban will not listen to their senior commanders. That may have led to the attack as well."[63] The official Abbey Gate Report did not even mention the word "Haqqani."

Taliban commander Abdul Hadi Hamdan later said, "When I came to Kabul, I was put in charge of the airport. We surrounded it with a thousand suicide bombers."[64]

On the day of the Abbey Gate bombing, Saleh said that "IS-K cells have their roots in Talibs & Haqqani network, particularly the ones operating in Kabul."[65] In late 2021, Andarabi said that the Abbey Gate bombing had been likely the result of collusion: "There is a tactical relationship between the Taliban and Deash in Kabul, as well as with the notorious Haqqani Network. I doubt that the attack on the Americans at Kabul airport would have happened without the involvement of lower-level groups."[66]

The Taliban's reaction to the Abbey Gate bombing was disconcerting: Lieutenant Colonel Brad Whited said he had seen the Taliban laughing at the chevron.[67]

"We take the position that ISIS–K may in fact be currently operating as a proxy force for the Taliban," an article in the US Air Force's *Journal of Indo-Pacific Affairs* in November 2021 noted. ". . . The Taliban may have leveraged ISIS-K as a proxy strawman layer of separation to oversee and/or facilitate the attack on US service members and Afghan civilians at HKIA on 26 August 2021."[68] In September 2021, Giustozzi wrote that the "alternative explanation" for the ISIS-K attack was collusion with the Haqqanis, noting "In the past, there was evidence of cooperation between the Haqqani network and IS-K, with the former facilitating attacks by the latter in Kabul."[69]

On the day of the bombing, H. R. McMaster, Trump's national security advisor, said that the suicide bombing had been the predictable outcome of the United States' entrusting the Haqqani Taliban to provide security at the Kabul airport and argued that it was likely that the bombing had been the product of collusion between ISIS-K and Haqqani elements in Kabul.

The Indian journalist Praveen Swami tweeted on the day of the Abbey Gate bombing, "ISIS-did-it is simple, linear and comfortable. There's a less elegant tale, too, worth thinking over: Fed up with the exodus, Taliban asked Haqqanis to end the crowds. Well, there was ISKP, old friends of the Haqqanis, right at hand and eager for blame."[70]

Former US intelligence officer Michael P. Pregent tweeted, "The Taliban killed the top IS-K leader at the Bagram prison & after establishing new rules for IS-K—the Taliban released IS-K fighters including the suicide bomber that made his way thru Haqqani & Taliban checkpoints with ease. The Taliban & The Haqqani Network are complicit."[71]

"Strange bedfellows are made in tactical situations," a former senior US intelligence official with time on the ground in Afghanistan told us when asked about possible collusion. "What they kept telling us—and even now are still telling people—was, oh, you know, 'ISIS-K and the Taliban don't like each other,'" Vargas-Andrews said. "Well, that might be the case—but they like Americans less."[72]

"WE WILL NOT FORGET"

The attack prompted a flood of calls from Republicans for Biden to resign or be impeached. Donald Trump said the bombing should never have been allowed to occur. Nancy Pelosi's first tweets after the bombing were related to celebrating Women's Equality Day, but she soon issued a statement mourning the dead and ordered that flags at the Capitol be flown at half-staff.

Psaki said, "What happened today... is a tragedy, is horrific, is one of the worst things, if not the worst thing, we've experienced during President Biden's time in office." When asked about Republican calls for Biden to resign, she replied, "It's not a day for politics."[73] When asked if the violence at the airport had been avoidable, she largely dodged the question.

General McKenzie said just after the bombing that "anytime you build a noncombatant evacuation plan like this, you bring in forces, you expect to be attacked" and "so, we expected—we thought this would happen sooner or later."[74] The general promised to go after those behind the Abbey Gate bombing.

Joe Biden gave a speech just hours after the bombing, responding to the attack, which had killed thirteen US service members, by quickly bringing up his deceased son, Beau Biden, a former officer with the Army Judge Advocate General, who had done a tour in Iraq in 2008 and 2009. Beau died of brain cancer in May 2015—something that Biden claims, without real evidence, was the result of his exposure to burn pits at his military base in Iraq. In his speech, he said, "We have some sense, like many of you do, what the families of these brave heroes are feeling today." When meeting with the families of the thirteen during the dignified transfer of the bodies of the fallen at Dover Air Force Base a few days later, he also repeatedly brought up his deceased son with the Gold Star families, much to the disgust of many of them. He has never spoken the names of the thirteen out loud in public. "They were part of the bravest, most capable, and the most selfless military on the face of the Earth. And they were part of, simply, what I call the 'backbone of America,'" he said of the thirteen. He added that in recent days "we've been made aware by our intelligence community that the ISIS-K . . . has been planning a complex set of attacks on the United States personnel and others." Biden also referred to ISIS-K as "an arch-enemy of the Taliban" even as he noted that ISIS-K members had been among those "who were freed when both those prisons were opened" by the Taliban.[75]

Biden backed away from his promise not to withdraw US troops until all other Americans had been gotten out, and when asked if he felt it had been a mistake to rely on the Taliban to secure the airport perimeter, he replied, "No, I don't." He then argued that it was "in the interest of the Taliban" that ISIS-K not metastasize and the United

States leave on time, and he largely defended the way the Taliban had acted during the evacuation. He confirmed that the United States had handed over evacuee information to the Taliban during the evacuation and simultaneously denied any knowledge of names being handed over to the Taliban. He also tried to blame the Trump administration and the Doha Agreement for the chaos that had unfolded in Kabul and for the attack that had killed thirteen Americans. He became combative as he tried to grill the reporter who had asked the question when the reporter noted that Trump was no longer president. The president said that Americans were unhappy that "people are likely to get hurt—some, as we've seen, have gotten killed—and that it is messy." He said that he stood by his withdrawal decision but that he had another meeting to go to.[76]

Biden vowed to ISIS-K, "We will not forgive. We will not forget. We will hunt you down and make you pay."[77] In the days after the Abbey Gate bombing, the United States conducted an air strike in Nangarhar province that killed two alleged ISIS-K leaders, followed by the botched air strike in Kabul, but from the end of August 2021 through the end of 2022, the United States did not conduct a single air strike against ISIS-K.

A "COMPLEX ATTACK"

The Pentagon immediately and repeatedly labeled the HKIA bombing a "complex attack." Numerous US service members said they had been shot at by gunmen after the bomb had gone off.

McKenzie said on the day of the bombing that the attack was conducted by two ISIS-K suicide bombers as well as a follow-on attack by ISIS-K gunmen. There had not actually been a secondary suicide bombing, but evidence indicates that US forces were fired upon. In February 2022, the Pentagon concluded that the attack had been conducted by a single ISIS-K bomber and that there had been no gunmen. But several US service members on the ground at HKIA insist that there were gunmen, either ISIS-K attackers or Taliban shooters or both. "The attack on the Abbey Gate was followed by a number of ISIS gunmen who opened fire on civilians and military forces," McKenzie said on August 26.[78] He later said that his comments on the day of the bombing had not been accurate.

Psaki repeatedly referred to "the attacks"—plural—during her press briefing the day of the bombing. Army Major General William "Hank" Taylor said the day after that the attack had been "followed by direct fire from an enemy position that is not exactly known" just north of Abbey Gate. Air Force Lieutenant Colonel Kristen Duncan wrote in October 2021 that, after the bombing, "the terrorists then engaged with small arms fire."[79]

"We now know that the explosively fired ball bearings cause wounds that look like gunshots, and when combined with a small number of warning shots, that lead many to assume that a complex attack had occurred," McKenzie said in February 2022.[80] But at least one gunman—dubbed a possible "rogue Taliban member" by Pentagon investigators—likely fired on a group of Marines. The Marines also fired on a suspicious man on a roof nearby who was wielding an AK-47. Another Marine shot rounds above a "suspicious individual" nearby. In September 2021, Marine Major Ben Sutphen said that he had been about fifteen feet from the blast and described what had happened to a Marine corporal: "He's blown off his feet and still has his wits about him. Shot through the shoulder. Immediately recovers his weapon and puts the opposing gunman down."[81] The Pentagon later said that Sutphen had been repeating what he had been told by fellow Marines.

Some U.S. service members at HKIA cast doubt on the idea that it had been a complex attack, but multiple Marines on the ground told Pentagon investigators they were certain that U.S. forces were fired upon after the blast. One service member who was part of a Marine Expeditionary Unit said that "the Marines had rounds impacting around them" and that "they could hear and see impact."[82] The Abbey Gate

Report also included this: "ISIS-K executed a complex attack with small arms fire immediately following the explosion. An eyewitness account from a field grade officer noted enemy gunmen in dominant overwatch positions from adjacent buildings. This threat is rapidly defeated. The large casualty count is directly attributed to the complex attack."[83]

Marine Sergeant Tyler Vargas-Andrews, who was severely wounded in the blast, recalled hearing shots being fired over his head at him and his fellow Marines after the bomb went off. A Marine sniper told us he had watched the blast go off, climbed the guard tower, and heard rounds being fired at their position from the northeast. "I heard three distinct shots hit the back windows of the tower. The third round impacted right in front of my face as I was closing the ballistic glass window," he told us. "I put the gun out the window and was looking for the gunman. He was coming from the northeast building with a single door. There was also someone in the alleyway, smiling and taking pictures. We could not find the actual shooter." A Marine squad leader said, "The bomb went off. It was very obvious that it was AK fire happening. And they said it was the Taliban shooting warning shots, which is bullshit. You heard like a big volley of AK fire, and then you heard kind of suppression rounds being shot as we were running up to the gate."

Curtis said that a "leading theory" behind the idea that there had been a complex attack was the lower extremity wounds on some of the victims.[84] A blast analysis graphic showed that the lowest frag mark on the wall opposite the blast was just two feet below the ledge, indicating that the bomb had gone off up and out more than down.

Medical staff at several hospitals in Kabul said that some victims of the attack had had bullet wounds.

Marines on the ground also saw a likely ISIS-K terrorist filming the attack from a water tower, and the Marines discussed a mysterious "man in the hat" who had appeared to be doing reconnaissance before and after the ISIS-K bombing, some Marines snapping photos of him, then shooting above his head to scare him off after the blast.

When the State Department in February 2022 announced $10 million in rewards for finding Muhajir and those responsible for the ISIS-K bombing, it initially stated, "A suicide bomber and gunmen attacked the airport." The website now states, "A suicide bomber attacked the airport" and makes no mention of gunmen. The prior claim of a complex attack was quickly scrubbed from the website.

WOULD NOT EXPECT A NAME TO BE RELEASED

The Biden administration announced in April 2023 that the Taliban had killed an ISIS-K member whom "we assess was most responsible for the August 26 bombing at Abbey Gate." In a now-familiar pattern, the Pentagon and White House refused to actually name the alleged mastermind, with a defense official saying that "I would not expect a name to be released" as he also doubled down on still not naming Logari as well. The official made it clear that dealing with the ISIS-K problem had been farmed out to the Taliban, saying that the U.S. "did not provide any assistance to the Taliban" and calling it "purely a Taliban operation." Family members of the thirteen told us the military also refused to provide them with the name of the alleged ISIS-K bombing planner. Darin Hoover, the father of Marine Corps Staff Sgt. Darin Taylor Hoover, warned that the Biden administration was attempting to take an undeserved "victory lap" and said the news did not change the need for "accountability" over the Biden's mishandling of the withdrawal.[85]

ELEVEN

A PUNCH IN THE GUT

A s dusk turned to darkness on the twenty-sixth of August, an eerie stillness hung over Abbey Gate. Bloodstains were prominent on the walls and pavement of the inner gate. Bodies and severed limbs floated in the sewage water in the canal below. The canal was mostly empty, save for a handful of Afghans wading through the carnage in search of family members. For the first time since the Marines had arrived, the area was silent.

Marines from 2/1's Echo and Weapons companies relieved Ghost Company immediately after the attack and continued to guard the now-shuttered gate. At 2:00 a.m. on the twenty-seventh, paratroopers from the 82nd Airborne's 5th Battalion, 201st Parachute Infantry Regiment arrived at the gate to take over for the hurting Marines. As the sun began to rise a few minutes after 5:00 a.m., the paratroopers were fully in charge of the gate, and the Marines rotated off shift for the final time.

During the relief in place from 1:00 to 7:00 a.m., soldiers from the United Kingdom's 1st and 2nd Parachute Battalions retrograded their troops and remaining evacuees through the gate. While the final UK personnel were crossing the threshold of Abbey Gate, the nineteen US service members who had been seriously wounded in the bombing were being loaded onto a C-17 bound for Landstuhl Regional Medical Center in Germany.

Abbey Gate was now closed for good and would soon be sealed off forever, as far as US forces were concerned, but limited evacuations continued through the airfield's remaining entrances. In midmorning on August 27, Ukrainian special operations forces maneuvered outside the wire to rescue two minibuses of Afghan evacuees who were surrounded by an unruly crowd and unable to make it to the gates. The nineteen evacuees, bound for Canada, included a former interpreter for the Canadian special forces and his family and an interpreter who had worked for the Toronto *Globe and Mail*.[1] Video of the operation shows Ukrainian forces approaching the crowd while shouting and firing volleys of automatic weapons fire just over their heads.[2] At first the crowd moved only a little, attempting to gauge the Ukrainians' level of commitment. When it became clear that the troops weren't messing around, the crowd parted just enough for the minibuses to surge forward and resume movement toward the gates. The Ukrainian forces escorted them the rest of the way in.

THE MOST SACRED GOODBYE

"Ramp ceremonies" are among the most intimate and sacred events of military life. Photos and videos are forbidden, but that standing order almost never needs to be emphasized. The event is not about the attendees or their observations; its sole purpose is to provide a final salute, a deeply felt recognition of the sacrifice of the fallen that words alone cannot quite capture. A military transport plane, its cargo bay empty, awaits on the tarmac. Every serviceman and -woman not on duty stands in a file on each side, creating a corridor for the fallen hero's last journey on foreign soil. A military vehicle approaches, the troops in attendance stand at attention, and an honor guard—frequently staffed by close friends of the fallen—lifts the casket from the vehicle and turns toward the plane. The men and women on each side of the corridor render a final salute as the six members of the honor guard carry the deceased to an aircraft destined for Dover Air Force Base. The unit chaplain prays over the casket, the ramp of the aircraft closes, and everyone in attendance spends a few moments alone with their thoughts and emotions.

And then they return to their mission because they have no other choice.

In form, the ramp ceremony on 1:00 p.m. on August 27 at HKIA was no different. Even in a chaotic, makeshift environment like the one at HKIA in August 2021, every available resource, every spare moment was dedicated to honoring the sacrifice of the fallen and providing a final measure of respect from those who had been privileged enough to serve alongside them. Still, the symbolism of the event hit home for everyone present, veterans of previous deployments in particular. Five of the troops were only twenty years old when they were killed in action. Three were twenty-two, three were twenty-three, one was twenty-five, and only one was in his thirties. The oldest among them had been in elementary school on 9/11. Yet they had all met their fates in Afghanistan, almost exactly twenty years after the attacks on their homeland.

A thousand troops flanked the runway as the thirteen began their journey home. Their close friends and platoonmates served as pallbearers, gently carrying them onto the plane one at a time. At one point, one of the pallbearers doubled over in grief, his hand on the casket. The waiting C-17 was crewed by the men of Reach 824, who had inserted special operators onto the airfield in a blind landing at the beginning of the evacuation, just over ten days before. The juxtaposition was heartbreaking. One of the crew members stated, "When I strapped those 13 cases down to the floor of my jet, I learned what it was to cry."[3] The crew had spent the first week and a half of the evacuation saving lives; now they would be taking home Americans who had been killed in service of that effort.

The Marines from 2/1 who remained were hurting, angry, and desperate for any opportunity to settle the score. But for the rest of the twenty-seventh, they had nowhere to channel their frustration and grief. One of the squad leaders recounted, "I remember sitting on the runway and just kinda talking to the boys, and we were all like 'I hope [the commander] comes out and says "Let's go." We're on a patrol, we're doing something.' We were ready for it, but it never happened." When they got the "slightest bit of intel that something would happen," he added, "guys were jumping, gnawing at the bit to go." A Marine from the same unit said, "It's just shitty to have that happen and then not to be able to do something about it. We're always taught if you get punched in the mouth, then you turn around and punch them back. But with this mission you couldn't really do that. You just had to eat it. . . . It was kind of shitty having to just sit there and take it like that." With nothing constructive to do, each tried to find his or her own way to cope. Some Marines went to the now-shuttered chow hall and cooked their own food. Others found a cooler of ice cream in the facility and brought tubs back to the rest of their units.

Eventually, battalion leadership ordered Ghost Company to accomplish pro forma tasks at the passenger terminal to try to keep their minds off the horror of the previous day.

THE FIGHT CONTINUES

The pace of evacuations may have slowed after the bombing, but the threats to the airfield persisted. In the late afternoon of the twenty-seventh, a platoon from Alpha Company, 2/504 was manning a sector on the southern perimeter of the airfield, halfway between the now-shuttered Abbey Gate and the Taliban-controlled South Gate. For all its troubles and vices, Afghanistan has some breathtaking terrain, and several of the men were taking pictures of the sunset over the mountains to the west.

Radio traffic from the SAW gunner in the guard tower quickly interrupted the rare moment of tranquillity: a squad-sized element of men with AK-47s was "trying to breach the fence line in vicinity of the UN Building." "UN Building" was how the platoon referred to a warehouse that had been used by the United Nations until Kabul had abruptly became inhospitable to diplomatic activities. The building was low, wide, and close to the fence, creating several dozen yards of "dead space" that the paratroopers were unable to view from their command post.

Several paratroopers piled into the hot-wired Toyota Hilux pickup truck they used to traverse the airfield and peeled out toward the gate. They approached the building from an angle to get a view of the fence behind it. Even from a distance, it was clear that the report from the tower was accurate; the intruders had leaned a ladder against the fence and had cut through the razor wire on top. As they closed the gap, the troops watched the Taliban fighters break the bolt on the interior gate and swiftly move in the opposite direction, using the warehouse for cover. The Talibs apparently failed to realize that doing so would place them directly in the observation tower's fields of fire.

The troops in the Hilux quickly changed course to meet the enemy on the other side, where they would have overlapping fields of fire with the guard tower. But things quickly hit a snag—literally. The early-2000s-era truck got tangled in an old string of concertina wire half submerged in the earth, leaving the paratroopers completely exposed halfway between their command post and the handful of armed Taliban fighters rounding the corner of the UN Building. They dismounted and attempted to close the hundred-yard gap on foot, while the SAW gunner in the tower pulled overwatch. By then, the Taliban had taken cover and dialed in.

The Americans quickly hit the dirt, and rounds flew overhead in both directions. In a pure ground fight, it would have been "advantage Taliban." They were shooting from covered positions, and the 82nd was caught in the open. Fortunately, it wasn't a pure ground fight. The SAW gunner in the tower opened up with a sustained burst of automatic fire, emptying his belt just feet above the Taliban fighters' heads. As soon as the tower went quiet, the squad of Talibs bolted back toward the gate.

The entire firefight lasted little more than thirty seconds, but there was no doubt that both sides had acted with hostile intent. The Alpha Company paratroopers were proud that they'd finally had an opportunity, however brief, to assert their agency against the Taliban. At the unit level, no one doubted that the men had done the right thing—a squad-sized element of men with AKs, moving tactically, had breached the airfield. They had been fired upon and returned in kind. Case closed. One of Alpha's medics remarked that the incident "wasn't a huge surprise," because the Taliban "had been poking around the whole time we were there." The company- and battalion-level leadership of 2/504 agreed; there was nothing offensive or improper about US soldiers defending themselves, especially on their own air base.

When reports of the incident made their way past the battalion level, however, attitudes changed. Officers and senior enlisted advisers at both the brigade and division levels harshly reprimanded the non-commissioned officers who had spearheaded the response. According to one of the NCOs who was dressed down, the senior-level leaders "were basically like 'Hey, the Taliban are our friends for right now.'" After a moment, he sarcastically added, "Wild times over there, trying to morally deal with that proposition."

"WE BASICALLY BROKE EVERYTHING WE COULD"

As a basic principle of military doctrine, units that are forced to abandon their positions destroy any abandoned equipment that might be useful to the enemy forces taking it over. The evacuation from HKIA was no different. The airport contained millions of rounds of ammunition, an untold number of weapons, countless military vehicles and aircraft, and all kinds of classified devices that couldn't be allowed to fall into the Taliban's possession.[4] As US forces prepared to withdraw on the twenty-eighth, the customary "demilitarization" order went out. Each unit was tasked with "demilitarizing" vehicles and all other useful equipment within various sectors of HKIA. The communications teams "ensured that computer systems were corrupted or destroyed," and the engineer units "dug trenches to cover [other sensitive] equipment with cement and bury it."[5]

When the directive to break things came down on the morning of the twenty-eighth, the Marines of 2/1 were more than ready. They grabbed hammers from a tool shed and fulfilled the order in its most literal sense. They bashed every bit of sensitive equipment in sight and quite a few windows to boot. One of the company commanders took the unit guidon (a guidon, for lack of a better description, is a flag on a staff with a pointy end that can be embedded in the turf when a unit stands in formation) and threw it like a spear through a flat-screen TV. A junior Marine involved described it—understandably—as a good release after the hell they'd encountered the previous two weeks.

The following day, the Marines doubled down on their efforts. A noncommissioned officer recounted, "We basically broke everything we could. We flipped cars into the roads and all kinds of shit." The Marines were hardly alone in that regard. In a briefing room previously used for mission planning, 82nd Airborne paratroopers scrawled a message on the whiteboard: "SUCK A DICK TALIBAN."

The destruction made sense to the soldiers and Marines on the ground—why should they leave the area and its amenities pristine for the Taliban? Senior leaders, however, found it positively distasteful. For example, Army Sergeant Major Garric Banfield complained that "penises were spray painted all over the place" by the Marines. He added, "Leadership, myself included, had spoken about how it was in American interest in leaving the airport functional" and that the Marines and paratroopers had failed to "[respect the] equipment on the ground."[6] He reported those concerns to higher headquarters.

THE FINAL INDIGNITY

In the early afternoon of the twenty-eighth, Ghost Company prepared to redeploy from Kabul. Its first stop would be Camp Buehring, Kuwait. The night before, military forces from Ukraine, Japan, Italy, Turkey, France, and every NATO country besides the United Kingdom had departed Kabul. The Norwegians, who were helping to man the hospital, insisted upon staying.

Before leaving, the Marines of 1st Platoon gathered for a final platoon photo in the country. That platoon had been on the wall when Abdul Rahman al-Logari had triggered his suicide vest, and they'd borne the brunt of the ensuing casualties. They had arrived at HKIA with forty-two Marines; their final photo contained only twenty.[7] The rest had been killed or wounded in action. A corporal in the platoon had been injured during training exercises in Jordan and told that he was ineligible to deploy with everyone else. As a result, he had been forced to observe the horrific events from afar. Now, as Ghost packed up, company leadership took pains to ensure that he would be flown from Jordan to Kuwait to be reunited with his brothers in arms once they landed.[8]

The remaining 2/1 units weren't supposed to be far behind Ghost Company. A few hours after Ghost went wheels up, Echo Company staged on a road just off the flight line, waiting their turn for an aircraft. Some Marines took final pictures with one another or chain-smoked cigarettes to pass the time; others leaned back against their equipment and dozed off to the extent possible. In the two days since the bombing, the airfield had been deluged with reports about the possibility of ISIS fighters disguising themselves among the crowds of evacuees and bringing suicide bombs on board evacuation flights. Commanders at the airfield had already been forced numerous times to evacuate planes and search every military-aged male on board.

Just after sundown, another false alarm came across the net. A C-17 preparing to take off had suddenly reversed course and returned down the runway. Once again, there was a credible threat that a suicide bomber had made it on board. Squad leaders kicked their guys awake, riflemen checked that they had rounds in the chamber, and commanders gave clipped instructions to subordinate leaders. Vehicles from other units on standby flew past at breakneck speeds. Rumors swirled that ten or more Taliban fighters had jumped the fence. Given the choice, that would have been the fight the Marines preferred: one final chance for retribution on behalf of their fallen. When we asked a junior Marine who had been present to describe the atmosphere, he responded, "The guys in my company were all like 'Let's go. Fuck these guys.'" But there were no fence jumpers to fight, only a plane that reportedly had a human bomb on board.

The remaining Marines from 2/1 hustled to the runway and took positions overwatching the plane from a few hundred yards away in case it blew. According to one of the Marines present, "We're thinking 'Here we go, this is round two. This guy's going to blow up, and then we're going to run down there to pick up body parts.'" The report about a suicide bomber turned out to be inaccurate. The passengers were hustled off the aircraft, and all the males were segregated to one side, where they were slowly cleared by explosive ordnance disposal (EOD) personnel. One at a time, they approached the techs from a relatively safe distance and raised their shirts (or, if they were wearing traditional Afghan garb, pulled their flowing tunics tight against their bodies). Once he showed no obvious signs of carrying a suicide vest or other weapons, each male moved forward for a more thorough pat down. At the same time, other EOD techs swept the plane for explosive devices. After some hours of tension, the search teams issued an all clear, the evacuees reboarded, and the plane departed.

Immediately after they received the all clear, the Marines left on the ground received "the biggest 'Fuck you' ever": they were ordered to police call the passenger terminal that had previously held all of the evacuees. In military jargon, to police call an area means to stand shoulder to shoulder and walk through it, picking up every stray piece of trash or debris in your path. Military units commonly police call training areas, parade grounds, and other areas they occupy in the civilized world. Police calling a section of turf in a war zone is unheard of.

Nevertheless, the order from on high was that the men and women of 2/1's final task at HKIA—after seeing thirteen fellow service members killed in action and dozens of others wounded in a suicide bombing—was to clean up the trash and human feces in the passenger terminal before it was transferred to the Taliban's control. The passenger terminal had housed close to a hundred thousand Afghan refugees in the previous week and a half, most of whom had defecated and urinated in place for lack of other options and discarded their trash, clothing, and other items wherever necessary. When we asked what the terminal had looked like, a junior Marine involved in the cleanup sarcastically replied, "It wasn't exactly clean." The Marines were also ordered to unflip all of the vehicles they had flipped over the previous day.

The Marines of 2/1 were certain that the order had come from higher headquarters because their battalion commander, Lieutenant Colonel Brad Whited, joined them in the cleanup effort and was as visibly displeased as they were. Marines at every level of the company were infuriated by the order, and the story has spread far beyond the units involved. (For example, during a conversation unrelated to this book, a Marine reserve officer asked one of us if we'd heard about the Marines at HKIA who had been "forced to scoop up human poop.")

The junior Marines' suspicions that the order had come from a higher level are corroborated by interviews published as part of the Army's investigation of the evacuation. When Army investigators asked 2/1's command sergeant major if he had anything to add at the end of his interview during the investigation into the Abbey Gate bombing, the senior enlisted leader independently raised the police call order as an injustice that had been imposed on his Marines. The order to clean the passenger terminal, he said, "came with a threat that we would not leave at all if it was not completed." More than 120,000 Afghans had camped in the area, "defecating and leaving trash, bags, clothes, and other unspeakable things." The twenty-two-year Marine simply couldn't fathom that the order was real. He said he had approached senior staff at the JOC to ask "if this was [a] serious" order. Once he had learned that the directive wasn't a terrible practical joke, he had looked for brooms and rubber gloves from remaining supplies on the airfield and led by example. "It was degrading and ridiculous. We took a lot of casualties and put a lot of effort into that mission and to close it out that way was wrong. Morale was really down at that point, and it was an extremely pointless effort."[9]

After cleaning up piles of trash, feces, and half-eaten food to prepare for the Taliban's arrival, the remaining Marines from 2/1 finally left the country a few minutes after midnight on the twenty-ninth.

A "RIGHTEOUS STRIKE"

Desperate to regain some semblance of credibility, the Biden administration quickly authorized a strike on an "ISIS planner," who later turned out to be Zemari Ahmadi, an Afghan civilian father of six kids who worked for an NGO and had assisted US troops. The strike, which occurred at 4:53 p.m. on August 29, in Kabul, killed ten civilians, including seven children. No one was punished or fired for the deadly mistake.

The Defense Department's top leaders acknowledged that they had known within hours that the air strike in Kabul had killed innocent civilians, but they falsely claimed that CENTCOM had quickly admitted to the deadly error. On September 1, General Milley described the operation as a "righteous strike."[10] In late September 2021, Defense Secretary Lloyd Austin and General McKenzie testified before the House Armed Services Committee. Austin said he had learned that civilians had been killed "several hours" after the strike when it had been reported to him by McKenzie.[11] Milley said it had been the "same thing" for him, adding "We knew that civilians were killed, we knew that noncombatants, and there was collateral damage."[12] McKenzie claimed, "We knew the strike hit civilians within four or five hours after the strike occurred, and U.S. Central Command released a press release saying that. We did not know, though, that the target of the strike was in fact in error, a mistake, until sometime later."[13] He was, at best, misinformed—CENTCOM had never issued a press release confirming that the air strike had hit civilians.

In the "period of darkness" between August 29 and August 30, the remaining State Department consular officers left the country.[14]

LEFT BEHIND

August 30 was largely characterized by US forces' last-ditch efforts to destroy the remaining batches of equipment and produce manifests for the final flights out of the country. In the late morning, a desperate American family showed up at the gates and managed to catch the attention of American guards, who dragged them through at the eleventh hour. Thousands of other Americans weren't so fortunate.

At 12:37 p.m., ISIS forces fired five rockets at the airfield. Some were shot down by the last two counterrocket systems at HKIA (known as C-RAMs). Fortunately, the ratio of US troops to HKIA landmass was now relatively small, and no one was injured by the others. At 8:00 p.m., US troops began the process of disabling those last two C-RAMs. The process was lengthy, and the US forces weren't scheduled to leave the airfield for another four hours. The timeline left the airfield vulnerable to rocket attacks without any prior notice or air defense as the final flights departed.

Any such attacks could potentially have disabled the runways and made C-17 departures impossible, but it was a necessary risk to take. Otherwise, US troops not only would have left sensitive antirocket defenses in the hands of the Taliban—a group that is famously fond of rocket attacks—but also risked letting US antirocket technology end up in the hands of Iran or foreign terrorist organizations eager to attack Americans stationed elsewhere in the Middle East.

To mitigate the risk, 82nd Airborne Division commander Chris Donahue and his staff conducted a final meeting with Taliban leaders while the C-RAMs were being disabled. Donahue and company told the Taliban that US forces were planning a formal handover of airport authority to Taliban officials in the morning and that everything would be in good order. The Taliban bought the ruse hook, line, and sinker, even asking if US forces would be willing to conduct a photo op of the handover. Donahue assured them that they would. They continued the head fake until the final C-17 was literally headed down the runway; Donahue's interpreter continued to coordinate the "details" of the handover with Taliban contacts until the plane took off and he lost service.

The Taliban saw the final planes go wheels up and realized that they finally had the run of the country once again. As the C-17s disappeared into the horizon, Taliban celebratory fire—from US-made weapons—echoed in the background. Minutes later, senior Pentagon brass watching on radar as the last US flights exited Afghan airspace also celebrated. Krummrich described watching "these generals clapping and cheering" for themselves as "some kind of bizarro land." He added, "I mean, this is the biggest embarrassment of their career. This is failure. . . . We lost this thing, and I'm watching all of our generals sit there and pretend like we won the game."

TWELVE

THE AFTERMATH

On August 17, 2021, the State Department concluded that ten to fifteen thousand Americans remained in Afghanistan.[1] Many of them were still in the country because they trusted the State Department's assurances that the security situation was under control. When the final US military aircraft departed HKIA on August 30, only six thousand Americans had been evacuated.[2] In short, the government's own numbers demonstrate that the Biden administration abandoned at least four thousand—and perhaps as many as nine thousand—US citizens to the mercy of the Taliban. The betrayal was unprecedented in US history. For decades, a US passport was the most valuable document in the world; it signaled that its holder was protected by the unmatched might of the most powerful country on Earth. In full view of the global community, the Biden administration knowingly torched that precedent.

Worse yet, the administration knew that it was betraying its commitment to thousands of US citizens but employed an aggressive public relations campaign characterizing the evacuation as "successful" and "historic" anyway. Twenty-four hours after the final C-17 exited Afghan airspace, Biden declared the withdrawal to have been an "extraordinary success."[3] The same day, Blinken claimed that only one to two hundred Americans who wanted to leave remained in the country. The brass peddled the myth, too: on August 30, 2021, General McKenzie admitted, "We did not get everybody out that we had wanted to get out" but claimed that the number of Americans left behind was in the "very low hundreds."[4]

The political appointees at the Pentagon were no more forthcoming. Lloyd Austin likewise described the mission as a success on September 1.[5] He attempted to double down on that claim four weeks later during a September 28 hearing in front of the Senate Armed Services Committee but ran into a buzz saw of opposition from Senator Josh Hawley. Hawley took issue with Austin's assertion that Americans hadn't been abandoned: "'We are not leaving anyone behind.' That was your quote a minute ago. With all due respect, sir, you have *left*—past tense—Americans behind. There are hundreds of Americans—and not just Americans generally, *civilians*—you left behind. Against the president's explicit commitment not to leave until all Americans were out and to safety." Austin demurred, stating again, "As you've seen, we've continued to facilitate" Americans' evacuations. Hawley drilled down: "Isn't it true that you left Americans behind on August the thirty-first?" Austin was forced to concede the point, admitting, that, yes, "there are Americans that were left in Afghanistan and still are."[6] Nevertheless, the undersecretary of defense for policy, Colin Kahl, repeated the false narrative a month later, claiming that "nobody was abandoned" and bragged that the State Department had helped facilitate the departures of 240 US citizens and another 157 permanent residents since September 1.[7] He did not explain how those figures could be consistent with the administration's prior claim that only one to two hundred Americans remained in the country.

On November 10, 2021, Secretary of State Blinken took the administration's attempt to gaslight the American people to the next level. During a press conference with Qatar's deputy prime minister, he claimed that every American who had wished to leave Afghanistan had "been offered an opportunity to do so."[8] He also claimed that the administration had evacuated more than 380 US citizens and 240 permanent residents. Like other administration officials, he made no attempt to reconcile those numbers with his prior claim that there were only two hundred Americans remaining in the country. Numerical inconsistencies aside, a State Department official appointed by the administration flatly described Blinken's claim that every American had been given an opportunity to leave Afghanistan as "not true." The official added, "I knew of a number of American children who were still there at that time. There were families trying to get out of the country. Like, there were probably at least a dozen at that point. And I imagine there were many, many more."

A government official with firsthand knowledge recounted the harrowing ordeal endured by one of those families. He had attempted to evacuate a stranded American family of three from Indiana who had been unable to escape before the thirty-first. The father was an employee of the World Bank and had been working in Kabul when the government collapsed. They'd received precious little guidance from the US government during the chaotic evacuation and had been unable to navigate the crowds with their young son. They had been deep in the back of the crowd at Abbey Gate when the suicide attack had occurred and had avoided its effects only because they had been late to the airport. The family had spent weeks stuck in Taliban-controlled territory before World Bank employees contacted them with a "plan"—of sorts. The World Bank had spoken with Pakistani authorities and urged the Americans to hire a driver to ferry them nine hours from Kabul to the Pakistani border and simply present themselves at the border checkpoint.

It wasn't much of a plan, but the family believed that they had no other options. The father contacted the US official and told him, "Hey, look, the World Bank says that we can go, and I don't know what the American government is going to do for us, so we're going to go." The official didn't trust the Pakistani government's word or competence. He immediately reached out to embassy authorities in Islamabad and told them, "There's going to be an American family with a child showing up on the Pakistan border at this time and this location. Please help them." The official also provided the father's cell phone number and the family's passport information. When the family arrived, however, there was nobody waiting for them. The official's fears about the Pakistani government's lack of reliability had been confirmed, but unfortunately, the State Department had proven no more reliable. The family received "no support, no response from the embassy, nothing."

Now the family was stuck at a Taliban checkpoint, where their young son—already traumatized by the suicide bombing on August 26—had to "watch the Taliban beat the living shit out of five or six people." They weren't allowed through—and it's unclear that they'd even have been able to find their way to their destination in Pakistan if they had been admitted. They had no choice but to make the nine-hour trip back to Kabul. Several days later, the World Bank made a second attempt to facilitate the beleaguered family's evacuation. They braved the trip once again, and this time, World Bank officials made sure that someone was waiting for them. Successfully out of the country, the Americans finally linked up with the embassy in Islamabad. Still, they had to find the State Department instead of vice versa. The official bitterly noted, "There were no State Department officials in touch with that family at any point in time—it was just me as a private citizen doing it. And that's fucked up."

REALITY

Roughly two years later, the White House is still trying to evade accountability. Under any standard, the administration's "under two hundred" figure, even if true, would represent a historic failure. When else in modern history has the US government, the most powerful entity in the world, willfully abandoned hundreds of its citizens to the whims of a maniacal regime? Previous administrations dispatched teams of special operators to rescue just *one* American held hostage by terrorists.

In October 2020, for example, the Pentagon tapped SEAL Team Six to rescue a twenty-seven-year-old American citizen named Philip Walton from Nigeria just five days after he was abducted by Islamist militants.[9] A counterterrorism official stated at the time, "They were all dead before they knew what happened."[10]

Historical context aside, the Biden administration's claims in September 2021 were flat-out lies. The State Department's own public figures indicate that more than *nine hundred* American citizens and permanent residents were evacuated from Afghanistan from September 2021 to March 2022—a figure nearly five times as great as that provided by the White House.[11] The true scale of the Biden administration's betrayal of US citizens is far greater. Defense Department documents obtained through Freedom of Information Act requests prove that the administration knew that *thousands* of Americans were still stuck inside Afghanistan on August 30, 2021.[12] The administration has still not accounted for these vast discrepancies, even though lives are on the line.

Moreover, we reviewed spreadsheets listing more than 1,400 US citizens, legal permanent residents, and their family members who were independently evacuated by a clandestine operation run by former special forces and intelligence community operatives. We randomly selected dozens of individuals listed on the spreadsheet and successfully confirmed their identities and the nongovernmental nature of their evacuations. The records show that the clandestine network successfully evacuated 117 Americans from Afghanistan on its very first postwithdrawal evacuation flight. According to one of the leaders of the network, government officials approached them after their first successful flight. "They were like 'Oh, can you do that again?'"

ALLIES ABANDONED

Meanwhile, tens of thousands of former interpreters, local partners of US intelligence agencies, and US Embassy employees remain in hiding in Afghanistan. Many of them are still stranded in safe houses, unable to return to their homes and relying on the generosity of friends or even strangers for shelter and their next meal. Others depend on family or tribal relations to keep them safe for the time being, while living with the knowledge that their luck could run out at any moment. Even under the most optimistic scenarios, many of them will never leave the country, much less reach US shores as promised. In August 2022, the Association of Wartime Allies estimated that "81,000 SIV applicants in Afghanistan had visa applications pending as of August 15, 2021 (the day Kabul fell) and that at least 78,000" of them—or 96 percent—had been left behind.[13]

The Taliban continues to hunt them down, one by one. Masoud Andarabi, a former general in Afghanistan's internal security service (the National Defense Service, or NDS) and Afghanistan's minister of the interior until March 2021, told us that the Chinese government is helping the Taliban track interpreters by providing cell phone location data on a broad scale through call detail records, or CDRs, and also on the tactical level by providing mobile direction-finding devices that allow Taliban fighters to connect to a specific cell phone tower and home in on the locations of targeted cell phones covered by that tower. Notably, Afghanistan's primary cellular company, Roshan, has used Huawei as its primary network provider since 2012. The United States and nearly every member of the European Union banned Huawei from expanding its operations within their borders after Western intelligence agencies determined that the Chinese company was essentially a proxy for the Chinese Communist Party (CCP).

According to several active and former US intelligence officials, China's primary motivation for assisting the Taliban is to secure the group's cooperation in crushing Uighur militant groups in the northeastern Afghan province of Badakshan, which borders the Xinjiang region of China. (Xinjiang, of course, is ground zero for the CCP's ongoing genocide of Uighurs.) The CCP's secondary interest, however, is to gain access to Afghanistan's wealth of untapped mineral resources. In either case, the result is the same: loyal Afghan allies are being methodically eliminated every day, with assistance from the Chinese government.

KEEPING THE PROMISE

The Biden administration packed up shop and hoped the world would move on, but the veterans and retired national security operatives who plugged the gap in August 2021 had other ideas. Several of the ad hoc evacuation networks formed out of necessity in mid-August formalized into professional organizations in early September. They shared a single goal: to rescue the men and women the Biden administration had callously left behind. But first they needed money. With no US airport left and the Taliban firmly in control of all societal institutions, future evacuations would require creativity. And in a country with an ancient legacy of corruption, creativity can get expensive.

The groups' long-term plan was to raise capital through private donations, and many have done so successfully. Their fundraising goals might be realized in less than a year in the best of circumstances, but Americans and Afghan allies were in danger *now*. They were scattered across safe houses or sheltering behind blackout curtains in the back rooms of friends' houses, shuddering at every knock on the door. Donations a few months in the future wouldn't cut it, so many of the founders emptied their 401(k)s and savings accounts to bridge the gap. The leaders of one such group, the Human First Coalition, pooled their retirement funds to provide $6 million to get their efforts off the ground. The efforts of these groups have been buttressed by discreet, targeted operations funded by independently wealthy individuals—including a number of well-known Wall Street executives—who prefer to keep their involvement out of the spotlight. Collectively, these private citizens are doing the job that the Biden administration should do but won't. We will not go into granular detail about these operations because they are still ongoing, but suffice it to say that their methods have been effective and have saved the lives of thousands of people.

In an ironic twist, one of those people was Aman Khalili. In 2008, Khalili was an interpreter assigned to the Arizona National Guard's 1st Battalion, 158th Infantry Regiment in Kapisa province in northeastern Afghanistan. For the previous eleven months, he had eaten with them, slept next to them, and survived more than a hundred firefights in the Hindu Kush mountains alongside them.[14] The assignment had often kept him away from his family for six or seven months at a time. The men considered him one of their own and even gave him a weapon—despite Army regulations prohibiting units from arming their interpreters—so he could fight alongside them when things got hairy.[15] By then, Khalili had worked for the military for six and a half years. Just weeks after US troops seized Bagram Air Base in the 2001 invasion, he had showed up at the front gates and told the soldiers guarding the entrance, "I can help you."[16]

On February 21, 2008, Khalili and the soldiers he served alongside were at Bagram for some long-overdue rest. Their R and R didn't last long. Two Black Hawk helicopters carrying senators Joe Biden, John Kerry, and Chuck Hagel had found themselves in the middle of a blizzard and were forced to conduct an emergency landing in a valley some twenty miles southeast of Bagram. The handful of soldiers and military contractors providing the senators' security detail quickly formed a perimeter and radioed for an emergency ground evacuation force to extract the VIPs.

Khalili didn't hesitate to answer the call. He joined a quick reaction force of several Army vehicles and armored SUVs manned by security contractors and helped guide the convoy through the mountains for several hours in whiteout conditions to rescue Biden and the other senators. After successfully linking up with the downed aircraft in the mountains of Parwan province, the force escorted the VIPs to safety. But the US aircraft and their crews were still on the ground, protected in part by local Afghan forces, and a crowd of local villagers had coalesced around the aircraft. The situation called for an interpreter. Khalili stayed put. He endured freezing temperatures alongside the US soldiers for more than thirty hours and frequently used a bullhorn to warn the crowd to keep its distance. He didn't have to be there—he wasn't assigned to the aviation unit flying the aircraft or the paratroopers guarding them—but he stayed anyway. And he did it all because an Army unit giving Joe Biden and two other senators a tour of the battlefield had found itself in desperate conditions.

Khalili retired from his interpreter position in late 2014, after assisting thousands of US troops for thirteen years. Almost seven years later, his visa application was still in limbo as Kabul collapsed. Like so many others, he was trapped. He knew that Biden remembered the incident; it had been a staple of his stump speeches in 2008 and 2012. In fact, just seven months after the incident, Biden had bragged to a group of national guardsmen, "If you want to know where bin Laden is, come back to Afghanistan with me. Come back to the area where my helicopter was forced down."[17] Based on Biden's frequent retellings of the incident, Khalili couldn't fathom that the man who was now president of the United States, the most powerful man in the world, would leave his family high and dry at the mercy of the Taliban—the same Taliban that he'd rescued Biden from all those years before.

In an interview with the *Wall Street Journal*, he publicly begged Biden, "Save me and my family. Don't forget me here."[18] The Biden administration, however, did just that.

THE STATE DEPARTMENT CONTINUES TO "PUT EVERYBODY'S LIFE IN DANGER"

Biden may have willfully forgotten Aman Khalili, but the men who served with him didn't. Using networks on the ground developed over more than a decade of service, they linked up with Khalili and his family at an Afghan safe house in a province that will remain undisclosed to protect some of the participants who remain in the country. They spent the next thirty hours transporting the family across the country in a circuitous route to avoid Taliban checkpoints, using a variety of tactics to keep them out of sight of villagers who might be tempted to curry favor with the Taliban by reporting American sympathizers attempting to flee. Khalili's identity was so sensitive—and his capture so valuable to the Taliban's propaganda efforts—that the locals facilitating his transfer were given a false name and backstory for him. A leak would be fatal, in the most literal sense.

For the same reasons, the collective of former national security operatives purposely avoided telling the US government about the evacuation until Khalili was safely out of the country. The motives of the State Department staffers handling the cases of stranded Americans and SIVs were more noble than those of the Taliban fighters searching for them, but the bureaucrats were no more reliable at keeping secrets. The former operatives informed Foggy Bottom about the operation only after Khalili was stashed at a farmhouse outside Islamabad, Pakistan, that the group used as a way station on their evacuation route. Even then, their fears were immediately vindicated.

The group had already arranged to fly the Khalili family and other evacuees from the safe house to a safe third country. They hadn't spent weeks coordinating every step of the evacuation in intricate detail just to wing it at the final hour. After making those preparations, they informed senior State Department officials that Khalili had been safely extracted from Afghanistan, was being housed in a secure location in Pakistan, and would be smuggled out in a few days alongside a hundred other evacuees. All they asked was that the State Department be prepared to receive the evacuees in the identified third country. According to one of the operatives involved, the State Department enthusiastically responded to the overture, asked for further details, and promised to support the effort "in any way possible." State Officials also specifically asked for Khalili's location, which the group reluctantly provided.

The State Department did not support the group's efforts, however; it tried to coopt them. It interrupted the process with the grace of the Kool-Aid Man bursting through the wall of a suburban home. The

Biden administration had been hammered about its failure to rescue stranded Americans and Afghan allies, and Khalili's story had been particularly damaging due to his connection to the president. State Department officials leaped at the opportunity to snatch the baton at the end of the race and carry it across the finish line for all to see. But in typical fashion, they never considered the secondary effects of their politically motivated actions.

Without warning, Deputy Secretary of State Wendy Sherman contacted the Pakistani government and informed it about the situation. She provided the location of the safe house and requested permission to send a State Department convoy to retrieve Khalili and his family from it. She also informed the Pakistanis that State planned to immediately fly the Khalilis to safety in Qatar. The group of former operatives protested that the government's plan "was not part of the deal," but there was little they could do about it. Shortly thereafter, several black State Department SUVs with diplomatic license plates rolled up to the farmhouse in a cloud of dust and escorted Khalili and his family—and only them—into the vehicles. They departed within minutes, leaving the remaining evacuees behind.

The incident demoralized the remaining evacuees in the safe house. Worse, it exposed them—and the Americans working to rescue them— to attacks from Islamic militants in the region. According to one of the operatives on the ground, the administration's self-serving antics "brought so much attention to our operation there" and "put everybody's life in danger."

A few days later, the Biden administration announced Khalili's evacuation and took credit for bringing his family to safety.[19] The State Department released a statement that the Khalili family had "safely departed Afghanistan and subsequently initiated onward travel from Pakistan" and "did so with extensive and high-level engagement and support from the US Government." The statement concluded, "We are grateful for the many others who also supported him along the way."[20]

"WE TRAINED SOME GREAT PRIVATE MILITARY CONTRACTORS"

For each success story like Ahmad Khalili's, there are several others of abandonment and desperation. For former Afghan commandos trained by US special operations and NDS operatives trained by the CIA and DIA, that abandonment comes with tempting opportunities. Most of them speak passable, if not fluent, English, and they have years of hands-on training by the United States' best operatives. At a minimum, those credentials make them attractive to wealthy contractors and other groups across the Middle East, many of whom are willing to pay a premium for their services. Scores of Afghan commandos—mid- to senior-level officers in particular—saw the train wreck to come and decided to cash in before the government collapsed and passage out of the country became more unreliable.

In the months following Biden's withdrawal announcement, scores of highly trained Afghan commandos accepted job offers from security contractors in wealthy Gulf countries and promptly abandoned their homeland before the battle had run its course. Most ended up in Dubai. An active member of the House Intelligence and Special Operations Committee with direct knowledge of the status of several dozen former Afghan commandos sarcastically told us, "Hey, at least we trained some great private military contractors over there." After Kabul fell, the incentives only intensified. For enlisted commandos concerned foremost about their bottom line, the choice was easy: they could stay in Afghanistan under Taliban rule and eke out a few dollars a day working manual labor jobs (assuming that they weren't executed first), or they could earn many times as much practicing their craft in other countries.

The demand for skilled and knowledgeable Afghan operatives isn't limited to private clients, however. The biggest player on the market is the Islamic Republic of Iran. Iran has a natural advantage in the bidding war: it shares a 582-mile-long border with Afghanistan, and tens of thousands of Afghans have already migrated there to escape Taliban rule. The Islamic Revolutionary Guard Corps (IRGC) could hardly have asked for a better recruiting scenario. Hundreds of former commandos and NDS officials stranded in Afghanistan had front-row seats to the US military and intelligence community's capabilities and their approach to sensitive operations. They possess a wealth of information about US forces' technical capabilities, mission planning protocols, and training and recruitment operations for host nation forces. More than a half-dozen sources, ranging from former Afghan officials to current and former US intelligence officials, independently told us that Iran has conducted extensive debriefing of those men and their families. Many of the debriefing "requests" were accompanied by offers of visas for the targeted Afghans and their families. Numerous US sources provided direct evidence of interactions between Afghan commandos and IRGC officials, including pictures from Iranian social media networks showing former senior Afghan commandos and their family members in Iran alongside known members of the IRGC.

FAILURE TO VET

Operation Allies Refuge, the initial US military operation to airlift US diplomats as well as SIV applicants and other Afghan allies out of Afghanistan, quickly morphed into Operation Allies Welcome, the US government's effort to resettle tens of thousands of Afghans in the United States, whether they had been our allies or not. Unsurprisingly, this has created significant security issues, much of which have escaped public notice.

Only weeks after the withdrawal, media outlets reported that several unvetted, military-age males had committed crimes of sexual violence against children, other refugees, and female service members *after* arriving at US military bases. In September 2021, two Afghan evacuees housed at Fort McCoy, Wisconsin, were accused of brutal crimes. According to the Department of Justice, twenty-year-old Bahrullah Noori was charged with "attempting to engage in a sexual act with a minor using force" and "three counts of engaging in a sexual act with a minor, with one count alleging the use of force."[21] The DOJ press release was sparing in its details, but the charging documents were not: Noori had allegedly sexually assaulted another evacuee's twelve-year-old son and fourteen-year-old nephew in a bathroom on the military installation.[22] In a separate case stemming from Fort McCoy, thirty-two-year-old Mohammad Haroon Imaad was charged with strangling and suffocating his wife.[23]

Those incidents were only the tip of the iceberg. An Afghan refugee staying at a refugee camp in Quantico, Virginia, twenty-four-year-old Mohammed Tariq, was convicted of sexually abusing a three-year-old girl. Four US Marines observed him forcibly kissing and sexually groping a three-year-old girl over her clothes as she attempted to push him away. Tariq defended his actions to police by saying that they were "part of his culture,"[24] and in April 2022 he was sentenced to just one year in prison—with credit for time served. Alif Jan Adil, another twenty-four-year-old Afghan refugee at Quantico, was charged with abusive sexual contact, coercion and enticement of a minor, and possession of child pornography for his attempts to force a fourteen-year-old Pashto-speaking female refugee to have sex with him in November 2021.[25]

At Camp Atterbury, Indiana, national guardsmen reported that male Afghan evacuees used pebbles to prop open the doors in women's barracks to access them at night. One of the military police logs, for example, noted that MPs "identified male Afghan evacuees in the women's barracks late at night, and the MPs successfully removed the men and issued them warnings."[26] Evacuees were also caught committing spousal and child abuse, assaults, thefts, prostitution, and other crimes, but no felony or misdemeanor charges have been brought, even though many of those incidents are recorded in military police logs.[27] Military personnel at Fort Pickett, Virginia, likewise caught several evacuees committing serious crimes, including vehicle theft and physical abuse.[28] Ominously, Fort Pickett security personnel reported that "there had been several instances of reported crimes, including knives stolen from the dining facility, weapons made from pipes, and nails found in an

Afghan evacuee's possession."[29] In response to those incidents, Army leadership requested additional security backup and by October 12, 2021, had been assigned twenty-eight Department of Homeland Security agents and twenty-one federal air marshals to "help mitigate the security risks." Still, no serious charges were ever filed, and misdemeanor offenses were not included in evacuees' State Department profiles. As a result, Fort Pickett personnel expressed concern that families who chose to sponsor Afghan evacuees and their families "would not have a full profile detailing incidents allegedly committed during an evacuee's time at Fort Pickett."[30]

Such incidents weren't limited to the military bases. As the unvetted evacuees moved into American neighborhoods, so did reports of sexual assault. In Las Cruces, New Mexico, Shah Mahmood Selab was charged with committing a sex crime against a twelve-year-old boy he had approached in a park. Similar assaults have occurred in Wausau, Wisconsin;[31] Brattleboro, Vermont;[32] and elsewhere.

We want to emphasize that we are not implying that most unvetted Afghan refugees pose a threat or engage in such behavior. Rather, these incidents underscore how little the Biden administration cared about who, precisely, it evacuated from Afghanistan. Furthermore, it was a grave injustice to give precious seat assignments to pedophiles and common criminals while leaving loyal interpreters behind.

THE TALIBAN CAME ALONG, TOO

Those weren't the only people who took seats from US citizens and SIV applicants. An American citizen of Tajik ancestry who served as the personal interpreter for a litany of commanding generals in Afghanistan and remained at HKIA until the final flight stated that he "know[s] for a fact some Taliban came in."[33] The interpreter, who asked to be described only as Gulam, personally intercepted two of them on the airfield on the US side of the South Gate—which, coincidentally, happened to be controlled by the Taliban.

The men had the distinctive long hair and untrimmed beards of Taliban fighters, and they were unaccompanied by any women and children. Gulam contacted the US commander in charge of the area, relayed his suspicions, and asked to interview the men. Upon questioning, the men were unable to produce visa paperwork, passports, or even Afghan national identity cards and were immediately ejected from HKIA. As the two would-be infiltrators walked off the airfield, the Taliban commander in charge of outer security for the gate called them by name. Both men then got into a Taliban truck and left the premises.[34]

But for every infiltrator identified by US forces, undoubtedly several more escaped detection. As of February 2022, the National Ground Intelligence Center (NGIC) had identified at least fifty Afghan military-age male evacuees—none of whom was an SIV applicant—who had been flagged as significant security risks by the Defense Department.[35] By August 2022, that number had risen to sixty-five. The NGIC identified them by matching their intake files with biometric data stored on Defense Department servers. The individuals identified by NGIC included men whose fingerprints had been found on IEDs defused by US troops. None had been flagged during the initial screening process because the administration had compared evacuee profiles only against U.S. Customs and Border Protection (CBP) databases. For obvious reasons, the databases did not include men who had spent their entire lives in Afghanistan. The US government is unable to account for the whereabouts of most of the evacuees flagged by the NGIC review.

CBP failed to collect biometric fingerprints from roughly 1,300 evacuees who entered the United States and frequently lacked elementary details such as evacuees' names, dates of birth, or identification numbers.[36] At least 417 evacuees' first names were listed as "unknown," and the last names of another 242 were likewise missing.[37] The records of another 11,110 evacuees listed their dates of birth as January 1.[38] Those discrepancies, of course, only reflect the universe of individuals that CBP actually vetted. The DHS report acknowledged that an untold number of evacuees had simply "traveled to the United States without undergoing established vetting processes."[39]

The DHS Inspector General also found that the department had not adequately or efficiently deployed its employees to US military installations in support of Operation Allies Welcome.[40] Personnel at four of the safe havens told the inspector general that DHS had not fulfilled requests for staff in most cases, including several leaders who said they had requested staff and received none.

Chillingly, the administration even imported an evacuee who had been "liberated from prison in Afghanistan by the Taliban" in August 2021. The evacuee cleared the screening and vetting processes at a third-country transit point and flew to the United States, where, despite derogatory information on him being identified by CBP officers during a primary inspection, a CBP supervisor "unreferred" him and let him into the United States.[41] The FBI didn't obtain the derogatory information on the evacuee until three weeks after he was let into the United States. U.S. Immigration and Customs Enforcement (ICE) then kicked him out of the country.

The Biden administration didn't learn from those failings, however. In the summer of 2022, the Department of Homeland Security and the State Department announced new exemptions for "vetted" applicants who would otherwise have been blocked from the United States—including some former members of the Taliban.[42] The exemptions included Afghans "who worked as civil servants under the Taliban" or "who provided only certain limited material support to the Taliban or other designated terrorist organizations."[43]

TALIBAN 2.0

The Biden administration repeatedly claimed throughout the summer of 2021 that soft-power considerations—a desire for "international legitimacy," for example—would keep the Taliban in line.[44] The months since the United States' withdrawal proved just how naive the administration's hopes were. By November 2021, widespread famine and starvation loomed over Afghanistan amid a broad economic collapse. Parents began selling their children into marriages just to afford food.[45] Murad Khan, a day laborer who sold his eight-year-old daughter for roughly $2,000, described the arrangement bluntly: "We are 10 people in the family. I'm trying to keep 10 alive by sacrificing one."[46] In some cases, fathers even sold their children without telling their mothers.[47]

However, even families fortunate enough to maintain their economic stability still faced the brutal reality of Taliban rule: revenge killings, religious oppression, and sharia law. Less than a month after US forces left, the Taliban announced that public floggings, amputations, and executions would return.[48] Next, the Taliban initiated a wave of religious persecution throughout the country. Fighters conducted numerous raids against Afghanistan's tiny Christian community[49] and the Hazaras, a Shiite Muslim minority that has long been persecuted in Afghanistan.[50] Finally, the Taliban initiated a comprehensive campaign to oppress women. The new regime began systematically jailing women across the country for petty or nonexistent offenses, such as appearing in public without male chaperones. Taliban leaders raped women and forced them into marriages.[51] In response, some women in Afghanistan created underground safe houses to help each other escape.[52]

On May 7, 2022, the Taliban decreed that women must wear head-to-toe clothing in public.[53] In November, it formally imposed sharia law on the country.[54] The next month, it officially banned all education for women across the country.[55] The order also forbade all local and foreign nongovernment organizations (NGOs) to use female staff in Afghanistan.

A month after the Taliban takeover, FBI director Christopher Wray testified that the US withdrawal could lead to an attack on the United States, including a homegrown terrorist attack inspired by the Taliban victory. Just such an attack occurred in Times Square on New Year's Eve 2022 when nineteen-year-old Trevor Bickford shouted "Allahu Akbar!" and attacked NYPD officers with a large kukri-style machete.

FUNDING THE TALIBAN

On August 18, three days after Kabul fell, State Department spokesman Ned Price confidently assured a gaggle of reporters that the Biden administration would "not give another cent to the Taliban, if the Taliban introduces Sharia law."[56] Like so many other administration claims regarding the Afghanistan evacuation and the subsequent Taliban takeover, Price's statement was either hopelessly naive or knowingly false. An October 2022 Special Inspector General for Afghan Reconstruction (SIGAR) report found that "the United States remains Afghanistan's single largest donor, having provided more than $1.1 billion in assistance" to Afghanistan since Kabul fell in August 2021.[57] Those funds are in addition to another $57 million in government funds that US agencies sent to the Afghan government almost immediately prior to the collapse. All of those are presumed to have fallen into Taliban hands.[58]

Those funds are only a drop in the bucket, compared to what the Biden administration has authorized. Last year, President Biden signed an executive order authorizing the systematic release of $3.5 billion in frozen Afghanistan central bank funds to "humanitarian groups" operating in the country.[59] Marshall Billingslea, who served as the assistant secretary for terrorist financing in the Treasury Department and tracked the Taliban's financial movements for years, told us that the Biden Treasury Department "has already issued a license to the UN and to nonprofit organizations that effectively authorizes the paying of bribes to the Taliban" pursuant to Biden's executive order. According to current and former government officials with direct knowledge of the situation, however, a sizable percentage—if not an outright majority—of those funds will be skimmed off by the Taliban. To paraphrase one national security official with more than twenty years of experience tracking terrorist-financing operations: nothing in Afghanistan today can move without the Taliban's say-so, and getting its approval means giving them a sizable cut of your funding.

AL-QAEDA AND ISIS ON THE REBOUND

ISIS-K continues to grow and conduct domestic attacks. Al-Qaeda has once again found the safe haven US forces sought to deny it two decades ago, and the terrorist Haqqani Network has been fully integrated into the governing apparatus of the Taliban regime. Their resurgence has no doubt been aided by the $7.12 billion worth of US aircraft, vehicles, weapons, munitions, and other equipment left in Afghan government inventories at the time of the Taliban takeover.[60] Sirajuddin Haqqani, the "deputy emir" of the Taliban, is designated as a terrorist by the US government, and there is a $10 million reward for his arrest. He is also a close al-Qaeda ally. Haqqani was named the Taliban's interior minister.

Despite the massive surrender of US equipment, the designated terrorists tapped for senior leadership in the Taliban regime, and the near-total absence of US intelligence resources on the ground to facilitate strikes anywhere outside Kabul, the Biden administration clung to its absurd claim that al Qaeda was not reconstituting its base of operations in Afghanistan. In May 2022, the Defense Intelligence Agency (DIA) director, Lieutenant General Scott Berrier, claimed that "Al Qaeda has had some problems with reconstituting leadership, and to a degree, the Taliban have held to their word about not allowing al Qaeda to rejuvenate."[61] There was no reason to believe that Berrier's claim was true. And as subsequent events demonstrated only weeks later, it wasn't.

Al-Qaeda's favored status under the new Taliban government was hardly a secret. The day US forces left Afghanistan, Osama bin Laden's personal bodyguard drove across the border from Pakistan and entered the country amid great fanfare. Less than a year after the Taliban took control, Ayman al-Zawahiri, Osama bin Laden's longtime deputy and the leader of al-Qaeda since 2011, was killed in a CIA drone strike in Kabul. He had been living in a residence that was once owned by USAID but is now controlled by none other than Sirajuddin Haqqani.

A senior Biden administration official said that senior Haqqani Taliban were aware that Zawahiri was in Kabul, and that Haqqani

Taliban members had taken quick action to try to conceal Zawahiri's presence in the safe house following the strike, including by restricting access to the house and the street for hours following the strike and by moving Zawahiri's wife, children, and grandchildren to another spot.[62]

Regarding ISIS-K, General Michael "Erik" Kurilla, the new commander of U.S. Central Command, estimated in March 2023 that ISIS-K could conduct "an external operation against U.S. or Western interests abroad in under six months, with little to no warning" and, although it would be "much harder" for the group to hit the U.S. homeland, he believed that was possible within six months too.[63]

SEE NO EVIL

The Biden White House has repeatedly attempted to gaslight the American people about the events of August 2021 and the injury, trauma, and loss of life that flowed from the administration's incompetence. SIGAR pointedly noted that Biden is the first president in the history of the war to refuse to cooperate with its inquiries. The IG accused the administration of "stonewalling" its investigation into the withdrawal—a refusal he described as "illegal"—and was particularly concerned with the administration's refusal to confirm that Americans' tax money was not flowing to the Taliban and the Haqqani Network. The administration's obstruction of the IG probe was only one aspect of a broader effort to suppress any discussion of its failure. Biden aides have likewise refused to comply with congressional investigations. The administration also attempted to create a new office within the Department of Homeland Security to police so-called misinformation on social media platforms. Lo and behold, one of the subjects targeted by the administration was "misinformation" about the US withdrawal from Afghanistan.[64] It rescinded the proposal in the wake of sustained public opposition.

The administration's suppression efforts appear to have extended even to the publication of individual merit awards given to troops for their service at HKIA. The military has traditionally publicized award ceremonies, especially when the awards are related to combat service. Curiously, that tradition has not applied to awards for heroism during the Afghanistan withdrawal—commendations issued by the Army and Navy, for example, can generally be found only on unit social media pages.[65] In keeping with this trend, the 82nd Airborne paratroopers who exchanged fire with Taliban fighters who breached the wire at HKIA on August 27 have never been awarded Combat Infantryman Badges (or Combat Action Badges, for the non-infantrymen). The exact reason for this omission is unclear, but a few paratroopers offered their informed speculation: Because those awards—like all military commendations—are accompanied by a factual narrative, issuing them would require the government to acknowledge, on paper, that American troops had engaged in a firefight with the supposedly cooperative Taliban.

"We have admitted and acknowledged that not everything about the withdrawal was done perfectly, that there were certainly mistakes made, we've investigated those mistakes, we've owned up for those mistakes," the State Department's John Kirby insisted in November 2022.[66]

UNPRECEDENTED

Afghan watchdog John Sopko said that "it is critical that our assistance not be diverted by the Taliban" during House testimony in April 2023, but "unfortunately, as I sit here today, I cannot assure this committee or the American taxpayer that we are not currently funding the Taliban, nor can I assure you that the Taliban are not diverting the money we are sending from the intended recipients, which are the poor Afghan people." Spoko blamed the "State Department and USAID's failure to fully cooperate with SIGAR audits and other inquiries." He called "the lack of cooperation" by the Biden administration as being "unprecedented" over the last two decades, and condemned the "obfuscation and delay" by the State Department and USAID. He warned that "if permitted to continue, it will end SIGAR's work in Afghanistan, but also Congress's access to independent and credible oversight of *any* administration."[67]

THIRTEEN

FROM KABUL TO KYIV

The Russian government swiftly signaled that the fall of Afghanistan did not bode well for Ukraine, its state-run media and key national security officials immediately linking the Taliban takeover to a possible invasion.

Russian military forces engaged in two major force buildups in 2021: in the spring, just before Biden's announcement of the withdrawal of US forces from Afghanistan, and in the fall, just after the Taliban takeover of Afghanistan. The latter resulted in the invasion in 2022. The former began just after Biden's inauguration, in an apparent test of the new president. Estimates of Russian forces on the border with Ukraine exceeded 100,000 in March and April 2021 before Vladimir Putin began to draw them down. The Biden administration responded in May by waiving congressionally mandated sanctions against the Nord Stream 2 gas pipeline, widely known to be one of Putin's personal pet projects. Many members of Congress and national security experts warned that Russia would interpret that as a sign of US weakness and feel emboldened. They were right.

After the searing experience of Kabul, the Biden administration assumed that the Ukrainian military would be as inept as the Afghan military and greatly outmatched by the Russians. As a result, it delayed sending military aid to Ukraine in June and December 2021.

Nevertheless, it has engaged in a sustained, premature victory lap, touting the US intelligence community's success in predicting the Russian invasion in February 2022 while papering over the fact that the US government did little, if anything, to deter the invasion, overrated the Russian military, and underestimated Ukraine's will to fight.

FORESHADOWED

Two days before Biden's Afghanistan withdrawal announcement in April 2021, Secretary of State Blinken spoke with NATO's secretary general, saying "We agreed Russia must end its dangerous military buildup and ongoing aggression along Ukraine's borders" and "also discussed prospects for advancing peace in Afghanistan."[1] He met with NATO's secretary general in person the day of Biden's withdrawal announcement, when they discussed both Afghanistan and Ukraine. National Security Advisor Sullivan said in a documentary that in late March 2021 and heading into April 2021, "we began to see indications of a massive Russian military buildup around Ukraine."[2] In August 2021, NATO allies lamented the Taliban takeover of Afghanistan, often blaming Biden, and warned about potential damage done to the transatlantic alliance.

Putin had been building up Russian forces on Ukraine's border at the exact time Biden was weighing his withdrawal decision. The Russian leader backed off from invading then, but he saw the debacle in Afghanistan, began building up troops again immediately after the fall of Kabul in August 2021, and pulled the trigger on his Ukraine invasion in February 2022.

Blinken would insist in December 2022, "When it comes to Russia's war against Ukraine, if we were still in Afghanistan, it would have, I think, made much more complicated the support that we've been able to give and that others have been able to give Ukraine."[3] There is little reason to believe that a small US/NATO presence in Afghanistan would have complicated allied efforts to support Ukraine but strong reason to believe that the debacle in Afghanistan was what pushed Putin over the line in his decision making about Ukraine, thinking the NATO alliance was reeling.

THE TALIBAN AND THE KREMLIN

In February 2021, Putin's special envoy for Afghanistan, Zamir Kabulov, spoke to the Russian state-run news agency Sputnik's Tajik service, using the interview to make excuses for the Taliban, trash the Afghan government, and encourage Biden to withdraw. He bragged about the strength of the Taliban in its fight against the Afghan government and falsely claimed, "The Taliban adhere to the agreement for all intents and purposes flawlessly . . . which cannot be said about the Americans." That was an obvious lie. He also made excuses for the Taliban's ongoing alliance with al-Qaeda as he downplayed the threat posed by the terrorist group. He added, "The new [Biden] administration. . . are looking for an excuse to explain why they are preparing to violate the agreement with the Taliban."[4]

Dmitry Zhirnov, Russia's ambassador to Afghanistan, praised the Taliban the day after they took Kabul. He called the Taliban's actions "good, positive, and business-like" and argued, "The situation is peaceful and good and everything has calmed down in the city. The situation in Kabul now under the Taliban is better than it was under (President) Ashraf Ghani."[5]

In September 2022, Kabulov expressed skepticism that US operatives had actually killed Zawahiri (saying he trusted the Taliban more in dealing with terrorism) and said that the Russians would prefer to rely on the Taliban rather than the United States for counterterrorism.[6] He continued to hammer away at the United States and NATO over Afghanistan in November 2022, mixing propaganda with bizarre conspiracy theories. He claimed that the Americans were trying to "blackmail" the Taliban and falsely claimed that the United States was working to "strengthen" ISIS-K in a (made-up) effort to push the Taliban away from Russia. Iranian state media uncritically repeated the false claims. He blamed the United States and its "collaborators" for the deplorable situation under Taliban rule, rather than the Taliban itself.[7]

During 2022, the Taliban and Russia signed a series of economic agreements.[8]

ALARM BELLS

Ivo Daalder, a former US ambassador to NATO, said a few days after Biden's April 2021 withdrawal announcement that "Moscow and Beijing will look closely at how we react in one situation to set the stage for the other" and argued that "we need greater strategic clarity on what we would do if Russia moved militarily against Ukraine, or China on Taiwan."[9] British Defense Secretary Ben Wallace said a few days after the fall of Kabul that "if the West is seen not to have resolve and it fractures, then our adversaries like Russia find that encouraging."[10]

Milley conceded in November 2021 that U.S. adversaries may have interpreted the US withdrawal from Afghanistan as a sign of weakness, but argued that would be a mistake by them.[11] The Poles saw the Kabul debacle as the United States bailing on Afghanistan, and it made them very concerned about the US stance on Russia invading Ukraine, and some US allies in Europe were alarmed that the fall of Kabul was the beginning of a cascade of security concerns.

RUSSIA SAYS UKRAINE IS NEXT

Putin's first public comments after the Taliban takeover were used to trash Western and NATO efforts in Afghanistan—and he made clear references to his designs on Ukraine. "I think a lot of politicians in the west are beginning to realize that you can't impose your standards for political life and behavior on other countries," he said on August 20, 2021.[12]

On August 19, Nikolai Patrushev, the secretary of Russia's Security Council and a close Putin ally, gave a lengthy interview to Russia's *Izvestia* newspaper in which he repeatedly warned that the Ukrainians would soon face the same fate as the Afghans, pointing to what he saw as the weaknesses of the US-led NATO alliance. He claimed, "Kyiv servilely serves the interests of overseas patrons, seeking to enter NATO. But did the overthrown pro-American regime in Kabul be saved by the fact that Afghanistan had the status of the main US ally outside NATO? A similar situation awaits supporters of the American choice in Ukraine." He accused the United States of abandoning its Afghan allies "to the whim of fate."[13]

The state-owned All-Russian State Television and Radio Broadcasting Company underscored Patrushev's remarks by writing that "Ukraine in the future is waiting for the Afghan scenario" and Ukraine was "moving towards disintegration, and its 'allies' in the West will not come to the rescue at the right time and will not remember supporters in Kyiv as well as in Kabul."[14]

On August 22, Andrey Kortunov, the director general of the government-established Russian International Affairs Council, went on CNN to warn Ukraine that it could not trust the United States' commitments following the Taliban takeover. "I think politicians in Kiev should be concerned about the credibility of the U.S. security assistance to this country because if the United States decided to let down one of its strategic allies in one part of the world, why wouldn't they do the same in another part of the world?" he asked.[15] He continued to trash the US withdrawal from Afghanistan and used the Taliban takeover to claim that the United States' credibility with its allies was shot.

Russian state-run media also used the Afghan withdrawal debacle to cast doubt on the United States' trustworthiness as an ally. On August 17, Viktoria Nikiforova, a columnist for the Russian state-owned propaganda agency RIA Novosti, wrote that "the fate of American collaborators" in Afghanistan "as we see is sad" and warned that a similar fate awaited the Ukrainians. She added, "Looking at what is happening in Afghanistan, the elites in Ukraine and the Baltics somehow trembled and became agitated."[16]

"It's those who helped the Stars and Stripes reach its ill-thought-out goals that slide off the sides of the departing planes as their nails give out," Margarita Simonyan, the editor in chief of the Russian government propaganda network RT, wrote on Telegram a few days after the Taliban takeover. "The lesson: Do not help the Stars and Stripes. It'll use you, then abandon you."[17]

Outlets allied with the Kremlin also joined in seizing on the fall of Kabul as a way of warning Ukraine that a similar fate awaited it. On August 16, *Strana*, a pro-Russian publication in Ukraine, headline an article, "The Americans Fly Away, the Afghans Cling to the Planes. How the US Is Fleeing Kabul and What Are the Implications for Ukraine."[18] The same day, RIA Novosti wrote, "In Ukraine, they changed their minds about angering Russia after the flight of the United States from Afghanistan."[19] The Russian broadcaster 360TV headlined an article "Ukraine Warned About the Danger of Participating in Anti-Russian Provocations After the US Withdrawal from Afghanistan."[20] Russia's *Moskovskij Komsomolets* wrote the next day, "Ukraine should draw certain lessons from the events unfolding in Afghanistan."[21]

A host of Kremlin-allied media outlets also quickly seized on an article in the *National Interest* published on August 14—the day before the Taliban took Kabul—titled "Afghanistan Is a Wake-Up Call for Major Non-NATO Allies" by Nikolas S. Gvosdev, a professor at the U.S. Naval War College.[22] The Russian state-owned news agency TASS promoted the story on August 16, writing "The situation in Afghanistan is a wake-up call for those countries that the United States calls its allies and partners outside of NATO" and stressing the portions about Ukraine specifically.[23] A host of other pro-Kremlin outlets also pushed the article with similar headlines and messaging about the similar doom awaiting Ukraine. Russia's 5-TV warned that "the defeat of the Afghan authorities, which did not receive US support in the armed conflict with the Taliban, should serve as a good example for Ukraine."[24]

"WE ARE VERY DIFFERENT FROM AFGHANISTAN"

Ukrainian government officials were clearly worried about what the US betrayal of Afghanistan to the Taliban meant relative to continued US support for Ukraine in the face of an impending Russian invasion. An anonymous adviser of Ukrainian president Volodymyr Zelenskyy said in late August 2021, "America's commitment to Ukraine's security is in doubt given everything that has happened in past months, from the US-German Nord Stream 2 agreement to the debacle in Afghanistan."[25] Zelenskyy's adviser Andrew Mac said at the end of August 2021, "The situation in Afghanistan seems to indicate a realignment of U.S. global commitments, and President Zelensky wants to hear from President Biden where Ukraine fits in." Another Zelenskyy adviser, Tymofiy Mylovanov, emphasized, "We are very different from Afghanistan, and we would like to emphasize this. We are an independent country, not a failed state, and our military has managed to resist the Russians, not the Taliban."[26] An article by Alyona Getmanchuk, the director of the New Europe Center in Kyiv, that appeared on August 16, the day after the Taliban takeover, warned that "for observers in Ukraine . . . the Taliban takeover of Afghanistan represents a particularly ominous sight" in Ukraine's fight against Russia.[27]

On September 12, 2021, Zelenskyy was asked about Putin's threats against Ukraine and the United States' abandonment of Afghanistan—and whether he was worried that the United States would abandon Ukraine, too. "First of all, we have to clearly understand that Ukraine, when compared to Afghanistan, I believe it's not an accurate comparison," he said. "I don't think we can compare that, Ukraine to Afghanistan, being that Ukraine is not so dependent on the United States like Afghanistan was. And I really believe that, in four or five or seven days, you can't take such a big country geographically as Ukraine with such a quite big population and simply occupy it like that."[28]

Zelenskyy was asked about Patrushev's claims that the United States would abandon Kyiv just as it had abandoned Kabul, and he emphasized that Ukraine had thus far stood strong despite Russia's annexation of Crimea and its incursions into the Donbas since 2014. Zelenskyy had repeatedly referenced Afghanistan in the days prior, focusing on Ukrainian military intelligence rescue operations in Kabul.

On September 13, 2021, Ukraine's foreign minister, Dmytro Kuleba, said that the United States was now in the middle of a "leadership crisis" after the Taliban takeover but added, "I spoke with one US senator who told me the United States should not screw up in Ukraine as it did in Afghanistan."[29]

On September 27, 2021, Mykhailo Minakov, who grew up in Ukraine and is the editor in chief of the Kennan Institute's Focus Ukraine blog, wrote that "Afghanistan syndrome was on full display in the responses of the Ukrainian elites . . . to the news of the US withdrawal from Afghanistan."[30]

In October 2021, Ukrainian defense minister Andriy Taran said, "I'm not going to compare relations between the U.S. and Ukraine with relations between the U.S. and Afghanistan. Ukraine is a country that fights for its own independence and territorial integrity. We have no doubt of the support from our strategic partner."[31]

THE BIDEN ADMINISTRATION'S AFGHANISTAN-UKRAINE MIX-UP

On the twentieth anniversary of 9/11, less than two weeks after the final US evacuation from Afghanistan, Under Secretary of State for Political Affairs Victoria Nuland was pressed at a Ukraine-focused political conference to say what the debacle meant for Ukraine. Carl Bildt, a former prime minister of Sweden, asked about the idea that the Afghan withdrawal had been a wise move because had it freed up the Biden administration to focus on "big issues" such as China and asked if that logic applied to other places in the world where the United States would need to "cut out" other issues—such as Ukraine.

Nuland responded by immediately mixing up Afghanistan and Ukraine—probably a disturbing sign to observers in Ukraine who had just witnessed the Taliban takeover. "Does our move out of Afghanistan mean that we don't care or have strategic interests in Ukraine anymore?" she asked. "I think there's no greater exemplar of our continuing commitment to Ukraine's sovereignty, territorial integrity, independence, and European aspirations than the summit we just had between President Biden and President Zelenskyy literally the day after our evacuation from Ukraine—our evacuation from Afghanistan—you've got me messed up now—concluded."[32]

Defense Secretary Austin was pressed in October 2021 about whether it was important to reassure the Ukrainians of the United States' commitment to them in the wake of the debacle in Afghanistan. He emphasized the United States' commitment to Ukraine—without mentioning Afghanistan.[33]

NORD STREAM 2

The Biden administration's failure to follow the law and shut down Russia's Nord Stream 2—a malign influence weapon the Kremlin intended to use to weaken Ukraine—likely contributed to Putin's decision to invade, as it indicated Biden's weakness and a NATO riven by divisions. (Germany was strongly in favor of the lucrative project, while the Poles were staunchly opposed.)

Under both Obama and Trump, the US government and Congress had opposed Nord Stream 2, designed to carry Russian natural gas to Europe under the Baltic Sea. The pipeline would bypass Ukraine, denying that US partner money as the Kremlin attempted to squeeze Ukraine and gain influence in Europe.

Sanctions the Trump administration had placed on the Russian pipeline, which was nearly finished, had forced construction to halt before its completion. But an early move by the Biden administration was to go weak on the sanctions while still claiming that it opposed the project. As early as February 2021, Blinken and the Biden administration were refusing to implement sanctions against Nord Stream 2 AG (the company behind Nord Stream 2), its CEO Matthias Warnig, and Nord Stream 2 AG's corporate officers.[34] Russian deputy foreign minister Sergei Ryabkov responded that that could indicate "a glimmer of normalcy in American politics."[35]

Throughout 2021, Ukraine and Poland continued to warn the Biden administration about the dangers of its Nord Stream 2 strategy.[36] They condemned the deal between the Biden administration and German chancellor Angela Merkel, a big proponent of Nord Stream 2, that had allowed Nord Stream 2 to inch forward.[37]

Republicans blasted the Biden administration's boneheaded decision, with Congressman Michael McCaul arguing, "The completion of this pipeline will threaten Ukraine's security, deepen Europe's dangerous energy dependence on the Kremlin, and further enrich the corrupt Putin regime."[38]

The White House attempted to soften the blow by announcing a meeting between Biden and Zelenskyy at the end of August 2021, when Biden would "affirm the United States's unwavering support for Ukraine's sovereignty."[39] Kabul fell two weeks before the meeting.

Even as Republicans continued to push the Biden administration to kill Nord Stream 2 as Russia made it clear in late 2021 and January 2022 that it was preparing to invade Ukraine, the Biden administration continued to refuse to do so. Republicans argued that punishing Putin could dissuade him from going through with the invasion, but their arguments fell on deaf ears.

Senator Ted Cruz introduced a bill voted on in January 2022 that would have forced the Biden administration to kill Nord Stream 2, but enough Democrats voted against it to stop it from hitting the sixty votes necessary for passage. "Today, the Senate rebuked Joe Biden's surrender to Vladimir Putin on Nord Stream 2," Cruz said. ". . . Only immediately imposing sanctions can change Putin's calculation, stop a Ukrainian invasion, and lift the existential threat posed by Nord Stream 2."[40] Biden refused to listen, and Putin invaded the next month.

It was only after Putin's February 2022 invasion that Biden imposed the sanctions and Germany killed the project. It was obviously too late. German justice minister Marco Buschmann said in November 2022, "The decision to pursue Nord Stream 2 following the annexation of Crimea in 2014 was Germany's contribution to the outbreak of the war in Ukraine."[41]

BOUNTIES

In April 2021, the White House said that the US intelligence community had only "low to moderate confidence" in intelligence suggesting that the Russian government had offered bounties to Afghan militants to kill US troops, despite Biden's having repeatedly hammered then president Trump about the issue on the campaign trail, including during their October 2020 debate.[42]

The controversy emerged after it was reported in June 2020 that a US intelligence assessment had concluded that Russian military intelligence might have paid Taliban-connected militants in Afghanistan to kill US and coalition troops, but US officials stressed that the intelligence was unverified.[43] They believed that Russia had supplied weapons to the Taliban for years, but offering bounties would have been a significant escalation of Russian targeting of the United States in Afghanistan.

In June 2020, Biden used the Russian bounty claims to assert that Trump "has continued his embarrassing campaign of deference and debasing himself before Vladimir Putin."[44] The future president continued to level similar attacks for the remainder of the race. It was Biden, though, who would abandon Afghanistan and on whose watch Russia would invade Ukraine.

ONE WAR ENDS, ANOTHER BEGINS

In mid-January 2022, Congressman Michael McCaul, then the ranking member on the House Foreign Affairs Committee, warned that the United States would need to do more to deter Russia from invading Ukraine and tied the situation to the Afghan debacle: "I think people, our foreign adversaries, like Putin, President Xi in China, the ayatollah, and Kim Jong-un, all view that as a moment of weakness."[45]

Star witnesses from the Ukraine-related, Democrat-led impeachment of Trump in 2019 also weighed in in January to reveal their assessments that Biden's debacle in Afghanistan had contributed to Putin's move toward invading Ukraine. Fiona Hill, a National Security Council expert on Russia during the Trump administration, wrote that Putin saw the United States as "weakened at home and in retreat abroad." She argued that, in Putin's analysis, when combining Trump's "disastrous presidency" and the "rifts" he had created with US allies and then "America's precipitous withdrawal from Afghanistan," it added up to a signal of "weakness."[46] Kurt Volker, the US Special Representative for Ukraine Negotiations under Trump, said that criticism of Biden over Afghanistan was "well founded" because it was a "completely unforced catastrophe" that showed a lack of resolve and of willingness to stand by allies—and "that in turn has given encouragement to both Putin concerning Ukraine and to Xi concerning Taiwan."[47]

On January 20, Michael Vickers, an undersecretary of defense for intelligence under Obama, wrote, "Our defeat in Afghanistan in August 2021 no doubt convinced Putin that our resolve to counter his aggression had weakened."[48]

Trump said a couple weeks before Putin's invasion of Ukraine that it was happening because Russia "got a lot more ambitious" following Biden's debacle in Afghanistan.[49] The same day, Republican Senate Minority Leader Mitch McConnell echoed those sentiments: "There's not a doubt in my mind that the Russians wouldn't be on the border of

Ukraine with 100,000 or more troops, had we not indicated to the rest of the world we were pulling the plug on Afghanistan."[50]

On February 18, retired general Jack Keane said that Putin was moving on Ukraine now because of US and European weakness, feeble pushback from Biden about Russia's military buildup the year before, and a lack of US assistance to Ukraine—adding "after Afghanistan, I think it became an accelerant."[51] On February 21, General Keith Kellogg, Trump's close adviser on Afghanistan, said that Putin had seen "weakness and opportunity" in deciding to invade Ukraine. He also said that Putin is "also a student of history" and pointed to Biden's being the lone vote against the Osama bin Laden raid.[52]

"Each time we fail to demonstrate American resolve, whether it is the debacle that was Afghanistan that caused thirteen Americans to perish as we exited, those are the kinds of things that convince people like Vladimir Putin that his dream—his dream of recreating the Soviet Union—is something he may well be able to do under this leadership's watch here in the United States," former secretary of state Mike Pompeo said on February 22.[53] Putin invaded Ukraine two days later.

"The Russian troops began moving in October. What happened in October? It was sort of the end of our Afghanistan debacle, and that incompetence has resonated around the world," retired brigadier general Anthony Tata said on February 24. "We left NATO out to dry, and Putin's saying, 'Well, you know what, NATO's fractured. America left all their NATO allies to fend for themselves in Afghanistan.' . . . The Afghanistan failure is resonating around the globe."[54]

On March 6, Andrei Kozyrev, a Russian foreign minister in the 1990s, argued that the invasion had been "rational for Putin" based on three main (flawed) premises: the West's fractured geopolitical condition, Ukraine's weak condition as a country, and Russia's military strength. He added that "the U.S. botched its withdrawal from Afghanistan, solidifying this narrative."[55]

On March 3, former French president François Hollande said that he believed the US-led disaster in Afghanistan had encouraged Putin to pull the trigger on his invasion of Ukraine.[56] On August 18, ex–Swedish prime minister Carl Bildt wrote that the debacle in Afghanistan "demonstrated that the US might not have the staying power or the strategic patience that is necessary" and that "the Kremlin certainly took note."[57]

Also in March, General Tod Wolters, the commander of the U.S. European Command (EUCOM), testified before the House of Representatives that the US/NATO debacle in Afghanistan might have led Putin to finally go ahead with his long-desired invasion of Ukraine. "I think he felt like he had the popular support of the citizens of Russia," he said. "I also felt like he was attempting to take advantage of fissures that could have appeared in NATO as a result of the post-Afghanistan environment."[58]

In April, General Milley conceded to the Senate that it was "possible" that the disastrous withdrawal from Afghanistan had contributed to Russia's decision to invade Ukraine. He added, "It's not clear. I think it certainly is possible, but I also know that Putin had aims on Ukraine long before the end of the war in Afghanistan."[59]

On August 16, the *Washington Post* reported that following the Taliban takeover, US intelligence analysts had assessed that Putin had "believed that the Biden administration was chastened by the humiliating U.S. withdrawal from Afghanistan and wanted to avoid new wars" and that the Russian dictator had made that part of his calculus in late summer 2021 when deciding to invade Ukraine.[60]

Congressman Mike Turner, the chairman of the House Intelligence Committee, told us he believed that Putin had "expedited invasion—probably to his own peril, because it was poorly planned and poorly executed—with him believing that this was his moment since the United States was in withdrawal and had a weak leader." He added, "Whenever you have a new president that has come in, world leaders—certainly of authoritarian regimes—look to assess the strength and the commitment of that leader. And when your first statement to the world is running from Afghanistan, it certainly emboldened our adversaries."

"I think, most dramatically, as all this was happening in August, we were looking at satellite technology and watching the Russian Federation encircling Ukraine," McCaul told us. "It was a dark moment of failure in American foreign policy that emboldened our enemies and projected weakness and invited aggression. And now we're seeing that today with Putin invading Ukraine, with Chairman Xi looking at Taiwan."

Andrew Hastie, the shadow defense minister for the Australian government and an Afghan war veteran, agreed with that assessment. "I surmise that Putin was emboldened by the US and NATO withdrawal from Afghanistan. I think he believed that morale and resolve was badly damaged by it, and that there wouldn't be great resistance to a Russian invasion of Ukraine," he told us, adding, "In this context, it is remarkable how quickly the US, NATO, and Australia and other allies were able to pivot to support Ukraine. Afghanistan was a bruising experience for all."

A former senior station chief in South Asia noted that the United States had not properly consulted with NATO allies on the Afghan withdrawal and told us, "That may have also influenced Putin's decision-making thinking like 'Hey, Europe and United States are having a lot of issues right now. And I can break them with the leverage I have because of the hydrocarbons I'm exporting to Europe. I can break them because they're angry at each other over Afghanistan.' So that may have been a factor for Putin."

BOTCHING IT AGAIN

Fresh off the Pentagon's vastly overstating the size and strength of the Afghan military and vastly underestimating the Taliban's power and de-termination ahead of its rapid takeover in 2021, the Biden administration promptly made the exact opposite mistake with Russia and Ukraine—vastly underestimating the strength and will to fight of the Ukrainian defenders and vastly overestimating the effectiveness of the invading Russians.[61]

The invasion of Ukraine came after weeks of warnings by the US intelligence community that Putin was likely to invade. They got that right, but the Biden administration horribly misjudged how the war would go, predicting a swift Kremlin victory.[62]

In mid-January 2022, Biden indicated that he believed a Russian victory in Ukraine would essentially be certain; he seemed to say that the United States might be okay with a limited invasion. "It's one thing if it's a minor incursion, and then, we end up having a fight about what to do and not do," he said during a press conference prior to the invasion. During that same press conference, he said that Russia would "be able to prevail over time."[63]

In early February 2022, Milley told Congress behind closed doors that Ukraine could be conquered by Russia within seventy-two hours of being invaded.[64] Anonymous US intelligence officials said that the Russian military would be able to march into Kyiv in two days.[65]

On February 22, two days before Putin's invasion, Ukrainian foreign minister Dmytro Kuleba traveled to the Pentagon to beg the Biden administration for Stinger antiaircraft missiles. Defense Secretary Austin said that the United States might help but pressed Kuleba about where Ukrainian government officials would flee to if the Russians took over: "If you get pushed out of Kyiv, where are you going to go?" Kuleba retorted, "We're not even going to talk about that or think about that." Austin said that he understood but added, "But you need a plan." Milley then jumped in with what a US defense official dubbed a "You're going to die" tirade. "They're going to roll into Kyiv in a few days," he predicted. "They're coming in with tanks and columns of formations. You need to be ready for that. You need to be prepared. If you're not, it's going to be a slaughter."[66]

Zelenskyy ended up saving Biden's ass and the collective credibility of the NATO alliance—as well as saving his own country—when he told the United States, "The fight is here. I need ammunition, not a ride." The Ukrainian military pushed back the Russian charge for Kyiv, and the ensuing war has been devastating for both sides—but Ukraine has survived.

On March 30, Wolters was asked if the United States had overestimated Russia or underestimated Ukraine, and he seemed to indicate that it had been "a little bit of both." He pointed to "the will and determination of the Ukrainian citizens" and said that the United States might have overestimated Russia's military.[67]

On March 18, General McKenzie weighed in when pressed about why the United States had underestimated the Ukrainians and overestimated the Afghans so badly. "What you can't give an Army is the fighting spirit of the individual soldier. Clearly, the Ukrainians have tremendous fighting spirit," he said, adding "The Taliban ultimately chose to fight, the Afghan Army, as part of what I would characterize as not just a military collapse but really a national collapse, ultimately couldn't find the will to stand and fight. And I think we're still—frankly, I'm still digesting that."[68]

On March 31, Wolters responded to questions about intelligence failures in Ukraine, saying "This one has been baffling as a result of Russia's challenges and the spirit of the Ukrainian citizens."[69]

On March 10, Republican senator Tom Cotton began a line of questioning by commending the intelligence community for "the outstanding work that it did leading up to the invasion" in warning about Putin's impending attack. But he noted that Director of National Intelligence Avril Haines had said that Putin had underestimated the skill of Ukraine's military and its willingness to fight and asked if US intelligence had made the same mistake. Haines replied, "So we assessed prior to the invasion that he was overestimating—or underestimating, rather—the Ukrainians' . . . resistance. So I think we did well there. We did not do as well in terms of predicting the military challenges that he has encountered with his own military."[70]

Cotton asked Defense Intelligence Agency director Berrier the same question, and he admitted that he had botched it. He said, "My view was that, based on a variety of factors, that the Ukrainians were not as ready as I thought they should be, therefore I questioned their will to fight. That was a bad assessment on my part because they have fought bravely and honorably and are doing the right thing." He added that the Defense Intelligence Agency had "made assumptions about Putin's assumptions that were wrong."

"These mistakes potentially had real world policy implications about the willingness of the president or other NATO leaders to provide weapons that they thought might've fallen into the hands of Russians in a matter of hours, or to impose sanctions for something that might have been a *fait accompli*," Cotton said.[71]

A PREMATURE VICTORY LAP

In mid-April 2022, the Biden administration took a premature victory lap over the US intelligence community's performance during Russia's invasion of Ukraine despite the war's still raging and despite US spy agencies' overestimating the might of the Kremlin military and under-estimating Ukrainian resistance.[72]

On March 26, Biden had criticized Putin as "not much of a student of history" for underestimating the Ukrainian military's will to fight, but Biden himself had botched that, too.[73] He made the comment during a speech in Warsaw during which he appeared to support regime change in Russia before the White House walked it back.

On April 5, Milley said, "This war has arguably been the most successful intelligence operation in military history, and it's really tremendous—and someday, that story will be told."[74] Unmentioned was his own horrible and repeated prediction that Ukraine would immediately lose.

Later that month, Brett Holmgren, the assistant secretary of state for intelligence and research, said that US spy agency actions related to the Russia-Ukraine war would be seen as among the best in US history, alongside discovering missiles in Cuba in 1962 and finding Osama bin Laden in 2011. But he soon conceded that the intelligence community had misjudged Russia and Ukraine. He added, "So I think there's an opportunity for us to kind of take a look back at what happened."[75]

"If we had known in advance how strong the Ukrainians would be and how weak the Russians would be, we might have been able to preposition more equipment and had aid to the Ukrainians flow in faster," Independent senator Angus King said in March.[76]

DETERRENCE FAILURE

In late February, Biden argued that US sanctions against Russia were not meant to deter Putin despite numerous high-ranking Biden administration officials arguing that the sanctions were meant to do so.[77]

"If Putin sees deterrence coming back from the United States and our NATO allies, he may second-guess his calculation to invade Ukraine," McCaul said on January 16. ". . . But I'm not seeing a lot of deterrence. I'm seeing some tough rhetoric, but not a lot of action. I would recommend—I talked to Deputy Secretary Wendy Sherman prior to her negotiations—that you have to put things on the table like sanctions. You have to talk about more arms sales, weapon sales to Ukraine. And this Nord Stream 2, the idea that the president waived congressionally mandatory sanctions on Putin's pipeline, I don't know how that's in the national interests of the United States. And it just emboldened and empowered Putin to start completing his pipeline."[78]

Biden, in Brussels for a meeting with NATO leaders, was asked on March 24 if US and international sanctions would prod Putin to alter course, and the president claimed that the sanctions weren't meant to deter the Russian strongman, even though his vice president, national security advisor, secretary of state, and other officials had said that that was indeed a goal. "I did not say that, in fact, the sanctions would deter him. Sanctions never deter. You keep talking about that. Sanctions never deter," he said. ". . . That's not what I said. You're playing a game with me. I know. The answer is no."[79]

On February 24, the day Putin launched his full-scale invasion, Biden said, "No one expected the sanctions to prevent anything from happening." "I didn't say sanctions couldn't stop him . . . The threat of the sanctions and imposing the sanctions and seeing the effect of the sanctions are two different things," Biden claimed.[80] During a briefing that afternoon, Psaki said that she believed "that's not exactly what he meant" to say. "We do see them as having a deterrent impact, right?" she asked. "It doesn't mean they're 100% foolproof."[81]

Deputy National Security Advisor Daleep Singh also said that day that the purpose of the sanctions threat was deterrence. However, on February 11, Jake Sullivan had said, "The president believes that sanctions are intended to deter." On February 20, Antony Blinken had said, "The purpose of the sanctions in the first instance is to try to deter Russia from going to war." On February 21, John Kirby had said of sanctions, "We want them to have a deterrent effect." On February 22, Vice President Kamala Harris had said, "The purpose of the sanctions has always been and continues to be deterrence."[82]

The disconnect over whether sanctions were even meant to deter Putin or not was strategically incoherent.

RECRUITMENT OF AFGHANS TO FIGHT IN UKRAINE

For several months after Putin's invasion of Ukraine, rumors swirled that former Afghan commandos had joined the Russian military as mercenaries in the battle against Kyiv. Pentagon officials refused to confirm their veracity. The claims were largely sourced to former Afghan generals.

We obtained direct evidence that Afghan commandos trained by the CIA and Army special forces have, in fact, joined Russia's offensive. Specifically, they have signed on with the Wagner Group, Russia's state-run paramilitary organization, staffed by mercenaries, which has been implicated in war crimes in Syria, Africa, and Ukraine. (The Wagner Group's leader, Yevgeny Prigozhin, reports to Putin himself.) That evidence includes a draft version of a classified report detailing Wagner Group recruitment efforts of Afghan personnel, most of whom are now based in Iran. The report specifies that former commandos are approached by Russian operatives who offer a monthly salary of $1,500 for six months of service, after which the commandos (if they survive) will also receive Russian citizenship. If a commando accepts the offer, the operatives facilitate his travel to Russia through a "visa invitation" issued by the Russian Ministry of Foreign Affairs. When the commandos arrive in Russia, they receive a crash course in Wagner Group tactics and are quickly inserted into the Wagner Group pipeline.

The report assessed that Wagner Group operatives coordinate with prospective recruits through a dedicated WhatsApp group. Screenshots of the group's members show several Russia-based phone numbers as well as confirmed phone numbers of "former Afghan military who are attempting to transit to Russia to support the Ukraine war effort." The report's contents are reinforced by firsthand accounts from numerous former Afghan commandos in Iran who rejected the Russian overtures. Each commando independently described the same recruiting approach. One of them provided pictures from the social media accounts of other commandos who had accepted the offer, depicting the commandos and their family members with Russian and Iranian officials.

The classified report includes a copy of a Wagner Group recruiting form created specifically for Afghan commandos and written in Pashtu. It also includes a copy of a Russian visa issued to a former Afghan commando. Finally, the report confirmed with "high confidence" that an Afghan passport issued by the US-era Afghan government had been recovered on a battlefield in the Mykolaiv region of Ukraine.

McCaul told us that one of the consequences of the botched Afghan withdrawal was the US-trained forces who had been left behind: "There were three thousand Afghan security forces that fled into Iran who are now being manipulated to fight in Ukraine with the Russians against the Ukrainians." A spokesman for Prigozhin lied that the recruitment allegations were "crazy nonsense."[83]

MERCHANT OF DEATH

Right around the time when Russia's Ukraine offensive stalled and Russia was in desperate need of more military weaponry, the Biden administration agreed to free the world's most famous arms dealer, a Russian named Viktor Bout—who, fittingly, had helped arm the Taliban and al-Qaeda with weapons that were used to fight Americans.

Russian officials arrested WNBA star Brittney Griner on February 17, 2022—less than a week before its Ukraine invasion—purportedly because of the less than a gram of medically prescribed hash oil she had in her luggage when passing through Russian customs. The real reason for the arrest? She was a useful hostage as Russia invaded.

For years, Putin had fought to spring Bout from an American prison, and now he had his chance. Trump had refused any hostage exchange involving Bout, but Biden was a willing partner, and the trade took place in early December 2022.

Bout had helped fuel civil wars in Africa, had armed terrorist groups around the world, and was eventually convicted of planning to arm left-wing Colombian revolutionary terrorists and of intending to kill Americans. There were key Afghanistan connections, too. The definitive book on Bout, *Merchant of Death: Money, Guns, Planes, and the Man Who Makes War Possible* by Douglas Farah and Stephen Braun, has an entire chapter on "The Taliban Connection." An associate of Bout said, "Yes he flew for the Taliban.... He was landing in Kandahar all the time." Bout had helped fuel a jihadist insurgency in Bosnia in the early 1990s as well, using the al-Qaeda-linked Third World Relief Agency, whose board members included al-Qaeda cofounder Wa'el Hamza Julaidan and which received funding from bin Laden himself, to supply weaponry.[84]

Beyond the help Bout could give to the Russian war effort against Ukraine, Putin had long sought to free him almost assuredly because he was a member of the Russian foreign intelligence service, the GRU.[85]

Donald Trump called Bout "one of the biggest arms dealers anywhere in the World" and argued that he had been "responsible for tens of thousands of deaths and horrific injuries."[86] John Bolton, who had been Trump's national security advisor, said that the Trump administration had rejected releasing Bout. "This is not a deal. This is not a swap. This is a surrender," he said, calling it "a huge victory for Moscow over Washington."[87]

Kirby said that no one in the Biden administration was doing "back flips" over Bout's being a free man but added that it had been a "difficult" yet "courageous" decision by Biden to make the trade. Derek Maltz, a former Drug Enforcement Agency agent who had helped lead the team that arrested Bout in 2008, lamented in December 2022, "The Lord of War is back in the game."[88]

Bout soon said that he "wholeheartedly" supported the "special military operation" in Ukraine and wished that Russia had invaded sooner. He said he was willing to share the skills he has and was willing to volunteer to fight.[89] He then traveled to the Russian-occupied city of Luhansk in eastern Ukraine and said that the region would be "peaceful" under Russian rule.[90]

Sullivan wouldn't call Bout a terrorist when asked, saying "Well, he's not listed as a specially designated national."[91] Sullivan was wrong; Bout had been on the Specially Designated Nationals and Blocked Persons List for many years, including when the Biden administration had let him walk.[92]

Bout was back in Russia and ready to help the Russian war machine—just as he had helped the Taliban conquer Afghanistan two decades prior.

INTEGRATED DETERRENCE

Congressman Mike Gallagher, now the head of the House Select Committee on China, believed that the Biden administration's defense policy of "integrated deterrence" was deeply flawed because it had failed to deter Russia from invading Ukraine, as the Pentagon promoted the strategy to deal with China.[93] In late March 2022, an anonymous senior Pentagon official praised the United States' successes against Russia, saying "I don't think there's any doubt that the model of integrated deterrence comes out smelling pretty good from this."[94]

Gallagher responded, "That the Biden Pentagon is spiking the football on the so-called success of integrated deterrence in Ukraine is a stunning show of hubris." Deterrence, specifically integrated deterrence, failed in Ukraine. . . . The same brave senior Pentagon official speaking on the condition of anonymity . . . should go to Kyiv or Mariupol and smell the rotting flesh of Putin's innocent victims."[95]

In March 2022, Gallagher asked Admiral William Lescher what the West had deterred in Ukraine. After a nine-second pause, the admiral replied, "Excellent question, I suppose. So we're deterring any expansion into the NATO territories that we're committed to defend." When asked if it was fair to say that the United States had failed to deter Putin's invasion of Ukraine, Lescher said, "Oh, absolutely."[96]

On March 30, Wolters told Gallagher that he considered it part of his mission to deter Putin from invading and considered himself part of an interagency effort to "deter and dissuade" Russia.[97] Gallagher asked if the general agreed that deterrence had failed, and Wolter replied, "I can't argue with your conclusion."

"So deterrence failed in Ukraine—specifically, integrated deterrence failed in Ukraine," Gallagher said on March 29, later adding "The administration's embrace of integrated deterrence is an abandonment of the Pentagon's previous strategy of deterrence by denial. That required the U.S. to maintain enough military strength to turn back an adversary's aggression, particularly in Taiwan and Eastern Europe."[98]

After the Taliban takeover in Afghanistan, enabled by Biden's poor decision making and his ill-planned withdrawal, and after Putin's invasion of Ukraine, which was prompted in part by the fall of Kabul and which Biden himself claimed he had not tried to deter, it was right to worry about what all of it portended for the looming threat posed by the Chinese Communist Party.

FOURTEEN

THE CCP AND THE KABUL MOMENT

The Chinese government had long quietly played a double-cross game in Afghanistan, reaching out to the Afghan government while sidling up to the Taliban. The fall of Kabul was a propaganda gift for the Chinese Communist Party (CCP), which immediately began touting the "Kabul moment" and threatening Taiwan with a similar fate.

When the Biden debacle in Afghanistan encouraged Russia to invade Ukraine, Chinese president Xi Jinping stood shoulder to shoulder with Putin just days beforehand, with the dictator duo declaring a "no limits" alliance. China continued to back Russia throughout the war in 2022.

The Chinese also quickly became the most powerful advocates for the Taliban on the world stage, pushing for the United States to unfreeze billions of dollars' worth of Afghan bank reserves (which would enrich the Taliban). In return, China wanted the Taliban to give it the green light to exploit Afghanistan's vast mineral wealth, providing resources China could use to fund its military buildup and minerals it saw as key for preparing to invade Taiwan.

"For China, everything revolves around Taiwan. In my view, I think Xi Jinping is deadly serious about taking Taiwan. I think he's laser focused on that. Having this withdrawal does call into question our credibility," David Sauer, a former CIA station chief in East Asia, told us. "I think Afghanistan, our withdrawal there, I'm sure they were quite happy."

Chinese state media quickly began exploiting the debacle in Afghanistan to push propaganda aimed at Taiwan, questioning the United States' commitment there.

Just after the Taliban took Kabul, Biden vowed that the United States would respond to any Chinese invasion of Taiwan, pushing back on criticism from Chinese state media that the United States' debacle and the Taliban takeover in Afghanistan should make the island of Taiwan question whether the United States would protect it. ABC's George Stephanopoulos said that China was already telling Taiwan, "See? You can't count on the Americans." Biden pushed back: "Why wouldn't China say that? Look, George, the idea that we—there's a fundamental difference between [Afghanistan and] Taiwan, South Korea, NATO.... We made a sacred commitment to Article Five that if in fact anyone were to invade or take action against our NATO allies, we would respond. Same with Japan, same with South Korea, same with—Taiwan."[1]

In fact, there was no such mutual defense treaty with Taiwan, and the White House walked back Biden's remarks. It became a pattern.

On August 17, 2021, Chinese senior colonel Shi Yi declared that the Chinese military had conducted live-fire drills in the airspace and sea area around Taiwan in order to "safeguard national security" in a "necessary action" to protect China from foreign foes and "independence forces" in Taiwan.[2] Those threatening actions ramped up throughout 2021 and 2022.

Sullivan said that day that "our commitment to Taiwan . . . remains as strong as it's ever been."[3] Taiwanese president Tsai Ing-wen said the next day that Taiwan needed to increase its strength in response to the Taliban takeover in Afghanistan. "Recent changes in the situation in Afghanistan have led to much discussion in Taiwan," she said. "I want to tell everyone that Taiwan's only option is to make ourselves stronger, more united, and more resolute in our determination to protect ourselves."[4]

The Biden administration insisted that the United States' position on Taiwan—which for decades has been one of so-called strategic ambiguity—had not changed, despite Biden's vowing that the United States would respond to a Chinese attack on the island similarly to the way it has promised to defend NATO allies.

On August 15, the day of the Taliban takeover, The Chinese state-run website Global Times said that the fall of Kabul was a signal that the United States would abandon its other allies (such as Taiwan). "When its interests require it to abandon allies, Washington will not hesitate to find every excuse to do so," the CCP outlet said. "A country as powerful as the US could not defeat the Afghan Taliban, which received almost no aid from outside, even in 20 years. This defeat of the US is a clearer demonstration of US impotence than the Vietnam War—the US is indeed like a paper tiger."[5] The next day, the outlet said that the "US will abandon Taiwan in a crisis given its tarnished credibility"[6] and asked, "Washington just left despite the worsening situation in Kabul. Is this some kind of omen of Taiwan's future fate?"[7] It also said that "[Chinese analysts] said that once the price for keeping its strategic interests with Taiwan becomes unbearable, the US will abandon Taiwan island without hesitation."[8] Two days later, the propaganda outlet said that the debacle "has dealt a heavy blow to the credibility and reliability of the US."[9]

The Chinese government outlet repeatedly pointed to the fall of Saigon in 1975 and the fall of Kabul in 2021, telling the Taiwanese in a lengthy tirade that the same thing would happen to them when China inevitably invaded. "How Washington abandoned the Kabul regime particularly shocked some in Asia, including the island of Taiwan," it said, adding that Taiwan's leaders "must have been nervous and feel an ominous presentiment. They must have known better in secret that the US is not reliable." It then stated, "Once a cross-Straits war breaks out while the mainland seizes the island with forces, the US would have to have a much greater determination than it had for Afghanistan." It also threatened, "From what happened in Afghanistan, [DPP authorities] should perceive that once a war breaks out in the Straits, the island's defense will collapse in hours and the US military won't come to help."[10]

Global Times editor in chief Hu Xijin also immediately commented on the Afghanistan withdrawal on Twitter: "After the fall of the Kabul regime, the Taiwan authorities must be trembling. Don't look forward to the US to protect them. Taipei officials need to quietly mail-order a Five-Star Red Flag from the Chinese mainland. It will be useful one day when they surrender to the PLA."[11]

On August 20, Chinese Foreign Ministry spokesperson Hua Chunying used the death of a young Afghan falling from a C-17 at Kabul airport, just after the Taliban takeover, to attack the US efforts to bring democracy to Afghanistan, saying "Zaki Anwari's fallen. American myth down. More and more people are awakening."[12]

The Global Times insisted that the Taliban takeover had been a "huge blow to US's reputation as an ally" and opined, "Taiwan will be tomorrow's Afghanistan being abandoned by the US."[13]

China continued its trolling of the United States about the debacle in Afghanistan into 2022 and beyond, with Chinese Foreign Ministry spokesman Zhao Lijian tweeting again on June 29 about the Afghans who had fallen from a US plane at HKIA. The Global Times matched that messaging by tweeting about "American military aircraft in #Afghanistan vs Chinese military aircraft in Afghanistan."[14] The tweet included a side-by-side of the C-17 that Afghans had fallen off of and a Chinese aircraft purportedly bringing supplies to Afghanistan in the wake of the earthquake on June 22. Unmentioned was the fact that the United States has remained the largest provider of humanitarian aid in Afghanistan, even after the Taliban takeover.

The Chinese government continued its criticism of the United States on the first anniversary of the fall of Kabul. "The 'Kabul moment' became a byword for the US's debacle in Afghanistan," Chinese Foreign Ministry spokesman Wang Wenbin said in August. "The 'Kabul moment' marks the failure of the 'democratic transformation' imposed by the US. . . . The so-called 'leader of the West' left its reputation in tatters when it decided to ditch its allies in the hurried retreat." Wang added, "More importantly, the 'Kabul moment' marks the failure of the US's strategy of hegemony. . . . Acting against the trend of the times will only lead to more 'Kabul moments.'"[15]

In late November, The Defense Department released its report on Chinese military power, concluding that the CCP had used the US debacle in Afghanistan to undermine US alliances as it turned its sights on Taiwan. "In 2021, the PRC employed multiple diplomatic tools in an attempt to erode U.S. and partner influence, such as highlighting the U.S. withdrawal from Afghanistan," Pentagon analysts noted, adding "PRC officials and state media outlets also repeatedly condemned the U.S. withdrawal from Afghanistan and cited the withdrawal as evidence that the U.S. is an unreliable partner and declining power."[16]

Kirby, however, tried to deny that the Pentagon had concluded that the US withdrawal from Afghanistan had been a propaganda gift to China.[17]

BACKING THE TALIBS

NATO analysts wrote that, for years, "Beijing . . . was hinting at their willingness to cooperate with a Taliban government if they were to take over." NATO said that the Chinese government was "apparently trying to play both sides, rhetorically supporting President Ashraf Ghani, while offering to host peace talks between the Afghan government and the Taliban."[18]

In late December 2020, the Trump administration declassified unconfirmed intelligence reports indicating that the Chinese government had offered bounties to nonstate actors in Afghanistan to attack US soldiers.[19] In mid-September 2007, the State Department had complained to Beijing about Chinese weapons shipments to Iran that had ended up in Taliban hands;[20] earlier that month, the British government had warned the Chinese government that Chinese-made weaponry was being used by the Taliban against UK troops.[21]

In December 2020, Afghanistan's National Directorate of Security (NDS) arrested ten Chinese nationals on charges of espionage and running a terror cell, saying that those arrested were linked to China's Ministry of State Security.[22] A senior diplomat in Kabul said that some of the Chinese nationals had been in contact with the Haqqani Network.[23] Afghan officials said that they had canceled oil and gas contracts with China in the wake of breaking up the spy ring and that they were also seeking to renegotiate the mining deal they had made with China a decade prior.

On June 4, 2021, the Chinese Foreign Ministry declared, "Foreign military forces should withdraw in a responsible and orderly manner," and the Afghan government should "welcome the Taliban back to the political mainstream."[24] In mid-July 2021, Xi Jinping held a call with Afghan president Ashraf Ghani, during which China said that Xi had (falsely) "emphasized that China firmly supports the Afghan government" and that China will support "the process of peace and reconciliation in Afghanistan."[25]

On July 28, China's minister of foreign affairs, Wang Yi, met with Taliban leader Abdul Ghani Baradar, and Wang said that the Taliban "is a pivotal military and political force in Afghanistan and is expected to play an important role in the process of peace, reconciliation, and reconstruction in Afghanistan." The Chinese government said that the Taliban commander had "said that China has always been a trustworthy and good friend of the Afghan people, and appreciates China's fair and active role in the process of peace and reconciliation in Afghanistan."[26] Baradar reportedly said that the Taliban "will never allow any forces to use Afghanistan's territory to do things that endanger China." The Chinese government said that Baradar "hopes that China will participate more in the Afghan peace reconstruction process and play a greater role in Afghan reconstruction and economic development in the future."[27]

On July 28 Taliban spokesman Mohammad Naeem tweeted, "China pledged to continue and expand its cooperation with the Afghan people."[28] Earlier that month, a senior Taliban official in Doha had said, "We care about the oppression of Muslims, be it in Palestine, in Myanmar, or in China, and we care about the oppression of non-Muslims anywhere in the world. But what we are not going to do is interfere in China's internal affairs."[29] Taliban spokesman Suhail Shaheen claimed not to know any specifics about how the Chinese government was repressing Uighur Muslims in Xinjiang. He said that the Taliban saw China as a friend and wanted China to invest in reconstruction work in Afghanistan "as soon as possible."[30] He also said that the Taliban would not allow any Uighur fighters to enter Afghanistan and also dismissed the al-Qaeda threat in Afghanistan, falsely claiming that al-Qaeda was no longer present in the country.

Global Times responded by making excuses for the Taliban and tried to divert attention from China's human rights abuses against the Uighurs by pointing the finger at the United States, saying "The West did not really care about Xinjiang Uygurs' human rights. It instead hoped to sow discord between Beijing and the Taliban."[31]

Despite all that, Blinken was asked about the Taliban-China meetings in late July, and he absurdly argued that China's role could be positive in Afghanistan. "Well, I think many countries immediately neighboring Afghanistan and in the broader region, including China, have interests in Afghanistan. And as it happens, those interests largely align," he said, adding "No one has an interest in a military takeover of the country by the Taliban. . . . And so if China is acting on those interests, if other countries are acting on those interests, that's a positive thing."[32] Ned Price was asked about the Taliban-China meetings in early August 2021, and he also said that the interests of the United States and China were aligned and that the United States welcomed China's role, adding "We are united in this."[33]

In the years leading up to the Taliban takeover, China increased its economic, intelligence, and military partnership with Pakistan; the Pakistani government has a large amount of influence over the Taliban.[34]

Afghanistan's ambassador in China, Javid Ahmad Qaem, futilely tried to push Beijing to pressure the Taliban, saying in mid-August that China should "be very clear to them that the way they want to govern is not going to be accepted" and "we believe China can use that leverage to convince Pakistan to see a peaceful Afghanistan."[35] Signaling where China thought things were headed, Global Times published a piece on August 13 in which it interviewed Dr. Latif Pedram, the leader of the National Congress Party (NCP) of Afghanistan, who lavished praise on China and added, "We are in agreement with the Taliban's position on the China projects."[36]

"THE WISHES AND CHOICES OF THE AFGHAN PEOPLE"

The Chinese Communist Party said it looked forward to continuing its "friendship and cooperation" with Afghanistan following the Taliban takeover of Afghanistan. Foreign Ministry spokeswoman Hua Chunying said that China "respects the wishes and choices of the Afghan people" following the Taliban's return to power. "China respects Afghan people's right to decide their own destiny and future, and is willing to continue to develop friendship and cooperation with Afghanistan," she said, adding, "Afghanistan's Taliban has expressed many times a desire for good relations with China, with an expectation that China will take part in Afghanistan's rebuilding and development process, and will not allow any forces to use Afghanistan's soil to harm China. We welcome this."[37]

On August 30, Chinese foreign minister Wang Yi told Blinken that the international community should establish relations with the Taliban and "guide it actively." A press release issued by the Chinese government said, "Blinken expressed his understanding of and respect for China's concerns on the Afghanistan issue."[38]

Taliban spokesman Zabihullah Mujahid said on September 2, "China is our most important partner and represents a fundamental and extraordinary opportunity for us, because it is ready to invest and rebuild our country." There are "rich copper mines in the country, which, thanks to the Chinese, can be put back into operation and modernised. In addition, China is our pass to markets all over the world."[39]

A former senior station chief in South Asia told us, "The Haqqanis are pretty close to the Chinese. And they've been shipping back Uighurs from Afghanistan. The Haqqanis were the guys who made everything run on time during the Taliban's insurgency, and that's also a concern. Eventually, if the Afghan government ever gets their shit together, they'll be an ally of China and let China just prey upon them economically."

SHOW ME THE MONEY

China has been the most powerful voice on the side of the Taliban arguing that the United States and the international community should lift all sanctions, unfreeze all bank accounts, and allow money to flow into Taliban coffers. Following the fall of Kabul, Chinese foreign minister Wang Yi said that all sanctions against the Taliban "must be stopped" and "all kinds of unilateral sanctions or restrictions" against Taliban-led Afghanistan should be lifted.[40] On December 22, at the United Nations, the Chinese demanded, "We once again call for the unfreezing of Afghanistan's overseas assets as soon as possible" and said that the funds "cannot be used as a bargaining chip for threats or coercion."[41]

On January 26, 2022, The Chinese government repeated the mantra at the United Nations, blaming Afghanistan's problems not on the Taliban but on the United States.[42] On March 30, the Chinese Foreign Ministry said that the United States and NATO should "earnestly assume the primary responsibility for the reconstruction and development of Afghanistan, and return the property of the Afghan people as soon as possible." Chinese foreign minister Wang Yi claimed that the United States had been the "initiator of Afghanistan's predicament" and said that the United States should "take the major responsibility" by ending its sanctions of the Taliban and handing over the frozen Afghan bank funds to them.[43]

CHINA COZIES UP TO THE TALIBAN

On March 31, Xi Jinping declared that China "is committed to supporting Afghanistan's peaceful and stable development."[44] On April 1, the State Department said that the Taliban had announced that the Chinese government had agreed to accept the credentials of Taliban diplomats to operate the Afghan Embassy in Beijing, and the Chinese government was "likely motivated to accept the diplomatic credentials of the Taliban's representatives by a desire to gain influence with the Taliban." It also said that Beijing "has promoted business opportunities in Afghanistan to PRC businesses, including in the natural resources sector" in an effort to "deepen relations with the Taliban."[45]

On August 2, Chinese Foreign Ministry spokesperson Hua Chunying criticized the United States for the air strike that had killed the Taliban leader Ayman al-Zawahiri because it had been done without permission from the Taliban (who were protecting the terrorist).[46]

EYES ON BAGRAM

After the fall of Kabul to the Taliban, concerns immediately began to be raised that China would seek to garner influence over Bagram for itself. In November 2021, an article in the US Air Force's *Journal of Indo-Pacific Affairs* said that China's priorities in Taliban-controlled Afghanistan "are likely to include the projection of regional airpower through Bagram Airfield."[47] The authors said that China had a goal of countering the United States and NATO in the region, possibly through securing Bagram to strengthen its regional airpower and to embarrass the United States.

After the United States abandoned Bagram in early July 2021, China quickly sent its state-run media to Bagram to check out the scene at the air base and to take photos of the mess left behind. The Chinese propaganda outlet Xinhua contended that "scrap was heaped up like garbage outside the base and their hasty withdrawal clearly speaks of defeat." The article concluded, "The status of Bagram as a stronghold quickly evaporated as the last troops scampered for home with their mission a failure and their standing in the eyes of Afghans lower than ever before. Militants have declared victory."[48] In a video posted on June 12, 2022, the Chinese state-run television network CGTN claimed that it had interviewed former Taliban prisoners at Parwan who said that the United States had conducted an air strike against the freed prisoners on August 15, 2021, killing dozens of them. The video went on to attack the United States' presence in Afghanistan at length.

On September 2, 2021, former UN ambassador Nikki Haley warned, "We need to watch China, because I think you are going to see China make a move for Bagram Air Force Base."[49] On November 7, 2021, Trump said that "We would have kept Bagram because it is next to China" but "now China is going to take over Bagram, in my opinion."[50] Trump later returned to this theme: "The reason we're keeping Bagram is because of China," he said on April 21, 2022. "It's one hour away from where China makes its nuclear weapons because billions and billions of dollars to build many years ago and right now it looks to me like China is going to end up owning and operating Bagram. We fled, left the lights on late at night, and we fled."[51]

In 2021, the Chinese military conducted a feasibility study on sending workers and troops to Bagram in the near future as part of the Belt and Road Initiative and at the invitation of the Taliban.[52] On September 20, an Indian news outlet reported that a Chinese military and intelligence delegation had recently visited Bagram and conducted reconnaissance there, collecting "evidence and data against Americans." Its sources said that China wanted to set up an intelligence facility in collaboration with the Taliban and Pakistan with the goal of hunting down anyone supporting Uyghur Muslims in western China.[53]

On September 7, the Chinese Foreign Ministry had called similar claims "purely fake news."[54] On October 3, the Taliban's Ministry of Information also denied the stories, claiming that "there are no foreign troops currently in Afghanistan, including Chinese."[55] But Bagram remains in China's sights. "You've got China in there, exploiting rare earth minerals. Trillion dollars of lithium and, under their Belt and Road Initiative, will most likely get access to Bagram Air Base," McCaul told us.

Bagram's strategic value had been huge—not just for keeping the Taliban at bay but also for keeping an eye on China—and the United States lost both when it was abandoned. Congressman Mike Waltz said that it was a "misleading" argument by the Biden administration to say that "we had to get out of Afghanistan to focus on China, again ignoring the fact that Bagram was the only base we have in the region—only base in the world—sandwiched between China, Russia, and Iran, kind of important on all three of those fronts." He said, "Twelve-thousand-foot runway, and oh, by the way, we're talking about China tripling its nuclear arsenal. It's right there in Xinjiang that Afghanistan borders. It's four hundred miles away."[56]

TAIWAN AND THE AFGHAN BELT AND ROAD SEGMENT

The CCP is maniacally focused on conquering Taiwan—and it believes that exploiting Afghanistan's natural resources (especially its critical rare-earth minerals) could be a small contribution to fueling the Chinese economic engine and building up the military strength needed to do so. An article in the US Air Force's *Journal of Indo-Pacific Affairs* said in November 2021 that "Beijing's priorities in Afghanistan include China's CPEC/BRI [China-Pakistan Economic Corridor and Belt and Road Initiative] interests, securing REE [rare-earth element] mining, and countering the Afghan-based Uighur ethnic minority." The article stressed that "China's planned REE mining operations in Afghanistan align with Beijing's intention to seize Taiwan for its semiconductor industry."[57]

In 2007, the U.S. Geological Survey concluded that Afghanistan has abundant mineral resources,[58] and in 2010, the US government said that there was nearly $1 trillion worth of untapped mineral deposits beneath the ground in Afghanistan, in an internal Pentagon memo that referred to the country as possibly the "Saudi Arabia of lithium."[59] In 2019, the Afghan government produced a mining sector road map that concluded that Afghanistan held "1.4 million [metric tons] of rare-earth minerals."[60]

China is interested in Logar province's Mes Aynak, which contains copper mines that are among the biggest in the entire world. In mid-July 2022, Global Times said that an Afghan government minister had held talks with a Chinese mining firm about the Aynak copper project.[61] On September 30, the Taliban's embassy in Beijing tweeted that the Taliban's head of embassy, Syed Muhyiddin Sadat, had met with Wang Hao, the deputy director of the Chinese contractor company behind the Mes Aynak project.[62] The Taliban said that dozens of Chinese companies, including state-owned ones, were bidding for Afghan mining concessions, and Chinese officials are regular visitors to the Afghan Ministry of Mines and Petroleum's headquarters in Kabul.[63]

Trump administration Treasury official Marshall Billingslea told us that "the Chinese were there" well before Kabul fell. "For instance, China was the dominant market for sales from the illicit mining trade. Now I would imagine that has ramped up substantially."

China had proudly touted its Belt and Road Initiative efforts in Afghanistan for years prior to the Taliban takeover.[64] NATO assessed in 2022 that "China has continued to indicate their interest in establishing relations with the Taliban and pushing for stability in the country." It also said that "Beijing is most likely concerned with extending the China-Pakistan Economic Corridor (CPEC) to Afghanistan" as part of the broader Belt and Road Initiative. The governments of China, Pakistan, and Afghanistan had announced in 2019 their intent to bring Afghanistan into the CPEC through a proposed highway running from Peshawar in Pakistan to Kabul in Afghanistan, and China had said it planned to put $62 billion into the project. "With the Taliban now in charge, China is expected to continue engagement in this project, with

the Taliban likely to agree," NATO said. "This would be mutually ben-
eficial: China gets to extend their economic corridor and gain access to
more regional markets, while the Taliban will get economic investment
to counter international sanctions."[65]

On March 24, 2022, Afghan acting foreign minister Amir Khan
Muttaqi said that "Afghanistan is ready to actively participate in Belt and
Road cooperation."[66] In mid-October, Taliban spokesman Zabihullah
Mujahid said, "In the last Cabinet meeting, it was decided that the Silk
Road, which will connect Afghanistan with China, must be built."[67]

The Chinese and the Taliban government inked a more-than-half-
billion-dollar deal at the start of January 2023, with Xinjiang Central
Asia Petroleum and Gas Company agreeing to develop the oil and
gas field in the Amu Darya basin in northern Afghanistan over the
following three years—yet another sign that China is serious about
exploiting Afghanistan's natural resources and the Taliban is eager
for Chinese cash.[68]

CHINA TOWN IN KABUL

In the wake of the Taliban takeover, China spent more than a year
repeatedly touting the money it was pouring into its "China Town in
Kabul."

On September 8, 2021, Global Times announced that "Chinese
business representatives in Afghanistan are to establish an industry
platform for investment promotion after the Taliban announced the
formation of an interim government." The Chinese business representative group China Town in Kabul said it was working to establish an
"Afghan institute" in the Taliban-led country.[69] On January 23, 2022,
Global Times said that "China's business representatives at China Town
in Kabul are to hold what could be the first large expo in Afghanistan
since the Afghan Taliban took power."[70] It then claimed on March 31
that "Chinese firms and businessmen are eyeing more opportunities in
Afghanistan, with an industrial park to be established in the Kabul New

City."[71] The groundbreaking ceremony for the China Town industrial park took place in April 2022, as the Chinese government sought to increase its economic foothold in Afghanistan and its influence in the capital city.[72]

ISIS-K CRASHES THE PARTY

Not to allow the China-Taliban friendship to proceed without a hitch, ISIS-K terrorists launched an attack on a Chinese-run hotel in Kabul in December 2022. Global Times said that "three armed people opened fire" on the Kabul hotel, in a more than hourlong gunfight with suicide bombers and more than ten explosions.[73] Videos showed fire and smoke rising from one of the lower-floor windows of the ten-floor hotel building, and videos showed hotel guests escaping out of a window, with one man hanging onto an air-conditioning unit before he fell to the ground from several floors up.

The Chinese outlet said the Kabul Longan Hotel was run by Chinese nationals, who had rented several floors of the building and remodeled it as a hotel and that it was the largest Chinese-run hotel in Afghanistan. The hotel also held the Chinese Embassy and the Kabul branch of the Chinese state-run news agency Xinhua; the website said that "some businesspeople, vloggers, scholars and Chinese nationals who travel to Kabul for business usually choose to stay in the hotel."[74] The eighth floor of the hotel had a small Chinese restaurant with a Chinese chef, and there was a Chinese hot pot place on the roof.[75]

The founder of the hotel said in November 2022, "Afghanistan is a popular country now. Our guests are mostly middle-class and elite Chinese people."[76] A Chinese businesswoman visiting the hotel assured him that many people from Chinese state-owned companies would be happy to stay at the hotel. Chinese Foreign Ministry spokesperson Wang Wenbin said that the attack had been "egregious in nature" and that China was "deeply shocked" by it. The Chinese government demanded a "thorough investigation" into the attack and urged the Taliban "to

take resolute and strong measures to ensure the safety of Chinese citizens, institutions, and projects in Afghanistan." China's ambassador
to Afghanistan, Wang Yu, "expressed his satisfaction over the overall
security in Afghanistan" but called on the Taliban to "pay more attention
to the security of the Chinese Embassy in Kabul."[77] ISIS-K said that its
attack had been aimed at "Communist China."

FEEDING THE DRAGON

Biden loves to brag about how much time he spent with Xi Jinping when
they were both vice presidents (actually exaggerating how many miles
the two traveled together, as if such a thing were a source of pride).
That relationship has yet to prove fruitful, at least for the United States.

In February 2022, the Biden administration ditched the Trump
Justice Department's China Initiative, which was aimed at combating
Chinese trade secret theft and industrial espionage, after pressure
campaigns by congressional Democrats, left-wing activists, university
professors, and the CCP itself.[78]

In September 2021, the Biden Justice Department had dropped its
fraud case against Huawei CFO Meng Wanzhou following hostage diplomacy conducted by China against Canada, where Meng was being held
pending extradition to the United States.[79] The United States entered into
a nonprosecution agreement with the Huawei criminal under Biden and
let her walk free, and China responded by freeing the two Canadians it
had wrongly imprisoned—with White House press secretary Jen Psaki
claiming that there had been "no link" between the two events.

The Biden Education Department has also largely backed off of its
predecessor's crackdown on Chinese influence on campus.[80] The United
States was also caught flat-footed in the South Pacific, where China
established a pact with the Solomon Islands in April 2022 and pushed
for other agreements with island nations.[81] The US government seems
to have largely given up on the hunt for covid-19's origins, and China

has successfully blocked a follow-up investigation while solidifying its influence at the World Health Organization and the United Nations.

In late January to early February 2023, Biden also allowed a Chinese spy balloon to traverse the continental United States, the CCP airship floating from Alaska's Aleutian islands into Canada, then into Idaho and Montana, then to the Eastern Seaboard, lingering near several military bases and installations before a US jet shot it down off the coast of the Carolinas.

DRAGONBEAR

In February 2022, Putin and Xi met at the start of the Beijing Olympics to announce a broad strategic partnership "without limits" amid Russia's military buildup on Ukraine's border. The State Department said that China has since "amplified" Russia's narrative on NATO. Once the full-scale invasion launched, China carefully avoided condemning Russia. Though the United States criticized China for its "at least tacit approval" of Russia's invasion, China repeatedly sought to lay the blame on the United States, calling it one of the "culprits of the crisis."[82]

In March 2022, the Russian government and media outlets ramped up their claims that the United States was operating bioweapon research facilities in Ukraine, with Chinese diplomats and propaganda outlets amplifying the story. The baseless allegations by Russia stretch back years. The United States has consistently denied the claims, and Russia has never provided any proof.[83]

China continually attempted to present itself as a peace mediator in Russia's war against Ukraine while amplifying the Kremlin narratives attempting to justify the war and pointing the finger at the United States.[84] Though claiming it stands for "peace" in Ukraine, the Chinese government repeatedly blamed the United States for the violence there, along with Western exuberance over the collapse of the Soviet Union during the Cold War, NATO's membership expansion over the years, and the United States' provision of weaponry to Ukraine both before and after Putin's invasion.[85]

The fact that the CCP amplified the Kremlin's claims wasn't surprising. Even before the Putin-Xi "no limits" partnership, the Chinese and Russian governments had quietly signed a secret deal in July 2021 to help promote propaganda being pushed by their respective state-run media outlets.[86] Russia and China also jointly spread covid-19 disinformation, claiming that the virus had originated with the US military.

On March 18, 2022, Biden and Xi spoke together at length, and the Chinese government's transcript contained no criticism of Russia but claimed, "China stands for peace and opposes war." It included the Chinese sayings "It takes two hands to clap" and "He who tied the bell to the tiger must take it off."[87] Both echoed Chinese efforts to blame the West for the war in Ukraine.

On March 20, 2022, China's ambassador to the United States, Qin Gang, said that it was "naive" to ask why Xi wasn't condemning Putin's invasion. But, he insisted, "China is part of the solution. It's not part of the problem."[88] Wrong.

In late March 2022, Russian foreign minister Sergey Lavrov made his first visit to China since the Ukraine invasion had begun in February, and he and his team engaged in discussions with Chinese foreign minister Wang Yi, in which the two sides reaffirmed their friendship despite calls from the United States and the West for China to pressure the Kremlin into ending its war. Wang blamed the war in Ukraine in part on "accumulated European security contradictions, Cold War thinking, and confrontations between groups." Reporting on the meeting, the Kremlin said that "the sides noted the counterproductive nature of the illegal unilateral sanctions imposed on Russia by the United States and its satellites." Wang also reportedly said that Moscow and Beijing are now "more determined" to build their strategic partnership and that their alliance is moving in the "correct" direction, even during the Ukraine invasion.[89]

Putin and Xi spoke via video link at the end of December 2022, reaffirming their alliance. Despite claims by some that China was backing off of its embrace of Russia because of the way the Ukraine invasion had gone, both dictators claimed that their friendship was stronger than ever. The Russian leader repeatedly touted the enduring "Russian-Chinese strategic partnership" as he praised "Dear Mr. Chairman" Xi and China's economic support for Russia during the war. He also said, "We aim to strengthen cooperation between the armed forces of Russia and China."[90]

Xi called Putin "my dear friend" and said, "I am very glad to see you again." "Under our joint leadership, China-Russia comprehensive partnership and strategic interaction in the new era is showing maturity and resilience," he said. "In the face of a difficult and far from unambiguous international situation, we are ready to build up strategic cooperation with Russia." Chinese state-run media said that Xi had told Putin that "China is ready to work with Russia and all progressive forces in the world that stand against hegemonism and power politics."[91]

The DragonBear alliance was strengthened even further when Xi traveled to Moscow to meet with Putin in March 2023, as China continued to provide Russia with rhetorical, economic, financial, and, at minimum, non-lethal military support for the Ukraine invasion.[92]

Just as Russia needed China in its corner when invading Ukraine, China knows it will need Russia to have its back when it goes after Taiwan.

STRATEGIC AMBIGUITY

Admiral Philip Davidson, a former commander of the U.S. Indo-Pacific Command (USPACOM), said in March 2021, before the Taliban takeover, "The PRC has adopted an increasingly assertive military posture to exert pressure and expand its influence across the region. This is particularly stark concerning Taiwan." He said that the "threat is manifest" this decade.

After the Taliban takeover (including days after the fall of Kabul), Biden repeatedly vowed that the United States would defend Taiwan if China invaded, only for the White House to ultimately walk that back (while claiming that wasn't what it was doing), insisting upon a posture of strategic ambiguity. Biden again declared during an October 2021 CNN town hall, "Yes, we have a commitment to do that" when asked if the United States would come to Taiwan's defense. Psaki quickly claimed that "the president was not announcing any change in our policy."[93] And when asked in May 2022 if the United States would "get involved militarily to defend Taiwan" after not having done so in Ukraine, Biden replied, "Yes, that's the commitment we made." Again, the White House rapidly backpedaled.[94] Biden was again asked in September if US forces would defend Taiwan if China invaded, and he said, "Yes, if in fact there was an unprecedented attack." He repeated his answer when asked again. The White House again walked it back.[95]

On December 27, Taiwanese president Tsai Ing-wen announced that Taiwan would be strengthening its military amid increased threats of invasion by China. She announced an expanded military, a new standing garrison force, a new civil defense system, an expanded reserve force, and mandatory one-year military service for Taiwanese men. She said, "No one wants war. . . . Taiwan stands on the frontlines of authoritarian expansion, at the vanguard of the global defense of democracy. Only by preparing for war can we avoid it—only by being capable of fighting a war can we stop one."[96]

On March 8, Director of National Intelligence Avril Haines and CIA director William Burns both testified before the House Intelligence Committee that the Russian invasion's going sideways for Putin had likely impacted Xi's calculus toward Taiwan, with Burns saying that Xi was likely "unsettled" by the way the war in Ukraine was going.[97]

David Sauer, the former CIA station chief in East Asia, told us that Russia's struggles in Ukraine likely had not shifted Xi's malign intentions toward Taiwan at all. "I doubt he's changed one bit. It's whether he can coerce Taiwan back to the negotiating table, and my view is, no, they're not going to give up their sovereignty. They've seen what's happened with Hong Kong, with the destruction of Hong Kong people's rights, and the Taiwan people are going to reject that," he said. "So he's going to bide his time. He's going to use United Front tactics inside Taiwan to try to get politicians that are more amenable elected, who are more amenable to China and try to slowly subvert, at least for the near term. But if he wants Taiwan, he's going to have to take it."

Should the CCP choose to invade Taiwan, Biden's debacle in Afghanistan will be one of the reasons Xi Jinping will doubt the will of the United States to stop him.

FIFTEEN

THE THIRTEEN

O n August 29, 2021, President Biden, First Lady Jill Biden, and other members of the military and his administration, stood on the tarmac of Dover Air Force Base as eleven metal caskets (two transfers were conducted in private) were carried from a military plane into vehicles ready to drive them to a facility at Air Force Mortuary Affairs Operations. An American flag covered each casket, and soldiers in fatigues, boots, white gloves, and black masks accompanied each casket down the ramp and into the waiting vehicles.

The attack had left so many dead, military officials said, that the Fisher House at Dover, which the Defense Department provides for the families of fallen, was not large enough to accommodate all the grieving families, so some loved ones lodged off base.

NO TIME FOR NAMES HE DIDN'T KNOW

On the day of the Kabul bombing, Biden had honored the thirteen, saying "These American service members who gave their lives—it's an overused word, but it's totally appropriate—they were heroes. Heroes who have been engaged in a dangerous, selfless mission to save the lives of others."[1]

But if he believed his own words, he certainly did not show it at Dover. As the flag-draped steel coffins were escorted off the plane, he repeatedly checked his watch. Several warriors' families claim that he checked his watch *at least five times*, as opposed to the three times previously reported.[2] "It was literally impossible to miss unless you had your eyes closed. Every single casket that came off up through the first five," said Mark Schmitz, the father of Lance Corporal Jared Schmitz. "I stopped looking at him after that because I was so disgusted by what I was seeing." Shana Chappell, the mother of Marine Lance Corporal Kareem Nikoui, told us that she also stopped watching Biden after he checked his watch for a fifth time.

Meanwhile, Darin Hoover, the father of Staff Sergeant Darin Taylor Hoover, told us that Biden had checked his watch every time he finished saluting one of the warriors. "I was watching Biden the entire time, and every single one of them—and I was there—when they released the salutes, he'd check that stupid watch. Every single time," he stated.

Whether he checked his watch five or eleven times, Biden sent the same message to the families gathered on the tarmac: he didn't have time for them or their fallen loved ones. Christy Shamblin, the mother-in-law of Marine Sergeant Nicole Gee, told us that the situation had been "heartbreaking." She added, "It's hard to believe it wasn't intentionally disrespectful."

After the ceremony concluded, Biden met privately with the Gold Star family members present that day. The families we interviewed had had disturbing yet remarkably similar encounters with the president. They told us that he had repeatedly interrupted family members to talk about his son Beau, who had died of brain cancer five years after a deployment to Iraq. Shamblin described her conversation with Biden, saying "It started with, 'My son, Beau. When my son Beau passed—' and I just looked at him and kind of tuned out at that point. It was very hard. We were close enough that we could hear what he said to other families, and he said the exact same thing. I mean, it was like he had memorized it. It was nauseating."

Chappell recalled a similar, albeit more contentious, conversation with the president, telling us "I explained to him that I'm never going to hug Kareem again. I'm never going to see a smile, I'm never going to hear his voice, and he interrupted me. He started talking about his son Beau." When she tried turning the conversation back to her son, Biden tried to justify his position, saying he wanted to show that he knew how she felt.

Finally, as if his actions were not already disgraceful enough, the whole time Biden spoke with the Gold Star parents, he *never said their children's names*. He said only "your son" or "your daughter," leading some parents to believe that he did not know the thirteen warriors' names. "He never once said Nicole's name. I can tell you who did, and it was members of the Marine Corps," Shamblin said. "He didn't know their names. It just felt so disingenuous." President Biden issued a written statement honoring the thirteen on August 26, 2021, and another honoring them by name on the one-year anniversary of the attack, but never spoke their names out loud in public.

Biden's behavior was not limited to that night in Dover. On Memorial Day, May 30, 2022, he met with Paula Knauss Selph, the mother of Army Staff Sergeant Ryan Christian Knauss. Like the other Gold Star parents we interviewed, Paula said Biden had never mentioned Ryan's name and that she's never heard him mention the names of the other fallen warriors. "I can't think of a president who's ever brought such shame to our country, for the whole fact that these men and women are standing up for the United States of America and our president doesn't have enough in him to speak their names. To say 'Sorry,' just out loud," she stated. "Never a word of sorrow or 'I'm sorry,' never did he say that. Nor did he say Ryan's name. A man of character is who I was looking for, as I stood at the Oval Office, to hear him express deep sorrow or deep hurt or pain for the situation he saw in front of him. But I saw an empty, soulless person."

Multiple family members also discussed their frustration with Biden over the impossible situation he had placed their sons and daughters in: a massive and chaotic evacuation which left Americans and Afghan allies behind, which relied upon a brutal and insidious Taliban enemy for security as ISIS-K ran wild and looked for an opportunity to strike, and which resulted in the deadly attack that murdered their loved ones. They were also angered by the Biden administration's continued stonewalling and silence, which they attributed to Biden's desire to put the debacle—and the deaths of their loved ones—squarely in the rearview mirror.

NEVER FORGET

The families we interviewed made one thing painfully clear: the president of the United States didn't just fail to pay proper respect to those thirteen fallen warriors, he actively disrespected them. To this day, he still hasn't said their names out loud and has mentioned them in only two written statements.

We can't possibly honor these thirteen the way they deserve, but their names must be known, and their memory must be preserved. The best way to do that is through the words of those who knew them best.

The remainder of this chapter features testimonies from family and friends of the thirteen warriors who died in Kabul. Though we attempted to contact members of each family, some asked for privacy, declined to be interviewed, or did not respond. In such cases, we collected publicly available testimonies given by family or friends.

Marine Lance Corporal David L. Espinoza

Lance Corporal Espinoza's official obituary:

In the words of the late President John F. Kennedy in his inaugural address, "Ask not what your country can do for you—ask what you can do for your country." Lance Corporal Espinoza embodied this treasured moment in history and carried it with him throughout his life's journey. As a toddler, he always wanted to play with his plastic soldiers, envisioning different scenarios. No matter how many years have passed since then, he always told everyone that knew him that he was going to become a US Marine. A dream he pursued into reality when he joined the ranks of the United States Marine Corps in August of 2019, two years ago. David was born in Laredo, Texas, and raised in Rio Bravo, Texas, his hometown. Never the outspoken type, he was shy at first, but when you got to know him, you got to know the beautiful, caring, honest, and loyal person he truly was.

He was educated in the United Independent School District, having attended Lyndon B. Johnson High School, graduating in the summer of 2019. Immediately after graduating, he went off to MCRD in San Diego, California for basic training. Lance Corporal Espinoza then went to the school of Infantry at Camp Pendleton and most recently, received his orders to Afghanistan for the withdrawal of the US forces after a 20 year-long conflict. David never once complained about his assignment, rather, took it to heart to give back to those whom he was sent to protect. He, alongside 12 other servicemen and women, was killed in action, doing what they were trained to do: protect and defend. Although that fateful day will forever be remembered and forged in our hearts and minds, comfort is taken in the amount of love, support, and encouragement the community, the nation has given to us, his beloved family.

David's memory will carry on in each and every one of us and we also hope that as the days, weeks, months, and years go by, we too might be of service to our brothers and sisters, neighbors and friends, near and far. In the words of the late President Ronald Reagan: "Some people spend an entire lifetime wondering if they made a difference in this world. Marines don't have that problem." David, you have made a difference in this world. Until we meet again, may you rest in peace, Semper Fi, Ooh-Rah!!![3]

Marine Sergeant Nicole Gee

Christy Shamblin, mother-in-law of Sergeant Gee:

Nicole was just truly the epitome of everything that can come from hard work and a positive attitude. It's hard to explain, and I don't have quite the right words for it. Things came to her because she worked her ass off for it. Because she was up at 5 a.m. going to the gym, when nobody else was there, so that she could then go to school and get straight As and then go work a job.

In high school when she was on deployment, right before Afghanistan, she was kind of like a legend on her ship. I think the Navy guys didn't like the Marine people working out in their gym, on the ship. So she would get as a 4am to go workout. She was going to get her workout in, you know? She was just everything that you can look at and go, "Here's what a positive attitude and hard work can do."

She just had such a heart for everybody. She volunteered to even be in Afghanistan because they needed women to serve the women and children. They went on her ship and said, "We need volunteers," and she was one of the first ones to say "Yes, send me," and that's just the kind of person she always was.[4]

Marine Staff Sergeant Darin Taylor Hoover

Kelly Hoover, mother of Staff Sergeant Hoover:

I want people to know how much of a good person he was. How much of a good leader he was. How much he loved this country and how much he loved his men. Loved his family, of course. That was his main thing was family. He had a strong conviction of being a leader, and not in the sense of title. It was a sense of always trying to make someone better than when you found them, if that makes sense.

When it comes down to getting the job done, taking care of the job, taking care of his family, taking care of his men, he was all 100 percent in, and that's what I want his legacy to be. His mantra was "Movement is life." You've got to keep moving, you've got to keep bettering yourself, you've got to keep bettering others and give 100 percent, and that's his legacy. His legacy is one of love, and of honor, courage, and commitment.

Darin Hoover, father of Staff Sergeant Hoover:

F irst and foremost, his sisters and his mom were everything to him. He's got quite a bit of an extended family on Kelly's side. And whenever he'd come home from a deployment or come home, you know, anytime, any given time during the year when he was working, everybody flocked to him. He was the center of attention and everybody from cousins, aunts, uncles, grandparents, obviously, and all of us, you know, he was the epitome of what a man is.

But he was the calm in the storm. He was the one that literally brought everybody together, and Kelly's right: he was anti-bully. He'd see somebody getting picked on that was smaller, even if that individual started the dustup, that he would be the calming force in everything. It didn't matter what it was.

Army Staff Sergeant Ryan Christian Knauss

Paula Knauss Selph, mother of Staff Sergeant Knauss:

R yan was something. He had this great smile that made you smile. It was a little smirky smile when Ryan thought he knew a little bit more than you or thought he had something clever to say. This confidence was part of Ryan's mark on people. But, it was serving in the armed forces that truly helped Ryan grow from a boy to a man of valor...

You just want to see someone like Ryan keep going in life, you know? You want to see what he is going to do with his life, because Ryan was trying to live life fully.

Therefore, The Respect and Remember Memorial Foundation, also known as The R2 Factor, was established after Ryan's untimely death to respect and remember Ryan, the 13 killed in Kabul, and the many men and women in uniform who are now bravely serving this nation. The foundation has a three-pronged effect. First, it encourages men and women who are enlisting into the armed forces with monetary stipends to help them buy needed comfort items that the armed forces does not supply.... Secondly, actively deployed military personnel are supported with community care packages while their dependent family members receive community support during organized fundraising events such as 5K races, group bike rides, and musical events. Thirdly, the foundation partners with other veteran organizations that promote brotherhood in such events as motorcycle rides, fishing, golfing, parades, and more. These efforts are aimed at combating the high suicide rate among veterans and the adjustments needed by veterans returning to civilian life.

Ryan really was something. I will always love him and never forget the sacrifice he and others heroically gave at the Abbey Gate. May we always respect and remember those in uniform who are willing to lay down their lives for our freedom, regardless of poor political or military decisions that can cost them their lives.

Marine Corporal Hunter Lopez

From Corporal Lopez's obituary, published in the Palm Springs Desert Sun:

Hunter was devoted to serving others and perfecting himself in order to be the best explorer and Marine possible. Whether at work or at home, Hunter strived for perfection, seeking knowledge and experience from those he respected and admired. When on leave, Hunter enjoyed being around family and friends and sharing his experiences with everyone. He lived life to the fullest and was often the reason why family and friends would bend over backwards to get together when he was around.

Hunter was a history buff and had many aspirations to pursue after completing his service to the country, among those was being part of a shooting and firearms company with several friends which is already underway and becoming a deputy with the Riverside County Sheriff's Department.

Always a fan of everything and anything Star Wars related, Hunter convinced countless friends, family and Marines to binge watch movies and would often quiz them on Star Wars trivia. As a child, Hunter shied away from photographs and it was a challenge to get him to smile in most photographs. As an Explorer Scout and especially as a Marine Hunter seemed to flourish and developed an infectious smile and amazing personality. Hunter lived a full life in a short amount of time, he impacted so many lives and has left a lasting impression on family, friends, and his brothers and sisters in arms.

May he rest in peace in the loving arms of his Savior.

Semper Fidelis.[5]

Marine Lance Corporal Rylee J. McCollum

Excerpts from Lance Corporal McCollum's obituary:

In Rylee's short 20 years and six months he lived a lifetime.

Rylee was born Feb. 26, 2001, in Riverton. His early years were spent in Dubois. At the age of 6, Rylee moved to Jackson with his father, Jim, and his sisters, Cheyenne and Roice. It was in this mountain community that Rylee learned about love, life, loss, hardships and hard work.

Life came at Rylee hard, but he found a way to meet the challenges and come out on the other side! Usually with his warm smile and great sense of humor! His infectious laugh and smile always lit up the room. . . .

Rylee had a desire to do something and be something greater than he was. He had always shown admiration and respect for the military, the country and in particular the USMC. Conversations often led to a desire to be a Marine. On Rylee's 18th birthday he made that choice, to offer his service to the country and do what it took to become one of the Few and the Proud. He graduated Marine Corps Boot Camp at Camp Pendleton, on Dec. 6, 2019. . . .

As his story unfolded and developed, he became the man that I knew he would be. Humble, selfless and heroic. He gave his life helping others. Meeting the challenges head-on and doing what he knew was right for another. Even those he didn't know. . . .

Growing up in western Wyoming afforded Rylee the opportunities to enjoy the beautiful country that he lived in. . . .

Shortly after his Marine Corps graduation, Rylee met his wife Jiennah (Gigi). They married on Valentine's Day 2021, and are expecting their baby Sept. 22. Rylee was excited to become a father. Rylee could not have found a better partner to share his life with. The family fell in love with her as well the very first time we met her. As the family has gotten to know her better, it has become apparent they share the same generous heart. Always thinking of others.

Some of the fondest memories of Rylee are the simplest times shared with him. Card games, stories, family trips and holidays. He always kept us laughing and smiling . . . usually at his expense![6]

Marine Lance Corporal Dylan R. Merola

Cheryl Rex, mother of Lance Corporal Merola:

Growing up, Dylan was a very happy child. He never let anything really bother him. He was always smiling and caring towards everybody around him.[7]

Clarinda Matsuoka, grandmother of Lance Corporal Merola:

Growing up knowing that it's God and Country, that was where he laid his thoughts. He was very enthralled with every aspect of the armed services.

I remember him running around with his little Nerf guns thinking he was a soldier. He just would laugh, and he goes, "one day I'm going to be in the service."[8]

Uncle (unnamed) of Lance Corporal Merola:

Dylan loved doing stage set up and technical theater at Los Osos High School in Rancho Cucamonga. He was the kind of person who would always be there for his friends and just enjoyed hanging out with family for family cook nights. They would hike, fish, kayak and spend time just being together. He will be truly missed and always in our hearts.[9]

Marine Lance Corporal Kareem Nikoui

Shana Chappell, mother of Lance Corporal Nikoui:

I think readers should know that Kareem was a really good person. There is nothing that he wouldn't do to help others. He was just very good.

He loved being a Marine. It was something he wanted to be since he was a child, and he took it really seriously. So seriously that when he'd come home on weekends, because we live close enough to Camp Pendleton that he could come home on weekends, and he would bring his Marine brothers and they would think that they were going to get to spend a weekend relaxing and partying. And he'd have them up bright and early Saturday morning hiking the hills because we live in a hill, and he'd be making them go hiking, and he'd take them down to the river bottom and make them run through the sand. Because he always knew he could be a better Marine than what he was. So he absolutely loved his job as a Marine.

Marine Corporal Daegan W. Page

Statement released by Corporal Page's family:

Our beloved son, Corporal Daegan William-Tyeler Page, 23, was killed in Afghanistan yesterday. Daegan joined the U.S. Marine Corps after graduating from Millard South High School. He loved the brotherhood of the Marines and was proud to serve as a member of the 2nd Battalion, 1st Marine Regiment at Marine Corps Base Camp Pendleton, California.

Daegan's girlfriend Jessica, his mom, dad, step-mom, step-dad, 4 siblings, and grandparents are all mourning the loss of a great son, grandson, and brother. Daegan was raised in Red Oak, Iowa and the Omaha metro area and was a longtime member of the Boy Scouts. He enjoyed playing hockey for Omaha West-side in the Omaha Hockey Club and was a diehard Chicago Blackhawks fan. He loved hunting and spending time outdoors with his dad, as well as being out on the water. He was also an animal lover with a soft spot in his heart for dogs.

Daegan always looked forward to coming home and hanging out with his family and many buddies in Nebraska. To his younger siblings, he was their favorite jungle gym and to his friends, he was a genuinely happy guy that you could always count on. After finishing his enlistment, Daegan planned to come home and go to a local trade school, possibly to become a lineman.

Daegan will always be remembered for his tough outer shell and giant heart. Our hearts are broken, but we are thankful for the friends and family who are surrounding us during this time. Our thoughts and prayers are also with the other Marine and Navy families whose loved ones died alongside Daegan.[10]

Marine Sergeant Johanny Rosario Pichardo

Yohervi Rosario Pichardo, brother of Sergeant Pichardo:

My older sister Johanny was such a beautiful person. She was just an amazing person. She was our family's backbone whenever my mom or siblings couldn't, she would find a way. My older sister taught me these wise words: "Not every situation needs a reaction," and that hit us all.[11]

From Sergeant Pichardo's obituary:

Marine Corps Sergeant Johanny Rosario Pichardo 25, a member of the 5th Marine Expeditionary Brigade, Naval Support Activity, Bahrain and that brigade's Female Engagement Team who was screening women and children at the

Abbey Gate of the Hamid Karzai International Airport, Kabul, Afghanistan died on Thursday, August 26, 2021 along with her 9 Marine Brothers, 1 Marine Sister, 1 US Navy Corpsman and 1 US Army soldier from a terrorist attack. In addition, nearly 200 Afghan men, women and children died that day. Her family honors the US service men and women who were injured in the attack and pray for their quick recovery.[12]

Marine Corporal Humberto A. Sanchez

Coral Briseno, mother of Corporal Sanchez:

I've shared this story before, and I'm not going to be tired of sharing it. He was making bad decisions, he was being a teenager, was a wild teenager, and people didn't believe in him. But somehow, I always said, "No matter what people say about you, I am proud of you. You are my everything, and you know it doesn't matter what you do, I'm going to be here for you." And one day he shows up after high school was done, and he's like "Hey, Mom, do you have something to do around four?" and I said, "No what do you need?" He's like "I have an appointment, and they need you to go" and I said "Appointment? What happened? What did you do?" and then he said, "I joined the Marines. I am seventeen, and they need your signature." And then I knew my kid was going to do something and be somebody.[13]

Carol Sanchez, sister of Corporal Sanchez:

He had such a beautiful soul. A lot of times when I was going through something, sometimes all I needed was just a hug from my brother because he was like my partner in everything.

Even though I hated that he was away because I just wanted him close, I was very proud of him for everything he was doing.

Even when he didn't try, he was just amazing at everything he did. Everything.[14]

Marine Lance Corporal Jared M. Schmitz

Suzanne Schmitz, mother of Lance Corporal Schmitz:

As far as what I want people to know is, I mean, the only way I can describe Jared is he was just a sweet guy and only thing he ever wanted to do was join the military. He told me that when he was in third grade. I thought he would outgrow it, but he didn't. He never did. He never talked about doing anything else with his life. This is what he wanted to do.

And, like, this was his whole life, being a Marine. It was, you know, that's all he ever wanted. He was so proud of himself. He loved it. He couldn't wait to deploy. He was just a goofy kid. Always joking, always laughing, always dancing, loved to dance. He went to a visual and performing arts school all through elementary school, so he was never serious about anything, unless it was about the Marines. This was his whole life.

Mark Schmitz, father of Lance Corporal Schmitz:

Jared was probably the best big brother anyone could ever ask for and I think he carried that on with him in his personal relationships. He was a friend to everyone. He looked out for the little guy. He always looked out for everybody that was getting bullied in school, for example, or having issues, he would stand up for him.

He was an incredible young man and to watch him growing into the man he was, it was just amazing. I had seen him through everything from being a little squirt to, you know, to blossoming into the young man he was, and it just tears me up to know that he'll never have the opportunity to be someone's husband, someone's father, because he would have been great at any of those things.

Our mission is to remember all of those who have gone before by paying the ultimate sacrifice by honoring those veterans that are still with us. . . . It's called The Freedom 13. . . . Our goal is to build recreational retreat villages in every state in the United States. . . . We want this to be a gift from our family to all the veterans out there.

Navy Corpsman Maxton W. Soviak

From Corpsman Soviak's obituary, published by his memorial foundation:

Maxton graduated from Edison High School in 2017 with a determined mind to join the Navy. He went to boot camp at Great Lakes Chicago and from there he went to Texas for A school. Once he graduated A school he was stationed in Guam. While in Guam he worked as a medic in vaccinations and surgery. Guam provided him with many opportunities to meet some amazing people and grow as a person. During his time there he enjoyed cliff diving, scuba diving, cross fit, wrestling, jujitsu, and was able to help start a wrestling program.

He dreamed of going greenside with the Marines and was looking forward to making that dream come true. He attended Corpsman school in California at Camp Pendleton. Upon graduation he was assigned to 2/1 Ghost company. He felt a sense of pride and excitement as things were falling into place. While on a routine deployment to Jordan the battalion was called to assist with the humanitarian effort to evacuate those trying to escape the Taliban in Kabul.

On August 26th, 2021, while at Abbey gate he along with 12 other service members as well as over 170 Afghans were killed by a suicide bomber. Maxton died doing what he felt passionate about. Serving his country regardless of who they were and where they were born, saving one person at a time.[15]

ACKNOWLEDGMENTS

JAMES HASSON: First and foremost, I want to thank my wife, Katie, who served as my "focus group of one" and patiently listened to my ramblings about this book throughout our first year of marriage. I also want to recognize my younger brother, John, who helped carry me over the finish line.

None of this would have been possible without the efforts of Jonathan Bronitsky and the entire team at Athos. I owe Jonathan more than a few rounds of good bourbon. And I'd be remiss if I didn't recognize Alex Pappas and his team at Center Street, who took the lump of marble we gave them and turned it into something worth paying attention to.

JERRY DUNLEAVY: I want to thank all of my friends and family— especially my Mom and Dad—who encouraged me during the course of writing this book. Thank you to Athos and to Jonathan Bronitsky for helping this project come to fruition, and many thanks to everyone at Center Street, with a special shout-out to Alex Pappas, for turning this idea into a reality. I will also be eternally grateful to everyone who was willing to trust us and speak with us for this book so that these important stories could be brought to light. Many thanks to my excellent coauthor, James, without whose hard work and friendship none of this could have been possible. And last but by no means least, thank you to Carly Roman, my insightful sounding board throughout this process, whose invaluable and loving support I will always remember and cherish.

NOTES

A good deal of information in this book comes from firsthand interviews conducted by the authors, or material supplied by our contacts. Where sources are not annotated in the text and cited below, readers can assume that the information or quotations were obtained in this way.

CHAPTER 1: WRONG ABOUT EVERYTHING

1. Jerry Dunleavy, "'The US has no obligation': Biden fought to keep Vietnamese refugees out of the US," *Washington Examiner*, July 4, 2019, https://www .washingtonexaminer.com/news/the-us-has-no-obligation-biden-fought-to-keep -vietnamese-refugees-out-of-the-us.

2. Ibid.

3. Memorandum of Conversation, April 14, 1975, Gerald R. Ford Presidential Library & Museum, https://www.fordlibrarymuseum.gov/library/document/0314/1553026 .pdf.

4. Jerry Dunleavy, "Afghanistan Debacle is Biden's Second Saigon Moment," *Washington Examiner*, August 19, 2021, https://www.washingtonexaminer.com /news/afghanistan-debacle-biden-second-saigon-moment.

5. Annie Linskey, "From Saigon to Kabul: Biden's Response to Vietnam Echoes in His Views of Afghanistan Withdrawal," *Washington Post*, August 15, 2021, https://www .washingtonpost.com/politics/biden-vietnam-afghanistan/2021/08/15/fd155518 -fdd5-11eb-ba7e-2cf966e88e93_story.html.

6. Joseph Simonson and Jerry Dunleavy, "'Joe Biden Has a Big China Problem': Trump Preps Campaign Assault on Fall Foe," *Washington Examiner*, April 20, 2020, https:// www.washingtonexaminer.com/news/joe-biden-has-a-big-china-problem-trump -preps-campaign-assault-on-fall-foe.

7. Jerry Dunleavy and Joe Simonson, "'Joe Biden has a big China problem': Trump preps campaign assault on fall foe," *Washington Examiner*, April 17, 2020, https://www.washingtonexaminer.com/news/joe-biden-has-a-big-china-problem -trump-preps-campaign-assault-on-fall-foe.

8. Ibid.

9. Ibid.

10. Ebony Bowden, "Inside Joe Biden's History of Falsely Claiming He Predicted 9/11 Attacks," *New York Post*, September 10, 2020, https://nypost.com/2020/09/10/inside -bidens-history-of-falsely-claiming-he-predicted-9-11/.

11. Michael Crowley, "Rhetorical Question," *The New Republic*, October 22, 2001, https://newrepublic.com/article/61756/rhetorical-question.

12. Mitt Romney, "Press Release: The Obama-Biden Record: Failed Overtures Toward Iran," The American Presidency Project, October 11, 2012, https://www.presidency.ucsb.edu/documents/press-release-the-obama-biden-record-failed-overtures-toward-iran.

13. Gabriel Debenedetti, "'It'd Be Fun to Let You Be President for Just 5 Minutes': Joe Biden's Afghanistan Policy Was Forged in Obama-Era Disappointment," *Vanity Fair*, September 13, 2022, https://www.vanityfair.com/news/2022/09/joe-bidens-afghanistan-policy-was-forged-in-obama-era-disappointment.

14. Bob Woodward and Robert Costa, *Peril*, (New York: Simon & Schuster, 2021), 336.

15. Ibid., 382.

16. Bob Woodward, *Obama's Wars* (New York: Simon & Schuster, 2011), 167.

17. "White House Stands by Biden Statement That Taliban Isn't U.S. Enemy," Fox News, January 27, 2015, https://www.foxnews.com/politics/white-house-stands-by-biden-statement-that-taliban-isnt-u-s-enemy.

18. Robert Gates, *Duty: Memoirs of a Secretary at War* (New York: Knopf, 2014), 288.

19. Ibid., 349.

20. George Packer, citing Richard Holbrooke's diary, in *Our Man: Richard Holbrooke and the End of the American Century* (New York: Knopf, 2019), 533.

21. Ibid.

22. Ibid.

23. Robert Gates, *Duty*, 410.

24. Jerry Dunleavy, "Biden Prepares to Blast Trump over Russia, a Threat He Dismissed in 2012," *Washington Examiner*, April 26, 2019, https://www.washingtonexaminer.com/news/joe-biden-prepares-to-blast-trump-over-russia-a-threat-he-dismissed-in-2012.

25. Joseph R. Biden, Jr., "Remarks by President Biden on the Way Forward in Afghanistan," White House, April 14, 2021, https://www.whitehouse.gov/briefing-room/speeches-remarks/2021/04/14/remarks-by-president-biden-on-the-way-forward-in-afghanistan/.

26. Jerry Dunleavy, "Biden's Shifting Story on His Bin Laden Raid Stance Conflicts with Obama's Own Telling," *Washington Examiner*, December 7, 2020, https://www.washingtonexaminer.com/news/bidens-shifting-story-on-his-bin-laden-raid-stance-conflicts-with-obamas-own-telling.

27. Barak Obama, *A Promised Land*, quoted in Jerry Dunleavy, "Biden's shifting story on his bin Laden raid stance conflicts with Obama's own telling," *Washington Examiner*, December 7, 2020, https://www.washingtonexaminer.com/news/bidens-shifting-story-on-his-bin-laden-raid-stance-conflicts-with-obamas-own-telling.

28. Gates, *Duty*, 543.

29. Daniel Halper, "Biden Once Called Iraq One of Obama's 'Great Achievements,'" *Weekly Standard*, June 12, 2014, https://www.washingtonexaminer.com/weekly-standard/biden-once-called-iraq-one-of-obamas-great-achievements.

30. Joe Biden, "Why I Chose Lloyd Austin as Secretary of Defense," *Atlantic*, December 8, 2020, https://www.theatlantic.com/ideas/archive/2020/12/secretary-defense/617330/.

31. Marc Caputo, "'Clever': Biden Plays the Obama Card," Politico, January 17, 2020, https://www.politico.com/news/2020/01/17/biden-plays-the-obama-card-100520.

CHAPTER 2: DOHA

1 Munir Ahmed, "US Envoy Lauds Pakistan's Role in Afghan Peace Talks Process," *Washington Post*, September 14, 2020, https://www.washingtonpost.com/world/middle_east/us-envoy-lauds-pakistans-role-in-afghan-peace-talks-process/2020/09/14/b5813586-f6b1-11ea-85f7-5941188a98cd_story.html.

2. Steve Coll and Adam Entous, "The Secret History of the U.S. Diplomatic Failure in Afghanistan," *New Yorker*, December 10, 2021, https://www.newyorker.com/magazine/2021/12/20/the-secret-history-of-the-us-diplomatic-failure-in-afghanistan.

3. Rupam Jain and Phil Stewart, "U.S. sees contours of peace accord with Taliban to end war in Afghanistan," Reuters, January 28, 2019, https://www.reuters.com/article/us-usa-afghanistan/u-s-sees-contours-of-peace-accord-with-taliban-to-end-war-in-afghanistan-idUSKCN1PM0UO.

4. Coll and Entous, "Secret History."

5. Antony Blinken, "Secretary of State Briefing," Department of State, January 27, 2021, https://www.state.gov/secretary-antony-j-blinken-at-a-press-availability/.

6. "Trump Wants to Get Out of Afghanistan 'as Quickly as He Can,'" TOLOnews, August 1, 2019, https://tolonews.com/afghanistan/trump-wants-get-out-afghanistan%C2%A0%E2%80%98%C2%A0quickly-he-can%E2%80%99.

7. Lynne O'Donnell, "Defying Peace Deal, Freed Taliban Return to Battlefield," *Foreign Policy*, September 3, 2020, https://foreignpolicy.com/2020/09/03/defying-peace-deal-freed-taliban-prisoners-return-battlefield-afghanistan/.

8. Special Inspector General for Afghanistan, *Quarterly Report to Congress*, July 30, 2020, https://www.sigar.mil/pdf/quarterlyreports/2020-07-30qr.pdf.

9. "Transcript: Mike Pompeo on 'Face the Nation,' March 1, 2020," CBS News, https://www.cbsnews.com/amp/news/transcript-mike-pompeo-on-face-the-nation-march-1-2020/.

10. Michael R. Pompeo, "Secretary Michael R. Pompeo Remarks to Traveling Press," U.S. Department of State, September 11, 2020, https://2017-2021.state.gov/secretary-michael-r-pompeo-at-a-press-availability/index.html.

11. Ayaz Gul, "US, Taliban Sign Historic Afghan Peace Deal," VOA, February 29, 2020, https://www.voanews.com/a/south-central-asia_us-taliban-sign-historic-afghan-peace-deal/6185026.html.

12. Bill Roggio, "Taliban Religious Decree Calls for Its Emir to Rule 'Islamic Government' in Afghanistan," FDD's Long War Journal, March 8, 2020, https://www.longwarjournal.org/archives/2020/03/taliban-religious-decree-calls-for-its-emir-to-rule-islamic-government-in-afghanistan.php.

13. Thomas Joscelyn, "Al-Qaeda Lauds Taliban's Great 'Victory' over America and Allies," FDD's Long War Journal, May 13, 2020, https://www.longwarjournal.org /archives/2020/03/al-qaeda-lauds-talibans-great-victory-over-america-and-allies .php.

14. Courtney Kube, Ken Dilanian, and Dan De Luce, "Officials: U.S. Has Intel Taliban Don't Plan to Abide by Peace Deal," NBC News, March 6, 2020, https://www .nbcnews.com/politics/national-security/officials-u-s-has-persuasive-intel-taliban -does-not-intend-n1150051.

15. United Nations Analytical Support and Sanctions Monitoring Team, "Eleventh report," May 27, 2020, https://documents-dds-ny.un.org/doc/UNDOC/GEN/N20 /110/60/PDF/N2011060.pdf?OpenElement.

16. Defense Department inspector general, Operation Freedom's Sentinel, *Quarterly Report*, May 15, 2020, https://www.dodig.mil/Reports/Lead-Inspector-General -Reports/Article/2191020/lead-inspector-general-for-operation-freedoms-sentinel -i-quarterly-report-to-th/.

17. "Department of Defense Press Briefing by Secretary Esper and General Milley in the Pentagon Briefing Room," Department of Defense, March 2, 2020, https://www .defense.gov/News/Transcripts/Transcript/Article/2099710/department-of-defense -press-briefing-by-secretary-esper-and-general-milley-in-t/.

18. Dan Lamothe et al., "Defense Secretary Sent Classified Memo to White House About Afghanistan Before Trump Fired Him," *Washington Post*, November 14, 2020, https://www.washingtonpost.com/national-security/trump-pentagon-afghan-war /2020/11/13/5ac54c7e-25cb-11eb-8599-406466ad1b8e_story.html.

19. "Here's Every Word from the 9th Jan. 6 Committee Hearing on Its Investigation," NPR, 13 October 2022, https://www.npr.org/2022/10/13/1125331584/jan -6-committee-hearing-transcript.

20. Jonathan Swan and Zachary Basu, "Off the Rails: Trump's Failed 11th-Hour Military Withdrawal Campaign," Axios, May 16, 2021, https://www.axios.com/2021/05/16/off -the-rails-trump-military-withdraw-afghanistan.

21. Jamie Gangel, Jeremy Herb, and Elizabeth Stuart, "New Woodward/Costa Book: Trump Secret Memo Ordering Withdrawal from Afghanistan Blindsided National Security Team," CNN, September 14, 2021, https://www.cnn.com/2021/09/14 /politics/woodward-costa-book-trump-afghanistan-memo.

22. Keith Kellogg, Testimony before the January 6th Committee, December 14, 2021. https://web.archive.org/web/20230103075949/https://january6th.house.gov/sites /democrats.january6th.house.gov/files/20211214_Keith%20Kellogg%2C%20Jr..pdf.

23. Christopher Miller, Testimony before the January 6th Committee, January 14, 2022, https://web.archive.org/web/20230103080118/https://january6th.house.gov/sites /democrats.january6th.house.gov/files/20220114_Christopher%20C.%20Miller.pdf.

24. Jonathan Swan and Zachary Basu, "Off the Rails: Trump's Failed 11th-Hour Military Withdrawal Campaign," Axios, May 16, 2021, https://www.axios.com/2021/05/16/off -the-rails-trump-military-withdraw-afghanistan.

25. Robert O'Brien, Testimony before the January 6th Committee, August 23, 2022, https://web.archive.org/web/20230103022620/https://january6th.house.gov/sites /democrats.january6th.house.gov/files/20220823_Robert%20O'Brien.pdf.

CHAPTER 3: HOW QUICKLY CAN WE GET OUT?

1. "The Presidential Candidates on the War in Afghanistan," Council on Foreign Relations, July 30, 2019, https://www.cfr.org/article/presidential-candidates-war-afghanistan.

2. Joseph R. Biden, Jr., "Why America Must Lead Again," *Foreign Affairs*, January 23, 2020, https://www.foreignaffairs.com/articles/united-states/2020-01-23/why-america-must-lead-again.

3. Linsey Davis, Monica Hernandez, David Muir, Adam Sexton, and George Stephanopoulos, "2020 Democratic Debates," ABC News, WMUR-TV, and Apple News, Democratic Primary Debate, February 7, 2020, https://www.rev.com/blog/transcripts/new-hampshire-democratic-debate-transcript.

4. "Transcript: Joe Biden on Face the Nation," CBS News, Face the Nation, February 23, 2020, https://www.cbsnews.com/news/transcript-joe-biden-on-face-the-nation-february-23-2020/.

5. "Secretary of State Confirmation Hearing," C-SPAN, January 19, 2021, https://www.c-span.org/video/?507953-1%2Fsecretary-state-nominee-antony-blinken-testifies-confirmation-hearing.

6. Coll and Entous, "Secret History."

7. Horne, Emily. "Statement by NSC Spokesperson Emily Horne on National Security Advisor Jake Sullivan's Call with National Security Advisor Hamdullah Mohib," U.S. Embassy in Afghanistan, January 23, 2021, https://af.usembassy.gov/statement-by-nsc-spokesperson-emily-horne-on-national-security-advisor-jake-sullivans-call-with-national-security-advisor-hamdullah-mohib/.

8. Woodward and Costa, *Peril*, 337.

9. Bob Woodward and Robert Costa, *Peril* (New York: Simon & Schuster, 2021), 339.

10. "TRANSCRIPT: ABC News' George Stephanopoulos interviews President Joe Biden," ABC News, March 16, 2021, https://abcnews.go.com/Politics/transcript-abc-news-george-stephanopoulos-interviews-president-joe/story?id=76509669.

11. Joe Biden, "Remarks by President Biden in Press Conference." White House, March 25, 2021, https://www.whitehouse.gov/briefing-room/speeches-remarks/2021/03/25/remarks-by-president-biden-in-press-conference/.

12. Coll and Entous, "Secret History."

13. Matthieu Aikins, "Inside the Fall of Kabul," *New York Times*, December 10, 2021, https://www.nytimes.com/2021/12/10/magazine/fall-of-kabul-afghanistan.html.

14. Antony Blinken, "Secretary of State Briefing," Department of State, January 27, 2021, https://www.state.gov/secretary-antony-j-blinken-at-a-press-availability/.

15. Afghanistan Study Group, *Afghanistan Study Group Final Report*, February 2021, https://www.usip.org/sites/default/files/2021-02/afghanistan_study_group_final_report_a_pathway_for_peace_in_afghanistan.pdf.

16. Office of the Director of National Intelligence, *Annual Threat Assessment of the U.S. Intelligence Community*, April 9, 2021, https://www.dni.gov/files/ODNI/documents/assessments/ATA-2021-Unclassified-Report.pdf.

17. Jonathan Schroden, "Afghanistan's Security Forces Versus the Taliban: A Net Assessment," *CTC Sentinal* 14, no. 1 (January 2021), https://ctc.westpoint.edu/wp-content/uploads/2021/01/CTC-SENTINEL-012021.pdf, 20.

18. Oversight Committee Democrats, "The Special Inspector General for Afghanistan Reconstruction's 2021 High-Risk List," YouTube, March 16, 2021, https://www.youtube.com/watch?v=qZA8BtLOoOI.

19. Missy Ryan et al., "Biden Administration Scrambled as Its Orderly Withdrawal from Afghanistan Unraveled," *Washington Post*, August 14, 2021, https://www.washingtonpost.com/national-security/biden-taliban-afghan-collapse/2021/08/14/da7cba66-fcf7-11eb-b8dd-0e376fba55f2_story.html.

20. Thomas F. Lynch III, "Deconstructing the Collapse of Afghanistan National Defense and Security Forces," *Parameters: The US Army War College Quarterly* 52, no. 3 (Autumn 2022), 51, https://press.Armywarcollege.edu/cgi/viewcontent.cgi?article=3168&context=parameters.

21. Karoun Demirjian and Dan Lamothe, "General's Classified Testimony Underscores Political Split over Afghanistan Exit," *Washington Post*, September 18, 2021, https://www.washingtonpost.com/national-security/afghanistan-general-austin-miller-testimony/2021/09/17/cb14c90e-1711-11ec-a5e5-ceecb895922f_story.html.

22. "Milley, McKenzie Say, We Assessed That 2,500-3,500 Troops Should Stay." *CNN Newsroom*, CNN, September 28, 2021, https://transcripts.cnn.com/show/cnr/date/2021-09-28/segment/04.

23. Voice of Jihad, "Kabul admin even lacks international legitimacy," February 7, 2021, https://web.archive.org/web/20210818032921/https://alemarahenglish.net/?p=42481.

24. Ryan et al., "Biden Administration Scrambled."

25. Gregory Sullivan, "Memorandum for Department of Defense Lead Inspector General," U.S. Department of the Treasury, January 4, 2021, https://oig.treasury.gov/sites/oig/files/2021-01/OIG-CA-21-012.pdf, 4, 5.

26. Voice of Jihad, "Remarks by spokesman of Islamic Emirate concerning report by US Treasury Department," January 27, 2021, https://web.archive.org/web/20210818124825/https://alemarahenglish.net/?p=42081.

27. Bill Roggio, "Taliban Celebrates 2002 Battle in Which It Defended Al Qaeda," FDD's Long War Journal, March 17, 2021, https://www.longwarjournal.org/archives/2021/03/taliban-celebrates-2002-battle-in-which-it-defended-al-qaeda.php.

28. Bill Roggio, "Analysis: Al Qaeda Continues to Operate Throughout Afghanistan," FDD's Long War Journal, April 8, 2021, https://www.longwarjournal.org/archives/2021/04/analysis-al-qaeda-continues-to-operate-throughout-afghanistan.php.

29. Roggio, Bill. "Al Qaeda Leaders Use Afghanistan as a Safe Haven," FDD's Long War Journal, December 7, 2022, https://www.longwarjournal.org/archives/2022/12/al-qaeda-leaders-use-afghanistan-as-a-safe-haven.php.

30. T. S. Tirumurti, "Letter Dated 20 May 2021 from the Chair of the Security Council Committee Established Pursuant to Resolution 1988 (2011) Addressed to the President of the Security Council," United Nations Security Council, June 1, 2021, https://static.poder360.com.br/2021/08/taliba-al-qaeda-onu.pdf, 3.

31. Franklin Blair, "Taliban Framing of the Peace Process, 15 February–10 March 2021," Readkong, https://www.readkong.com/page/taliban-framing-of-the-peace-process -15-february-10-6452263.

32. Voice of Jihad, "Statement of Islamic Emirate regarding recent American Elections," November 10, 2020, https://web.archive.org/web/20210302200233/http:// alemarahenglish.net/?p=39175.

33. Franklin Blair, "Taliban Framing of the Peace Process, 15 February–10 March 2021," Readkong, https://www.readkong.com/page/taliban-framing-of-the-peace-process -15-february-10-6452263.

34. Vice News, "The Taliban's Message to President Biden," YouTube, March 5, 2021, https://www.youtube.com/watch?v=1lr8_OUa58c.

35. Voice of Jihad, "Statement of Islamic Emirate regarding vague remarks by the American President," March 26, 2021, https://web.archive.org/web/20210410191020 /https://alemarahenglish.net/?p=44102.

36. Ayaz Gul, "Taliban See Ghani as 'Obstacle' to Afghan Peace," VOA, January 9, 2021, https://www.voanews.com/south-central-asia/taliban-see-ghani-obstacle-afghan -peace.

37. Thomas Gibbons-Neff, David Zucchino, and Lara Jakes, "U.S. Pushes U.N.-Led Peace Conference in Letter to Afghan Leader," *New York Times*, August 15, 2021, https://www.nytimes.com/2021/03/07/world/asia/afghanistan-blinken-troop -withdrawal.html.

38. Antony Blinken, @SecBlinken, Twitter, January 28, 2021, https://twitter.com /SecBlinken/status/1354852782491262976.

39. Alex Ward, "The Biden Administration's Leaked Afghanistan Peace Plan, Explained," *Vox*, March 8, 2021, https://www.vox.com/2021/3/8/22319420 /afghanistan-blinken-letter-leak-peace-plan.

40. Afghanistan Peace Agreement, February 28, 2021, TOLOnews, https://tolonews.com /pdf/pdf.pdf.

41. Ward, "Biden Administration's Leaked Afghanistan Peace Plan."

42. Dan Lamothe, "Pentagon Chief in Afghanistan on Unannounced Visit as Deadline to Withdraw U.S. Troops Looms," *Washington Post*, March 21, 2021, https://www .washingtonpost.com/national-security/2021/03/21/lloyd-austin-afghanistan-us -withdrawal/.

43. "Oral Evidence: Work of the Chief of Defence Staff, HC 842," House of Commons Defence Committee, November 9, 2021, https://committees.parliament.uk /oralevidence/2978/html/.

44. Ayaz Gul, "NATO Chief: No Troop Withdrawal from Afghanistan 'Before the Time Is Right,'" VOA, February 15, 2021, https://www.voanews.com/a/south-central-asia _nato-chief-no-troop-withdrawal-afghanistan-time-right/6202075.html.

45. Joseph R. Biden, Jr., "Remarks by President Biden at the 2021 Virtual Munich Security Conference," White House, February 19, 2021, https://www.whitehouse.gov /briefing-room/speeches-remarks/2021/02/19/remarks-by-president-biden-at-the -2021-virtual-munich-security-conference/.

46. Woodward and Costa, *Peril*, 376.

47. Ibid., 376.

48. Coll and Entous, "Secret History."

49. "North Atlantic Council Ministerial Statement on Afghanistan," North Atlantic Treaty Organization, April 14, 2021, https://www.nato.int/cps/en/natohq/official _texts_183146.htm.

50. Jens Stoltenberg and Antony Blinken, "Remarks," North Atlantic Treaty Organization, April 14, 2021, = https://www.nato.int/cps/en/natohq/opinions _183079.htm?selectedLocale=en.

51. Jens Stoltenberg, Antony Blinken, and Lloyd Austin, "Joint press point," North Atlantic Treaty Organization. Meeting of NATO Foreign Affairs and Defence Ministers, April 14, 2021, https://www.nato.int/cps/en/natohq/opinions_183061.htm ?selectedLocale=en.

52. Kate Ng, "'Not what we'd hoped for': UK military chief disappointed over US withdrawal from Afghanistan," *The Independent*, April 16, 2021, https://www .independent.co.uk/news/uk/home-news/afghanistan-military-troops-withdrawal -defence-b1832722.html.

53. Dan Sabbagh, "Boris Johnson struggles to justify Afghanistan stance to hostile MPs," *The Guardian*, August 18, 2021, https://www.theguardian.com/world/2021 /aug/18/boris-johnson-struggles-to-justify-afghanistan-stance-to-hostile-mps.

54. Joseph R. Biden, Jr., "Remarks by President Biden on the Way Forward in Afghanistan," White House, April 14, 2021, https://www.whitehouse.gov/briefing -room/speeches-remarks/2021/04/14/remarks-by-president-biden-on-the-way -forward-in-afghanistan/.

55. Joseph R. Biden, Jr., "Remarks by President Biden on the Drawdown of U.S. Forces in Afghanistan," White House, July 8, 2021, https://www.whitehouse.gov/briefing -room/speeches-remarks/2021/07/08/remarks-by-president-biden-on-the-drawdown -of-u-s-forces-in-afghanistan/.

56. Biden, "Remarks on the Way Forward in Afghanistan."

57. "Full Transcript of ABC News' George Stephanopoulos' Interview with President Joe Biden," ABC News, August 19, 2021, https://abcnews.go.com/Politics/full-transcript -abc-news-george-stephanopoulos-interview-president/story?id=79535643.

58. Biden, "Remarks on the Way Forward in Afghanistan."

59. Jerry Dunleavy, "Pentagon Quickly Refutes Biden's Claim al Qaeda Is No Longer in Afghanistan," *Washington Examiner*, August 20, 2021, https://www .washingtonexaminer.com/news/pentagon-refutes-biden-claim-al-qaeda-no-longer -afghanistan.

60. Jerry Dunleavy, "Biden and Milley misled about Afghan army numbers," *Washington Examiner*, August 18, 2021, https://www.washingtonexaminer.com /news/biden-milley-misled-afghan-Army-numbers.

61. Biden, "Remarks on the Way Forward in Afghanistan."

62. Ibid.

63. Joseph R. Biden, Jr., "Remarks by President Biden After Wreath Laying at Section 60 of Arlington Cemetery," White House, April 14, 2021, https://www.whitehouse

.gov/briefing-room/speeches-remarks/2021/04/14/remarks-by-president-biden-after
-wreath-laying-at-section-60-of-arlington-national-cemetery/.

64. Woodward and Costa, *Peril*, 391.

65. Ibid., 388.

66. Antony Blinken, @SecBlinken, Twitter, April 15, 2021, https://twitter.com
/SecBlinken/status/1382801616382914562.

67. "Taliban Statement on U.S. Troops Withdrawal Postponement, Apr 15, 2021," Social
Transformation Group, April 15, 2021, https://stgroup.in.ua/index.php/en/watches
/terrorismwatch/taliban-statement-on-u-s-troops-withdrawal-postponement-apr-15
-2021.

68. Special Inspector General for Afghanistan Reconstruction, *Why the Afghan
Government Collapsed*, November 2022, https://www.sigar.mil/pdf/evaluations
/SIGAR-23-05-IP.pdf.

69 Special Inspector General for Afghanistan Reconstruction, *Collapse of the Afghan
National Defense and Security Forces: An Assessment of the Factors That Led to Its
Demise*, May 2022, https://www.sigar.mil/pdf/evaluations/SIGAR-22-22-IP.pdf.

CHAPTER 4: BAGRAM

1. Brian Bennett, "Biden Faces the Fallout for Chaotic Retreat in Afghanistan," *Time*,
September 2, 2021, https://time.com/6094786/biden-afghanistan-fallout/.

2. Afghanistan Study Group, *Afghanistan Study Group Final Report*, February 2021,
https://www.usip.org/sites/default/files/2021-02/afghanistan_study_group_final
_report_a_pathway_for_peace_in_afghanistan.pdf.

3. "Secretary of State Blinken Arrives in Afghanistan," *New Day*, CNN, April 15, 2021,
https://transcripts.cnn.com/show/nday/date/2021-04-15/segment/03.

4. Joseph R. Biden, Jr., "Remarks by President Biden on the Drawdown of U.S. Forces
in Afghanistan," White House, July 8, 2021, https://www.whitehouse.gov/briefing
-room/speeches-remarks/2021/07/08/remarks-by-president-biden-on-the-drawdown
-of-u-s-forces-in-afghanistan/.

5. Joseph R. Biden, Jr., "Remarks by President Biden on Afghanistan," White House,
August 16, 2021, https://www.whitehouse.gov/briefing-room/speeches-remarks/2021
/08/16/remarks-by-president-biden-on-afghanistan/.

6. Dunleavy, "Biden and Milley misled."

7. Anthony H. Cordesman, "The Reasons for the Collapse of Afghan Forces," Center
for Strategic & International Studies, August 17, 2021, https://csis-website-prod.s3
.amazonaws.com/s3fs-public/publication/210816_Cordesman_Sudden_Collapse.pdf
?VersionId=zRVgOSgKB0l7l3Ph_lTVpkO79ajBG2PJ, 8.

8. David R. Winston, *Narco-Insecurity, Inc.: The Convergence of the Narcotics
Underworld and Extremists in Afghanistan and Pakistan and Its Global Proliferation*,
Defence Education Enhancement Programme, 2022, https://deepportal.hq.nato.int
/eacademy/wp-content/uploads/2022/05/Narco-Insecurity-Inc..pdf, 152.

9. Glenn Kessler, "Biden's bogus claim that Afghanistan's military was larger than
those of many of our NATO allies," *Washington Post*, August 18, 2021, https://www

.washingtonpost.com/politics/2021/08/18/bidens-bogus-claim-that-afghanistans
-military-was-larger-than-nato-allies/.

10. Heineman, *Retrograde*.

11. Ibid.

12. Ibid.

13. Kirby, John F. "Pentagon Press Secretary John F. Kirby Holds a Press Briefing," Department of Defense, May 3, 2021, https://www.defense.gov/News/Transcripts /Transcript/Article/2594232/pentagon-press-secretary-john-f-kirby-holds-a-press -briefing/.

14. Altman, "CENTCOM Commander Vows to Keep the Pressure on Adversaries.

15. "Secretary of Defense Lloyd J. Austin III Remarks Before the Senate Armed Services Committee (As Prepared)," Defense Department, September 28, 2021, https://www .defense.gov/News/Speeches/Speech/Article/2791954/secretary-of-defense-lloyd -j-austin-iii-remarks-before-the-senate-armed-service/.

16. Altman, "CENTCOM Commander Vows to Keep Pressure on Adversaries."

17. Ibid.

18. C-SPAN, "Defense Department Fiscal Year 2022 Budget Request," June 17, 2021, https://www.c-span.org/video/?512498-1/defense-department-fiscal-year-2022 -budget-request.

19. Carla Babb, "VOA Exclusive: CENTCOM Head Says US Will Not Support Afghan Forces with Airstrikes After Troop Withdrawal," Voice of America, June 14, 2021, https://www.voanews.com/a/usa_voa-exclusive-centcom-head-says-us-will-not -support-afghan-forces-airstrikes-after-troop/6206992.html.

20. John Kirby, "Pentagon Press Secretary John F. Kirby Holds a Press Briefing," Defense Department, June 21, 2021, https://www.defense.gov/News/Transcripts /Transcript/Article/2665540/pentagon-press-secretary-john-f-kirby-holds-a-press -briefing/.

21. "Operation Freedom's Sentinel Lead Inspector General Report to the U.S. Congress," April 1, 2021 - June 30, 2021, https://media.defense.gov/2021/Aug/17/2002832926/ -1/-1/1/LEAD%20INSPECTOR%20GENERAL%20FOR%20OPERATION %20FREEDOM%E2%80%99S%20SENTINEL%20I%20QUARTERLY%20REPORT %20TO%20THE%20UNITED%20STATES%20CONGRESS%20I%20APRIL%20I ,%202021%20-%20JUNE%2030,%202021.PDF.

22. Jeff Zients, Gov. Jim Justice & Gen. Austin 'Scott' Miller, "*This Week* Transcript 7-4-21," ABC News, July 4, 2021, https://abcnews.go.com/Politics/week-transcript-21 -jeff-zients-gov-jim-justice/story?id=78659208.

23. James Kitfield, "The Last Commander," Politico, July 16, 2021, https://www.politico .com/news/magazine/2021/07/16/scott-miller-general-afghanistan-profile-499490.

24. John Kirby, "Pentagon Press Secretary John F. Kirby Holds a Press Briefing," Defense Department, July 12, 2021, https://www.defense.gov/News/Transcripts /Transcript/Article/2691684/pentagon-press-secretary-john-f-kirby-holds-a-press -briefing/.

25. Lloyd J. Austin III, Mark Milley, and John F. Kirby, "Secretary of Defense Austin and Chairman of the Joint Chiefs of Staff Gen. Milley Press Briefing," U.S. Department

of Defense, July 21, 2021, https://www.defense.gov/News/Transcripts/Transcript/Article/2702966/secretary-of-defense-austin-and-chairman-of-the-joint-chiefs-of-staff-gen-mille/.

26. J. P. Lawrence, "US Forces Leave Kandahar Airfield as Drawdown Continues in Afghanistan," *Stars and Stripes*, May 13, 2021, https://www.stripes.com/theaters/middle_east/us-forces-leave-kandahar-airfield-as-drawdown-continues-in-afghanistan-1.673297.

27. Geir Moulson and Kathy Gannon, "Most European Troops Exit Afghanistan Quietly After 20 Years," Associated Press, June 30, 2021, https://apnews.com/article/europe-afghanistan-health-coronavirus-pandemic-9c1c4f5732c032ba85865aab0338a7a3.

28. "Another Forgotten War: America's Experience in Afghanistan," *Irregular Warfare Podcast*, Modern War Institute at West Point, September 12, 2022, https://podcasts.apple.com/us/podcast/another-forgotten-war-americas-experience-in-afghanistan/id1514636385?i=1000579189083.

29. Coll and Entous, "Secret History."

30. Special Inspector General for Afghanistan Reconstruction (SIGAR), *Quarterly Report to the United States Congress*, July 30, 2021, https://www.sigar.mil/pdf/quarterlyreports/2021-07-30qr-section2-security.pdf, 52.

31. Nabih Bulos, "Afghanistan's Air Force Is a Rare US-Backed Success Story. It Might Soon Fail," *Stars and Stripes*, June 21, 2021, https://www.stripes.com/theaters/middle_east/2021-06-21/Afghanistan-air-force-is-a-rare-US-backed-success-story-but-it-might-soon-fail-1757450.html.

32. SIGAR, *Quarterly Report to the United States Congress*, July 30, 2021.

33. John Kirby, "Pentagon Press Secretary John F. Kirby Holds a Press Briefing," Department of Defense, January 18, 2022, https://www.defense.gov/News/Transcripts/Transcript/Article/2903079/pentagon-press-secretary-john-f-kirby-holds-a-press-briefing/.

34. Coll and Entous, "Secret History."

35. Ibid.

36. Office of Inspector General, Department of Defense, *Operation Enduring Sentinel, Operation Freedom's Sentinel: Lead Inspector General Report to the United States Congress, April 1, 2022–June 30, 2022*, August 16, 2022, https://media.defense.gov/2021/Aug/17/2002832926/-1/-1/1/LEAD%20INSPECTOR%20GENERAL%20FOR%20OPERATION%20FREEDOM%E2%80%99S%20SENTINEL%20I%20QUARTERLY%20REPORT%20TO%20THE%20UNITED%20STATES%20CONGRESS%20I%20APRIL%201,%202021%20-%20JUNE%2030,%202021.PDF.

37. SIGAR, *Quarterly Report to the United States Congress*.

38. Office of Inspector General, Department of Defense, *Operation Enduring Sentinel*.

39. *House Republican Interim Report: A "Strategic Failure:" Assessing the Administration's Afghanistan Withdrawal*, August 2022, https://gop-foreignaffairs.house.gov/wp-content/uploads/2022/08/HFAC-Republican-Interim-Report-A-22Strategic-Failure22-Assessing-the-Administrations-Afghanistan-Withdrawal.pdf, 16.

40. CENTCOM, "Contractor Support of U.S. Operations In The USCENTCOM Area of Responsibility," July 2021, https://web.archive.org/web/20220818003050/https://www.acq.osd.mil/log/LOG_CSD/.CENTCOM_reports.html/FY21_3Q_5A_Jul2021.pdf.

41. Carla Babb, "VOA Exclusive: Former CENTCOM Commanders Say the US Not Safer Following Troop Withdrawal from Afghanistan," Voice of America, August 23, 2022, https://www.voanews.com/a/voa-exclusive-us-not-safer-following-troop-withdrawal-from-afghanistan-former-centcom-commanders-say/6712729.html.

42. "Senate Armed Services Committee Hearing on Afghanistan Withdrawal," C-SPAN, September 28, 2021, https://www.c-span.org/video/?514537-1/senate-armed-services-committee-hearing-afghanistan-withdrawal.

43. Abbey Gate Report, Enc. 2, 105.

44. Abbey Gate Report, 1.

45. Lynzy Billing, "U.S. Is Leaving Afghanistan? Tell That to the Contractors," Intelligencer, May 12, 2021, https://nymag.com/intelligencer/2021/05/u-s-contractors-in-afghanistan-are-hiring-amid-withdrawal.html.

46. Kathy Gannon, "US Left Afghan Airfield at Night, Didn't Tell New Commander," Associated Press, July 6, 2021, https://apnews.com/article/bagram-afghanistan-airfield-us-troops-f3614828364f567593251aaaa167e623.

47. Emma Graham-Harrison and Peter Beaumont, "Afghan Anger over US's Sudden, Silent Bagram Departure," Guardian, July 6, 2021, https://www.theguardian.com/world/2021/jul/06/afghan-anger-over-uss-sudden-silent-bagram-departure.

48. Zabihullah Mujahid, @ Zabehulah_M33, Twitter, July 2, 2021, https://twitter.com/Zabehulah_M33/status/1410887120600932352.

49. Richard Engel, @RichardEngel, "Taliban says 'for now' no plans to try to take Bagram. . . . Taliban spokesman Zabihullah Mujahid told @NBCNews," Twitter, July 2, 2021, https://twitter.com/RichardEngel/status/1410832300120719371.

50. Mike Waltz, @MichaelGWaltz, Twitter, July 1, 2021, https://twitter.com/michaelgwaltz/status/1410737699296739330.

51. John Kirby, "Pentagon Press Secretary John F. Kirby Holds a Press Briefing." Department of Defense, July 6, 2021, https://www.defense.gov/News/Transcripts/Transcript/Article/2683654/pentagon-press-secretary-john-f-kirby-holds-a-press-briefing/.

52. Ibid.

53. Joseph R. Biden, Jr., "Remarks by President Biden on the June Jobs Report," White House, July 2, 2021, https://www.whitehouse.gov/briefing-room/speeches-remarks/2021/07/02/remarks-by-president-biden-on-the-june-jobs-report/.

54. Jerry Dunleavy, "Milley says there were no indications that Taliban would take over this quickly." Washington Examiner, August 18, 2021, https://www.washingtonexaminer.com/news/milley-no-indications-taliban-take-over-so-quickly.

55. Lloyd Austin, "Secretary of Defense Lloyd J. Austin III Prepared Remarks before the House Armed Services Committee." September 29, 2021, https://www.defense

.gov/News/Speeches/Speech/Article/2791954/secretary-of-defense-lloyd-j-austin-iii
-remarks-before-the-senate-armed-service/.

56. "Another Forgotten War: America's Experience in Afghanistan," *Irregular Warfare Podcast*, Modern War Institute at West Point, September 12, 2022, https://podcasts
.apple.com/us/podcast/another-forgotten-war-americas-experience-in-afghanistan
/id1514636385?i=1000579189083.

57. Kathy Gannon, "Top US General Says Security in Afghanistan Deteriorating,"
Military Times, June 29, 2021, https://www.militarytimes.com/flashpoints/2021/06
/29/top-us-general-says-security-in-afghanistan-deteriorating/.

58. CENTCOM, "Update on the Withdrawal of U.S. Forces from Afghanistan July 26,
2021," U.S. Central Command, July 27, 2021, https://www.centcom.mil/MEDIA
/PRESS-RELEASES/Press-Release-View/Article/2708638/update-on-the-withdrawal
-of-us-forces-from-afghanistan-july-26-2021/.

59. Michael R. Gordon et al., "Inside Biden's Afghanistan Withdrawal Plan: Warnings,
Doubts but Little Change," *Wall Street Journal*, September 5, 2021, https://www
.wsj.com/articles/inside-the-biden-administrations-push-to-exit-afghanistan
-11630855499.

60. "Combined Forces Air Component Commander 2014–2021 Airpower Statistics,"
United States Air Forces Central Command, December 31, 2021, https://www.afcent
.af.mil/Portals/82/December%202021%20Airpower%20Summary_FINAL.pdf.

61. Senate Armed Services Committee Hearing on Afghanistan Withdrawal," C-SPAN,
September 28, 2021, https://www.c-span.org/video/?514537-1/senate-armed-services
-committee-hearing-afghanistan-withdrawal.

62. Office of Inspector General, Department of Defense, *Operation Enduring Sentinel*, 15.

63. Ruchi Kumar, "Afghanistan: Taliban Fires Missiles at Coalition Military Base." *The National*, July 1, 2021, https://www.thenationalnews.com/world/asia/afghanistan
-taliban-fires-missiles-at-coalition-military-base-1.1194296.

64. Zabihullah Mujahid, @ Zabehulah_M33, Twitter, March 30, 2021, https://twitter
.com/Zabehulah_M33/status/1376932590863724549.

65. Office of Inspector General, Department of Defense, *Operation Enduring Sentinel*, 15.

66. Zabihullah Mujahid, @ Zabehulah_M33, Twitter, April 7, 2021, https://twitter.com
/Zabehulah_M33/status/1379737577499004928.

67. John Kirby, "Pentagon Press Secretary John F. Kirby Holds a Press Briefing."
Department of Defense, April 7, 2021, https://www.defense.gov/News/Transcripts
/Transcript/Article/2565280/pentagon-press-secretary-john-f-kirby-holds-a-press
-briefing/.

68. Sonny Leggett, @USFOR_A, Twitter, May 1, 2021, https://twitter.com/USFOR
_A/status/1388474917495185410.

69. Zabihullah Mujahid, @ Zabehulah_M33, Twitter, May 1, 2021, https://twitter.com
/Zabehulah_M33/status/1388421451422699522.

70. "1 Killed, 24 Injured in an Explosion Inside Bagram Airfield," The Khaama Press
News Agency, May 1, 2021, https://www.khaama.com/1-killed-24-injured-at-an
-explosion-inside-bagram-airfield-7643322/.

71. John Kirby, "Pentagon Press Secretary John F. Kirby Holds a Press Briefing," Department of Defense, May 3, 2021, https://www.defense.gov/News/Transcripts /Transcript/Article/2594232/pentagon-press-secretary-john-f-kirby-holds-a-press -briefing/.

72. Dan Lamothe, "He Spent Years at War in Afghanistan. Now He Commands the U.S. Withdrawal," *Washington Post*, June 7, 2021, https://www.washingtonpost.com /national-security/2021/06/07/afghan-war-general-miller/.

73. Abbey Gate Report, Exhibit 174.

74. Kate Clark, "Afghanistan's Conflict in 2021 (2): Republic Collapse and Taleban *[sic]* Victory in the Long-View of History," Afghanistan Analysts Network, January 12, 2022, https://www.afghanistan-analysts.org/en/reports/war-and-peace/afghanistans -conflict-in-2021-2-republic-collapse-and-taleban-victory-in-the-long-view-of -history/.

75. Office of Inspector General, Department of Defense, *Operation Enduring Sentinel*.

76. SIGAR, *Quarterly Report to the United States Congress*.

77. Bill Roggio, "Taliban Doubles Number of Controlled Afghan Districts Since May 1," FDD's Long War Journal, June 29, 2021, https://www.longwarjournal.org/archives /2021/06/taliban-doubles-number-of-controlled-afghan-districts-since-may-1.php.

78. Mark Milley, House Armed Services Committee testimony, June 23, 2021, https:// www.youtube.com/watch?v=GZCvXUtbn1g.

79. Roggio, "Taliban Doubles Number of Controlled Afghan Districts Since May 1."

80. Bill Roggio and Andrew Tobin, "Half of Afghanistan's provincial capitals under threat from Taliban," FDD's Long War Journal, July 15, 2021, https://www .longwarjournal.org/archives/2021/07/nearly-half-of-afghanistans-provincial -capitals-under-threat-from-taliban.php.

81. Special Inspector General for Afghanistan Reconstruction (SIGAR), *Collapse of the Afghan National Defense and Security Forces*, May 2022, https://www.sigar.mil/pdf /evaluations/SIGAR-22-22-IP.pdf.

82. Ibid.

83. Clark, "Afghanistan's Conflict in 2021 (2)."

84. Massoud Ansar, "Hundreds More Take Up Arms as Clashes Intensify," TOLOnews, June 27, 2021, https://tolonews.com/afghanistan-173126.

85. Ibid.

86. "Ghani, Political Leaders Agree to Build Consensus on Peace," TOLOnews, June 21, 2021, https://tolonews.com/afghanistan-172989.

87. Ali Yawar Adlii, "Preparing for a Post-departure Afghanistan: Changing Political Dynamics in the Wake of the US Troop Withdrawal Announcement," Afghanistan Analysts Network, June 22, 2021, https://www.afghanistan-analysts.org/en/reports /war-and-peace/preparing-for-a-post-departure-afghanistan-changing-political -dynamics-in-the-wake-of-the-us-troop-withdrawal-announcement/.

88. "Taliban Call Recent Gains as Victory of 'Mujahid Afghan Nation,'" The Correspondent PK, June 23, 2021, https://www.thecorrespondent.pk/world/taliban -call-recent-gains-as-victory-of-mujahid-afghan-nation/.

89. Kitfield, "The Last Commander."

90. "Afghanistan's Interior Minister Reveals Plan to Push Back Taliban," Al Jazeera, August 11, 2021, https://www.aljazeera.com/news/2021/8/11/afghanistans-interior -minister-reveals-plan-to-push-back-taliban.

91. Pamela Constable, "Death of Famed Afghan Commander in Taliban Massacre Highlights the Country's Struggles and Fears," *Washington Post*, June 20, 2021, https://www.washingtonpost.com/world/asia_pacific/afghanistan-taliban -commando-killed/2021/06/19/ebd748fc-d03e-11eb-a224-bd59bd22197c_story.html.

92. "Taliban call recent gains as victory of 'Mujahid Afghan nation,'" The Correspondent, June 23, 2021, https://www.thecorrespondent.pk/world/taliban-call -recent-gains-as-victory-of-mujahid-afghan-nation/.

93. Heineman, *Retrograde*.

94. Sami Sadat, "I Commanded Afghan Troops This Year. We Were Betrayed," *New York Times*, August 25, 2021, https://www.nytimes.com/2021/08/25/opinion /afghanistan-taliban-Army.html.

95. Matthieu Aikins, "Inside the Fall of Kabul," *New York Times*, December 10, 2021, https://www.nytimes.com/2021/12/10/magazine/fall-of-kabul-afghanistan.html.

96. VICE News, "The Fall of Kandahar," YouTube, August 24, 2021, https://www .youtube.com/watch?v=vGQ34RCv7Pc.

97. "US Pledged 37 Black Hawks, 2 Fixed-Wing Attack Aircraft: Sources," TOLOnews, June 28, 2021, https://tolonews.com/afghanistan-173144.

98. "Afghanistan's Interior Minister Reveals Plan to Push Back Taliban," Al Jazeera.

99. "Afghanistan: Ghani Blames 'Abrupt' US Exit for Worsening Security," Al Jazeera, August 2, 2021, https://www.aljazeera.com/news/2021/8/2/afghanistan-ghani -blames-abrupt-us-exit-for-worsening-security.

100. John Hayward, "Afghan President Blames 'Sudden' U.S. Pullout for Taliban Advances," Breitbart, August 2, 2021, https://www.breitbart.com/national-security /2021/08/02/afghan-president-sudden-u-s-pullout-after-20-years-fueling-taliban -wins/.

101. Joshua Kaplan et al., "Hell at Abbey Gate: Chaos, Confusion and Death in the Final Days of the War in Afghanistan," ProPublica, April 2, 2022, https://www .propublica.org/article/hell-at-abbey-gate-chaos-confusion-and-death-in-the-final -days-of-the-war-in-afghanistan.

102. Susannah George, "Final Weeks of Fighting Among Deadliest for Afghan Security Forces, Former Official Says: 4,000 Dead and 1,000 Missing," *Washington Post*, December 29, 2021, https://www.washingtonpost.com/world/2021/12/30 /afghanistan-security-forces-deaths/.

103. "Afghanistan: Red Cross–Supported Health Facilities Treat More than 4,000 People Wounded by Weapons Since 1 August," International Committee of the Red Cross, January 10, 2023, https://www.icrc.org/en/document/afghanistan-red -cross-supported-health-facilities-treat-more-4000-people-wounded-weapons.

104. Susannah George, "Final weeks of fighting among deadliest for Afghan security forces, former official says: 4,000 dead and 1,000 missing," *Washington Post*,

December 30, 2021, https://www.washingtonpost.com/world/2021/12/30
/afghanistan-security-forces-deaths/.

105. Jonathan Schroden, "Lessons from the Collapse of Afghanistan's Security Forces,"
CTC Sentinel 14, no. 8 (August 2021), https://ctc.usma.edu/wp-content/uploads
/2021/10/CTC-SENTINEL-082021.pdf, 54.

106. "Hamdullah Mohib on 'Face the Nation,'" CBS News, December 19, 2021, https://
www.cbsnews.com/news/transcript-hamdullah-mohib-face-the-nation-12-19-2021/.

107. Kate Clark, "Afghanistan's Conflict in 2021 (2): Republic collapse and Taleban
victory in the long view of history," Afghanistan Analysts Network, December
30, 2021, https://www.afghanistan-analysts.org/en/reports/war-and-peace
/afghanistans-conflict-in-2021-2-republic-collapse-and-taleban-victory-in-the
-long-view-of-history/.

108. Lloyd Austin, "Secretary of Defense Lloyd J. Austin III Prepared Remarks before
the Senate Armed Services Committee," September 28, 2021, https://www.defense
.gov/News/Speeches/Speech/Article/2791954/secretary-of-defense-lloyd-j-austin
-iii-remarks-before-the-senate-armed-service/.

109. Babb, "VOA Exclusive: CENTCOM Head Says US Will Not Support Afghan Forces
with Airstrikes After Troop Withdrawal."

110. Schroden, "Lessons from the Collapse of Afghanistan's Security Forces."

111. Lynch III, "Deconstructing the Collapse of Afghanistan National Security."

112. SIGAR, *Collapse of the Afghan National Defense and Security Forces*, October 2022,
https://www.sigar.mil/pdf/quarterlyreports/2022-10-30qr.pdf.

113. Schroden, "Lessons from the Collapse of Afghanistan's Security Forces," 46, 53.

114. Ibid., 53.

CHAPTER 5: KABUL FALLING

1. Abbey Gate Report, Enc. 2, 86.

2. Abbey Gate Report, 54.

3. Abbey Gate Report, Enc. 3, Pg. 48.

4. Special Inspector General for Afghanistan Reconstruction (SIGAR), "Department
of State Anti-Terrorism Assistance Program in Afghanistan: Security Concerns
Prevented State from Fully Monitoring and Evaluating the Program, and Up to $32
Million in Assets May Be in the Taliban's Possession," October 2022, https://www
.sigar.mil/pdf/audits/SIGAR-23-01-AR.pdf.

5. Antony Blinken, @SecBlinken, Twitter, May 14, 2021, https://twitter.com/SecBlinken
/status/1393236670091235332.

6. Antony Blinken, @SecBlinken, Twitter, June 4, 2021, https://twitter.com/SecBlinken
/status/1400854806051360768.

7. Joseph R. Biden, Jr., "Remarks by President Biden on the COVID-19 Response and
Vaccination Program," White House, June 2, 2021, https://www.whitehouse.gov
/briefing-room/speeches-remarks/2021/07/08/remarks-by-president-biden-on-the
-drawdown-of-u-s-forces-in-afghanistan/.

8. "Rep. McCaul Presses Secretary Blinken on Evacuation Plan for Afghans Awaiting Special Immigrant Visas," House Foreign Affairs Committee Republicans, June 7, 2021, https://foreignaffairs.house.gov/press-release/rep-mccaul-presses-secretary-blinken-on-evacuation-plan-for-afghans-awaiting-special-immigrant-visas/.

9. Nick Schifrin and Dan Sagalyn, "Biden Wants to Leave Some U.S. Troops in Afghanistan. The Taliban Isn't Happy," PBS, June 25, 2021, https://www.pbs.org/newshour/show/biden-wants-to-leave-some-us-troops-in-afghanistan-the-taliban-isnt-happy.

10. "Readout of President Joseph R. Biden, Jr. Meeting with President Ghani and Chairman Abdullah of Afghanistan," White House, June 25, 2021, https://www.whitehouse.gov/briefing-room/statements-releases/2021/06/25/readout-of-president-joseph-r-biden-jr-meeting-with-president-ghani-and-chairman-abdullah-of-afghanistan/.

11. Ibid.

12. Lloyd Austin, President Mohammmad Ashraf Ghani, and Dr. Abdullah Abdullah, "Remarks by Secretary of Defense Lloyd J. Austin III with President of Afghanistan Mohammad Ashraf Ghani and Dr. Abdullah Abdullah, Chairman of the High Council For National Reconciliation," June 25, 2021, https://www.defense.gov/News/Transcripts/Transcript/Article/2672773/remarks-by-secretary-of-defense-lloyd-j-austin-iii-with-president-of-afghanista/.

13. Biden: "Remarks by President Biden on the Drawdown of U.S. Forces."

14. Antony Blinken, @SecBlinken, Twitter, July 9, 2021, https://twitter.com/SecBlinken/status/1413493186987806721.

15. Ned Price, "Senior Leaders from Afghanistan Hold Peace Talks," Department of State, July 19, 2021, https://www.state.gov/senior-leaders-from-afghanistan-hold-peace-talks/.

16. Ned Price, "Transfer of GTMO Detainee to Morocco," Department of State, July 19, 2021, https://www.state.gov/transfer-of-gtmo-detainee-to-morocco/.

17. "Excerpts of call between Joe Biden and Ashraf Ghani July 23," Reuters, August 31, 2021, https://www.reuters.com/world/excerpts-call-between-joe-biden-ashraf-ghani-july-23-2021-08-31/.

18. Ibid.

19. Aram Roston and Nandita Bose, "Exclusive: Before Afghan Collapse, Biden Pressed Ghani to 'Change Perception,'" Reuters, August 31, 2021, https://www.reuters.com/world/exclusive-call-before-afghan-collapse-biden-pressed-ghani-change-perception-2021-08-31/.

20. Office of Inspector General, United States Department of State, "Information Report: Afghan Special Immigrant Visa Program Metrics," September 2022, https://www.stateoig.gov/report/aud-mero-22-38.

21. Brian McKeon and Tracey Jacobson, Department of State, July 21, 2021, https://www.state.gov/briefing-with-deputy-secretary-for-management-and-resources-brian-p-mckeon-and-afghanistan-task-force-director-ambassador-tracey-jacobson-with-on-background-qa-by-senior-state-department-officials-o/.

22. Gordon Lubold and Yaroslav Trofimov, "Afghan Government Could Collapse Six Months After U.S. Withdrawal, New Intelligence Assessment Says," *Wall Street Journal*, June 23, 2021, https://www.wsj.com/articles/afghan-government-could-collapse-six-months-after-u-s-withdrawal-new-intelligence-assessment-says-11624466743.

23. "Elizabeth Zentos and Anton Cooper: Dissenting from Kabul," *Foreign Service Journal*, American Foreign Service Association, December 2022, https://afsa.org/sites/default/files/fsj-2022-12-december.pdf, 37.

24. Jerry Dunleavy, "'We got all kinds of cables': Biden tries to explain why Kabul embassy warning wasn't heeded," *Washington Examiner*, August 20, 2021, https://www.washingtonexaminer.com/politics/got-all-kinds-cables-biden-explain-kabul-embassy-warning-not-heeded.

25. Michael R. Gordon et al., "Inside Biden's Afghanistan Withdrawal Plan: Warnings, Doubts but Little Change," *Wall Street Journal*, September 5, 2021, https://www.wsj.com/articles/inside-the-biden-administrations-push-to-exit-afghanistan-11630855499.

26. Senate Foreign Relations Committee, "Examining the U.S. Withdrawal from Afghanistan," September 14, 2021, https://www.foreign.senate.gov/imo/media/doc/09%2014%2021%20Examining%20the%20U.S.%20Withdrawal%20from%20Afghanistan.pdf.

27. Jerry Dunleavy, "Bullshit excuses: McCaul threatens to subpoena State Department over Kabul dissent cable," *Washington Examiner*, March 27, 2023, https://www.washingtonexaminer.com/news/policy/defense-national-security/mccaul-threatens-subpoena-state-department-kabul-dissent-cable.

28. Antony Blinken, @SecBlinken, Twitter, August 3, 2021, https://twitter.com/SecBlinken/status/1422578000751628291.

29. Helene Cooper, Thomas Gibbons-Neff, and Eric Schmitt, "U.S. Airstrikes in Afghanistan Could Be a Sign of What Comes Next," *New York Times*, August 3, 2021, https://www.nytimes.com/2021/08/03/us/politics/us-airstrikes-afghanistan.html.

30. Antony Blinken, @SecBlinken, Twitter, August 5, 2021, https://twitter.com/SecBlinken/status/1423297752608350209.

31. Philip Wegmann, "White House Defends Tiktok Outreach amid Bipartisan Security Concerns," RealClear Politics, November 5, 2022, https://www.realclearpolitics.com/articles/2022/11/05/white_house_defends_tiktok_outreach_amid_bipartisan_security_concerns_148433.html.

32. John Kirby, "Pentagon Press Secretary John F. Kirby Holds a Press Briefing," August 9, 2021, Department of Defense, https://www.defense.gov/News/Transcripts/Transcript/Article/2725063/pentagon-press-secretary-john-f-kirby-holds-a-press-briefing/.

33. Dan Lamothe, John Hudson, Shane Harris, and Anne Gearan, "U.S. officials warn collapse of Afghan capital could come sooner than expected," *Washington Post*, August 10, 2021, https://www.washingtonpost.com/national-security/2021/08/10/afghanistan-intelligence-assessment/.

34. Ned Price, "Department Press Briefing – August 10, 2021," Department of State, August 10, 2021, https://www.state.gov/briefings/department-press-briefing-august -10-2021/.

35. Jen Psaki, "Press Briefing by Press Secretary Jen Psaki, August 10, 2021," White House, August 10, 2021, https://www.whitehouse.gov/briefing-room/press-briefings /2021/08/10/press-briefing-by-press-secretary-jen-psaki-august-10-2021/.

36. Ibid.

37. Blinken, Antony. Twitter, August 12, 2021, https://twitter.com/secblinken/status /1425957770843627521.

38. "Readout of Secretary of Defense Lloyd J. Austin III's Call With President of the Islamic Republic of Afghanistan Ashraf Ghani," White House, August 12, 2021, https://www.defense.gov/News/Releases/Release/Article/2730358/readout-of -secretary-of-defense-lloyd-j-austin-iiis-call-with-president-of-the/.

39. Katherine Doyle, "Kamala Harris's NASA Video Featured Child Actors," *Washington Examiner*, October 11, 2021, https://www.washingtonexaminer.com /news/nasa-kamala-harris-child-actors-space.

40. "Senate Armed Services Committee Hearing on Afghanistan Withdrawal," C-SPAN, September 28, 2021, https://www.c-span.org/video/?514537-1/senate-armed-services -committee-hearing-afghanistan-withdrawal/.

41. House Armed Services Committee, "Statement of General Mark A. Milley USA, 20th Chairman of the Joint Chiefs of Staff, Ending the U.S. Military Mission in Afghanistan, September 29, 2021," https://www.congress.gov/117/meeting/house /114096/witnesses/HHRG-117-AS00-Wstate-MilleyM-20210929.pdf, 5.

42. "Senate Armed Services Committee Hearing on Afghanistan Withdrawal," C-SPAN, September 28, 2021.

43. John Kirby, "Pentagon Press Secretary John F. Kirby Holds a Press Briefing," August 13, 2021, Department of Defense, https://www.defense.gov/News/Transcripts /Transcript/Article/2731940/pentagon-press-secretary-john-f-kirby-holds-a-press -briefing/.

44. National Security Council, "(U//FOUG) Summary of Conclusions for Meeting of the Deputies Small Group on Relocations out of Afghanistan," August 14, 2021, https:// www.documentcloud.org/documents/21195411-afghanistan-memo.

45. Ibid.

46. Antony Blinken, @SecBlinken, Twitter, August 14, 2021, https://twitter.com /SecBlinken/status/1426703449903796229.

47. Joseph R. Biden, Jr., "Statement by President Biden on Afghanistan," White House, August 14, 2021, https://www.whitehouse.gov/briefing-room/statements-releases /2021/08/14/statement-by-president-joe-biden-on-afghanistan/.

48. Tina Sfondeles and Sam Stein, "Biden Tries to Avoid the August Curse," Politico, August 9, 2021, https://www.politico.com/newsletters/west-wing-playbook/2021/08 /09/vacation-all-i-ever-wanted-493912.

49. Joseph R. Biden, Jr., "Statement by President Biden on the Senate Passage of the Bipartisan Infrastructure Investment and Jobs Act Bill," White House, August 10, 2021, https://www.whitehouse.gov/briefing-room/speeches-remarks/2021

/08/10/remarks-by-president-biden-on-the-senate-passage-of-the-bipartisan
-infrastructure-investment-and-jobs-act/.

50. John Maggio, director, *Year One: A Political Odyssey*, HBO, https://www.hbo.com
/movies/year-one-a-political-odyssey.

51. Ibid.

52. Jerry Dunleavy, "Top Biden Spokeswoman, Jen Psaki, 'Out of the Office' as
Afghanistan Falls to Taliban," *Washington Examiner*, August 15, 2021, https://www
.washingtonexaminer.com/news/top-biden-spokeswoman-jen-psaki-out-office
-afghanistan-falls-taliban.

53. Scott Wong, "Pelosi Circulates WH Talking Points after Afghanistan Collapse," *The
Hill*, August 16, 2021, https://thehill.com/homenews/house/568052-pelosi-circulates
-wh-talking-points-after-afghanistan-collapse/.

54. Dan Lamothe and Alex Horton, "Documents Reveal U.S. Military's Frustration
with White House, Diplomats over Afghanistan Evacuation," *Washington Post*,
February 2, 2022, https://www.washingtonpost.com/national-security/2022/02/08
/afghanistan-evacuation-investigation/.

55. Matthieu Aikins, "Inside the Fall of Kabul," *New York Times Magazine*, December
10, 2021, https://www.nytimes.com/2021/12/10/magazine/fall-of-kabul-afghanistan
.html.

56. Coll and Entous, "Secret History."

57. VOA, "Afghan President Ghani: 'Remobilization of Armed Forces Top Priority,'"
Voice of America (VOA News), August, 14, 2021, https://www.voanews.com/a/us
-afghanistan-troop-withdrawal_afghan-president-ghani-remobilization-armed
-forces-top-priority/6209570.html.

58. Aikins, "Inside the Fall of Kabul."

59. Matin Bek, Twitter, August 15, 2021, https://twitter.com/MatinBek/status
/1426808641521340418.

60. "Taliban declare not to enter Kabul for now, wait for transition," WION, August 15,
2021, https://www.wionews.com/south-asia/taliban-declare-not-to-enter-kabul-for
-now-wait-for-transition-405574.

61. Maggio, *Year One: A Political Odyssey*.

62. Special Inspector General for Afghanistan Reconstruction, *Theft of Funds from
Afghanistan*, August 2022, https://www.sigar.mil/pdf/evaluations/SIGAR-22-35-IP
.pdf

63. "Remarks by President Biden on Afghanistan," White House, August 16, 2021,
https://www.whitehouse.gov/briefing-room/speeches-remarks/2021/08/16/remarks
-by-president-biden-on-afghanistan/.

64. "Hamdullah Mohib on 'Face the Nation,'" CBS News, December 19, 2021, https://
www.cbsnews.com/news/transcript-hamdullah-mohib-face-the-nation-12-19-2021/.

65. Aikins, "Inside the Fall of Kabul."

66. Jerry Dunleavy, "US reliance on Taliban security was 'original sin' that led to suicide
bombing, GOP Rep. says," *Washington Examiner*, September 30, 2021, https://www
.washingtonexaminer.com/news/us-reliance-taliban-security-original-sin-gallagher.

67. Ibid.

68. Jerry Dunleavy, "Biden: Afghan government collapsed 'more quickly than we anticipated,'" *Washington Examiner*, August 16, 2021, https://www .washingtonexaminer.com/politics/biden-afghanistan-more-quickly-anticipated.

69. Marco Rubio, @MarcoRubio, Twitter, August 16, 2021, https://twitter.com /marcorubio/status/1427260151015383040.

70. Naomi Lim, "Biden Insists No Mistakes Were Made in US Exit from Afghanistan," *Washington Examiner*, August 18, 2021, https://www.washingtonexaminer.com /politics/biden-mistakes-afghanistan.

71. Joseph R. Biden, Jr., "Remarks by President Biden on Evacuations in Afghanistan," White House, August 20, 2021, https://www.whitehouse.gov/briefing-room/speeches -remarks/2021/08/20/remarks-by-president-biden-on-evacuations-in-afghanistan/.

72. Jerry Dunleavy, "Intel Community Defends Itself After US Was Caught Out by Speed of Taliban Takeover," *Washington Examiner*, August 17, 2021, https://www .washingtonexaminer.com/news/intel-community-defends-itself-us-caught-speed -taliban-takeover.

73. James Gordon Meek, "Afghanistan's Collapse: Did US Intelligence Get It Wrong?," ABC News, August 15, 2021, https://abcnews.go.com/amp/US/afghanistans-collapse -us-intelligence-wrong/story?id=79470553&id=79470553.

74. Abbey Gate Report, Enc. 3, Pg. 50.

75. Gordon et al., "Inside Biden's Afghanistan Withdrawal Plan."

76. Mark Mazzetti, Julian E. Barnes, and Adam Goldman, "Intelligence Warned of Afghan Military Collapse, Despite Biden's Assurances," *New York Times*, August 17, 2021, https://www.nytimes.com/2021/08/17/us/politics/afghanistan-intelligence -biden-administration.html.

77. Lubold and Trofimov, "Afghan Government Could Collapse Six Months After U.S. Withdrawal, New Intelligence Assessment Says."

78. "Transcript: NPR's Full Conversation with CIA Director William Burns," NPR, July 22, 2021, https://www.npr.org/2021/07/22/1017900583/transcript-nprs-full -conversation-with-cia-director-william-burns.

79. Special Inspector General for Afghanistan Reconstruction (SIGAR), *Quarterly Report to the United States Congress*, July 30, 2021.

80. "Senate Armed Services Committee Hearing on the Posture of United States Central Command and United States Africa Command, March 15, 2022," U.S. Central Command, March 15, 2022, https://www.centcom.mil/MEDIA/Transcripts/Article /2968166/senate-armed-services-committee-hearing-on-the-posture-of-united -states-central/.

81. Gordon et al., "Inside Biden's Afghanistan Withdrawal Plan."

82. Missy Ryan et al., "Biden Administration Scrambled as Its Orderly Withdrawal from Afghanistan Unraveled," *Washington Post*, August 14, 2021, https://www .washingtonpost.com/national-security/biden-taliban-afghan-collapse/2021/08/14 /da7cba66-fcf7-11eb-b8dd-0e376fba55f2_story.html.

83. Dan Lamothe et al., "U.S. Officials Warn Collapse of Afghan Capital Could Come Sooner than Expected," *Washington Post*, August 10, 2021, https://www .washingtonpost.com/national-security/2021/08/10/afghanistan-intelligence -assessment/.

84. Luis Martinez and Conor Finnegan, "US Military Analysis Says Kabul Could Fall to Taliban in 90 Days: Official," ABC News, August 12, 2021, https://abcnews.go.com /Politics/us-military-analysis-kabul-fall-taliban-90-days/story?id=79404085.

85. Lamothe et al., "U.S. Officials Warn Collapse Could Come."

86. Authors' interview with Jerry Dunleavy and Mike McCaul, December 22, 2022.

87. Senate Foreign Relations Committee, "Special Representative for Afghanistan Reconciliation Zalmay Khalilzad Opening Statement for Afghanistan Briefing, Senate Foreign Relations Committee, April 27, 2021," https://www.foreign.senate.gov /imo/media/doc/042721_Khalilzad_Testimony.pdf.

88. Ayaz Gul, "US Envoy: Afghanistan Will Become 'Pariah State' if Taliban Takes Country by Force," VOA, August 2, 2021, https://www.voanews.com/south-central -asia/us-envoy-afghanistan-will-become-pariah-state-if-taliban-takes-country -force.

89. "Hamdullah Mohib on 'Face the Nation,'" CBS News, December 19, 2021, https:// www.cbsnews.com/news/transcript-hamdullah-mohib-face-the-nation-12-19-2021/.

90. Abbey Gate Report, Enc. 3, Pg. 50.

91. "Statement of General Mark A. Milley," Senate Armed Services Committee, September 28, 2021, https://www.armed-services.senate.gov/imo/media/doc/Printed %2028%20Sep%20SASC%20CJCS%20Written%20Statement.pdf.

92. Maggio, *Year One: A Political Odyssey.*

93. Chris Whipple, *The Fight of His Life: Inside Joe Biden's White House* (New York: Scribner, 2023), 106-107.

94. Ibid., 90, 107-108.

95. Senate Armed Services Committee Hearing on Afghanistan Withdrawal," C-SPAN, September 28, 2021, https://www.c-span.org/video/?514537-1/senate-armed-services -committee-hearing-afghanistan-withdrawal.

CHAPTER 6: NIGHT OF THE ZOMBIES

1. Phil Stewart, "Special Report: Pilots detail chaotic collapse of the Afghan Air Force," Reuters, December 29, 2021, https://www.reuters.com/business/aerospace-defense /pilots-detail-chaotic-collapse-afghan-air-force-2021-12-29/.

2. Abbey Gate Report, Enc. 4, Pg. 26.

3. Abbey Gate Report, Enc. 12, Pg. 66.

4. Abbey Gate Report, Enc. 3, Pg. 14.

5. Abbey Gate Report, Enc. 2, Pg. 109.

6. Abbey Gate Report, Enc. 2, Pg. 4.

7. Abbey Gate Report, Enc. 3, Pg. 25.

CHAPTER 7: CHAOS AT THE GATES

1. Jake Sullivan, @JakeSullivan46, Twitter, August 17, 2021, https://twitter.com/JakeSullivan46/status/1427758984254078977.

2. Lucas Tomlinson, @LucasFoxNews, Twitter, August 18 2021, https://twitter.com/LucasFoxNews/status/1428062047770664971.

3. Mark Nicol, "Revealed: How Elite SAS Troops Launched Dramatic Operation to Save 20 Comrades Trapped by Advancing Taliban Hordes as Kandahar Fell—Landing a Hercules Plane on the Desert Floor in Pitch Darkness in 'Textbook' Raid," *Daily Mail*, August 22, 2021, https://www.dailymail.co.uk/news/article-9917109/SAS-dramatic-desert-raid-save-troops-Taliban.html.

4. Ibid.

5. Ibid.

6. Joshua Kaplan et al., "Hell at Abbey Gates," ProPublica, April 2, 2022, https://www.propublica.org/article/hell-at-abbey-gate-chaos-confusion-and-death-in-the-final-days-of-the-war-in-afghanistan.

7. Abbey Gate Report, Enc. 7, 11.

8. Haley Britzky, "They Were Children When the Afghanistan War Ended. As Soldiers They Carried the Burden of Ending It," Task & Purpose, November 10, 2021, https://taskandpurpose.com/history/Army-soldiers-stories-kabul-withdrawal/?amp.

9. Haley Britzky, "The True Story of How Army Paratroopers Traded Dip for a Toyota Gun Truck Used to Secure the Kabul Airport," Task & Purpose, October 12, 2021, https://taskandpurpose.com/news/Army-paratroopers-toyota-technical-kabul-airport/.

10. oarfoundation, Instagram, August 22, 2022, https://www.instagram.com/p/Chk2x-bOaUh/?hl=en.

11. Ibid.

12. Ibid.

13. Abbey Gate Report, Enc. 7, 26.

14. Ibid.

15. Abbey Gate Report, Enc. 3, 1.

16. Source interview, 2022.

17. Kristina Wong, "Biden's Order to 'Get F-cking Asses in Seats' Contributed to August 26 Afghanistan Attack That Killed 13 Americans," Breitbart, March 26, 2022, https://www.breitbart.com/politics/2022/03/26/bidens-order-asses-seats-contributed-afghanistan-attack-killed-13-americans/.

18. Abbey Gate Report, Enc. 3, Pg. 68.

19. Abbey Gate Report, Enc. 2, Pg. 88.

20. Josh Hawley, @HawleyMO, Twitter, October 26, 2021, https://twitter.com/HawleyMO/status/1453054643420995584.

21. Abbey Gate Report, Enc. 12, Pg. 5.

22. Source interview, 2022.

23. The White House, @WhiteHouse, Twitter, August 18, 2021, https://twitter.com /whitehouse/status/1428079918303301641?lang=en.

24. Ibid.

25. Abbey Gate Report, Enc. 8, 36.

26. Abbey Gate Report, Main Conclusions, 30.

27. oarfoundation, Instagram, August 24, 2022, https://www.instagram.com /p/ChpIYT9Lj3f/?hl=en.

28. Abbey Gate Report, Enc. 8, 37.

29. Helene Cooper and Eric Schmidt, "Witnesses to the End," *New York Times*, November 7, 2021, https://www.nytimes.com/2021/11/07/us/politics/afghanistan -war-Marines.html.

30. Abbey Gate Report, Enc. 8, 60.

31. oarfoundation, Instagram, August 24, 2022, https://www.instagram.com /p/ChpIYT9Lj3f/.

32. Abbey Gate Report, Enc. 4, 32.

33. Matthew Lee, "Afghan Evacuation Raises Concerns About Child Trafficking," Associated Press, September 3, 2021, https://apnews.com/article/middle-east-child -trafficking-27d93a340c4834d497eb36e22bb72f42.

34. Ibid.

35. Jana Winter, "DHS Monitoring for Cases of 'Child Brides' Among Afghan Refugees," Yahoo! News, September 8, 2021, https://news.yahoo.com/dhs-monitoring-for-cases -of-child-brides-among-afghan-refugees-202425854.html.

36. "Senator Cruz Confronts Secretary Blinken," C-SPAN, September 15, 2021, https:// www.c-span.org/video/?c4977099/user-clip-senator-cruz-confronts-secretary-state -antony-blinken.

37. Ibid.

38. Abbey Gate Report, Enc. 9, 23.

39. See, e.g., DHS and DOS Announce Exemptions Allowing Eligible Afghans to Qualify for Protection and Immigration Benefits, Department of Homeland Security, (June 14, 2022), https://www.dhs.gov/news/2022/06/14/dhs-and-dos -announce-exemptions-allowing-eligible-afghans-qualify-protection-and.

40. Abbey Gate Report, Enc. 4, 16.

41. Abbey Gate Report, Enc. 9, 63.

42. oarfoundation, Instagram, August 17, 2022, https://www.instagram.com /p/ChXOESIL1LU/.

43. Abbey Gate Report, Enc. 9, 63.

44. Abbey Gate Report, Enc. 3, Pg. 62.

CHAPTER 8: SEEING THINGS THAT NO PERSON SHOULD HAVE TO SEE

1. Abbey Gate Report, Enc. 8, 66.

2. Abbey Gate Report, Enc. 3, 11.

3. oarfoundation, Instagram, October 6, 2022, https://www.instagram.com/p/CjYZX
   _nLO3h/?hl=en.

4. Abbey Gate Report, Enc. 4, 47.

5. Ibid.

6. Ibid., 44–45.

7. Abbey Gate Report, Enc. 7, 20.

8. Abbey Gate Report, Enc. 10, 20.

9. "Amid Desperation at Kabul Airport, Evacuation Picks Up Pace," August 20,
   2021, *New York Times*, https://www.nytimes.com/live/2021/08/20/world/biden
   -afghanistan-taliban.

10. Andrew Quilty, "The CIA's Afghan Proxies, Accused of War Crimes, Will Get a
    Fresh Start in the U.S.," October 5, 2021, https://theintercept.com/2021/10/05/zero
    -units-cia-afghanistan-taliban.

11. Abbey Gate Report, Enc. 3, 30.

12. Abbey Gate Report Enc. 9, 21.

13. Kristen Duncan, "Air Force Rescue Personnel Support NEO Weeks Before the Fall of
    Kabul," United States Air Force, October 12, 2021, https://www.af.mil/News/Article
    -Display/Article/2807037/air-force-rescue-personnel-support-neo-weeks-before-the
    -fall-of-kabul/.

14. OARFoundation, Instagram, October 13, 2022, https://www.instagram.com/p/Cjp
    _SfUsa9x/?hl=en.

15. Abbey Gate Report, Enc. 8, 36.

16. Ibid.

17. Nicole Gee, Instagram, August 20, 2021, https://www.instagram.com
    /p/CS0LAGFh35Y/.

18. Abbey Gate Report, Enc. 3, 11.

19. Abbey Gate Report, Enc. 8, 67.

20. Abbey Gate Report, Enc. 3, 12.

21. Ibid., 86.

22. Ibid., 61–62.

23. Abbey Gate Report, Enc. 12, 16.

24. Abbey Gate Report, Enc. 3, Pg. 22.

25. Abbey Gate Report, Enc. 4, 17.

26. Abbey Gate Report Enc. 8, 32.

27. Abbey Gate Report, Enc. 12, 15.

28. Abbey Gate Report, Enc. 11, 33.

29. Mary Louise Kelly, Erika Ryan, and Patrick Jarenwattananon, "The U.S. Lost Track
    of Why It Was in Afghanistan, Former Commander Says," KUOW, August 10,
    2022, https://www.kuow.org/stories/the-u-s-lost-track-of-why-it-was-in-afghanistan
    -former-commander-says.

30. Abbey Gate Report, Enc. 9, 7.

31. Abbey Gate Report, Enc. 7, 69.

32. oarfoundation, Instagram, August 21, 2021, https://www.instagram.com /p/ChhadB9OlCB/?hl=en.

33. Abbey Gate Report, Enc. 7, 69.

34. Ibid.

35. Chargé d'Affaires Karen Decker, @USAmbKabul, Twitter, August 22, 2021, https:// twitter.com/USAmbKabul/status/1429424966286684165.

36. Twitter, @UsAmbKabul, August 22, 2021, https://twitter.com/USAmbKabul/status /1429443476421292034.

37. "Pentagon Press Secretary John F. Kirby and General Kenneth F. McKenzie Jr. Hold a Press Briefing," U.S. Department of Defense, August 30, 2021, https://www.defense .gov/News/Transcripts/Transcript/Article/2759183/pentagon-press-secretary-john -f-kirby-and-general-kenneth-f-mckenzie-jr-hold-a/.

38. "President Biden on Afghanistan Withdrawal, Taliban Takeover Intelligence Decisions," ABC News, August 18, 2021, https://abcnews.go.com/WNT/video /president-biden-afghanistan-withdrawal-taliban-takeover-intelligence-decisions -79526276.

39. *Good Morning America*, "Biden Says He Did Not See a Way to Withdraw from Afghanistan Without 'Chaos Ensuing,'" August 19, 2021, https://www.youtube.com /watch?v=i2nwusq_WcM.

40. Ibid.

41. Ibid.

42. Abbey Gate Report, Enc. 4, 10.

43. Christina Wilkie, "U.S. consulting with Taliban on 'every aspect' of Kabul evacuation, says Biden national security advisor," CNBC.Com, August 23, 2021, https://www.cnbc.com/2021/08/23/us-is-consulting-with-taliban-on-every-aspect -of-kabul-evacuation.html.

44. Ibid.

45. Ibid.

46. Abbey Gate Report, Enc. 3, 9-10.

47. Abbey Gate Report, Enc. 10, 21.

48. Joseph R. Biden, Jr., "Remarks by President Biden on the Ongoing Evacuation Efforts in Afghanistan and the House Vote on the Build Back Better Agenda," White House, August 24, 2021, https://www.whitehouse.gov/briefing-room/speeches-remarks /2021/08/24/remarks-by-president-biden-on-the-ongoing-evacuation-efforts-in -afghanistan-and-the-house-vote-on-the-build-back-better-agenda/.

49. Steven Nelson and Juliegrace Bruske, "Psaki claims it's 'irresponsible' to say Americans 'are stranded' in Afghanistan," *New York Post*, August 23, 2021, https://nypost.com/2021/08/23/psaki-irresponsible-to-say-americans-stranded-in -afghanistan/.

50. John Bowden, "Psaki says Afghanistan evacuation cannot be called 'anything but a success,'" *The Independent*, August 24, 2021, https://www.independent.co.uk/news /world/americas/us-politics/jen-psaki-kabul-evacuations-success-b1908193.html.

51. Sky News Australia, "Biden Smirks at Reporter Who Asks Him Tough Question on Afghanistan," YouTube, August 25, 2021, https://www.youtube.com/watch?v= 8hFYc5zsOcY&t=13sf.

52. Abbey Gate Report, Enc. 4, 31.

53. Abbey Gate Report, AG Enc. 2, 86.

54. Abbey Gate Report, Enc. 2, 86.

55. Abbey Gate Report, Enc. 3, 26.

56. Source interview, 2022.

57. Abbey Gate Report, Enc. 4, 8.

58. Ibid., 31.

59. Abbey Gate Report, Enc. 4, 8.

60. Gordon Lubold, "CIA, U.S. Troops Conduct Missions Outside Kabul Airport to Extract Americans, Afghan Allies," *Wall Street Journal*, August 25, 2021, https:// www.wsj.com/amp/articles/cia-u-s-troops-conduct-missions-outside-kabul-airport -to-extract-americans-allies-11629915605.

61. Abbey Gate Report, 21.

CHAPTER 9: ANSWERING THE CALL

1. Joseph R. Biden, Jr., "Remarks by President Biden on the Drawdown of U.S. Forces in Afghanistan," White House, July 8, 2021, https://www.whitehouse.gov/briefing -room/speeches-remarks/2021/07/08/remarks-by-president-biden-on-the-drawdown -of-u-s-forces-in-afghanistan/.

2. Ned Price, "Department Press Briefing—July 8, 2021," U.S. Department of State, July 8, 2021, https://www.state.gov/briefings/department-press-briefing-july-8-2021/.

3. Barbara Starr and Kylie Atwood, "Pentagon Examining How to Evacuate Thousands Who Worked for US from Afghanistan," CNN, May 27, 2021, https://www.cnn.com /2021/05/26/politics/pentagon-examining-afghanistan-evacuation/index.html.

4. George Packer, "The Betrayal," *Atlantic*, July 7, 2022, https://www.theatlantic.com /magazine/archive/2022/03/biden-afghanistan-exit-american-allies-abandoned /621307/.

5. Haidee Eugenio Gilbert and Phill Leon Guerrero, "Guam 'Will Support' Hosting Afghan Evacuees, If Needed," *Guam Daily Post*, June 7, 2021, https://www.postguam .com/news/local/guam-will-support-hosting-afghan-evacuees-if-needed/article _9012332c-c2a8-11eb-8123-57dfff6e0d15.html.

6. Packer, "The Betrayal."

7. Ibid.

8. Ibid.

9. Ibid.

10. Ibid.

11. Ibid.

12. Abbey Gate Report, Enc. 3, 47.

13. "Denver-Based Group 'Team America' Helping People Trapped in Afghanistan," CBS News, August 26, 2021, https://www.cbsnews.com/colorado/news/team -america-afghanistan-taliban/.

14. Abbey Gate Report, Enc. 4, 29.

15. Emily Horne, "Statement by NSC Spokesperson Emily Horne on Qatar Airways Charter Flight from Kabul," White House, September 9, 2021, https://www .whitehouse.gov/briefing-room/statements-releases/2021/09/09/statement-by-nsc -spokesperson-emily-horne-on-qatar-airways-charter-flight-from-kabul/.

16. *House Republican Interim Report: A "Strategic Failure:" Assessing the Administration's Afghanistan Withdrawal*, August 2022, https://gop-foreignaffairs .house.gov/wp-content/uploads/2022/08/HFAC-Republican-Interim-Report -A-22Strategic-Failure22-Assessing-the-Administrations-Afghanistan-Withdrawal .pdf,, 93–94.

17. Ibid.

18. Ibid.

19. Mark Landler and Megan K. Stack, "Taliban Reject Extended Deadline as U.S. Races to Finish Evacuation," *New York Times*, August 23, 2021, https://www.nytimes.com /2021/08/23/world/asia/afghanistan-evacuation-americans-biden.html.

20. Christopher Eberhart, "Pelosi Filmed at Lavish Napa Valley Fundraiser Where Tickets Sold for Up to $29K as Kabul Crumbles," *Daily Mail*, August 23, 2021, https://www.dailymail.co.uk/news/article-9917827/Pelosi-filmed-lavish-Napa-Valley -fundraiser-tickets-sold-29K-Kabul-crumbles.html.

21. Mark Moore, "Schumer Slammed for Dancing at NYC Concert amid Afghanistan Strife," *New York Post*, August 22, 2021, https://nypost.com/2021/08/22/schumer -attends-we-love-nyc-concert-amid-afghanistan-covid/.

22. Joshua Q. Nelson, "Sen. Cotton Helps American Get Out of Afghanistan, Knocks State Department for Lack of Assistance," Fox News, August 23, 2021, https://www .foxnews.com/media/tom-cotton-helps-american-leave-afghanistan-dc.

CHAPTER 10: KNOWN WOLF

1. Abbey Gate Report, Enc. 8, Pg. 52.

2. Jeff Schogol, "Americans were promised an 'orderly and safe' withdrawal from Afghanistan. US troops say it was anything but," Task and Purpose, February 10, 2022, https://taskandpurpose.com/history/marines-investigation-afghanistan-abbey -gate-attack/.

3. Abbey Gate Report, Enc. 11, Pg. 1.

4. "Marine Sgt. Tyler Vargas-Andrews Recalls Kabul Airport Suicide Bombing," House Foreign Affairs Committee, C-SPAN, March 8, 2023, https://www.c-span.org/video/ ?c5060848/marine-sgt-tyler-vargas-andrews-recalls-kabul-airport-suicide-bombing.

5. "One Year Later: Chico's Tristan Hirsch recalls the horrors of suicide bomb attack at Kabul's Abbey Gate," *Enterprise-Record*, August 21, 2022, https://

www.chicoer.com/2022/08/21/one-year-later-chicos-tristan-hirsch-recalls
-the-horrors-of-suicide-bomb-attack-at-kabul-airports-abbey-gate-on-aug-26-2021/.

6. Heidi Hatch, "Gravely injured Utah Marine saves life of fellow Marine in U.S. exit from Afghanistan," KUTV, February 16, 2023, https://kjzz.com/news/local/utah-marine-gravely-injured-saves-life-of-fellow-marine-in-us-exit-from-afghanistan.

7. Jonathan Eby, @ghost.1b, Instagram, July 13, 2022, https://www.instagram.com/p/Cf-FVXOLhpz/.

8. Abbey Gate Report, Enc. 9, 67.

9. Abbey Gate Report, Enc. 2, 16.

10. Jerry Dunleavy, "Six Months On, Biden Administration Won't Identify Kabul Airport Bomber," *Washington Examiner*, February 26, 2022, https://www.washingtonexaminer.com/policy/defense-national-security/six-months-on-biden-administration-wont-identify-kabul-airport-bomber.

11. Jerry Dunleavy, "Biden Administration Refuses to Identify Kabul Airport Bomber Who Killed 13 Americans," *Washington Examiner*, August 25, 2022, https://www.washingtonexaminer.com/policy/defense-national-security/biden-administration-still-wont-identify-kabul-airport-bomber.

12. Ibid.

13. Ibid.

14. Eric Schmitt, "U.S. Military Focusing on ISIS Cell Behind Attack at Kabul Airport," *New York Times*, January 1, 2022, https://www.nytimes.com/2022/01/01/us/politics/afghan-war-isis-attack.html.

15. CENTCOM investigation documents obtained by the *New York Times*, https://int.nyt.com/data/documenttools/kabul-strike-investigation-ar15-6/189578e886367589/full.pdf.

16. Abbey Gate Report, Enc. 2, 87.

17. "Senate Armed Services Committee Hearing on Afghanistan Withdrawal," C-SPAN, September 28, 2021, https://www.c-span.org/video/?514537-1/senate-armed-services-committee-hearing-afghanistan-withdrawal.

18. Jerry Dunleavy, "ISIS threat in Afghanistan is 'real' and 'persistent,' Biden national security adviser says," *Washington Examiner*, August 22, 2021, https://www.washingtonexaminer.com/news/isis-afghanistan-taliban-united-states-sullivan-biden.

19. Maggio, *Year One: A Political Odyssey.*

20. Ibid.

21. Joe Biden, White House, August 24, 2021, https://www.whitehouse.gov/briefing-room/speeches-remarks/2021/08/24/remarks-by-president-biden-on-the-ongoing-evacuation-efforts-in-afghanistan-and-the-house-vote-on-the-build-back-better-agenda/.

22. "Secretary Antony J. Blinken On Afghanistan," State Department, August 25, 2021, https://www.state.gov/secretary-antony-j-blinken-on-afghanistan/.

23. "UK advises against all travel to Afghanistan amid 'high threat of terrorist attack,'" https://www.reuters.com/world/uk/uk-advises-against-all-travel-afghanistan-amid -high-threat-terrorist-attack-2021-08-25/.

24. "Afghanistan: US, allies warn of 'terror threat' at Kabul airport," https://www .aljazeera.com/news/2021/8/26/us-uk-australia-warn-of-terror-threat-at-kabul -airport.

25. "Afghanistan: Lethal attack is highly credible and imminent, says armed forces minister," Sky News, August 26, 2021, https://news.sky.com/video/lethal-attack -is-highly-credible-and-imminent-in-afghanistan-says-armed-forces-minister -12390874.

26. Abbey Gate Report, Enc. 2, Pg. 88.

27. Abbey Gate Main Report, Pg. 33.

28. United Nations Analytical Support and Sanctions Monitoring Team, "Twenty-eighth report," July 21, 2021, https://www.securitycouncilreport.org/atf/cf/ %7B65BFCF9B-6D27-4E9C-8CD3-CF6E4FF96FF9%7D/S_2021_655_E.pdf.

29. Jeff Seldin, "Islamic State Poised for Possible Resurgence in Afghanistan, US Officials Warn," Voice of America, February 9, 2021, https://www.voanews.com /a/south-central-asia_islamic-state-poised-possible-resurgence-afghanistan-us -officials-warn/6201815.html.

30. United Nations Analytical Support and Sanctions Monitoring Team, "Twenty-seventh report," February 3, 2021, https://digitallibrary.un.org/record/3899838 ?ln=en.

31. Zabihulalh Mujahid, @Zabehulah_M33, Twitter, August 15, 2021, https://twitter .com/Zabehulah_M33/status/1426827365393518592.

32. "Defense Department Briefing on Afghanistan," C-SPAN, August 27, 2021, https:// www.c-span.org/video/?514309-1/pentagon-suicide-bomber-kabul&live#&vod.

33. Thomas Joscelyn, "Islamic State claims responsibility for suicide bombing in Kabul," FDD's Long War Journal, August 26, 2021, https://www.longwarjournal.org /archives/2021/08/islamic-state-claims-credit-for-suicide-bombing-in-kabul.php.

34. Lolita Baldor, "Pentagon: Deadly Afghan airport attack was not preventable," Associated Press, February 5, 2022, https://apnews.com/article/afghanistan-islamic -state-group-bombings-evacuations-kabul-cf040d942b2c0eee88f71b556143388a.

35. Praveen Swami, "Kabul Airport Suicide Attacker Was Freed by Taliban After Four Years in CIA Custody for New Delhi Terror Plot," Firstpost, September 19, 2021, https://www.firstpost.com/india/kabul-airport-suicide-attacker-was-freed-by -taliban-after-four-years-in-cia-custody-for-new-delhi-terror-plot-9976961.html.

36. Ibid.

37. Kyle Orton, "Islamic State Says the Massacre at Kabul Airport Shows They Are the True Jihadists," Kyle Orton's Blog, September 9, 2021, https://kyleorton.co.uk/2021 /09/09/islamic-state-says-the-massacre-at-kabul-airport-shows-they-are-the-true -jihadists/.

38. Jerry Dunleavy, "Taliban and Haqqani Network have close relationship despite State Department claiming otherwise," Washington Examiner, August 27, 2021, https://

www.washingtonexaminer.com/news/taliban-haqqani-network-close-state-claiming
-otherwise.

39. Al Jazeera, "Badri-313: The Taliban's brigade patrolling Kabul airport," October 26, 2021, https://www.youtube.com/watch?v=L7Ah0I4pYbc.

40. Yaroslav Trofimov, "In Its Last Days in Kabul, U.S. Turns to Taliban as a Partner," *Wall Street Journal*, August 27, 2021, https://www.wsj.com/articles/in-its-last-days-in -kabul-u-s-turns-to-taliban-as-a-partner-11630105650.

41. "Joe Biden orders US military to prepare strikes against Kabul bomb attackers," *The Telegraph*, August 27, 2021, https://www.telegraph.co.uk/world-news/2021/08/26/afghanistan-threat-attack-kabul-airport-severe-imminent-warns/.

42. "13 U.S. troops killed in ISIS attacks on Kabul airport," Politico, August 26, 2021, https://www.politico.com/news/2021/08/26/explosion-rocks-kabul-airport-as-us -tries-to-evacuate-thousands-506937.

43. Joe Biden, White House, August 26, 2021, https://www.whitehouse.gov/briefing-room/speeches-remarks/2021/08/26/remarks-by-president-biden-on-the-terror-attack-at-hamid-karzai-international-airport/.

44. Jen Psaki, White House, August 26, 2021, https://www.whitehouse.gov/briefing -room/press-briefings/2021/08/26/press-briefing-by-press-secretary-jen-psaki -august-26-2021/.

45. "Defense Department Briefing on Afghanistan," C-SPAN, August 26, 2021, https:// www.c-span.org/video/?514298-1/pentagon-confirms-12-services-members-killed -suicide-bombing-kabul.

46. "Defense Department Briefing on Afghanistan," C-SPAN, August 26, 2021, https:// www.c-span.org/video/?514298-1/pentagon-confirms-12-services-members-killed -suicide-bombing-kabul.

47. "General Kenneth F. McKenzie Jr., Commander, U.S. Central Command, Holds a Press Briefing," Defense Department, February 4, 2022, https://www.defense.gov /News/Transcripts/Transcript/Article/2924617/general-kenneth-f-mckenzie-jr -commander-us-central-command-holds-a-press-briefi/.

48. Ibid.

49. Abbey Gate Report, Enc. 10, 31.

50. Praveen Swami, @PraveenSwami, Twitter, August 26, 2021, https://twitter.com /praveenswami/status/1430918134563844102.

51. Thomas Joscelyn, "An ISIS Jailbreak in Afghanistan," *The Dispatch*, August 7, 2020, https://www.fdd.org/analysis/2020/08/07/an-isis-jailbreak-in-afghanistan/.

52. United Nations Analytical Support and Sanctions Monitoring Team, "Twelfth report," June 1, 2021, https://www.ecoi.net/en/file/local/2053487/S_2021_486_E.pdf.

53. Antonio Giustozzi, *The Islamic State in Khorasan*, (London: Hurst & Company, 2018), 61.

54. Sajjan M. Gohel, "The Taliban Are Far Closer to the Islamic State than They Claim," *Foreign Policy*, August 26, 2021, https://foreignpolicy.com/2021/08/26/afghanistan -kabul-airport-attack-taliban-islamic-state/.

55. Massoud Andarabi, @Andarabi, Twitter, August 3, 2020, https://twitter.com
/andarabi/status/1290271098743869440.

56. Zabihullah Ghazi and Mujib Mashal. "29 Dead after ISIS Attack on Afghan Prison."
New York Times, August 3, 2020, https://www.nytimes.com/2020/08/03/world/asia
/afghanistan-prison-isis-taliban.html.

57. "The Haqqani Network: The New Kingmakers in Kabul," November 12, 2021,
https://warontherocks.com/2021/11/the-haqqani-network-afghanistans-new-power
-players/.

58. UN Security Council Monitoring Team, "Twenty-seventh report," February 3, 2021,
https://web.archive.org/web/20210305104848/https://undocs.org/S/2021/68.

59. UN Security Council Analytical Support and Sanctions Monitoring Team, "Taliban
and other associated individuals and entities constituting a threat to the peace
stability and security of Afghanistan," June 1, 2021, https://static.poder360.com.br
/2021/08/taliba-al-qaeda-onu.pdf.

60. Amira Jadoon, Abdul Sayed, and Andrew Mines, "The Islamic State Threat in
Taliban Afghanistan: Tracing the Resurgence of Islamic State Khorasan," *CTC
Sentinal* 15, no. 1 (January 2022), https://ctc.westpoint.edu/wp-content/uploads
/2022/01/CTC-SENTINEL-012022.pdf, 36.

61. "Twelfth report of the Analytical Support and Sanctions Monitoring Team," June 1,
2021, https://static.poder360.com.br/2021/08/taliba-al-qaeda-onu.pdf.

62. "Taking Action against ISIS-K – United States Department of State," U.S.
Department of State, 22 Nov. 2021, https://www.state.gov/taking-action-against-isis
-k/.

63. Abbey Gate Report, Enc. 4, Pg. 50.

64. Jamie Roberts, director, *Escape from Kabul*, HBO, 2022, https://www.hbo.com
/movies/escape-from-kabul.

65. Amrullah Saleh, @AmrullahSaleh2, Twitter, August 26, 2021, https://twitter.com
/AmrullahSaleh2/status/1431078856207785984.

66. Brian Brivati, *Losing Afghanistan: The Fall of Kabul and the End of Western
Intervention* (London: Biteback Publishing, 2022), 113.

67. Abbey Gate Report, Enc. 5, 58.

68. Buck Elton and Joshua Fruth, "Evacuation Operations, Great-Power Competition,
and External Operations Terror Threats in Post-drawdown Afghanistan: Mapping
Out the Path Ahead," *Journal of Indo-Pacific Affairs*, Air University, November 1,
2021, https://www.airuniversity.af.edu/JIPA/Display/Article/2828397/evacuation
-operations-great-power-competition-and-external-operations-terror-th/.

69. Antonio Giustozzi, "Afghanistan: Who Are IS-K and What Was the Motivation
Behind Kabul Airport Attack?," *Scotsman*, August 27, 2021, https://www.scotsman
.com/news/opinion/afghanistan-who-are-is-k-and-what-was-the-motivation-behind
-kabul-airport-attack-dr-antonio-giustozzi-3362554.

70. Praveen Swami, @praveenswami, Twitter, August 26, 2021, https://twitter.com
/praveenswami/status/1430970826564661251.

71. Michael P Pregent, @MPPregent, Twitter, October 6, 2021, https://twitter.com
/MPPregent/status/1445839378664722433.

72. "The Bridge – the True Story about the Evacuation of Kabul, Afghanistan with Tyler Vargas-Andrews," YouTube, September 16, 2022, https://www.youtube.com/watch?v=V24WSED1oHs.

73. Jen Psaki, White House, August 26, 2021, https://www.whitehouse.gov/briefing-room/press-briefings/2021/08/26/press-briefing-by-press-secretary-jen-psaki-august-26-2021/.

74. John Kirby, U.S. Central Command, August 26, 2021, https://www.centcom.mil/MEDIA/Transcripts/Article/2789438/pentagon-press-secretary-john-f-kirby-holds-a-press-briefing-aug-26-2021/.

75. Joseph R. Biden, Jr., "Remarks by President Biden on the Terror Attack at Hamid Karzai International Airport," White House, August 14, 2021, https://www.whitehouse.gov/briefing-room/speeches-remarks/2021/08/26/remarks-by-president-biden-on-the-terror-attack-at-hamid-karzai-international-airport/.

76. Ibid.

77. Ibid.

78. "Pentagon Press Secretary John F. Kirby Holds a Press Briefing," U.S. Department of Defense, August 26, 2021, https://www.defense.gov/News/Transcripts/Transcript/Article/2752126/pentagon-press-secretary-john-f-kirby-holds-a-press-briefing/.

79. Kristin Duncan, "Air Force Rescue Personnel Support NEO Weeks before the Fall of Kabul," Air Force, https://www.af.mil/News/Article-Display/Article/2807037/air-force-rescue-personnel-support-neo-weeks-before-the-fall-of-kabul/.

80. Jim Garamone, "U.S. Central Command Releases Report on August Abbey Gate Attack," DOD News, February 4, 2022, https://www.defense.gov/News/News-Stories/Article/Article/2924398/us-central-command-releases-report-on-august-abbey-gate-attack/.

81. "U.S. Marine Wounded in Kabul Attack Gives Eyewitness Account," CBS News, September 15, 2021, https://www.cbsnews.com/news/Marine-wounded-kabul-attack-eyewitness-account/.

82. Abbey Gate Report, Enc. 10, 52.

83. Abbey Gate Report, Enc. 6, 73.

84. Abbey Gate Report, Enc. 11, 56.

85. Jerry Dunleavy, "ISIS leader behind deaths of 13 US service members in Kabul is killed by Taliban," Washington Examiner, April 25, 2023, https://www.washingtonexaminer.com/policy/defense-national-security/isis-leader-13-deaths-kabul-airport-killed-taliban.

CHAPTER 11: A PUNCH IN THE GUT

1. Marco Levytsky, "Ukraine Boldly Goes Where No NATO Member Dared Go," Ukrainian Weekly, October 1, 2021, https://www.ukrweekly.com/uwwp/ukraine-boldly-goes-where-no-nato-member-dared-go/.

2. The Globe and Mail, "Dramatic Footage of Ukrainian Soldiers Escorting Canada-Bound Afghans into Kabul Airport," YouTube, September 10, 2021, https://www.youtube.com/watch?v=FiEGbM7HfAk.

3. Corey Berke, Instagram, August 31, 2021, https://www.instagram.com/p/CTQFJBnJtpe/?hl=en.

4. Abbey Gate Report, 14.

5. Abbey Gate Main Report, 13.

6. Abbey Gate Report, Enc. 9, 43.

7. Jonathan Eby, Instagram, August 28, 2022, https://www.instagram.com/p/Chzs9MIr0rW/.

8. Jonathan Eby, Instagram, August 23, 2022, https://www.instagram.com/p/ChmfF2vrmWH/.

9. Abbey Gate Report, Enc. 5, 69–76.

10. "Secretary of Defense Austin and Chairman of the Joint Chiefs of Staff Gen. Milley Press Briefing on the End of the U.S. War in Afghanistan," U.S. Department of Defense, September 1, 2021, https://www.defense.gov/News/Transcripts/Transcript/Article/2762169/secretary-of-defense-austin-and-chairman-of-the-joint-chiefs-of-staff-gen-mille/.

11. John Haltiwanger, "Top General Says US Military Was Aware Within Hours That Kabul Drone Strike Killed Civilians, but Pentagon Took Weeks to Fully Acknowledge It," Business Insider, September 29, 2021, https://www.businessinsider.com/general-mckenzie-military-aware-within-hours-kabul-drone-strike-killed-civilians-2021-9.

12. Dunleavy, "Military Brass Claim They Knew."

13. Ibid.

14. Abbey Gate Report, Enc. 4, 33.

CHAPTER 12: THE AFTERMATH

1. Senate Foreign Relations Committee, "Risch Publishes Report on Biden Administration's Strategic Failures During Afghanistan Withdrawal," February 3, 2022, https://www.foreign.senate.gov/press/rep/release/risch-publishes-report-on-biden-administrations-strategic-failures-during-afghanistan-withdrawal.

2. Ibid.

3. Emily Crane, "Biden Claims Afghanistan Withdrawal 'Extraordinary Success' in Address to Nation," New York Post, August 31, 2021, https://nypost.com/2021/08/31/biden-to-address-end-of-afghan-war/.

4. Brigid Kennedy, "Number of Americans Left in Afghanistan Is in the 'Very Low Hundreds,' Says Gen. McKenzie," The Week, August 30, 2021, https://theweek.com/news/1004331/number-of-americans-left-in-afghanistan-is-in-the-very-low-hundreds-says-gen-mckenzie.

5. Secretary of Defense Lloyd J. Austin, @SecDef, Twitter, September 1, 2021, https://twitter.com/SecDef/status/1433119871940837378.

6. MRCTV, @MRCTV, Twitter, September 28, 2021, https://twitter.com/mrctv/status/1442888114234552324.

7. Andrew Clevenger, "Hundreds of Americans Remain in Afghanistan, Pentagon Official Says," Roll Call, October 26, 2021, https://rollcall.com/2021/10/26/hundreds -of-americans-remain-in-afghanistan-pentagon-official-says/.

8. Nicole Gaouette, Jennifer Hansler, and Alex Marquardt, "Blinken Says All U.S. Citizens in Afghanistan Who Want to Leave 'Have an Opportunity to Do So,'" CNN, November 12, 2021, https://www.cnn.com/2021/11/12/politics/us-qatar -afghanistan/index.html.

9. James Gordon Meek, Aicha El Hammar Castano, and Conor Finnegan, "American Hostage Philip Walton Rescued in Dramatic Military Operation: Officials," ABCNews, October 31, 2020, https://abcnews.go.com/International/american -hostage-philip-walton-rescued-dramatic-military-operation/story?id=73940195.

10. Ibid.

11. Senate Foreign Relations Committee, "Risch Publishes Report on Biden Administration's Strategic Failures."

12. Ibid.

13. Association of Wartime Allies, "The Left Behind Afghans," August 15, 2022, https:// www.wartimeallies.co/_files/ugd/5887eb_55744a02be434163a5f60c09a89648b9.pdf.

14. Dion Nissenbaum, "Afghan Interpreter Who Rescued Biden in 2008 Left Behind After U.S. Exit," Wall Street Journal, August 31, 2021, https://www.wsj.com/articles /afghan-interpreter-who-helped-rescue-biden-in-2008-left-behind-after-u-s-exit -11630429285.

15. Ibid.

16. Greg Woodfield, "EXCLUSIVE: 'If He Recognized Me I'd Be Dead.' Afghan Interpreter Who Saved Joe Biden in 2008 Tells How Heavily Armed Taliban Extremist Looked Him in the Eye as He Made His Terrifying Escape to the United States," Daily Mail, February 10, 2022, https://www.dailymail.co.uk/news/article-10498515/Afghan -interpreter-saved-Joe-Biden-says-feels-safe-excited-arriving-US.html.

17. "National Guard Association Conference," C-SPAN, September 22, 2008, https:// www.c-span.org/video/?281272-1/national-guard-association-conference.

18. Nissenbaum, "Afghan Interpreter Who Rescued Biden in 2008 Left Behind."

19. Mariana Alfaro, "Afghan Interpreter Who Helped Rescue Biden in 2008 Is Evacuated from Afghanistan," Stars and Stripes, October 13, 2021, https://www .stripes.com/theaters/middle_east/2021-10-12/aman-khalili-afghan-interpreter -biden-evacuated-3224554.html.

20. "Interpreter Who Helped Rescue Biden in 2008 Leaves Afghanistan," BBC, October 14, 2021, https://www.bbc.com/news/world-us-canada-58879441.

21. "Grand Jury Returns Indictments Charging 2 Afghan Evacuees with Crimes While at Fort McCoy & Wisconsin Residents with Gun & Drug Crimes," U.S. Department of Justice, September 22, 2021, https://www.justice.gov/usao-wdwi/pr/grand-jury -returns-indictments-charging-afghan-evacuees-crimes-while-fort-mccoy.

22. Emily Hamer, "Afghan Man Sexually Assaulted Boys Ages 12, 14, in Fort McCoy Bathroom, Affidavit Alleges," Stars and Stripes, September 24, 2021, https://www .stripes.com/theaters/us/2021-09-23/bahrullah-noori-afghan-evacuee-fort-mccoy -sexual-abuse-charges-2999542.html.

23. U.S. Department of Justice, "Grand Jury Returns Indictments Charging 2 Afghan Evacuees with Crimes While at Fort McCoy & Wisconsin Residents with Gun & Drug Crimes," September 22, 2021, https://www.justice.gov/usao-wdwi/pr/grand-jury-returns-indictments-charging-afghan-evacuees-crimes-while-fort-mccoy.

24. Gabrielle Fonrouge, "Afghan Evacuee Convicted of Molesting Child at Marine Refugee Camp," *New York Post*, January 25, 2022, https://nypost.com/2022/01/25/afghan-evacuee-convicted-of-molesting-child-at-Marine-refugee-camp/.

25. *United States v. Adil*, 1:21-cr-277, E.D. Va., June 15, 2022, https://casetext.com/case/united-states-v-adil-1.

26. Inspector General, U.S. Department of Defense, "Management Advisory: DoD Support for the Relocation of Afghan Evacuees at Camp Atterbury, Indiana," March 9, 2022, https://media.defense.gov/2022/Mar/11/2002954675/-1/-1/1/DODIG-2022-070.PDF, 19.

27. Ibid., 20.

28. Ibid., 16, n.19.

29. Inspector General, U.S. Department of Defense, "Management Advisory: DoD Support for the Relocation of Afghan Evacuees at Fort Pickett, Virginia," January 20, 2022, https://media.defense.gov/2022/Jan/24/2002926228/-1/-1/1/DODIG-2022-055.PDF,16.

30. Ibid.

31. Renee Hickman, "'One individual doesn't necessarily reflect on the wider group': Resettlement group responds to arrest of Afghan refugee," *Wausaw Daily Herald*, February 7, 2022, https://www.wausaudailyherald.com/story/news/2022/02/07/one-individual-doesnt-necessarily-reflect-wider-group-resettlement-group-responds-sexual-assault-arr/6693516001/.

32. Susan Smallheer, "Refugee Charged with Attempted Sexual Assault," *Brattleboro Reformer*, August 15, 2022, https://www.reformer.com/local-news/refugee-charged-with-attempted-sexual-assault/article_1fd85f1c-1a6f-11ed-8dde-7f06db41b69c.html.

33. Abbey Gate Report, Enc. 4, 53.

34. Ibid.

35. Inspector General, U.S. Department of Defense, "Evaluation of the Screening of Displaced Persons from Afghanistan," February 15, 2022, https://media.defense.gov/2022/Feb/17/2002940841/-1/-1/1/DODIG-222-065.PDF10.

36. Office of Inspector General, Department of Homeland Security, "DHS Encountered Obstacles to Screen, Vet, and Inspect All Evacuees During the Recent Afghanistan Crisis (Redacted)," September 6, 2022, https://www.oig.dhs.gov/sites/default/files/assets/2022-09/OIG-22-64-Sep22-Redacted.pdf.

37. Ibid., 14.

38. Ibid.

39. Ibid.

40. Office of Inspector General, Department of Homeland Security, "DHS Did Not Adequately or Efficiently Deploy Its Employees to U.S. Military Installation in

Support of Operation Allies Welcome," July 27, 2022, https://www.oig.dhs.gov/sites
/default/files/assets/2022-07/OIG-22-54-Jul22.pdf.

41. Office of Inspector General, Department of Homeland Security, "DHS Encountered
Obstacles to Screen, Vet, and Inspect All Evacuees During the Recent Afghanistan
Crisis (Redacted)," September 6, 2022, https://www.oig.dhs.gov/sites/default/files
/assets/2022-09/OIG-22-64-Sep22-Redacted.pdf, 11.

42. Office of Inspector General, Department of Defense, *Operation Enduring Sentinel,
Operation Freedom's Sentinel: Lead Inspector General Report to the United States
Congress, April 1, 2022–June 30, 2022,* August 16, 2022, https://www.oversight.gov
/sites/default/files/oig-reports/DoD/LEAD-INSPECTOR-GENERAL-OPERATION
-FREEDOM%E2%80%99S-SENTINEL-AND-OPERATION-ENDURING
-SENTINEL-APRIL-1-2022-%E2%80%93.PDF.

43. U.S. Department of Homeland Security, "DHS and DOS Announce Exemptions
Allowing Eligible Afghans to Qualify for Protection and Immigration Benefits,"
June 14, 2022, https://www.dhs.gov/news/2022/06/14/dhs-and-dos-announce
-exemptions-allowing-eligible-afghans-qualify-protection-and.

44. Michael Crowley, "Biden Officials Place Hope in Taliban's Desire for Legitimacy and
Money," *New York Times,* April 23, 2021, https://www.nytimes.com/2021/04/23/us
/politics/biden-afghanistan-taliban.html.

45. Richard Engel, "Desperate for Cash, Afghan Families Are Selling Young Daughters
into Marriage," NBC News, November 21, 2021, https://www.nbcnews.com/news
/world/afghan-families-sell-daughters-marriage-economy-collapses-rcna5829.

46. Ibid.

47. "Parents Selling Children Shows Desperation in Afghanistan," Associated Press,
December 31, 2021, https://www.npr.org/2021/12/31/1069428211/parents-selling
-children-shows-desperation-in-afghanistan.

48. "Taliban Says Strict Punishment and Execution Will Return," Associated Press,
September 24, 2021, https://www.npr.org/2021/09/24/1040339286/taliban-official
-says-strict-punishment-and-executions-will-return.

49. U.S. Department of State, "2021 Report on International Religious Freedom:
Afghanistan," June 2, 2022, https://www.state.gov/reports/2021-report-on
-international-religious-freedom/afghanistan/.

50. Ibid.

51. Sahar Fetrat and Heather Barr, "#JusticeForElaha Takes on Taliban Violence Against
Women," Human Rights Watch, September 1, 2022, https://www.hrw.org/news/2022
/09/01/justiceforelaha-takes-taliban-violence-against-women.

52. Patrice Taddonio, "18 Essential Documentaries on Afghanistan and the Taliban,"
PBS Frontline, August 15, 2022, https://www.pbs.org/wgbh/frontline/article/18
-documentaries-afghanistan-taliban-streaming/.

53. "The Taliban Orders Women to Wear Head-to-Toe Clothing in Public," National
Public Radio, May 7, 2022, https://www.npr.org/2022/05/07/1097382550/taliban
-women-burqa-decree.

54. "Afghanistan: Taliban Leaders Order Sharia Law for All Punishments," BBC,
November 14, 2022, https://www.bbc.com/news/world-asia-63624400.

55. Esmatullah Kohsar, "Afghanistan's Taliban Ban All Education for Girls," *Wall Street Journal*, December 21, 2022, https://www.wsj.com/articles/afghanistans-taliban-ban -all-education-for-girls-11671642870.

56. Ned Price, "Department Press Briefing—August 18, 2021," U.S. Department of State, August 18, 2021, https://www.state.gov/briefings/department-press-briefing-august -18-2021/.

57. Special Inspector General for Afghan Reconstruction (SIGAR), *Quarterly Report to the United States Congress*, October 2022, https://www.sigar.mil/pdf /quarterlyreports/2022-10-30qr.pdf, i.

58. Ibid.

59. Aamer Madhani, "Biden Frees Frozen Afghan Billions for Relief, 9/11 Victims," Associated Press, February 11, 2022, https://apnews.com/article/joe-biden-business -united-states-terrorism-b2743737c3286dbba95a7663615e37be.

60. Office of Inspector General, Department of Defense, *Operation Enduring Sentinel, Operation Freedom's Sentinel*.

61. Mike Brest, "Intelligence Community Chiefs Give Update on Afghan Terrorist Threat," *Washington Examiner*, May 11, 2022, https://www.washingtonexaminer .com/policy/defense-national-security/intelligence-community-chiefs-give-update -on-afghan-terrorist-threat.

62. "Background Press Call by a Senior Administration Official on a U.S. Counterterrorism Operation," White House, August 1, 2022, https://www .whitehouse.gov/briefing-room/press-briefings/2022/08/01/background-press-call -by-a-senior-administration-official-on-a-u-s-counterterrorism-operation/.

63. CENTCOM, "Senate Armed Services Committee Hearing," March 16, 2023, https:// www.centcom.mil/MEDIA/Transcripts/Article/3332606/senate-armed-services -committee-hearing-on-posture-of-uscentcom-and-usafricom-i/.

64. Kim Klippenstein and Lee Fang, "Truth Cops: Leaked Documents Outline DHS's Plans to Police Disinformation" The Intercept_, October 31, 2022, https:// theintercept.com/2022/10/31/social-media-disinformation-dhs/.

65. Jeff Schogol, "The 82nd Airborne Awarded Soldiers for the Kabul Evacuation, ThenTook the Medals Back for Now," Task and Purpose, August 9, 2022, https:// taskandpurpose.com/news/Army-awards-afghanistan-evacuation-82nd-airborne/.

66. Bailee Hill, "Kilmeade presses Biden spokesman on Pentagon's new findings on Afghanistan exit: 'Disaster'," FoxNews.Com, November 30, 2022, https://www .foxnews.com/media/kilmeade-presses-biden-spokesman-pentagon-findings -afghanistan-exit-disaster.

67. Mike Brest, "Afghanistan inspector general unsure if American taxpayers are 'funding the Taliban,'" *Washington Examiner*, April 19, 2023, https://www .washingtonexaminer.com/policy/defense-national-security/afghan-inspector -general-unsure-taliban-funds.

CHAPTER 13: FROM KABUL TO KYIV

1. Antony Blinken, @SecBlinken, Twitter, April 12, 2021, https://twitter.com /SecBlinken/status/1381660008463667200.

2. Blinken, @SecBlinken, Twitter, April 12, 2021.

3. Antony Blinken, "Secretary Antony J. Blinken at a Press Availability," Department of State, December 22, 2022, https://www.state.gov/secretary-antony-j-blinken-at -a-press-availability-27/.

4. Kyle Orton, "Russia's View of the Endgame in Afghanistan," Kyle Orton's Blog, November 1, 2022, https://kyleorton.co.uk/2021/02/23/russias-view-of-the-endgame -in-afghanistan/.

5. Andrew Osborn, "Russia Says Kabul Seems Safer Under Taliban than It Was Under Ghani," Reuters, August 16, 2021, https://www.reuters.com/world/russia-says-kabul -seems-safer-under-taliban-than-it-was-under-ghani-2021-08-16/.

6. Adrienne Cuffley, "Afghanistan Under the Taliban: Findings on the Current Situation," Stimson Center, November 21, 2022, https://www.stimson.org/2022 /afghanistan-under-the-taliban-findings-on-the-current-situation/.

7. "US, Britain strengthening Daesh terrorists' foothold, destructive potential in Afghanistan: Russian diplomat," PressTV, November 4, 2022, https://www.presstv.ir /Detail/2022/11/04/692139/US,-Britain-strengthening-Daesh-terrorists%E2%80%99 -foothold,-destructive-potential-in-Afghanistan--Russian-diplomat.

8. Aaron Y. Zelin, "New Statement from the Islamic Emirate of Afghanistan: 'Ministry of the Economy: Explanations Regarding Contracts with Russia,'" September 28, 2022, https://jihadology.net/2022/09/28/new-statement-from-the-islamic-emirate -of-afghanistan-ministry-of-the-economy-explanations-regarding-contracts-with -russia/.

9. Gideon Rachman, "After Afghanistan, China and Russia Will Test Biden," *Financial Times*, April 19, 2022, https://www.ft.com/content/0116d3ab-9c97-45d8-97ef -8ba86254c4dc.

10. Guy Faulconbridge and Andrew Osborn, "Afghanistan's Fate Means West Now Perceived as Weak, UK Minister Says," Reuters, August 19, 2021, https://www .reuters.com/world/uk/afghanistans-fate-means-west-is-now-perceived-weak-british -minister-says-2021-08-19/.

11. NBC News, "Aspen Security Forum Discussion with Lester Holt and Gen. Mark Milley," YouTube, November 3, 2021, https://www.youtube.com/watch?v= vSBN5xBC1L4.

12. Guy Chazan, "Afghanistan Shows Folly of Western Interference, Says Putin," *Financial Times*, August 20, 2021, https://www.ft.com/content/8299983e-0bcb-42fa -a192-1b564e1ac5bd.

13. *Izvestia*, August 19, 2021, https://iz.ru/1209165/aleksei-zabrodin/pokhozhaia -situatciia-ozhidaet-i-storonnikov-amerikanskogo-vybora-na-ukraine.

14. "Ukraine in the future is waiting for the Afghan scenario," Russian Television and Radio Broadcasting Company, August 19, 2021, https://web.archive.org/web /20210922213100/https:/vesti-k.ru/news/2021/08/19/ukrainu-v-budushem-zhdyot -afganskij-scenarij/.

15. "Thousands of Afghans Attempt to Flee Taliban Rule" (transcript), *Fareed Zakaria GPS*, CNN, August 22, 2021, https://transcripts.cnn.com/show/fzgps/date/2021-08 -22/segment/01.

16. Victoria Nikiforova, "US strikes at Russia's best people," *RIA Novosti*, August 17, 2021, https://ria.ru/20210817/amerika-1745956827.html.

17. Leonid Bershidsky, "The Agony of Afghans Left Behind," Bloomberg, August 19, 2021, https://www.bloomberg.com/opinion/articles/2021-08-19/the-agony-of -afghans-left-behind.

18. Maxim Minin, "The Americans fly away, the Afghans cling to the planes. How the US is fleeing Kabul and what are the implications for Ukraine," Strana.ua, August 18, 2021, https://strana.news/news/348850-kak-ssha-ubehajut-iz-afhanistana-i-chto -budet-dalshe.html.

19. "In Ukraine, they changed their minds about angering Russia after the flight of the United States from Afghanistan," *RIA Novosti*, August 16, 2021, https://ria.ru /20210816/begstvo-1745985738.html.

20. "Ukraine warned of the danger of participating in anti-Russian provocations after the US withdrawal from Afghanistan," *360 TV*, August 16, 2021, https://360tv.ru /news/mir/ukrainu-predupredili/.

21. "Ukrainian journalist advised Kyiv not to anger Russia," *Moskovskij Komsomolets*, August 16, 2021, https://www.mk.ru/politics/2021/08/16/ukrainskiy-zhurnalist -posovetoval-kievu-ne-zlit-rossiyu.html.

22. Nikolas K. Gvosdev, "Afghanistan Is a Wake-up Call for 'Major Non-NATO Allies,'" *National Interest*, August 14, 2021, https://nationalinterest.org/feature/afghanistan -wake-call-%E2%80%98major-non-nato-allies%E2%80%99-191864.

23. "The Expert Called the Events in Afghanistan a Wake-up Call for US Partners Outside NATO," TASS, August 16, 2021, https://tass.ru/mezhdunarodnaya -panorama/12147625.

24. Hope Kvashenko, "The United States considers the situation in Afghanistan a 'black mark' for Ukraine," Channel 5, August 16, 2021, https://www.5-tv.ru/news/354775 /vssa-scitaut-situaciu-vafganistane-cernoj-metkoj-dla-ukrainy/.

25. Roman Olearchyk, "Ukraine Feels the Chill of Biden's Foreign Policy," *Financial Times*, August 29, 2021, https://www.ft.com/content/3a7f3282-2db5-47dc-84d5 -1c50f5295d8d.

26. Andrew E. Kramer, "Ukraine's Leader, Meeting Biden, Seeks Security Assurances After Afghan Pullout," *New York Times*, August 31, 2021, https://www.nytimes.com /2021/08/31/world/europe/ukraine-biden-zelensky.html.

27. Alyona Getmanchuk, "Afghanistan Collapse Sparks Wave of Alarm in Ukraine," Atlantic Council, August 16, 2021, https://www.atlanticcouncil.org/blogs /ukrainealert/afghanistan-collapse-sparks-wave-of-alarm-in-ukraine/.

28. Interview with Ukraine's President Volodymyr Zelensky" (transcript), *Fareed Zakaria GPS*, CNN, September 12, 2021, https://transcripts.cnn.com/show/fzgps /date/2021-09-12/segment/01.

29. Oliver Carroll, "Kyiv's Foreign Minister Says Ukraine Needs to Militarise to Survive," *Independent*, September 13, 2021, https://www.independent.co.uk/news /world/europe/ukraine-russia-war-west-b1919145.html.

30. Mykhailo Minakov, "The Afghanistan Syndrome and U.S.-Ukraine Relations," Wilson Center, September 27, 2021, https://www.wilsoncenter.org/blog-post /afghanistan-syndrome-and-us-ukraine-relations.

31. Joe Gould, "Ukraine Defense Minister: Don't Compare Us to Afghanistan," Defense News, August 18, 2022, https://www.defensenews.com/pentagon/2021/10/19 /ukraine-defense-minister-dont-compare-us-to-afghanistan/.

32. Victor Pinchuk Foundation, "The United States' Foreign Policy and What It Means for Ukraine," YouTube, September 11, 2021, https://www.youtube.com/watch?v= BMNfUW_G3-w.

33. Lloyd J. Austin III, "Secretary of Defense Lloyd J. Austin III's Remarks at Ukraine Ministry of Defense Post-Bilat Joint Press Event," U.S. Department of Defense, October 19, 2021, https://www.defense.gov/News/Transcripts/Transcript/Article /2815310/secretary-of-defense-lloyd-j-austin-iiis-remarks-at-ukraine-ministry-of -defense/.

34. Jerry Dunleavy, "GOP Says Biden Admin Actions on Russian Nord Stream 2 Pipeline Don't Go Far Enough," *Washington Examiner*, February 19, 2021, https:// www.washingtonexaminer.com/news/gop-says-biden-admin-actions-on-russian -nord-stream-2-pipeline-dont-go-far-enough.

35. Jerry Dunleavy, "GOP bill would reimpose sanctions on Kremlin-backed Nord Stream 2 after Biden waiver," *Washington Examiner*, May 20, 2021, https://www .washingtonexaminer.com/news/gop-bill-reimpose-sanctions-nord-stream-2-biden -waiver.

36. Joel Gehrke, "Ukraine and Poland Protest Biden's Nord Stream 2 Deal with Germany," *Washington Examiner*, July 21, 2021, https://www.washingtonexaminer .com/policy/defense/national-security/ukraine-poland-protest-biden-nord-stream.

37. Jerry Dunleavy, "Lawmakers Blast Biden Administration Sanctions Waiver for Kremlin-Backed Russian Pipeline to Germany," *Washington Examiner*, May 19, 2021, https://www.washingtonexaminer.com/news/lawmakers-blast-biden -administration-sanctions-waiver-for-kremlin-backed-russian-pipeline-to-germany.

38. Jerry Dunleavy, "GOP Bill Would Reimpose Sanctions on Kremlin-Backed Nord Stream 2 After Biden Waiver," *Washington Examiner*, May 20, 2021, https://www .washingtonexaminer.com/news/gop-bill-reimpose-sanctions-nord-stream-2-biden -waiver.

39. Joel Gehrke, "Ukraine and Poland Protest Biden's Nord Stream 2 Deal with Germany," *Washington Examiner*, July 21, 2021, https://www.washingtonexaminer .com/policy/defense/national-security/ukraine-poland-protest-biden-nord-stream.

40. "Sen. Cruz on Nord Stream 2 Vote: Today the Senate Rebuked Joe Biden's Surrender to Vladimir Putin on Nord Stream 2," Ted Cruz, U.S. Senator for Texas, January 13, 2022, https://www.cruz.senate.gov/newsroom/press-releases/sen-cruz-on-nord -stream-2-vote-today-the-senate-rebuked-joe-bidens-surrender-to-vladimir-putin -on-nord-stream-2.

41. Marco Buschmann, "Welcoming Address at the Meeting of the G7 Justice Ministers," Bundesministerium Der Justiz, November 29, 2022, https://www.bmj.de /SharedDocs/Reden/DE/2022/1129_G7_Welcoming_address.html;jsessionid=A336 B72F85B7ABD5005FF7E8BFABB201.1_cid334.

42. Jerry Dunleavy, "Biden Administration Says Intelligence Community Has 'Low to Moderate Confidence' in Russian Bounties Intelligence," *Washington Examiner*, April 15, 2021, https://www.washingtonexaminer.com/news/biden-intelligence -community-low-moderate-confidence-russian-bounties-intelligence.

43. Haley Victory Smith, "US Spy Agencies Believe Russian Operatives Secretly Offered Afghan Militants Bounties to Kill American Troops," *Washington Examiner*, June 26, 2020, https://www.washingtonexaminer.com/news/us-spy-agencies-believe -russian-operatives-secretly-offered-afghan-militants-bounties-to-kill-american -troops.

44. Ibid.

45. "Interview with Rep. Michael McCaul (R-TX)" (transcript), *State of the Union*, CNN, January 16, 2022, https://transcripts.cnn.com/show/sotu/date/2022-01-16 /segment/01.

46. Fiona Hill, "Putin Has the U.S. Right Where He Wants It," *New York Times*, January 24, 2022, https://www.nytimes.com/2022/01/24/opinion/russia-ukraine-putin-biden .html.

47. CEPA, "Kurt Volker: US Afghanistan Withdrawal Encourages Putin in Ukraine and Xi in Taiwan," YouTube, January 21, 2022, https://m.youtube.com/watch?v= DcLwaIzgdWA.

48. Michael Vickers, "Biden Must Show That the U.S. Stands Ready to Support Ukraine, Militarily if Necessary," *Washington Post*, January 20, 2022, https://www .washingtonpost.com/opinions/2022/01/20/biden-must-show-that-us-stands-ready -support-ukraine-militarily-if-necessary/.

49. Adam Shaw, "Trump Says Russia 'Emboldened' on Ukraine After 'Incompetent' US Afghanistan Withdrawal," Fox News, February 12, 2022, https://www.foxnews .com/politics/trump-russia-emboldened-ukraine-incompetent-us-afghanistan -withdrawal.

50. David Catanese, "McConnell: Abrupt Afghanistan withdrawal led to Russian march on Ukraine," McClatchy, February 16, 2022, https://www.stripes.com /theaters/us/2022-02-16/mitch-mcconnell-afghanistan-pullout-led-russian-march -ukraine-5043637.html.

51. "'Your World' on Global Impact of Russia-Ukraine Conflict," Fox News, February 22, 2022, https://www.foxnews.com/transcript/your-world-global-impact-of-russia -ukraine-conflict.

52. "'Hannity' on Biden and Putin, Canada Truckers," Fox News, February 22, 2022, https://www.foxnews.com/transcript/hannity-biden-putin-canada-truckers.

53. "Mike Pompeo: Biden Could Have Used 'Strategic Deterrence' to Stop Putin," *America's Newsroom*, Fox News, February 22, 2022, https://www.foxnews.com/video /6298494153001.

54. *Mornings with Maria Bartiromo*, Fox Business Channel, February 24, 2022, https:// archive.org/details/FBC_20220224_110000_Mornings_With_Maria_Bartiromo.

55. Andrei V. Kozyrev, @andreivkozyrev, "To understand why the invasion was rational for Putin, we have to step into his shoes. Three beliefs came together at the same time in his calculus: 1. Ukraine's condition as a country 2. Russian military's

condition 3. The West's geopolitical condition," Twitter, March 6, 2021, https://twitter.com/andreivkozyrev/status/1500610891842146306.

56. Mashup par HugoDécrypte, "Interview: François Hollande Analyzes Putin's Strategy," YouTube, March 3, 2022, https://www.youtube.com/watch?v=oI0qLLm3-T4.

57. Carl Bildt, "Did the Afghan Failure Lead to the Ukraine War?," Project Syndicate, August 18, 2022, https://www.project-syndicate.org/commentary/afghanistan-us-failure-set-stage-for-russia-invasion-ukraine-by-carl-bildt-2022-08.

58. Jerry Dunleavy, "Afghanistan debacle played role in Putin's Ukraine decision, general says," *Washington Examiner*, March 31, 2022, https://www.washingtonexaminer.com/policy/defense-national-security/afghanistan-debacle-played-role-in-putins-ukraine-decision-general-says.

59. Jerry Dunleavy, "Milley concedes Afghanistan withdrawal may have influenced Putin's Ukraine move," *Washington Examiner*, April 9, 2022, https://www.washingtonexaminer.com/news/milley-concedes-afghanistan-withdrawal-may-have-influenced-putins-ukraine-move.

60. Shane Harris et al., "Road to War: U.S. Struggled to Convince Allies, and Zelensky, of Risk of Invasion," *Washington Post*, August 16, 2022, https://www.washingtonpost.com/national-security/interactive/2022/ukraine-road-to-war/.

61. Jerry Dunleavy, "Botched Assessment of Ukraine's Will to Fight Mirrors Afghan Intel Failures," *Washington Examiner*, March 15, 2022, https://www.washingtonexaminer.com/policy/foreign/botched-assessment-of-ukraines-will-to-fight-echoes-afghan-intel-failures.

62. Ibid.

63. Joe Biden, White House, January 19, 2022, https://www.whitehouse.gov/briefing-room/speeches-remarks/2022/01/19/remarks-by-president-biden-in-press-conference-6/.

64. Jacqui Heinrich and Adam Sabes, "Gen. Milley Says Kyiv Could Fall Within 72 Hours if Russia Decides to Invade Ukraine: Sources," Fox News, February 5, 2022, https://www.foxnews.com/us/gen-milley-says-kyiv-could-fall-within-72-hours-if-russia-decides-to-invade-ukraine-sources.

65. Julian E. Barnes, "Why the U.S. Was Wrong About Ukraine and the Afghan War," *New York Times*, March 24, 2022, https://www.nytimes.com/2022/03/24/us/politics/intelligence-agencies-ukraine-afghanistan.html.

66. Michael Schwirtz et al., "Putin's War," *New York Times*, December 16, 2022, https://www.nytimes.com/interactive/2022/12/16/world/europe/russia-putin-war-failures-ukraine.html.

67. Jerry Dunleavy, "Afghanistan Debacle Played Role in Putin's Ukraine Decision, General Says," *Washington Examiner*, March 31, 2022, https://www.washingtonexaminer.com/policy/defense-national-security/afghanistan-debacle-played-role-in-putins-ukraine-decision-general-says.

68. Kenneth F. McKenzie, Jr., "CENTCOM Commander Gen. Frank McKenzie Holds a Press Briefing, March 18, 2022," U.S. Department of Defense, March 18, 2022, https://www.defense.gov/News/Transcripts/Transcript/Article/2971495/centcom-commander-gen-frank-mckenzie-holds-a-press-briefing-march-18-2022/.

69. Jerry Dunleavy, "Afghanistan Debacle Played Role in Putin's Ukraine Decision, General Says," *Washington Examiner*, March 31, 2022, https://www .washingtonexaminer.com/policy/defense-national-security/afghanistan-debacle -played-role-in-putins-ukraine-decision-general-says.

70. "Intelligence Directors Testify on National Security Threats and Ukraine," C-SPAN, March 10, 2022, https://www.c-span.org/video/?518379-1/intelligence-directors -testify-national-security-threats-ukraine&live=&vod=.

71. Dunleavy, "Botched Assessment of Ukraine's Will to Fight Mirrors Afghan Intel Failures."

72. Jerry Dunleavy, "Biden Admin Takes Premature Victory Lap on Russian Invasion Intelligence," *Washington Examiner*, April 17, 2022, https://www .washingtonexaminer.com/news/biden-admin-takes-premature-victory-lap-on -russian-invasion-intelligence.

73. Jerry Dunleavy, "Biden Criticizes Putin for Underestimating Ukraine— but US Did the Same," *Washington Examiner*, March 26, 2022, https://www .washingtonexaminer.com/policy/defense-national-security/biden-criticizes-putin -for-underestimating-ukraine-but-u-s-did-the-same.

74. "Defense Department Fiscal Year 2023 Budget Request," C-SPAN, April 5, 2022, https://www.c-span.org/video/?519185-1/defense-department-fiscal-year-2023 -budget-request.

75. "Top State Department Intelligence Official Brett Holmgren," *Intelligence Matters*, CBS News Radio, April 13, 2022, https://podcasts.apple.com/us/podcast/top-state -department-intelligence-official-brett-holmgren/id1286906615?i=1000557444594.

76. Barnes, "Why the U.S. Was Wrong About Ukraine and the Afghan War."

77. Sarah Westwood, "Five Times the White House Said Sanctions Could Deter Putin," *Washington Examiner*, February 26, 2022, https://www.washingtonexaminer.com /politics/five-times-the-white-house-said-sanctions-could-deter-putin.

78. "Interview with Rep. Michael McCaul (R-TX)" (transcript), *State of the Union*, CNN, January 16, 2022, https://transcripts.cnn.com/show/sotu/date/2022-01-16 /segment/01.

79. Jerry Dunleavy, "Biden Says Russia Sanctions Weren't Meant to Deter Putin—but His Admin Said They Were," *Washington Examiner*, March 24, 2022, https://www .washingtonexaminer.com/news/biden-says-russia-sanctions-werent-meant-to-deter -putin-but-his-admin-said-they-were.

80. https://www.whitehouse.gov/briefing-room/speeches-remarks/2022/02/24/remarks -by-president-biden-on-russias-unprovoked-and-unjustified-attack-on-ukraine/.

81. https://www.whitehouse.gov/briefing-room/press-briefings/2022/02/24/press -briefing-by-press-secretary-jen-psaki-and-deputy-national-security-advisor-for -international-economics-and-deputy-nec-director-daleep-singh-february-24-2022/.

82. Jerry Dunleavy, "Biden says Russia sanctions weren't meant to deter Putin — but his admin said they were,"*Washington Examiner*, March 24, 2022, https://www .washingtonexaminer.com/news/biden-says-russia-sanctions-werent-meant-to-deter -putin-but-his-admin-said-they-were.

83. Bernard Condon, "Russia recruiting U.S.-trained Afghan commandos, vets say," *Associated Press*, October 31, 2022, https://apnews.com/article/afghanistan-russia-ukraine-iran-europe-taliban-30e2b1ffc7c5ecf2847b654f862723b8.

84. Thomas Joscelyn, "On the 'Merchant of Death,'" FDD's Long War Journal, April 6, 2012, https://www.longwarjournal.org/archives/2012/04/a_brief_note_on_viktor_bout.php.

85. Nicholas Schmidle, "Disarming Viktor Bout," *New Yorker*, March 5, 2012, https://www.newyorker.com/magazine/2012/03/05/disarming-viktor-bout.

86. Donald.Trump, Truth Social, December 8, 2022, https://truthsocial.com/@realDonaldTrump/109479448656764721.

87. "Trump turned down Viktor Bout-for-Paul Whelan prisoner swap, John Bolton says," *New York Post*, December 8, 2022, https://nypost.com/2022/12/08/trump-turned-down-viktor-bout-for-paul-whelan-prisoner-swap-john-bolton/.

88. Erin Banco, Alexander Ward, and Matt Berg, "'The Lord of War Is Back in the Game,'" Politico, December 9, 2022, https://www.politico.com/newsletters/national-security-daily/2022/12/09/the-lord-of-war-is-back-in-the-game-00073254.

89. Darya Tarasova and Sharon Braithwaite, "Freed Russian Arms Dealer Viktor Bout Says He 'Wholeheartedly' Supports Ukraine War and Would Volunteer if He Could," CNN, December 13, 2022, https://www.cnn.com/2022/12/10/europe/viktor-bout-supports-ukraine-war-intl/index.html.

90. Kathleen Magramo et al., "December 19, 2022 Russia-Ukraine News," CNN, December 19, 2022, https://www.cnn.com/europe/live-news/russia-ukraine-war-news-12-19-22/h_1cabf2db32a130e8fd85b7a93f1f90c5.

91. Tim Haines, "Sullivan: Administration Considered the National Security Implications of Releasing Viktor Bout," *RealClearPolitics*, December 12, 2022, https://www.realclearpolitics.com/video/2022/12/12/sullivan_administration_considered_the_national_security_implications_of_releasing_viktor_bout.amp.html.

92. "Sanctions List Search," Office of Foreign Assets Control, https://sanctionssearch.ofac.treas.gov/Details.aspx?id=8279.

93. Jerry Dunleavy, "'Integrated Deterrence': GOP Charges Pentagon's New Buzzy Strategy Is Broken," *Washington Examiner*, April 3, 2022, https://www.washingtonexaminer.com/news/integrated-deterrence-gop-charges-pentagons-new-buzzy-strategy-is-broken.

94. Greg Jaffe and Dan Lamothe, "Russia's Failures in Ukraine Imbue Pentagon with Newfound Confidence," *Washington Post*, March 26, 2022, https://www.washingtonpost.com/national-security/2022/03/26/russia-ukraine-pentagon-american-power/.

95. "Gallagher: Officials Claiming Integrated Deterrence Succeeded in Ukraine Should Go to Kyiv or Mariupol," Congressman Mike Gallagher, March 28, 2022, https://gallagher.house.gov/media/press-releases/gallagher-officials-claiming-integrated-deterrence-succeeded-ukraine-should-go.

96. Jerry Dunleavy, "'Integrated Deterrence': GOP Charges Pentagon's New Buzzy Strategy Is Broken," *Washington Examiner*, April 3, 2022, https://www

.washingtonexaminer.com/news/integrated-deterrence-gop-charges-pentagons-new
-buzzy-strategy-is-broken.

97. "U.S. European Commander and Assistant Defense Secretary Testify on War in Ukraine," C-SPAN, https://www.c-span.org/video/?519012-1%2Fus-european -commander-assistant-defense-secretary-testify-war-ukraine.

98. Mike Gallagher, "Biden's 'Integrated Deterrence' Fails in Ukraine," *Wall Street Journal*, March 29, 2022, https://www.wsj.com/articles/biden-integrated-deterrence -fails-ukraine-russia-invasion-taiwan-xi-china-diplomacy-sanctions-hard-power -defense-spending-budget-negotiations-11648569487.

CHAPTER 14: THE CCP AND THE KABUL MOMENT

1. "Full Transcript of ABC News' George Stephanopoulos' Interview with President Joe Biden," ABC News, August 19, 2021, https://abcnews.go.com/Politics/full-transcript -abc-news-george-stephanopoulos-interview-president/story?id=79535643.

2. "PLA Conducts Drills Around Taiwan in Response to External Provocations," CGTN, August 17, 2021, https://news.cgtn.com/news/2021-08-17/PLA-conducts -drills-around-Taiwan-in-response-to-provocations-12NqJzMFyZq/index.html.

3. "Press Briefing by Press Secretary Jen Psaki and National Security Advisor Jake Sullivan, August 17, 2021," White House, August 17, 2021, https://www.whitehouse .gov/briefing-room/press-briefings/2021/08/17/press-briefing-by-press-secretary-jen -psaki-and-national-security-advisor-jake-sullivan-august-17-2021/.

4. "Taiwan needs to be 'stronger' after U.S. Afghanistan exit, says President Tsai Ing-wen," *Straits Times*, August 18, 2021, https://www.straitstimes.com/asia/east -asia/taiwan-needs-to-be-stronger-after-us-afghanistan-exit-says-president-tsai-ing -wen.

5. "US Stumbles as Afghan Situation Cycled in 20 Years," Global Times, August 15, 2021, https://www.globaltimes.cn/page/202108/1231549.shtml.

6. "Afghanistan Today, Taiwan Tomorrow? US Treachery Scares DPP," Global Times, August 16, 2021, https://www.globaltimes.cn/page/202108/1231635.shtml.

7. "Afghan Abandonment a Lesson for Taiwan's DPP: Global Times Editorial," Global Times, August 16, 2021, https://www.globaltimes.cn/page/202108/1231636.shtml.

8. Liu Caiyu and Liu Xin, "US Reaffirming Commitment Only to 'Fool Taiwan Separatists' in Face of Its Afghan Fiasco," Global Times, August 18, 2021, https:// www.globaltimes.cn/page/202108/1231897.shtml.

9. "Afghan Abandonment a Lesson for Taiwan's DPP: Global Times Editorial."

10. Ibid.

11. Hu Xijin, @HuXijin_GT, Twitter, August 16, 2021, https://twitter.com/HuXijin_GT /status/1427286890835705860?ref_src=twsrc%5Etfw.

12. "Foreign Ministry Spokesperson Hua Chunying's Regular Press Conference on August 20, 2021," Ministry of Foreign Affairs of the People's Republic of China, August 20, 2021, https://www.fmprc.gov.cn/mfa_eng/xwfw_665399/s2510_665401 /2511_665403/202108/t20210820_9170802.html.

13. Jerry Dunleavy, "Biden vowed US would 'respond' to Chinese invasion of Taiwan after Afghanistan debacle," *Washington Examiner*, August 19, 2021, https://news .yahoo.com/biden-vowed-us-respond-chinese-171900595.html.

14. Global Times, @globaltimesnews, Twitter, June 29, 2022, https://twitter.com /globaltimesnews/status/1542025067525132291.

15. "Foreign Ministry Spokesperson Wang Wenbin's Regular Press Conference on August 15, 2022," Ministry of Foreign Affairs of the People's Republic of China, August 15, 2022, https://www.fmprc.gov.cn/mfa_eng/xwfw_665399/s2510_665401 /2511_665403/202208/t20220815_10743533.html.

16. U.S. Department of Defense, *Military and Security Developments Involving the People's Republic of China: A Report to Congress Pursuant to the National Defense Authorization Act for Fiscal Year 2000*, November 29, 2022, https://media.defense .gov/2022/Nov/29/2003122279/-1/-1/1/2022-MILITARY-AND-SECURITY -DEVELOPMENTS-INVOLVING-THE-PEOPLES-REPUBLIC-OF-CHINA.PDF, iv, 14.

17. Fox News, "'Disaster': Kilmeade Throws Down with White House Spokesman," YouTube, November 30, 2022, https://www.youtube.com/watch?v=bOlyzO2K6Z8.

18. David R. Winston, *Narco-Insecurity, Inc.: The Convergence of the Narcotics Underworld and Extremists in Afghanistan and Pakistan and Its Global Proliferation*, Defense Education Enhancement Programme, 2022, https://deepportal.hq.nato.int /eacademy/wp-content/uploads/2022/05/Narco-Insecurity-Inc..pdf, 164.

19. Jerry Dunleavy, "Trump Briefed on Unverified Intelligence About China Offering Bounties in Afghanistan," *Washington Examiner*, December 31, 2020, https://www .washingtonexaminer.com/news/trump-briefed-unverified-intelligence-china -bounties-afghanistan.

20. Ron Synovitz, "Afghanistan: U.S. Worried Iran Sending Chinese Weapons to Taliban," Radio Free Europe/Radio Liberty, February 2, 2012, https://www.rferl.org /a/1078675.html.

21. Paul Danahar, "Taleban 'Getting Chinese Arms,'" BBC, September 3, 2007, https:// news.bbc.co.uk/2/hi/south_asia/6975934.stm.

22. Shishir Gupta, "Apologise, Afghanistan Tells China After Busting Its Espionage Cell in Kabul," *Hindustan Times*, December 25, 2020, https://www.hindustantimes.com /india-news/chinese-espionage-ring-in-afghanistan-busted-10-spies-detained/story -qyPsZY1wUoD2flp9UIYMrK.html.

23. Lynne O'Donnell, "Afghanistan Wanted Chinese Mining Investment. It Got a Chinese Spy Ring Instead," *Foreign Policy*, January 27, 2021, https://foreignpolicy .com/2021/01/27/afghanistan-china-spy-ring-mcc-mining-negotiations-mineral -wealth/.

24. "Wang Yi: Chinese, Afghan and Pakistani Foreign Ministers Reach Eight-Point Consensus," Ministry of Foreign Affairs of the People's Republic of China, June 4, 2021, https://www.fmprc.gov.cn/mfa_eng/gjhdq_665435/2675_665437/2757_663518 /2759_663522/202106/t20210604_9168735.html.

25. "Xi Jinping Speaks on the Phone with Afghan President Ghani," Ministry of Foreign Affairs of the People's Republic of China, July 16, 2021, https://web.archive.org/web

/20211026115934/https://www.fmprc.gov.cn/web/wjdt_674879/gjldrhd_674881
/t1892731.shtml. [in translation]

26. "Wang Yi Meets with Head of Taliban Political Council Baradar in Afghanistan,"
Ministry of Foreign Affairs of the People's Republic of China, July 28, 2021, https://
web.archive.org/web/20210906182313/https://www.mfa.gov.cn/web/wjbzhd
/t1895584.shtml.

27. "Wang Yi Meets with Head of Taliban Political Council Baradar in Afghanistan,"
Ministry of Foreign Affairs of the People's Republic of China, July 28, 2021, https://
web.archive.org/web/20210924062309/https://www.mfa.gov.cn/web/wjbzhd
/t1895584.shtml. [in translation]

28. Mohammed Naeem, Twitter, July 28, 2021, https://twitter.com/IeaOffice/status
/1420422251065774082/.

29. Yaroslav Trofimov, "Afghanistan's Taliban, Now on China's Border, Seek to Reassure
Beijing," *Wall Street Journal*, July 8, 2021, https://www.wsj.com/articles/afghanistans
-taliban-now-on-chinas-border-seek-to-reassure-beijing-11625750130.

30. Amy Chew, "China a 'Welcome Friend' in Afghanistan: Taliban Spokesman," *South
China Morning Post*, August 16, 2021, https://www.scmp.com/week-asia/politics
/article/3140399/china-welcome-friend-reconstruction-afghanistan-taliban.

31. Yu Ning, "Shameless for US to Question Taliban on China's Xinjiang Policy," Global
Times, July 12, 2021, https://www.globaltimes.cn/page/202107/1228479.shtml.

32. "Secretary Antony J. Blinken with Zakka Jacob of CNN-News18." Department of
State, July 28, 2021, https://www.state.gov/secretary-antony-j-blinken-with-zakka
-jacob-of-cnn-news18/.

33. "Department Press Briefing – August 4, 2021 - United States Department..."
Department of State, August 4, 2021, https://www.state.gov/briefings/department
-press-briefing-august-4-2021/.

34. Jerry Dunleavy, "China Likely to Recognize Taliban as Afghan Rulers with Fall of
Kabul," Yahoo! News, August 15, 2021, https://www.yahoo.com/video/china-likely
-recognize-taliban-afghan-180900159.html.

35. Kinling Lo, "Exclusive: China Should Pressure Taliban in Two Ways, Afghanistan's
Envoy Says," *South China Morning Post*, August 16, 2021, https://www.scmp.com
/news/china/diplomacy/article/3144974/china-should-pressure-taliban-2-ways
-afghanistans-envoy-says.

36. Hu Yuwei, "Afghan Party Leader Lambasts US for Leaving a Devastated Land
Tainted with Hatred, Eyes Stronger Role for China," Global Times, August 13, 2021,
https://www.globaltimes.cn/page/202108/1231388.shtml.

37. Sarah Zheng and Kinling Lo, "Risks and Opportunities for China in Taliban's
Return to Power in Afghanistan," *South China Morning Post*, August 16, 2021,
https://www.scmp.com/news/china/diplomacy/article/3145142/china-russia
-embassies-stay-put-afghanistan-us-and-allies-flee.

38. "Wang Yi Speaks with U.S. Secretary of State Antony Blinken on the Phone,"
Embassy of the People's Republic of China in the United States of America, August
30, 2021, http://us.china-embassy.gov.cn/eng/zmgxss/202108/t20210830_9014379
.htm.

39. "Afghanistan: Taliban to Rely on Chinese Funds, Spokesperson Says," Al Jazeera, September 3, 2021, https://www.aljazeera.com/news/2021/9/2/afghanistan-taliban -to-rely-on-chinese-money-spokesperson-says.

40. "Wang Yi Attends the G20 Foreign Ministers Video Conference on Afghanistan," Ministry of Foreign Affairs of the People's Republic of China, September 23, 2021, https://www.fmprc.gov.cn/mfa_eng/gjhdq_665435/2675_665437/2676_663356/2678 _663360/202109/t20210923_9580095.html.

41. "Explanation of Vote by Ambassador Zhang Jun on the Security Council Draft Resolution on Humanitarian Assistance to Afghanistan," Permanent Mission of the People's Republic of China to the UN, December 22, 2021, http://un.china-mission .gov.cn/eng/hyyfy/202112/t20211223_10474521.htm.

42. "Remarks by Ambassador Zhang Jun at Security Council Briefing on UNAMA," Ministry of Foreign Affairs of the People's Republic of China, January 26, 2022, https://www.fmprc.gov.cn/eng/wjb_663304/zwjg_665342/zwbd_665378/202201 /t20220127_10634859.html.

43. "China's XI Strongly Backs Afghanistan at Regional Conference," Associated Press, March 31, 2022, https://apnews.com/article/russia-ukraine-afghanistan-business -china-beijing-5b052ab24bf9d245beac99f83bfa3e9c.

44. "China Diplomacy: Afghanistan Neighbors Committed to Strengthening Regional Cooperation," CGTN, April 2, 2022, https://news.cgtn.com/news/2022-04-02 /VHJhbnNjcmlwdDY0MTI1/index.html.

45. Office of Inspector General, Department of Defense, *Operation Enduring Sentinel, Operation Freedom's Sentinel: Lead Inspector General Report to the United States Congress, April 1, 2022–June 30, 2022*, August 16, 2022, https://www.oversight.gov /sites/default/files/oig-reports/DoD/LEAD-INSPECTOR-GENERAL-OPERATION -FREEDOM%E2%80%99S-SENTINEL-AND-OPERATION-ENDURING -SENTINEL-APRIL-1-2022-%E2%80%93.PDF, 25.

46. "Foreign Ministry Spokesperson Hua Chunying's Regular Press Conference on August 2, 2022," Ministry of Foreign Affairs of the People's Republic of China, August 2, 2022, https://www.fmprc.gov.cn/mfa_eng/xwfw_665399/s2510_665401 /2511_665403/202208/t20220802_10732302.html.

47. Buck Elton and Joshua Fruth, "Evacuation Operations, Great-Power Competition, and External Operations Terror Threats in Post-drawdown Afghanistan: Mapping Out the Path Ahead," *Journal of Indo-Pacific Affairs*, Air University, November 1, 2021, https://www.airuniversity.af.edu/JIPA/Display/Article/2828397/evacuation -operations-great-power-competition-and-external-operations-terror-th/.

48. "U.S. Bagram Legacy Nothing but 'Piles of Scrap,'" Xinhua, July 4, 2021, http://www .xinhuanet.com/english/2021-07/04/c_1310041951.htm.

49. PTI, "China Trying to Take Over Bagram Air Force Base, Use Pakistan Against India: Nikki Haley," *Indian Express*, September 2, 2021, https://indianexpress.com /article/world/china-trying-to-take-over-bagram-air-force-base-use-pakistan -against-india-nikki-haley-7483862/.

50. Brooke Singman, "Trump Slams Biden's 'Surrender' of Afghanistan, Warns China Could Take Bagram," Fox News, November 7, 2021, https://www.foxnews.com

/politics/trump-slams-bidens-surrender-of-afghanistan-warns-china-could-take
-bagram.

51. Donald Trump, "Former President Donald Trump's Keynote Speech," Heritage
Foundation's Annual Leadership Conference, April 21, 2022, https://www.youtube
.com/watch?v=0bEhjIO0Duo.

52. Paul D. Shinkman, "China Weighing Occupation of Former U.S. Air Base at
Bagram: Sources," *US News & World Report*, September 7, 2021, https://www.usnews
.com/news/world-report/articles/2021-09-07/china-weighing-occupation-of-former
-us-air-base-at-bagram-sources.

53. Manoj Gupta, "Exclusive: Chinese Team Conducts Recce at Afghanistan's Bagram
Airbase; India Concerned," News18, September 20, 2021, https://www.news18.com
/news/world/chinese-delegation-conducts-recce-at-afghanistans-bagram-airbase
-india-concerned-4224605.html.

54. "Foreign Ministry Spokesperson Wang Wenbin's Regular Press Conference on
September 7, 2021," Ministry of Foreign Affairs of the People's Republic of China,
September 7, 2021, https://www.fmprc.gov.cn/mfa_eng/xwfw_665399/s2510_665401
/2511_665403/202109/t20210907_9721300.html.

55. Shirshah Rasooli, "Cultural Ministry Says No Chinese Troops at Bagram,"
TOLOnews, October 3, 2021, https://tolonews.com/index.php/afghanistan-174890.

56. Authors' interview with Jerry Dunleavy and Mike Waltz, December 22, 2022.

57. Elton and Fruth, "Evacuation Operations, Great-Power Competition, and External
Operations Terror Threats in Post-drawdown Afghanistan."

58. U.S. Geological Survey, "Preliminary Assessment of Non-Fuel Mineral Resources of
Afghanistan, 2007," https://web.archive.org/web/20090219110933/https://pubs.usgs
.gov/fs/2007/3063/fs2007-3063.pdf.

59. James Risen, "U.S. Identifies Vast Mineral Riches in Afghanistan," *New York Times*,
June 14, 2010, https://www.nytimes.com/2010/06/14/world/asia/14minerals.html.

60. Afghanistan's Ministry of Mines and Petroleum, *Mining Sector Roadmap*, 2019,
https://momp.gov.af/sites/default/files/2020-07/MoMP%20Roadmap-1-merged.pdf.

61. Global Times, @globaltimesnews, "An Afghan government minister holds talks with
a Chinese mining firm about operations of Aynak copper project, as more progress
is expected," Twitter, July 18, 2022, https://twitter.com/globaltimesnews/status
/1549036280209584128.

62. Embassy of Afghanistan—Beijing, @beijing_embassy, "Yesterday, A.A. Emirate
acting head of embassy Syed Muhyiddin Sadat met with Wang Hao, deputy director
of the Chinese contractor company of the Mes Aynak project. During the visit,
emphasis was placed on the practical start of the work of the said project and a
request was made to solve the remaining technical problems," Twitter, September 30,
2022, https://twitter.com/beijing_embassy/status/1575713178297978880.

63. Nabih Bulos, "The World Needs Chromite and Lithium. Afghanistan Has Them.
What Happens Next?," *Los Angeles Times*, November 3, 2022, https://www.latimes
.com/world-nation/story/2022-11-03/afghanistan-mining-minerals-economic-hope.

64. "China, Afghanistan Pledge to Jointly Promote Belt and Road Initiative," Xinhua,
April 28, 2020, https://www.xinhuanet.com/english/2020-04/28/c_139014660.htm.

65. Winston, *Narco-Insecurity, Inc.*, 164.

66. "Wang Yi Holds Talks with Acting Foreign Minister of the Afghan Interim Government Amir Khan Muttaqi," Ministry of Foreign Affairs of the People's Republic of China, March 25, 2022, https://www.fmprc.gov.cn/mfa_eng/wjdt_665385/wshd_665389/202203/t20220325_10655541.html.

67. "Taliban Say Afghanistan Secure Enough for Big Projects," Associated Press, October 12, 2022, https://apnews.com/article/afghanistan-business-china-taliban-foreign-aid-316bf5adf1c29e1e08e466a9765f98f6.

68. Saeed Shah, "Chinese Firm Signs $540 Million Oil-and-Gas Deal in Afghanistan," *Wall Street Journal*, January 5, 2023, https://www.wsj.com/articles/chinese-firm-signs-540-million-oil-and-gas-deal-in-afghanistan-11672934543.

69. Chinese Firms Plan Afghan Platform to Examine Opportunities and Pitfalls of Investment," Global Times, September 8, 2021, https://www.globaltimes.cn/page/202109/1233748.shtml.

70. Yin Yeping, "Chinese Businesses to Hold First Large Expo in Afghanistan to Boost Trade," Global Times, January 23, 2022, https://www.globaltimes.cn/page/202201/1246684.shtml.

71. "Chinese Industrial Park to Be Built in Kabul New City," Global Times, March 31, 2022, https://www.globaltimes.cn/page/202203/1257334.shtml.

72. "Chinese Industrial Park Project Wins Approval in Afghanistan: Source," Global Times, April 28, 2022, https://www.globaltimes.cn/page/202204/1260570.shtml.

73. "Gunfight in Kabul Hotel Run by Chinese Businesspeople Lasts One Hour, over 10 Explosions Occurred: Source," Global Times, December 31, 2022, https://www.globaltimes.cn/page/202212/1281729.shtml.

74. Ibid.

75. "The Chinese Entrepreneurs Chasing an Afghan 'Gold Rush,'" Al Jazeera, November 24, 2022, https://www.aljazeera.com/program/101-east/2022/11/24/the-chinese-entrepreneurs-chasing-an-afghan-gold-rush.

76. "The Chinese Entrepreneurs Chasing an Afghan 'Gold Rush,'" Al Jazeera, November 24, 2022, https://www.youtube.com/watch?v=Ssc5PUm8a-Q.

77. Deutsche Welle, "Afghanistan: Armed Gunmen Target Hotel in Kabul," *Taiwan News*, December 12, 2022, https://www.taiwannews.com.tw/en/news/4748314.

78. Jerry Dunleavy, "Biden DOJ Scuttles Trump's China Crackdown amid Criticism from the Left and CCP," *Washington Examiner*, February 23, 2022, https://www.washingtonexaminer.com/news/biden-doj-scuttles-trumps-china-crackdown-amid-criticism-from-the-left-and-ccp.

79. Jerry Dunleavy, "Jen Psaki Claims 'No Link' Between Huawei CFO's Release and China Freeing Two Canadians," *Washington Examiner*, September 27, 2021, https://www.washingtonexaminer.com/news/psaki-no-link-huawei-cfo-release-china-freeing-canadian-michaels.

80. Jerry Dunleavy, "House GOP Leaders Demand Answers from Biden Education Department About Combating CCP Influence on Campus," *Washington Examiner*, June 16, 2021, https://www.washingtonexaminer.com/news/house-gop-leaders

-demand-answers-from-biden-education-department-about-combating-ccp
-influence-on-campus.

81. Michael E. Miller, "China's Growing Reach Is Transforming a Pacific Island Chain," *Washington Post*, August 11, 2022, https://www.washingtonpost.com/world/2022/08 /11/solomon-islands-china-australia-pacific/.

82. Jerry Dunleavy, "The DragonBear alliance: How China has been parroting Russian justifications for Ukraine invasion," *Washington Examiner*, February 23, 2023, https://www.washingtonexaminer.com/policy/defense-national-security/dragonbear -china-echoes-russian-justifications-ukraine-invasion.

83. Jerry Dunleavy and Mike Brest, "'Malarkey': US Denies Russian and Chinese Claims of Bioweapon Labs in Ukraine," *Washington Examiner*, March 9, 2022, https://www .washingtonexaminer.com/news/justice/hunter-biden-criminal-fbi-investigation -whistleblower-ukraine-china.

84. Jerry Dunleavy, "China Plays 'Peacemaker' While Amplifying Russian Justifications for Ukraine War," *Washington Examiner*, March 21, 2022, https://www .washingtonexaminer.com/news/china-plays-peacemaker-while-amplifying-russian -justifications-for-ukraine-war.

85. Ibid.

86. Mara Hvistendahl and Alexey Kovalev, "Hacked Russian Files Reveal Propaganda Agreement with China," The Intercept, December 30, 2022, https://theintercept.com /2022/12/30/russia-china-news-media-agreement/.

87. Jerry Dunleavy, "China plays 'peacemaker' while amplifying Russian justifications for war," *Washington Examiner*, February 23, 2023, https://www .washingtonexaminer.com/news/china-plays-peacemaker-while-amplifying-russian -justifications-for-ukraine-war.

88. "Transcript of Ambassador Qin Gang's Interview with CBS Face the Nation," Ministry of Foreign Affairs of the People's Republic of China, March 20, 2022, https://www.fmprc.gov.cn/mfa_eng/wjb_663304/zwjg_665342/zwbd_665378 /202203/t20220321_10653844.html.

89. Jerry Dunleavy, "'Peacemaker' China Stands by Russia Partnership," *Washington Examiner*, March 21, 2022, https://www.washingtonexaminer.com/policy/foreign /peacemaker-china-stands-by-russia-partnership.

90. "Russian-Chinese Negotiations," President of Russia, December 30, 2022, http:// www.kremlin.ru/events/president/news/70303.

91. "Xi Meets Putin via Video Link," Xinhua, December 30, 2022, https://english.news .cn/20221230/5c64594f97af4f2fb0abb6304f9fa1b8/c.html.

92. Jerry Dunleavy, "GOP warns of 'vacuum' filled by China following Xi-Putin meetings," *Washington Examiner*, March 24, 2023, https://www .washingtonexaminer.com/policy/defense-national-security/gop-warns-vacuum -filled-china-following-xi-putin-meetings.

93. "Press Briefing by Press Secretary Jen Psaki, October 22, 2021," White House, October 22, 2021, https://www.whitehouse.gov/briefing-room/press-briefings/2021 /10/22/press-briefing-by-press-secretary-jen-psaki-october-22-2021/.

94. Kevin Liptak, Donald Judd, and Nectar Gan, "Biden Says US Would Respond 'Militarily' if China Attacked Taiwan, but White House Insists There's No Policy Change," CNN, May 23, 2022, https://www.cnn.com/2022/05/23/politics/biden -taiwan-china-japan-intl-hnk.

95. "Biden Tells 60 Minutes U.S. Troops Would Defend Taiwan, but White House Says This Is Not Official U.S. Policy," CBS News, September 18, 2022, https://www .cbsnews.com/news/president-joe-biden-taiwan-60-minutes-2022-09-18/.

96. "President Tsai Announces Military Force Realignment Plan," Office of the President, Republic of China (Taiwan), December 27, 2022, https://english.president .gov.tw/NEWS/6417.

97. Jerry Dunleavy, "Ukraine Invasion May Give China Pause over Taiwan, Spy Chiefs Suggest," *Washington Examiner*, March 8, 2022, https://www.washingtonexaminer .com/policy/defense-national-security/ukraine-invasion-may-give-china-pause-over -taiwan-spy-chiefs-suggest.

CHAPTER 15: THE THIRTEEN

1. Joseph R. Biden, Jr., "Remarks by President Biden on the Terror Attack at Hamid Karzai International Airport," White House, August 26, 2021, https://www .whitehouse.gov/briefing-room/speeches-remarks/2021/08/26/remarks-by-president -biden-on-the-terror-attack-at-hamid-karzai-international-airport/.

2. Daniel Funke, "Fact Check: Biden Honored Service Members Killed in Kabul, Checked Watch During Ceremony," *USA Today*, September 3, 2021, https://www .usatoday.com/story/news/factcheck/2021/09/01/fact-check-biden-checked-watch -after-ceremony-dover-air-force-base/5663427001/.

3. "Lance Corporal David Lee Espinoza Obituary 2021," Joe Jackson Funeral Chapels, https://www.joejacksonfuneralchapels.com/obituaries/lancecorporaldavid -leeespinoza.

4. Jerry Dunleavy, interview with Christy Shamblin, 2022.

5. "Hunter Lopez," *Desert Sun*, https://www.desertsun.com/obituaries/pds028481.

6. Jim McCollum, "McCollum, 20, Met Challenges Head-On," Jackson Hole News&Guide, September 15, 2021, https://www.jhnewsandguide.com/valley /obituaries/mccollum-20-met-challenges-head-on/article_df94245a-9346-52a7-906b -0b394bbdb77a.html.

7. Matt Leach, Megan Myers, and Eli Steele, "Heroes of Kabul: Lance Cpl. Dylan Merola Wanted to Help Afghans Escape the Taliban. That Was His Final Mission," Fox News, August 26, 2022, https://www.foxnews.com/us/heroes-of-kabul-lance-cpl -dylan-merola-wanted-help-afghans-escape-taliban-final-mission.

8. Ibid.

9. Jason Kandel, "Three SoCal Marines Among American Service Members Killed in Afghanistan Suicide Bombing," NBC Los Angeles, August 28, 2021, https://www .nbclosangeles.com/news/local/three-u-s-Marines-from-southern-california-among -american-service-members-killed-in-afghanistan-suicide-bombing/2681439/.

10. "Marine from Red Oak Among Those Killed in Afghanistan Airport Bombing," *Des Moines Register*, August 30, 2021, https://www.desmoinesregister.com/story/news